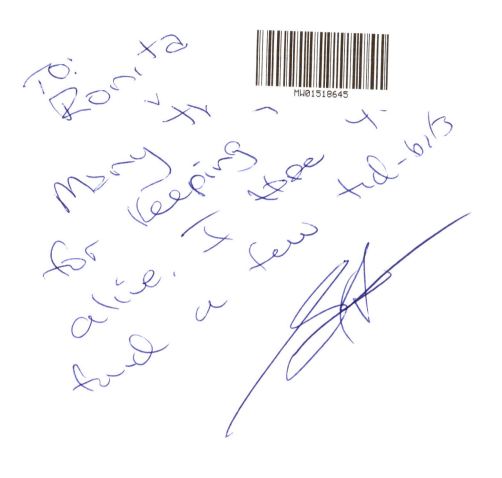

To:
Ronita

Many thanx
for keeping
alive. Y tree
find a few txd - b/3

WILLIAM FOX

A STORY OF EARLY HOLLYWOOD

1915-1930

WILLIAM FOX

A STORY OF EARLY HOLLYWOOD

1915-1930

by

SUSAN FOX

and

DONALD G. ROSELLINI

Midnight Marquee Press, Inc.
Baltimore, Maryland, USA

ISBN 1-887664-62-9
Library of Congress Catalog Card Number 2006922452
Manufactured in the United States of America
Printed by Thomson-Shore, Inc., Dexter, Michigan
First Printing by Midnight Marquee Press, Inc., March 2006

Acknowledgments: Linda J. Walter

*To those fearless men who
founded Hollywood*

TABLE OF CONTENTS

INTRODUCTION

I begin this story with some hesitation, because to recount the rise and fall of my great-grandfather, William Fox, I must refer to those other important figures who created the motion picture industry. A group of young, fearless businessmen who through performers, stories, sets, cameras and theaters waged an unceasing and bitter war for supremacy.

The only constant in the motion picture industry of the silent era was unrelenting change.

The period between 1915 and 1925 was a time of constant progress for Fox Film, the result of the release of a profitable run of pictures that brought William Fox to a prominent, but by no means dominant, position.

The industry consisted of many studios competing for a share of the theatergoing public. Barriers to entry were low, which meant that anyone with a flair for the theatrical, a story, the wherewithal to lease studio space, and a ramshackle old camera could and did make pictures.

A.P. Giannini's Bancamerica, along with the prestigious Wall Street investment houses of Goldman Sachs, Kuhn, Loeb, and Lehman Brothers, were ready and willing to finance the production of pictures.

Money was there for the asking. As a result, a colossal mound of debt would build on studio balance sheets—a debt that would feed and swell through the easy-money days of the 1920s until it would reach staggering proportions.

In their day-to-day lives, silent film producers faced the ever-present threat of insolvency. A bad film here, a poor showing there, and it was over. There were plenty of casualties strewn across the fruited Hollywood landscape, with changing studio signs testifying to the intense rivalry that existed in the industry. The possibility of extinction was no more than a thousand feet of film away.

Industry fundamentals could be summed up in two sentences: Pull patrons into theaters; sell them things they want to eat and drink, a formula that hasn't changed to this day.

Though his early pictures were not considered major artistic accomplishments, William Fox patched together a simple formula that featured cowboys and Indians, or vampires, with an occasional journey to the melodramatic. Most importantly, the top line usually exceeded costs, because Fox Film turned out pictures quickly and inexpensively.

Even if critics panned Fox pictures, who really cared? Audiences were flocking to theaters to see them, and that was all that mattered to William Fox.

He learned that to build a studio on one or two stars was like playing roulette. Fame was fleeting, scandal lurked around every corner, an irreconcilable difference with a director could and did stop production, illness could paralyze a project, and the public's taste could and did change with frightening speed. In response to the constant threat of business interruption, William Fox diversified his roster of players and replenished it with new faces on a regular basis. Early stars like Theda Bara, Tom Mix, William Farnum and Buck Jones kept the studio afloat.

To keep up with the undisputed industry leader, Paramount's Adolph Zukor, William Fox expanded capacity both in film production and film exhibition, vertically integrating the company. Over time, he was forced to dilute his original 51 percent stake to something less substantial. To avoid a loss of management control, he followed the practice of the time and kept more than half of the voting shares of both Fox Film and Fox Theaters in his name. All voting power in Fox Film lay in 100,000 shares of Class B stock, of which William Fox owned 50,101 shares. All voting power in Fox Theaters lay in a corresponding 100,000 shares of Class B stock, the entire issue of which belonged to my great-grandfather.

In 1927, while his business was still expanding, William Fox began to acquire theaters by the chain instead of by the unit, and the studio began experimenting with the talking picture. It came time for him to hire an investment banker, because the conversion to sound and the acquisition of theaters could no longer be financed through internally generated funds. Thus the firm of Halsey, Stuart and the venerable Harold Leonard Stuart, its president, entered the scene.

Following closely behind was the Electrical Research Products Company (an AT&T subsidiary) and its president John Otterson, a company very much interested in William Fox's development of Ted Case's sound-on-film technology, a process that came to be known as Movietone.

On Chicago's La Salle Street, the highbrow Halsey, Stuart was considered an excellent bond-selling organization, never once having shown the disposition to interfere in the affairs of its clients, which had great appeal to William Fox.

Fox, Stuart and Otterson were the best of friends and business associates, and it was under their auspices that William Fox embarked on the creation of his "great enterprise." The Fox Film and Fox Theaters companies expanded dramatically, so that by the end of 1928 the studio rose to a position of prominence among the big four of cinema (Warner Bros., Paramount, Fox and Loew's).

Fox Theater in San Francisco

In 1929, William Fox embarked upon an expedition a bit too ambitious for his resources and fell victim to his own voracious appetite for growth. In response to Paramount's theater-acquisition spree, he attempted to swallow the entire Loew's organization, which at the time controlled MGM and many first-run theaters, aggravating MGM studio boss L.B. Mayer.

To make matters worse, he also managed to antagonize his two major financial backers, AT&T and Halsey, Stuart, insisting that the Movietone sound patents belonged exclusively to him and were not to be shared royalty-free with AT&T.

During the most serious part of the negotiation for the Loew's shares, William Fox was immobilized as the result of a near-fatal automobile crash. While he lay recovering from his injuries, Louis B. Mayer connived with the newly elected Hoover administration to thwart William Fox's acquisition of Loew's and Mayer's beloved MGM. Mayer wanted no part of the crafty William Fox. To pay for the purchase of the controlling interest in Loew's, William Fox loaded his companies with short-term debt.

The final blow came in October 1929 when the stock market crashed. Stock prices tumbled and margins were called on the Loew's shares. In this time of acute need, his financial backers were nowhere to be found. It was payback time.

It was now a question of survival. My great-grandfather was about to lose control of the companies he had created and expanded over a 15-year time span. In his mind the plot was thus: A considerable group of very influential people wanted to unseat him and confiscate his controlling interest in the Fox companies.

But why?

I hope I can correct several misconceptions regarding my great-grandfather's role in the silent and early sound era, particularly those related to the Loew's acquisition and its aftermath. Most treatises on the subject dismiss William Fox's attempt to acquire Loew's as sheer folly, or an act of insanity. The truth was that the deal's fundamentals were sound and made good economic sense. What had changed was the environment.

While they were still alive, I spent time conversing about William Fox with my grandmother, Belle, my father's first cousin, Bill T., and my father, William Fox, Jr. It is through their story-telling that I am able to reconstruct many of the scenes I portray in this book.

I use *Upton Sinclair Presents William Fox* as both a timeline and source for William Fox's most intimate thoughts and words on many pertinent subjects. My great-grandfather is quoted throughout the Sinclair book. William Fox hired Sinclair to write a book and establish a public record of what had happened to him and why he lost control of the Fox enterprises. William Fox spent hours upon hours recounting to Sinclair what had taken place in those pivotal years 1929 and 1930. It is unfortunate that a stockpile of data given to Upton Sinclair by William Fox has been lost. The William Fox-Upton Sinclair file at Indiana University contains a trial record and not much else.

I'm particularly grateful to Carla Winter and the Wurtzel family for preserving correspondence between Sol Wurtzel and William Fox. These letters are published and are now available in their entirety. I use these letters to create several scenes in the book.

Dr. Lillian Lodge Kopenhaver, Dean of Florida International University's School of Journalism, courageously accepted the task of editing a preliminary draft of the manuscript. A special thanks to Scott Kass of the University's library for uncovering scarce background material on Halsey, Stuart, Harold Stuart, John Otterson and Harley Clarke.

Samuel Untermyer

Thanks to Alan Adler, former director of 20th Century-Fox's film library and archives, for a rare copy of the catalogue of films and stories owned by the Fox Film Corporation at the time of the merger with 20th Century.

As I was about to finish this book, I discovered that the Samuel Untermyer family had created an archive of the famed litigator's personal papers. His grandson Frank Untermyer kindly shared an unpublished manuscript with me, dealing with the intense litigation of early 1930. Throughout this tumultuous period, Samuel Untermyer ably defended William Fox and was instrumental in reaching a settlement with his opposition.

Douglas Taussig's whereabouts remained a mystery for over 60 years until his son from a second marriage, John Taussig, surfaced out of the blue. Surprisingly, John lived near his half brother, Bill T. John provided useful insight on his father Douglas, who had been married to William Fox's oldest daughter, Mona.

As for Belle's husband, Milton J. Schwartz, I have no idea what became of him. Possibly a reader will know something about him.

This biographical novel is documented by an extensive bibliography. I am deeply indebted to those wonderful writers at *Fortune* who so skillfully described some of the events that took place between 1915 and 1930.

A special thanks to our agent, Debbie Fine for her perseverance. We are particularly grateful to Susan and Gary Svehla for believing in our work.

I want to specially thank my great-grandfather, William Fox, for without him there would be no me. As I write these words, my sister Jo-Ann and I remember him. It was 50 years ago, May 8, 1952, that he passed away.

—Susan Eva Fox

CHAPTER 1
1915

The year was 1915. Woodrow Wilson was President of the United States. In America alone, more than 400 films of four reels—each with 60 minutes of running time—were being produced by more than 100 different companies.

One of those producers was a young entrepreneur by the name of William Fox.

On February 1, Fox rose at an early hour and went through his daily ritual of shaving, protecting as best he could the small, close-trimmed mustache under his rather prominent nose. William Fox was 36 years old.

The portly man of medium height stood before a mirror, stirred his brush in a shaving mug, lathered his skin and then shaved carefully with a finely honed razor.

"William?" called his wife, Eve, rapping on the bathroom door. "We'd better hurry."

Whenever a sense of urgency appeared about her, Eve called him William. Otherwise, he was just plain Bill. To those who had the good fortune to work for him, he became W.F.

Rinsing his face clean of lather, he opened the door. There stood his wife, the light of his life. Eve's light brown eyes sparkled, and her smile was contagious. She tenderly kissed him on his ample forehead.

A wave of nostalgia engulfed him. For a long moment, W.F. stood there looking at her, thinking all the way back to when they had first met in that Lower East Side tenement. Their pasts were intertwined in such complex ways that they could now almost read each other's minds. Married for 15 years, they had two lovely daughters, Caroline, whom they referred to as Mona, and the youngest, Isabelle, who became Belle. W.F. loved those girls more than his life, and he was determined to shelter them from the hardship and deprivation he'd felt growing up as a child.

Padding into the master bedroom, Eve picked a fresh white shirt from the highly polished chest of drawers, helped him into it and buttoned the starched collar that fit snugly around his neck. She wrapped a dark cravat around the high collar, tying a respectable bow in the front much as she did every morning. Then she stuck a pin through the collar.

When he was 10 or so, W.F. had lost the use of his left elbow due to an unfortunate accident in which he'd tumbled off the back end of an ice wagon, breaking his arm. Since the Fox family had had no money to speak of, the fracture had been poorly set.

William Fox

Flattening his eyebrows with her soft finger, Eve said, "Today is the day we've been waiting for, Bill."

W.F. didn't respond immediately, his mind wandering off to an earlier time when putting bread on the table for his four younger siblings seemed an interminable chore. Young William Fox had sold shoe polish and newspapers and had grubbed for a living like most of the tenants in the ghetto.

"What are you thinking about, dearest?"

"I was just thinking of my father," he replied. "He never saved any money. We'll do things differently."

Brushing a thick swath of graying hair over his balding head, Eve made sure it covered the shiny spot. She was careful about it, as though she were combing a baby's hair. Then she helped him slip into a suit coat.

Taking stock of the dapper image in the dresser mirror, W.F. saw a man of some prosperity. Now, he told himself, for the first time, he was on the road to financial independence.

Indeed, W.F. was putting the exhibition company he'd built from one modest theater acquired in 1904, everything he owned in this world, into a corporation to be called Fox Film. As a consequence, he'd wind up controlling 50 percent of this stock company, with an outside investor group from New Jersey controlling the other half.

"These people are trusting us with their money, Eve."

"I know," she said. "Do you have any doubts?"

"None!" W.F. replied in a firm voice, assuaging her concern, while at the same time reaffirming to himself that they were doing the right thing. "No doubts, whatsoever!"

Such a statement was a little white lie, because W.F. was used to complete control and now he would have to report to a board of directors who were disparate in thought. He told himself if he could control the board, then nothing would change. W.F. kept that thought uppermost in his mind, particularly when, several years later, he'd take the company public and suffer a substantial dilution in his ownership.

"We're going to work harder than we ever have in our lives, Eve."

Keeping in step with the practice of the time, he didn't want to arrive late for the important meeting. Extending his good right arm, W.F. said, "Let's go, my dear. Our investors are waiting for us."

Linking arms, they moved deliberately and quickly to the foyer.

Because it was the dead of winter, Eve wore a mink coat, and W.F. slipped on a cloth coat with a dark fur collar, topping his head with a dignified homburg.

In the gravel sweep before the house a spiffy chauffeur named Harold stood erectly by a shiny motorcar. The Foxes made their way to the car, edging themselves into the rear seat.

The Pierce-Arrow was solid and quiet, with a fully equipped umbrella holder and chauffeur telephone, one of the fine luxury motor carriages of the era. It had six cylinders and 48 horsepower, and cost $6,000.

The Foxes were living at Mt. Hope in the Bronx. The ride to Lower Manhattan would take nearly an hour. There was a steep hill, and then the chauffeur guided the motorcar, applying its brakes until it hit pavement. The rest of the ride was relatively smooth. Once in the city, Harold maneuvered the automobile through clustered pedestrians, trolley cars and motorcars. Dynamite blasted in underground excavations in an annoyingly monotonous fashion. New York City was building another length of subway line.

People hunched their shoulders against a chilly wind blowing down Fifth Avenue. Policemen directed competing flows of traffic at busy intersections. A crude electric traffic semaphore hung at Fifth Avenue and 42nd Street.

There it was. The swank Waldorf-Astoria looming in the distance, 11 stories of ornate architectural display at 34th Street and Fifth Avenue.

"There's a bit of traffic this morning, Mr. Fox."

"Drop us at the 33rd Street entrance, Harold."

"Yes, Mr. Fox."

Harold pulled the great motorcar to a complete stop in front of the canopied entrance on 33rd Street. The Foxes got out of the car with the assistance of a footman and sauntered into the hotel.

Meeting at the Waldorf-Astoria gave W.F. a certain cachet. All of the presidents from McKinley on spent time there. The hotel's manager—George C. Boldt, a bearded, urbane man—ran the place masterfully, steadily enhancing guest service. With its tastefully furnished rooms and its artistically tiled baths, the Waldorf had become New York's foremost hotel for public entertainments, charity balls and foreign dignitaries.

A regally uniformed houseman who had been with the Waldorf for ages, or so it seemed, was there to greet them. Dressed in satin knee pants, he spoke only when spoken to.

"Please follow me, Mr. Fox. Madam."

The houseman escorted them into a well-appointed sitting room. Upholstered chairs cushioned with velvet were distributed nicely throughout the room and an immense marble-top table was located in the center, with several straight-backed chairs around it.

Meeting the Foxes were Winfield Richard Sheehan, Jack G. Leo and Saul Rogers. Eve and W.F. instantly shed their coats, which were carried off by a houseman.

"W.F., Mrs. Fox."

"Winnie, isn't this wonderful?" The lively tone of Eve's voice said everything.

"Yes, it is. I think it's beginning to dawn on the motion picture industry that William Fox is a force to be dealt with, Mrs. Fox."

"It's much too early to stand up and be counted, Winnie," W.F. grumbled.

Turning, Eve went over to the far side of the room to join her brother, Jack Leo, who was beaming from ear to ear. Balding, with a now prominent forehead, Leo was W.F.'s right-hand man, managing day-to-day business affairs and supervising the office when W.F. was out of town or in one of the Fox theaters. Energetic, enthusiastic, completely wrapped up in his job, Leo was there when W.F. needed him.

"Jack, my darling," Eve said.

"Sweetheart."

They kissed each other on both cheeks. There was a genuine warmth there that W.F. did not share with his own siblings. But that was another matter.

Without notice or warning, a thick-chested man stuck his nose in the door, and W.F. signaled that he should enter. It was Oscar Tschirky, the *maitre d'hotel,* who had worked for the Waldorf since its opening. Smooth, affable, with a flawless memory for names and the gift for ingratiating himself with prominent guests, he was known to everyone who was anyone.

"Mr. Fox, what a wonderful day."

"Yes, it is, Oscar."

"I hope everything is to your liking?"

"Perfect for the occasion."

"Good. Good. If there is anything more you require, please do not hesitate to call upon me. I am at your service."

"I will, Oscar."

That said, Oscar left W.F. with one of his specially engraved cards and swiftly departed.

Having burdened himself for over a week with an exhaustive examination of *pro forma* financial statements, W.F. was satisfied that each and every number fell into place. As president and chief executive of Fox Film, W.F. knew that he was ultimately responsible for the financial results presented to stockholders and directors.

"Is everything in order?"

"We're ready, W.F.," Rogers responded.

On a small table rested a stack of bound booklets. Snatching one, W.F. sat in one of the chairs positioned around the table and began flipping through the pages. He read the story of how William Fox had grown a single theater he'd purchased in 1904 into a string of second-class vaudeville houses. Earlier, managing his affairs from an austere office at 24 Union Square, Fox purchased the interests of partners B.S. Moss and Sol Brill. Before long, former partner Moss joined Adolph Zukor, the man who would create Paramount.

The prospectus spoke of W.F.'s plans for expansion in the three vital areas of the movie business: exhibition, distribution and film production. Rogers' down-to-earth writing style pleased him, for he had painted a rosy picture for Fox Film without having made any false representations.

Short of stature with the steely bespectacled look of a litigator, Saul Rogers was the company's in-house attorney and had been W.F.'s personal secretary since 1905. W.F. had first met Rogers when he'd invited his older brother Gustavus to join him as a partner on the Dewey Theatre lease. Today, he was promoting Rogers to general counsel of Fox Film at the not so modest sum of $30,000 a year. Putting the booklet aside, W.F. lit a cigar and said, "Damn fine job, Saul."

"I'm happy you approve, W.F.," he replied.

Nearly a decade before, Winfield Sheehan came into W.F.'s life because W.F. needed someone with strong connections in city hall. Theater managers were regularly being harassed on safety issues by the city's fire department. Fire inspectors were shutting theaters down for days at a time, putting a sizeable dent in revenues.

Born in 1883, a onetime *New York World* reporter, "Winnie" was connected to the police department and seemed to know how to "fix" things, so W.F. hired him as his secretary at $100 a week. He seemed to have an extraordinary fund of political contacts, which would prove useful for the business.

W.F. saw great promise for the blue-eyed, vivacious Irishman, who, because he had the gift of gab, would serve as the front man for the company. Outwardly congenial and business-like, Sheehan fit the bill for studio spokesman. Although he had a charming manner with people, Sheehan was capable of rages at which strong men turned pale. Most importantly, he was a Gentile and America was a Gentile nation, and W.F. was a Jew.

The truth was that like so many of the uneducated young men of his generation, Sheehan had joined Fox Film partly from a need to improve his financial situation, and partly from the calculation that it was the best way to advance a career that had reached a dead end. Over time, he became a deferential manager, leaving policy decisions to W.F. Even when he disagreed with this or that decision, he never risked his career by doing something foolish. The only one who dared question W.F. on policy decisions was his brother-in-law Jack Leo.

Most nights, after around-the-clock work marathons, Sheehan could be found drinking at Jack's all-night bar on 6th Avenue, just off the Tenderloin.

Apart from his theater assets, W.F. owned Box Office Attractions, from which he distributed moving pictures made by the many studios shooting film. Most of these were short-subject films supplied by American, Beauty, Balboa, Broncho and a host of smaller studios. These studios ranged in size from one-car garages to multiple-stage operations. As for distribution, the exchange of films among theater owners made more sense than individual purchases from producers.

At the other end of the spectrum, the General Film Company, the giant distribution arm of the Motion Picture Patents Company, was still exclusively merchandising the products of Biograph, Edison, Essanay, Kalem, Lubin, Mina, Selig, Pathé and Vitagraph, the big studios of that time. These studios were the Edison licensees and formed part of what became known as "the Trust."

St. Elmo starring John Gilbert and Bessie Love (1923)

Unless a theater owner agreed to pay the General Film Company's schedule of costly fees, there were no big pictures. Not playing by Trust rules was never a safe business. Absolutely nothing gentle occurred in the way the Trust enforced its monopolistic policies. Examples of coercion abounded, and stories of physical violence were spawned.

Because W.F. fought the Trust tooth and nail, Box Office Attractions was unable to secure pictures from these big studios. W.F. was frozen out of the inner circle and had to rely on the lesser-known studios for pictures.

Another formidable barrier for the production of motion pictures by the small independent film producer was an interruption in the regular supply of raw film. The Motion Picture Patents Company signed an agreement under which Eastman Kodak became the exclusive supplier of raw film to the Edison licensees, and as a quid pro quo agreed not to supply the independents. In due course this agreement was amended to permit Kodak to sell to whomever it wanted, since the net result of the embargo was to encourage foreign raw film stock suppliers to enter the American market.

It was about this time that W.F. decided he needed to produce his own pictures, and the Box Office Attractions Company made his first movies. The very first picture was *Life's Shop Window*, adapted from a novel written by Victoria Cross in 1907. It cost Box Office Attractions $6,000 to film and was shot on Staten Island in a rented studio. Box Office's second picture was *St. Elmo*. Both films were profitable, and W.F. saw that as a good sign.

A group referred to as the New Jersey contingent was going to invest $400,000 in the Fox Film Corporation. The consortium comprised an engaging young man, Forrest F. Dryden, who had followed in his father John F. Dryden footsteps to become president of the Prudential Life

Insurance Company; Anthony R. Kuser, Forrest's brother-in-law; a sister, Susan Dryden Kuser; Uzal McCarter; and Martin Usar.

The "Pru" became a leader in the insurance business. It was told that John Fairfield Dryden did his first business in industrial insurance for the workingman, policies that cost pennies per week for up to $500 worth of coverage. The "Pru" had 10 million policyholders on its rolls. Upon his death in 1911, John F. Dryden bequeathed a family fortune estimated at $15 million, which was divided into five parts. Three-fifths was left in trust to Dryden's widow Mrs. Cynthia F. Dryden, one-fifth to Mr. Dryden's son Forrest, and one-fifth in trust to his daughter Susan Dryden Kuser. Two smaller investors, Nathaniel King and John Eisele, were backing Fox Film through their New Jersey investment house.

The investors were ushered in by a houseman who hastily carted off their coats, hats and scarves to a hatcheck.

"Welcome, everyone," Eve said.

"It's so good to meet you, Mrs. Fox," Forrest Dryden replied, his eyes lighting up.

"I've heard so much about you, Mr. Dryden."

"Most of it is true, I'm afraid."

They laughed.

Dryden set his briefcase down beside one of the straight-backed chairs.

A butler wheeled in glistening silver pots of tea. Another servant trailed behind, pushing a two-tiered cart stacked with a colorful assortment of finger sandwiches, fresh fruit and pastry. Everyone filled a plate and took assigned places around the marble-top table.

Mrs. Usar stuffed her mouth with a chocolate éclair. "This is so delicious, Susie."

"It's lovely."

It was not hard to discern that W.F. felt things couldn't be better. He was grateful just to be in the sophisticated company he was in, and there seemed to him no limit to the heights to which Fox Film could soar. This was truly a good beginning, something he'd thought about for a long time—an association with men of means, investors willing to finance his dream of moving picture expansion.

As the guests savored hot tea and pastry, Jack Leo passed out copies of the prospectus.

"I believe we're ready to start the meeting, Saul," Jack Leo said.

Dryden's demeanor turned serious as he sat down in a chair opposite W.F. A man of average height with a stomach kept down by plenty of golf, Dryden was dressed in a gray suit, a rather high collar and a dark tie.

Saul Rogers rose. "Ladies and gentlemen."

One could hear a pin drop.

"Mr. Fox is contributing his leases and ownership of 10 theaters in the greater New York area, another 12 theaters outside of New York."

W.F. fished a smoke from the row of long brown cigars he kept in his breast pocket, and lighted up.

"Mr. Fox's contribution includes real estate in California, a vaudeville booking company and Box Office Attractions. The officers of the Fox Film company are William Fox, president, Winfield R. Sheehan, vice president and general manager, Jack Leo, vice president, and yours truly, Saul Rogers, vice president and general counsel."

There was a drawn-out period of heated discussion, after which W.F. accepted the appointment of John Eisele as treasurer of the company. In effect, Eisele would become the New Jersey contingent's insider. Before closing the meeting, W.F. created a spot for Nathaniel King as well.

After the stockholders unanimously approved the nominations, a nice, warm round of applause erupted. With its management slate in place, Fox Film was now officially in existence.

Although Eve Fox would never occupy an official capacity in the company, whatever success was enjoyed at Fox Film and Fox Theaters was due in large part to her personal dedication and sacrifice. Besides tying W.F.'s necktie every morning and brushing his hair, she put a lot of time into reading scenarios for Fox pictures.

A film started with a good story. For years no one knew the work Eve was doing; when scenarios were submitted, W.F. packed them up every evening and brought them home to his wife. She plowed through them and gave him a brief critique. She read in bed, at meals, and in the motorcar. She rushed out and bought all the new novels. Later, she reviewed stage plays in a never-ending search for film-worthy material.

There was no question in W.F.'s mind that Forrest Dryden would lead the New Jersey contingent as far as business matters were concerned. He had that look of confidence that comes to a man who has achieved a certain status in life and was not in the least bit self-conscious.

Dryden stood up. "Since we are all neophytes in the picture business, I wonder if Mr. Fox would be kind enough to tell us what future he sees for Fox Film."

Dryden sat down and lit a cigarette.

For the next 10 minutes, W.F. enthusiastically described the opportunities in the motion picture business. This was a subject he thoroughly understood. "Back when I started, the motion picture began to appeal to everyone. One day some wise men in this country decided to monopolize the business and formed the Motion Picture Patents Company. Names you should remember: Edison, Kalem, Vitagraph, Lubin, Biograph, Selig, Essanay, Méliés and Pathé. No man was allowed to use a motion picture camera unless he received a license from that company. No man who wrote a story and gave his brains to create material for motion pictures was entitled to more than $25. The highest salary they agreed to pay a performer was $60 a week. These wise men controlled theaters and drove owners out of business. I refused to sign. I brought suit and they settled with me out of court."

Facing Forrest Dryden, W.F. said, "You ask Mr. Dryden what does William Fox see for the future? The motion picture will continue to provide entertainment for people from all walks of life. The industry will spread news around the world. We will one day teach not by books but by motion pictures."

"Fox Film will need theaters, studios—including one in California—stories, and talent."

W.F. lifted his right arm, his sleeve drawn back, revealing a bare wrist. "William Fox doesn't wear a watch. Our day will end when our work is done. That will be our philosophy at Fox Film."

"The Prudential Insurance Company of America represents New Jersey's largest pool of capital—most of our policyholders' dollars are invested in power and traction securities, or lent outright. New Jersey is an excellent state in which to do business, and I hope, Mr. Fox, that you will keep this in mind."

"I will, Mr. Dryden."

Jack Leo's beady eyes circled the table as he peered over a puff of smoke from his cigarette; he quickly bounced to his feet.

"Since you're now in the film business, we thought it wise that you meet one of your players. Theda Bara is a success in her first film, *A Fool There Was*. She has everyone in America saying, 'Kiss me, my fool!'"

That drew a hard laugh and Mrs. Usar blushed.

On cue, a houseman opened the door. Parading into view came Theda Bara, the epitome of the svelte, wide-eyed siren. Dressed flamboyantly for the occasion, she was draped in dark silks with her white shoulders and arms bare; she looked as if she had just walked off the silver screen.

There were indistinguishable "oohs" and "aahs."

Susan Kuser said, "Oh, my God!"

Theda Bara

Her delicate jaw gone rigid, Mrs. Usar said, "That's Theda Bara?"

A smiling Anthony Kuser whispered, "In flesh and blood."

There was never any question that Theda Bara would become the very first *femme fatale* in filmdom. In fact, she created the genre. All of five feet, six inches tall, Bara weighed 135 pounds and was a rather robust woman like so many of that era. Pitch-black hair and brown, heavy-lidded eyes added to the vamp image that the Fox Studio aggressively cultivated for her. Naturally blonde, Bara perpetually dyed her hair and used exotic makeup to accentuate her beauty.

Standing very erect, she allowed her big, dark eyes to circle the table, and raised her right hand in a plea for silence.

"Please. Please."

In that instant, some of the lights were turned off, dimming the room and fabricating a theatrical mood. Frowning with intrigue, Theda began reciting Kipling's famous poem, "The Vampire."

A fool there was and he made his prayer.
Even as you and I.
To a rag and a bone and a hank of hair,
We called her the woman who did not care.
But the fool, he called her his lady fair.
Even as you and I.

When the lights came up, those around the marble-top table lurched to their feet and applauded enthusiastically. W.F. noticed that Forrest Dryden was particularly effusive in his reaction to Theda Bara, and he took that to be a good sign.

"That was wonderful," Dryden said.

"Outstanding!" Anthony Kuser added.

With a devilish twinkle in her eyes, Bara gazed at Dryden. She was told that he was extremely wealthy, but she knew precious little about his private life.

"Thank you, one and all," Bara said.

Dryden looked at her wistfully. "That was wonderful, Theda."

In response, Theda Bara clasped her nicely manicured hands together tightly. Everything about her seemed fragile and gentle.

"Thank you, Mr. Dryden."

"Please call me Forrest, Theda."

"You're so sweet, Forrest."

Next on the agenda was a private showing of Theda Bara's highly popular film, *A Fool There Was.* The picture is a six-reeler that runs for 58 minutes and 26 seconds. Bara appears in about one-third of the frames.

Delighting in the moment, for this was the first real job he had ever had, Winfield Sheehan said, "Ladies and gentlemen!"

WILLIAM FOX
Presents

A FOOL THERE WAS

FOUNDED ON PORTER EMERSON BROWNE'S
DRAMATIC MASTERPIECE

It got quiet. One could hear the brassy sounds of klaxons outside the hotel.

"Next door, in the adjacent room, we've prepared a private screening of *A Fool There Was*. Please join Miss Theda Bara and the Fox family."

Theda Bara hooked her arm through Forrest Dryden's. He was all smiles.

A Fool There Was premiered in January and was an instant box office success, making Theda Bara a star. The story is about a vampire who ensnares a diplomat, causing him to give up his family and his very soul, all for Theda Bara's character.

While the guests found their seats, a pianist who was hunched over the keyboard came to life and struck up background music.

Bara perched next to Forrest Dryden. "I hope you like my picture, Forrest."

"I know I will, Theda."

The unmistakable purr of a film projector filled the room. A pale screen turned to a brighter shade of white marked with the black lettering of film credits.

In the final scene, Theda Bara, wearing a black velvet gown and a string of pearls, holds a long-stemmed rose in her teeth and calmly tosses rose petals onto the fool's broken body.

"Kiss me, my fool!" she mocks.

Then on the screen appears a Kiplingesque title: The Fool Was Stripped To His Foolish Hide.

When it was over, Dryden put his arm around Theda, a look of approval in his eyes.

"That was a wonderful performance, Theda."

"I'm so happy that you think so, Forrest."

As far as W.F. could tell, day one of Fox Film was a total success, thanks to Theodosia Goodman, "the most wickedly beautiful face in the entire world."

Film critics praised the picture. *Variety* reported that the "strong man caught in the meshes of the wicked woman makes an interesting theme."

"Vamp" became part of the lexicon. Vamp was defined as "a woman who uses her charm or wiles to seduce and exploit men."

W.F. signed Theda Bara to a five-year contract. She would go on to make 39 films for the studio.

CHAPTER 2

In the beginning, Fox Film occupied the sixth and seventh floors of the Leavitt Building at 130 West 46th Street between Sixth and Seventh Avenues. It was an edifice populated with the stuffy offices of traders, lawyers, real estate agents and physicians.

The routine was rigid. At 8:00 sharp in the morning, six days a week, W.F.'s staff had to be at their desks. Incoming mail was sorted and divided into two piles. One pile was the general correspondence that was assigned to several junior clerks for a first reading. Intermingled with ordinary correspondence was fan mail, which was promptly sorted, bagged and shipped to the respective star. The other stack was a series of in-house memos, which staff members were expected to read and channel to the proper person in the organization for immediate response or action. W.F.'s personal mail was left unopened on top of his desk.

Each morning W.F. made his way to a large corner office whose austere interior was more roll-top than Victorian. As a rule, he was difficult to see. To get there one had to go through a sequence of outer guards, tough-looking fellows who impeded the entry of unannounced visitors. They guarded a series of offices, all interconnecting, in which a handful of executives sat perusing production reports and theater-attendance statistics. The atmosphere was one of business conservatism and secrecy, with a small dose of art-minded discussion during frequent coffee klatches.

No industry was so reluctant to reveal its inner workings as the motion picture business. Paranoia dominated when it came to the competition. It was relatively easy to pilfer an idea or entice a player to abandon a studio for a competitor. Continuous experimentation in filmmaking techniques encouraged technical staff to bounce from lot to lot.

The people who occupied the Leavitt Building directed the affairs of Fox Film. Among film studios at the time, it was one of the top 10 producers of motion pictures. One unadorned fact of the motion picture industry was that there did not exist a clear-cut leader. It was highly fragmented. No studio had more than 10 percent of the market.

A male secretary managed a daily agenda and handled W.F.'s correspondence. It took a lot of telephoning and a lot of requisitions to satisfy the demands of the theaters. W.F. signed off on every purchase order. After reading the mail and signing letters, W.F. began to see those who had scheduled appointments.

In his role as president and chief executive, W.F. made decisions that aroused the envy of the artistic types, ultimately choosing what to film and what not to film. As part of his responsibility, he passed on expensive hires, no matter how talented the directors said they were, and sorted through story ideas, of which about a third were bought as novels, plays and stories.

Rather swiftly, W.F. discovered an essential truth about the economics of the motion picture industry. The successful long-term producers and directors, those who turned out a high percentage of box-office winners over an extended period of time, were those who united the tried and true stars, plots and situations in just the right proportions. It was precarious, indeed, to go out on a limb time and time again with unheard-of players, particularly if the studio was operating on a shoestring.

Shortly after setting up shop in Manhattan, Fox Film leased the old Willat Studio in Fort Lee, New Jersey as its main production facility. "Doc" Willat's facility had two large shooting stage areas resembling glass barns. Forrest Dryden was instrumental in brokering a great rental price. Because the company filmed 36 pictures during 1915, it became necessary to use other studios in places like Hoboken, New Jersey; Flushing, New York; and, later in the year, Edendale, California.

Most of Fort Lee's studios were located on Main Street, which was known as "studio row." The first company to operate there was the Champion Film Company.

In those early days travel to Fort Lee was by ferryboat. Harold chauffeured W.F. to 125th Street and the Hudson River where he joined the rest of the crew and boarded a ferry to New Jersey. Once on the other side, several cars met the players and crew and transported them to the top of the Palisades where Fort Lee was perched.

Not only did the variety of scenery lend itself to good photography, more importantly, the costs in New Jersey were reasonable. The great period of Fort Lee's film industry was from 1914 to 1919. By the end of the decade, California became the primary locus for film production.

For good reason directors were becoming more important in filmmaking, so W.F. hired one with considerable theatrical experience, J. Gordon Edwards. To W.F., he became "Jack." Edwards started his varied career as a stage actor and later directed stage plays. Sheehan assigned Edwards to direct the studio's expensive spectacles. Equipped with restless energy, he took great pride in his work. Between 1916 and 1917, Jack Edwards would direct nearly all of Theda Bara's pictures.

Since Edwards thought the best pictures were being made in Europe, W.F. dispatched him there. He returned with an improved approach to camera work, principally difficult exterior shots. The Bell & Howell 2709 camera began replacing the

J. Gordon Edwards directed Theda Bara in *Romeo and Juliet* for Fox in 1916.

older Pathé model, which the industry had used since its inception. The new camera had a turret lens that acted like a zoom, assisting greatly in close-ups.

Over time, the silent film director became a little dictator on the set, which indeed he had to be since he was critical to the production of successful pictures. It was the director's job to convert an underdeveloped story page into little celluloid frames of visual entertainment, helped along by the infrequent use of title cards, all at a modest cost.

Early images of this distinctive breed of motion picture director were of showy figures wearing breeches and puttees or seven-league boots, while brandishing their most important tool, the megaphone. A sole cameraman busily cranked a camera by hand, rotating at 16 frames per second or so, to record the scenes as they materialized. A top-flight director was one who could fit together a series of scenes and actors without wasting time, without backpedaling once during the making of a film.

Time was money. And there only was so much of it.

At this early stage of industry development, the average length of a motion picture was quite short. Throughout the United States there were 17,000 theaters with an average size of 500 seats. Many reminded audiences of the nickelodeons of an earlier time. Because the industry produced mainly short subjects, theaters were constantly changing their programs to keep the interest of the audience. Purposeful techniques for whipping up public interest in a given picture arose, many of them pirated from the stages of vaudeville. A mighty tide of jugglers, magicians and dancers were employed in large-scale, live stage presentations. Exhibitors used stunts to promote longer runs.

To promote its pictures, Fox Film used lithographed posters including one-sheets (27 by 41 inches), three-sheets (41 by 81 inches), and six-sheets (81 by 81 inches). Within the theater itself lobby cards, inserts and half-sheets were displayed, all colorfully created by companies like H.C. Kinet Litho Company, Alpha Litho and J.H. Tooker. Some of the more routine posters were printed in the company's shop. W.F.'s youngest brother, Maurice, a friendly little man with no apparent pretensions, was put in charge of printing and controlling the manufacture of posters. His job was to see that posters were distributed to theaters in a timely fashion. Before long, W.F. added his personal trademark to his pictures, "William Fox Presents."

From its very inception, silent film had been accompanied by music. The piano, of course, was the instrument of choice. It was a lot easier to find a piano player than just about any other instrumentalist. Besides, pianos didn't take a lot of room, and most of the theaters were rather small at that time.

In the larger first-run theaters, musical accompaniment ran the gamut, from pianos and mighty Wurlitzers to full-string orchestras.

In essence, the silent movie was never really silent, at least not to theater audiences. When the lights went out, the first images appeared on the screen, accompanied by the singular tones from a piano. Most background music was classical. Later, with the advent of the feature film, customized music came into vogue. Full scores were written to accompany specific scenes in a picture.

The 3,000-seat Strand made its debut on April 11, 1914 on the former site of the Brewster Carriage Factory. Occupying an entire block on Broadway between 47th and 48th Streets, the Strand was the Great White Way's first true movie palace, constructed for film rather than the stage.

Opening night featured *la creme de la creme* of New York's high-toned society. Attendees included Vincent Astor and his fiancée, Helen Dinsmore Huntington; the fat man of comedy, John Bunny; George M. Cohan; Sam Harris; Daniel Frohman; Al Erlanger; and the star of the main feature, William Farnum.

To be sure, other Broadway theaters converted to film, like the old Broadway Theater at 41st Street, The Astor—which went over to film with *Quo Vadis*—and the Criterion. But none

The lobby of the magnificent Strand in New York City

of these edifices could hold a candle to the Strand's elegance. The investors Mitchell and Moe Mark wanted to attract "high-class" patrons to their new theater.

On opening night Mitchell Mark told a gathering of reporters: "From the first moment we conceived of erecting the Strand, we made studies of all the best theaters in Europe and America, and we selected Thomas W. Lamb for the task of putting all their best features into making the Strand a national institution which would stand for all time as the model for moving picture palaces."

At the helm of the Strand was S.L. Rothapfel, better known as "Roxy." The Marks discovered him working at the Regent up in Harlem. For the inaugural event, Roxy organized a small army of ushers, doormen and ticket takers to deal with the overflowing crowd.

The Strand Tropical Review was an early precursor to the newsreel, which fascinated audiences with scenes of a baseball game that had taken place earlier that same day. The first feature film to be shown at the Strand was a Western from Selig called *The Spoilers*, which at nine reels set a record for length.

As was customary, W.F. was holding one of his late-night conferences with Jack Leo and Winfield Sheehan in attendance. It was about one in the morning and it was cold outside.

His eyes cloudy and a little puffy, Leo yawned. "What time is it anyway?"

Pacing around as he liked to do, puffing on a cigar, W.F. said, "Forget the damn time, Jack! What's this about a 12-reel picture, Winnie?"

"D.W. Griffith has made this epic about the Civil War. It opens at the Liberty, W.F."

The press article W.F. was referring to said that the picture had previewed on February 8, 1915, at Clune's Auditorium in Los Angeles. The article added that the queues had been so long that four other theaters had to be equipped to show the picture.

"How did it play in Los Angeles, Winnie?"

"It more than sold out every night, W.F."

"I can't believe it. The Aitkens invested over $100,000 in this film. Is this true, Winnie?"

"That's what I heard, too."

"That's too much to risk on one damn picture, Jack, isn't it?"

"I'd say so, W.F."

"They'll never get their money back! The sons-a-bitches will go broke!"

What concerned William Fox most was that an upstart named Harry Aitken was upping the ante to produce a negative, sharply increasing the running time of a single film. In the motion picture business, there was something new every day. Now it was this 12-reel film.

"Let's go see the goddamn picture!" W.F. said.

Initially operators of film exchanges in the Midwest, Harry Aitken and his brother Roy were Protestants born and raised on a farm near Goerke's Corners, east of Waukesha, Wisconsin. Like many silent era film distributors, they had gone from cooperation with, to opposition to, Edison's Trust. In pursuit of product to satisfy the insatiable thirst of theaters, Harry Aitken founded Majestic and bought a half-dozen independent filmmakers like the Reliance Company that owned an outmoded studio on the former Clara Morris Estate in Yonkers. If the picture was good, it was released on Majestic. If it was lousy, it was released on Reliance.

Most of the Reliance and Majestic pictures were made at the Fine Arts Studio, which was located at the corner of Sunset Boulevard and Vine Street in Hollywood.

It was about this time that D.W. Griffith began looking for a new studio from which to produce elaborate pictures. "Elaborate" in Griffith's mind meant longer pictures with more complicated plots. He'd gone so far as to make a four-reel film, *Judith of Bethulia*. J.J. Kennedy's Biograph thought Griffith's big-picture idea risky and decided not to renew his contract unless he agreed to restrict himself to shorter, more commercial films.

Because of the film monopoly, Griffith did not turn to other members of Edison's Trust for employment. They had agreed not to poach key employees from one another.

D.W. Griffith met briefly with Adolph Zukor, who offered him $50,000 a year but would not grant him the free choice of stories or control over casting and production costs. Although Zukor firmly believed in Griffith's talent, he was reluctant to let go of the purse strings.

That's when Griffith reached out to Harry Aitken who, at the time, owned and managed a studio deemed on par with that of Zukor. Although Harry Aitken's salary offer was substantially lower than Zukor's, Aitken reluctantly granted Griffith stock, plus a percentage in his films, and, most importantly for the inventive genius, the right to produce two independent films a year. Aitken's earlier hesitancy now gave way to boldness.

Upon discovering the deal Harry Aitken had struck with D.W. Griffith, Roy Aitken warned his brother, "Does Griffith know we have very little available capital and an oversupply of nerve?"

"I think he likes our nerve."

Without so much as a scenario to indicate what Griffith's treatment would be, the Aitken brothers set out to finance the cost of producing what would become *The Birth of a Nation,* estimated at $100,000, a healthy sum in those days.

As part of his contribution, Thomas Dixon—the author of the story—offered to forgo an up-front fee of $25,000 and accepted $2,000 plus 25 percent of the producer's gross.

Over lunch at the Alexandria Hotel, Harry Aitken agreed to give Griffith 37 percent after Dixon's royalty was paid. The rest of the stockholders would share whatever money was left. To round off the financing of the picture, the investment banker Felix Kahn, Wall Streeter Otto Kahn's younger brother, got the Aitken brothers to pledge part of their stock and salaries against a loan. In spite of an equity dilution, Harry and Roy Aitken kept a substantial piece of the action for themselves. Tired of delays, Harry Aitken insisted that Griffith get started on the picture.

On February 28, 1915, a large crowd of well-dressed patrons gathered in front of the Liberty Theater at 234 West 42nd Street for the invitational matinee of *Birth.*

The who's who list included society leaders, stage personalities, politicians, writers, artists, producers and businessmen. It appeared to be a sold-out performance.

As their motorcar approached the theater, W.F. and Winnie could see a man up on a ladder putting in the last few letters on the marquee. Liberty's manager deftly steered them through the surging crowd into the theater. Outside, people were waving invitations, while others tried to push their way in.

On the far side of the lobby, W.F. could see a solemn-looking Harry Aitken pacing up and down, chatting with dignitaries while barking commands to ushers and other theater personnel. On another side, a sort of receiving line was taking shape. In the background, a robust, 40-piece orchestra played a classical piece. Griffith had worked many hours scheduling the music and tempo he required for certain scenes.

W.F. saw the very tall and imposing D.W. Griffith at the head of the line directly alongside a more taciturn-looking gentleman, greeting important guests. Now and again, Griffith's sharp eyes panned the room looking for familiar faces.

Irrespective of the time of day, everyone was dressed formally as befit the occasion.

Like everyone else, W.F. and Winnie would just have to wait their turn.

Now 40 years of age, David Wark Griffith began his career as a stage actor and later wrote stories, poems and plays, but with little success. To survive he toured with road shows as Lawrence Griffith. He was stranded in one-horse towns, fired and routinely overworked. Often, he lived on day-old bread and hard-boiled eggs. It had been a long hard road from the genteel poverty of the Kentucky farm where Griffith was born in 1875 to the place they called Hollywood.

Like many other thespians, Griffith took a pragmatic turn to directing and found an opening at Biograph where he was instantly assigned to a film. He invested a good deal of his personal charm and ability into his new job. Griffith's understanding of the dramatic effect of close-ups, coupled with a more natural way of acting, quickly distinguished his filmmaking techniques from those of his peers. To create realistic spectacles, he placed his camera in the middle of the action. The still-photo look of early silents slowly gave way to more realistic action.

Fortuitous discoverer of talent that he was, Griffith worked with gifted actresses like Mary Pickford, Blanche Sweet, Mae Marsh and Lillian Gish and through them demonstrated the vast assortment of material he was capable of transforming into pictures. Players rehearsed and were coached in every movement. While the camera rolled, Griffith fired rapid commands to his players, indicating how they should pose, smile, gesture or stand.

Averaging close to two films a week, D.W. Griffith demonstrated he was ready to produce films by the dozen, mostly in a single reel. By the time Griffith left Biograph in 1913, he'd directed 450 films. However, it was not quantity that set Griffith apart, but his unique photographic style and the distinct quality of his work. Over the years, he developed and perfected numerous camera techniques, many of which emanated from his outstanding cameraman, Billy Bitzer. It was Griffith who pioneered new ideas of scenic arrangement or "cutting" as it was called, possibly making him the first to use creative editing as a filmmaking tool. It was Griffith who first discovered the close-up, the cutback, the fade-out and the truck shot.

If early Hollywood had a standard for the "science" of filmmaking, it was David Wark Griffith's camera techniques.

After joining Reliance-Majestic, Griffith secretly prepared for the filming of *Birth*.

It was Harry Aitken who first caught sight of W.F. standing at the very end of the long receiving line. He darted through the crowd and extended a grateful hand. "Bill! I knew you'd come! We're making history here today."

"I'm happy to be here, Harry."

Aitken edged W.F. and Winnie toward Thomas Dixon, a tall, thin man with shiny gray hair, black eyebrows and a long narrow face. Along the way, Aitken explained that Dixon was a Baptist preacher.

"Perfectly cast for the part of a preacher man," W.F. told Aitken.

"This is William Fox, the owner of Fox Film, and Winfield Sheehan. Thomas Dixon wrote the story, Bill."

Dixon smiled politely. "My pleasure, gentlemen."

The clergyman looked at W.F. for a moment, then sneered at Winnie. Turning, he focused on another guest. Names didn't seem to impress him in the least.

Harry Aitken tapped D.W. Griffith on the shoulder and he swung around, facing W.F. and Sheehan. Smiling broadly, Griffith towered over them like a giant from the forest.

W.F. could recognize in him all the nuances of the grand pose of what would come to be known as the Hollywood Type.

"Have you ever met William Fox?" Aitken asked.

Contorting his face, which made his big aquiline nose seem even bigger, Griffith responded, "I don't believe I've ever had that pleasure, Harry."

Topping W.F.'s list of questions was the steep ticket price Harry Aitken proposed to charge the public. As it was in the beginning, 25 cents was still the most prevalent single price.

"Do you really think people will pay more than 25 cents to see a picture, Mr. Griffith?"

"We're charging two dollars a ticket, Mr. Fox."

Aitken inserted himself. "One of our backers, Felix Kahn, I think you know him, he—"

"I remember the man," W.F. said. "Kuhn, Loeb."

"Well, he says, 'let's get what it's worth.' We're showing 12 reels of film. It's an epic, Bill. It'll change the way pictures are made."

Griffith said, "See the picture, Mr. Fox. Watch the box office. It'll speak for itself."

No doubt existed in anyone's mind that Griffith was the center of attention, and like most creative people, he craved recognition and admiration. There was also no question in W.F.'s mind that Griffith would begin to exert undue influence over Harry Aitken, cloud his judgment and, that before long, Griffith would make a fatally bad picture.

When Griffith turned away from them, Harry Aitken said, "Griffith has this uncanny sense of knowing if something is wrong with a picture."

After a long pause that seemed to give W.F.'s statement a foreboding tone, he said, "I'll be honest with you, Harry. There's no way of telling when you've got a bad picture until it's up on the screen."

"If anyone knows, Griffith knows, Bill."

A pretty usherette came into view and was prepared to escort W.F. and Winnie into the auditorium. She was 21 going on 40 and had a mischief-loving smile on her face.

"Take these two gentlemen to their seats, please," Harry Aitken said.

"Yes, Mr. Aitken."

Almost as an afterthought, Aitken asked, "How about joining us for dinner tonight, Bill?"

Not at all social, W.F. entertained sparingly at this stage of his career.

"I'll take a rain check, but I'm sure Winnie would be pleased to go, isn't that so, Winnie?"

"I'd love to join you, Harry."

"Call me next week, Bill. I'd like to hear your personal critique of the picture."

"I'll do that, Harry. I'll do that."

Through some puzzling mix-up, too many invitations had been issued and one could see maintenance men frenetically placing folding chairs in the aisles to deal with the overflow. Guests were upset and tempers flared.

As befit their lofty status in the industry, W.F. and Winnie were led to a row of roped-off empty seats reserved for special guests, third-row front.

"Here are your seats, gentlemen."

Winnie dug deeply into a vest pocket and found a dime that he gladly handed to the pretty young girl. He could tell the acting bug had bitten her.

"Thank you, sir."

No matter how many rushes one had seen, no matter how many private screenings one had put a film through, nothing substituted for a live audience. Quite simply, it was make-or-break time for *Birth of a Nation,* and possibly the feature film as a medium of entertainment.

As the house lights darkened and the orchestra swung into theme music, W.F. and Winnie settled back into their chairs. The screen brightened and the orchestra keyed in.

On the screen appeared the first slaves arriving in America, and the ensuing abolition movement. Then came the Civil War, showing Phil and Tod Stoneman of Pennsylvania visiting their old friends, the Cameron boys of South Carolina. Margaret Cameron is in love with Phil Stoneman, and Elsie Stoneman is deeply in love with Colonel Ben Cameron.

A rising star by the name of Lillian Gish plays the role of Elsie. Some of the minor roles are played by the likes of Wallace Reid, Elmo Lincoln, who became the first Tarzan, Raoul Walsh and Donald Crisp, all names that later would shine on a theater marquee.

In the middle of the first half of the picture many battle scenes erupt, including the charge of Klan horsemen who, Aitken said later, ride directly over cameraman Billy Bitzer, who has buried himself in a basin in the ground.

The musical score is many-faceted and calls for a 40-piece orchestra, an offstage chorus and sound effects. The material includes pieces from Schubert, Dvorak, Schumann, Mozart, Tchaikovsky, Grieg and Mahler. Of course, echoes of Wagner are heard. Throughout the film the orchestra plays bits and pieces of Stephen Foster's musical creations.

After intermission came the Reconstruction Era. In Walthall's homecoming scene, women patrons groaned as delicate hands pulled the debilitated colonel into his battered house.

The final scene shows the remnants of the two families in a double wedding. The closing subtitle says: "The establishment of the South in its rightful place is the birth of a new nation."

When the lights came on, the applause was deafening. Guests crowded around Griffith, Aitken and Dixon, who were basking in their apparent triumph. Promoters and exchange men tried to corner Aitken and Griffith to request propositions for the exhibition of the film.

The audience slowly filed out and W.F. went over in his head what he'd learned that afternoon. D.W. Griffith was a great director, and Fox Film would have to pay more attention to its cadre of directors. The exteriors were marvelous, and W.F. needed to move some of his production outdoors. But for that, camera technology would have to improve.

W.F. also thought, in spite of what appeared to be a sure thing, Harry Aitken would one day go broke. Anyone who bet $100,000 on a single picture was betting the store.

After climbing into the front seat of the motorcar, Harold started the engine and gunned it away from the sidewalk, a second car following close behind. For a time, they bumped along behind a streetcar. Then Harold swerved the motorcar off in another direction, and all was quiet once again.

W.F. turned to look at Winnie and saw that he was pensive, sitting quietly with his hands in his lap. He said, "Aitken went out on the limb for this picture, Winnie."

Nodding, Winnie didn't say anything. His mind was moving in another direction.

"Harry Aitken will be gone in a couple of years, Winnie."

Shortly after *Birth's* preview, W.F. received a call from the bit player who performed the part of John Wilkes Booth in *Birth,* a young man named Raoul Walsh. He'd played in five or six one and two reels at Biograph and said he wanted to direct. An expert rider, he'd migrated onto the Biograph lot as an extra, moving up to assistant director.

It just so happened that W.F. had purchased an outdoor story and had no one in particular to direct the picture. "Raoul, I've just bought a great story for you. It's called *The Honor System.* I've been in touch with Governor Hunt of Arizona and he wants the picture made and will give all the assistance we need. Are you interested?"

Raoul Walsh as John Wilkes Booth in *Birth of a Nation*

"Hell, yes, Mr. Fox."

Not long after the call, Raoul Walsh boarded a train to Arizona where he met with a delighted Governor Hunt. After a few minutes of conversation, Walsh surmised that what the governor really wanted was to see his name spread all over the press for this wonderful social idea he was promoting.

To get things started, Walsh handed him a draft of the scenario he'd worked up.

The governor began reading and started making observations even before he came to the end of the two-page story line.

"That is just what I'm after, *The Honor System.* I believe in turning prisoners loose in the daytime, so they can go to various towns and return at night on their honor. This picture is just what I want."

"Let's make it then, Governor."

On his way back to Los Angeles, Walsh thought about a male lead and decided he'd propose his dashing younger brother George for the part.

Winnie took one look at several stills of the muscular George Walsh and said, "Try him for the part."

"Thanks," Raoul said.

"How about the female lead, Raoul?"

"Do you have any ideas?"

"Yeah. Gladys Brockwell. She comes cheap."

A stage-trained actress, Gladys Brockwell was from Brooklyn and had made several garden-variety two-reelers at Lubin's studio.

"I'll get in touch with her, Winnie."

It wasn't long before the picture was finished and in the can. Raoul Walsh traveled to Arizona and found himself in Governor Hunt's office. The rustic-looking, rough plastered walls reminded him of a sheriff's office back in Texas.

"If the Fox company will pay for the man's expenses, I'll turn a life prisoner loose to go back to New York for the opening of *The Honor System.*"

The next evening, Raoul Walsh was on the phone with W.F. He told him of the governor's idea.

"Raoul, that's great. We'll pay the expenses."

The lifer went to New York, attended the premiere and got up on the stage to make an appeal for the idea expressed in the film. Audience response was good, and Raoul thought the staged event would buy free publicity for the picture. He put the lifer on the Limited and sent him to Arizona, or so he thought. The lifer got as far as Chicago and was not seen again.

Mortified, W.F. phoned Walsh and asked, "Raoul, who picked that prisoner?"

"I think the governor did, Mr. Fox. Will this hurt the picture?"

"Hell, no. It'll help the picture."

And it did. Besides, W.F. found a director and a promising young player in the Walsh brothers.

Over the years, W.F. repeated the tale of Harry Aitken's trajectory to illustrate how risky the motion picture business really was.

"Imagine, if you will, the scenario of a great tragedy, one we shall title, 'The Rise and Fall of a Hollywood Tycoon,' the story of a man who loses everything in a few short years as the result of bad judgment, bad luck and timing.

"As his brother Roy Aitken once said, 'Harry didn't, and perhaps couldn't, consolidate. He was brimming over with ideas to develop the movie industry, and these ideas drove him.'

"The fact was that Harry Aitken was a quick read, but was very impatient. Bored by the day-to-day tasks of running a business, he was always off somewhere looking for new challenges.

"Our story begins right after the successful first-run appearances of his epic film.

"First scene: On the heels of *Birth's* success, Harry Aitken contracts a bloated thespian, Sir Herbert Beerbohm-Tree, and offers him $100,000 to make a couple of films. Both pictures are dismal box-office failures.

"'Those things will happen,' Harry says.

"Undaunted, Harry Aitken decides he needs a first-run theater on Broadway, so he leases the Knickerbocker. About this time, one of the most celebrated scenario writers of silent film, Gardiner Sullivan, winds up on Aitken's payroll.

"Roy Aitken admonishes, 'Watch your expenses, Harry.'

"Second scene: *Birth's* continuing box-office appeal generates a steady and appreciable cash flow. Unshaken by the Sir Herbert fiasco Harry Aitken forms another studio, an important studio, one he calls, 'Triangle Films.'

"To accomplish this objective, Harry floats a $5 million stock issue and decides to use other people's money to help him realize his dream of becoming a motion picture tycoon. Harry surrounds himself with exceptional talent. Hooking up with his old friend, D.W. Griffith, he contracts the gifted Thomas Ince and the comedy genius Mack Sennett. They all sign on to make pictures for Triangle Films.

"Roy Aitken warns him, 'Don't forget. Triangle will be costly to run if Griffith, Ince and Sennett get their way.'

"What Harry overlooks is that Ince and Sennett have prior commitments with other studios, and consequently there won't be enough time to make films for Triangle in the short term. He forgets the importance of managing time.

"But not all is bleak. Bathing beauties are part and parcel of Sennett's inventory, and he goes ahead and puts the girls on film in spite of the hundreds of protest letters from women's organizations. And the films generate cash that Harry Aitken never seems to have enough of.

"Third scene: around this time, Harry Aitken has under contract a promising young actor named Douglas Fairbanks, a former star of the Broadway stage. Aitken arbitrarily assigns Doug's program to the old warrior, D.W. Griffith, whose ego is even bigger than Doug's. Instead of attending to the promising actor like he should, Griffith farms 'the jumping Jack' out to the lesser known writer/director team of Anita Loos and John Emerson, and this enrages Douglas Fairbanks. It becomes patently evident that Douglas Fairbanks is disgruntled and he begins looking for greener pastures.

"Griffith says: 'He's got a face like a cantaloupe, and he can't act.'

"Fourth scene: Triangle shapes a rich and talented portfolio of players, including Mae Marsh, Lillian and Dorothy Gish, William S. Hart, H.B. Warner, Wallace Reid, Mabel Normand, Ford Sterling, Fatty Arbuckle, and, of course, Douglas Fairbanks.

"Fifth scene: Things are moving along nicely and Harry Aitken feels confident again. He returns to the stock market for more money. Armed with buckets of cash, he purchases control of the New York Motion Picture Corporation.

1915 Triangle stock certificate

"Space is a problem. Enough space for stages and outdoor sets where his producers, directors and players can make good pictures.

"Sixth scene: A nice piece of land, part of a Spanish land grant, *La Ballena,* is acquired by a developer, Harry H. Culver, who makes a gift of 12 acres to Thomas Ince, one of Aitken's associates.

"Feeling the pinch from producing a string of bad pictures, Ince decides to unload the property on Triangle Films. On this barren site Harry Aitken constructs a state-of-the-art studio at the cost of $500,000 that translates into a material increase in Triangle's fixed cost, raising its break-even point.

"To absorb this cost increment, Harry Aitken must produce profitable pictures as quickly as possible. From this moment on, Harry Aitken can't afford to miss a beat.

"Seventh scene: One fine day Douglas Fairbanks shows Harry Aitken a telegram from Adolph Zukor, offering him a $10,000 weekly advance and 50 percent of the profits from his pictures.

"After going over the numbers, Harry Aitken decides he can't match the offer and Fairbanks breaks his contract to sign with Zukor. The young actor with the devil-may-care attitude will go on to become a major star.

"Eighth scene: The pundits anoint Adolph Zukor as the single most important driving force behind the emerging motion picture industry. Harry Aitken hears the intelligentsia talk in glowing terms about Adolph Zukor's business acumen. Aitken says to himself, 'Why not merge Triangle with Zukor's company?'

"Ninth scene: A combine of Zukor's Famous Players and Triangle Films is what's on Harry Aitken's mind. Think of it. The industry's most popular players laboring under the tutelage of an outstanding cadre of directors, making good pictures in Harry's brand-new Culver City studio.

"'A match made in heaven,' Harry tells his brother, Roy. 'Hell, we'll even get Douglas Fairbanks back on the lot.'

"Unbeknownst to Harry Aitken, Adolph Zukor has more pressing matters to resolve. Zukor decides to buy out Sam [Goldfish] Goldwyn, an irritable personality forced upon him when he merges his Famous Players with Jesse Lasky's studio.

"When approached by Harry Aitken on his 'match made in heaven,' Zukor asks himself, 'Why pay good money for Triangle's underproducing assets when I can randomly pick and choose from Aitken's impressive roster of talent?'

"Good healthy rats don't want to die on a sinking ship, do they? Of course they don't. By offering inflated salaries, Adolph Zukor is able to lure away Triangle's Gloria Swanson, Fatty Arbuckle and William S. Hart. One, two, three.

"Tenth scene: From the very start, Ince, Griffith and Sennett make dreadful pictures. Harry Aitken asks his brother, Roy, 'Is it possible that these three icons have run out of gas at the same time?' This horrendous thought sends a cold chill down Harry Aitken's spine, and for the first time, he begins to doubt. Harry's judgment is questioned and he feels lethargic.

"To further complicate things, D.W. Griffith sinks a respectable chunk of Aitken's money into the inevitable sequel to *Birth,* which Griffith calls *Intolerance.* More to the point, Harry's got $200,000 riding on the picture. *Intolerance* is a dismal failure at the box office.

"Where is that uncanny sense of what is wrong with a picture?

"Eleventh scene: Thomas Ince gets cold feet and decides to bail out, turning a former associate into a competitor. Almost overnight, Ince forms his own company. Before long Ince is joined by Mack Sennett and together they create Associated Producers. The studio eventually merges into Tom Talley's First National.

"Twelfth scene: A predictable consequence of Harry Aitken's bad decisions is that he runs out of money. To satisfy jittery lenders, he's pressured into signing secured notes in order to get money to offset operating losses. As part of the deal, a few remaining precious assets are pledged to lenders. The lenders want to be sure they're not throwing good money after bad, so they insist upon an audit. After its completion, brackets are placed around Triangle's equity account. The studio is now leveraged to the hilt. Things don't improve. Aitken refuses to confront the stark reality facing him. Triangle is not only making bad pictures but also *fewer* of them.

"With their borrowing capacity exhausted and faced with insolvency, Harry and Roy Aitken have no other choice but to shut down some of their superfluous facilities, like the Fine Arts Studio in Los Angeles and the Keystone Studio.

"Thirteenth scene: There comes the day when there's not even enough money in the till to pay for power and light. Triangle collapses. Despite the romantic setting around the Culver City lot, Aitken is in the midst of a liquidation. A hungry flock of vultures swoop over Triangle's remaining assets, hoping to salvage something of value. The only thing that's left of the formerly lucrative enterprise is put up for sale.

"Using some of the money he gets from Zukor, Sam Goldwyn buys the Culver City studio for $325,000 in what he considers to be 'the backwater of Hollywood.' The very next day, a new sign goes up, Goldwyn Pictures. Majestic, Reliance, Thanhouser and the New York Motion Picture Company bankrupt. Their film catalogues sell for pennies. Aitken is broke."

CHAPTER 3

To celebrate the New York debut of *Birth*, a party was held in Harry Aitken's seven-room apartment on West 57th Street. Piled high in three bedrooms were fur coats, expensive jewelry, neckpieces, bowler hats and scarves. The English butler Dunstan and his wife Nellie quietly attended to guests as they circulated through the apartment eating and drinking highballs and eagerly talking about the picture.

Of course, the center of attention was David Wark Griffith (D.W. for short). Mostly jubilant throughout the evening, a flicker of uncertainty would now and then temper the excitement in his expression. Everything he owned was riding on this one picture, and he wasn't able to forget it.

Long after most of the guests had departed, Dunstan and Nellie were picking up glasses and dishes, as Harry Aitken invited those few who remained to join him for a drink in his study.

Felix Kahn wondered what W.F. thought of the picture. "Did he like it?"

"He thought it was too expensive," Winnie replied.

Now it was Harry Aitken who became embittered, and said, "That cheap bastard will be producing crap when we're on top of the world, Felix!"

They were in a jovial mood—smoking cigars and sipping cognac.

Suddenly the phone rang, and Aitken answered it. "Harry Aitken."

"Mr. Aitken, this is Louis B. Mayer, Boston. I've got a couple of theaters here. I've heard the story of *Birth*'s successful matinee opening. How about selling me the New England distribution rights?"

Covering the mouthpiece with his left hand Aitken turned to face his expectant investors. "It's a Louis B. Mayer from Boston. He wants to buy distribution rights."

"Perhaps," chuckled Griffith, "for a big price. All of us need money."

"Mayer, how much will you offer?"

"Maybe $50,000 with a $25,000 down payment. And a 50-50 split after I get my investment back."

"Come to New York as soon as you can, and we'll talk to you about the deal, Mr. Mayer. But hurry. You'll have competitors. Our $2 grand opening will be next week, and if it's a sellout, our distribution prices may go up."

As for Louis B. Mayer, he'd make more than half a million dollars on the deal and become a major player in film exchange.

Throughout his professional life, W.F. referred to Carl Laemmle as the grand old man of the motion picture industry.

By 1915, Laemmle was 48 years old and controlled an important studio—Universal. Because he'd inundated his payroll with relatives, most from his homeland in Germany, Laemmle was referred to around the lot as "Uncle Carl."

From the Gothic Dearborn Station in Chicago on March 7, 1915 a special train with a diner, buffet and drawing room cars departed on a long journey to the West Coast for the opening of Universal Studio. The train stopped at Kansas City and Denver. From Denver's Santa Fe Station the group left en route to the Grand Canyon, a side excursion that lasted another day and a half. Six days after leaving Grand Central Station, Uncle Carl and his coterie reached Los Angeles where players of all sorts—cowboys, cavalrymen and Indians—met them.

On March 15, the inaugural ceremony for the official opening of Universal Studio was in full swing. At W.F.'s request Sol Wurtzel, W.F.'s point man on the West Coast, represented Fox Film at the occasion.

Everything on the Universal lot was on levels. The hilly terrain was perfect for outdoor shooting. Universal City sprawled amid acres of chicken farms. It was the perfect place to make Westerns. Most of the structures in Universal City were painted white and contrasted sharply with their green surroundings. Weeds were hacked to an even level and the whole area was scrupulously gardened.

Sol wrote that there were 500 cars parked on the lot, maybe more. "I'm amazed at the number of people who came to see the new studio."

At 10:15 a.m. Laura Oakley, chief of the Universal Studio police, handed Carl Laemmle a gold key giving him entrance to the new municipality. When he placed it in the lock it released a super flashlight connection, of which he was given no warning, momentarily upsetting him.

Uncle Carl, a small, bespectacled man, maintained a gap-toothed smile on his face. "I hope I didn't make a mistake in coming out here."

In reality, Carl Laemmle had a dislike of ballyhoo. But it was an integral part of the film business.

Carl Laemmle

Much like William Fox, Carl Laemmle was one of the embattled independents who had fought Edison's Trust. For that fact alone, William Fox was indebted to him. W.F. thought Laemmle's fortitude admirable.

Laemmle rented an office at 111 East 14th Street in New York and started making moving pictures. Originally his filmmaking company was called IMP (Independent Motion Picture Company). The company's output soon reached one film a week and Laemmle was making money.

In spite of pervasive industry skepticism about the fittingness of his pictures, Laemmle's timing was better than most. For example, he acquired the services of talented director Thomas H. Ince and lured the glamorous Florence Lawrence away from Biograph.

Throughout this building period Laemmle persistently disputed the stranglehold Edison's Trust had cast over the industry. Over a period of five years, no fewer than 289 lawsuits were brought against him.

As a result of his persistent rejection of Edison's Trust, on April 15, 1912 the U.S. Government filed a petition against the Motion Picture Patents Company and the General Film Company demanding their dissolution. The Motion Picture Patents Company's reign of terror finally ended in 1915 with the implementation of a court decree.

Laemmle's lucky streak continued when he hired innocent-looking Mary Pickford, whose first picture for IMP was *Their First Misunderstanding*. Prior to Mary Pickford's association with Laemmle, Mary had acted at Biograph, earning a measly $100 a week. As part of the IMP deal, Laemmle upped her salary to $175 a week and gave Mary Pickford name recognition in IMP's publicity.

It was shortly thereafter that Laemmle merged the IMP company with Pat Power's Picture Plays, Adam Kessel and Charles Bauman's Bison Life Motion Pictures, as well as Nestor Champion and William Swanson's Rex companies. Kessel and Bauman's claim to fame was the creation of Keystone Comedies directed by Mack Sennett, whom they'd rescued from anonymity at Biograph.

After several years in the role of treasurer, Laemmle emerged as the undisputed boss. It was he who had picked the name for the new company: Universal.

Mona and Belle with their father, William Fox, in their garden.

If W.F. wanted to stay in the picture business, Fox Film required a studio in California. The cost of leasing a studio in Hollywood and the operating expense it entailed to make pictures were a lot less than on the East Coast. Despite its belated origin it was a good plan.

The evening before W.F.'s departure for California, the Fox family partook of the traditional Sunday family dinner. Of course Mona and Belle were there. By now Mona was a gangling girl of 15 and Belle was 11 years old. Over time Belle flowered into the free spirit of the family and was completely adored by her doting father.

Belle wore a blue dress and white stockings and had a serious look on her face.

As was customary, W.F. presided at the head of the table and sat in a ladder-back chair made of fine mahogany. Mona was seated on his right, with Belle to the left of him and Eve opposite.

Head servant Elsa and several other servants attended the family. They all ate heartily of roast beef, sauerkraut and dumplings.

"This is wonderful, Elsa."

Elsa replied in her Swedish-accented English, "Thank you, Mrs. Fox. I hope the girls like it."

"We do, Elsa. Honest," Mona volunteered.

Throughout the meal, W.F. noticed Belle's uncharacteristic silence as if her mind were a million miles away. "What are you thinking about, Belle?"

At first, Belle didn't answer him. Then she grunted something incoherent. Whatever was going through her mind, it had captivated her.

Following the main course, W.F. was served a thin slice of white layer cake, one of the chef's best recipes.

Looking over at Belle, Eve asked, "Belle, do we have anything special for Father?"

Mona gestured with one hand and it finally registered what it was that Belle was supposed to retrieve.

Belle disappeared into an adjacent room. After a few moments she surfaced clutching a decoratively wrapped little box. She handed W.F. the small package and planted a kiss on his ready cheek.

"What do we have here?"

"A gift for your trip to California, Daddy," Belle replied.

W.F. carefully untied the ribbon, tore off the paper wrapping and discovered a small leather case. Feigning surprise he opened the case and saw the elements of a traveling kit: a strop razor, nail clippers, a hair brush and some other shiny metal paraphernalia whose purpose he wasn't quite sure of.

"We all wish Father a very successful trip to California, don't we, girls?"

"Are there lots of Indians in California, Daddy?" Mona mused.

"Only in the moving pictures, darling."

Then it finally dawned on him that this would only be the second time he would leave the family for such a long time. True, he usually arrived late at night or early morning, but there was always the kiss good night, the kind of warmth that recharged his battery for another day of hard work.

W.F. looked at each of them and said, "I want to say how much I love all of you, and I shall miss you terribly."

Down on the platform chief red cap Jim Williams met every important person who came to Grand Central Station and supervised the handling of their luggage. He followed W.F. and Winfield Sheehan as they made their way along track 34.

"Anything I can do for you, Mr. Fox?" Williams asked.

"I hope you put tender steaks on board, chief."

"Now you know that's not my department, Mr. Fox."

"I know, chief."

They boarded the Limited, found their way to their seats and made themselves comfortable for the first leg of the trip to Chicago.

The trip to California would take several days; the longest leg, Chicago to Los Angeles, was nearly 70 hours running time. Passenger trains had every accommodation available at the time: air brakes, central heat, electric light and flush toilets. There was a dining car and sleeper cars. The only luxury missing was air conditioning, which was not used until the 1930s.

W.F. would learn the hard way that his frequent jaunts to the West Coast had to be planned during the fall and winter months when it was cooler.

About three hours into the second leg of the trip, W.F. decided to barrage Winnie with some of his concerns. "What about other players? We've got Theda Bara, William Farnum and Betty Nansen. That's not good enough!"

William Farnum, one of Fox's major players, was now 39 years old and had been on the stage since he was 12. He'd toured the vaudeville circuit in an athletic act with his brother Dustin Farnum. His first film, *The Spoilers*, was one of William Selig's most spectacular productions and enjoyed a good run at the Strand in New York.

It was strange in a way that Fox Film had hired Farnum away from Selig, because now W.F. and Winnie were on their way to California to lease one of Selig's studios.

Betty Nansen was Danish and famed as an Ibsen interpreter, but she'd never make it big in pictures. Fox was paying her a good deal of money, $2,000 a week.

"I hear Fairbanks may be looking, W.F."

"Too expensive! I'm not paying for big names. One bad picture and Fox Film is out of business!"

The growing popularity of Mary Pickford—who was now working for Famous Players—taught producers like Adolph Zukor that a good actor could offset a lot of mediocre films. The exhibitors would do just about anything to get a Pickford picture, so Zukor dictated terms on other films to them. This kind of leverage pushed the salaries of Chaplin, Pickford, Fairbanks and others through the roof.

W.F.'s thought was a little different. Fox Film would nurture unknowns to stardom under a tight rein, much as it had with Theda Bara. W.F. wasn't going to spend scarce funds to acquire some temperamental star who might bolt the very next day. Many believed this stringent policy would turn into William Fox's Achilles heel.

Whenever questioned on the subject of big stars, W.F. simply said, "Look at my record as head of Fox Film."

Somewhat disturbed by the trend of their conversation Winnie Sheehan shuffled his bulk in his seat and lit a cigarette. W.F. was never sure whether the Irishman liked traveling with him, but it didn't matter. What counted was staying on top of things. The backbone of the business was talent. The more of it a studio had the better off it was.

"How about Westerns, W.F.?"

"What about them?"

"William S. Hart is drawing a big audience."

W.F. thought about that for a moment. Some said Hart was the creator of the Western picture. "Broncho Billy" Anderson had made a lot of one-reelers but Hart, a former stage actor, brought a new dimension to the Western.

W.F. said, "So find us a cowboy, Winnie. Preferably one who can ride a horse."

Winnie chuckled and so did W.F.

"We're looking, W.F."

"What's our production schedule for the rest of the year, Winnie?"

"We'll make over 30 pictures."

"How about Theda Bara?"

"She'll shoot at least 10."

"Like all things, Winnie, there's a time, and then that time passes."

It was time for sleep and W.F. pushed a buzzer. A black man in a white jacket appeared. "Yes, Mr. Fox?"

"Get our berths ready George."

"Yes sir."

In Europe one had first, second and third class. In America one had the day coach and the Pullman. By 1920 over 20 million people rode sleepers. More extravagant was the private car. Their use came into fashion for people like Henry Ford, Paul Block, E.F. Hutton, John Raskob, C.M. Schwab and Harry Sinclair. Still at the lower rung of the social ladder, W.F. didn't measure up to their wealth and kind of power.

The train rocked gently from side to side. Every so often a train whistle blared a mournful sound. Sitting on the edge of a lower berth, W.F. removed his shoes and clothing except for his trousers. He slipped into the lower berth and traded a pajama bottom for his trousers and handed the trousers to a porter, who whisked them away.

A moment passed and the train was taking a sharp curve. The conductor steadied himself. "Good night, all." The conductor switched off the common light. W.F. fell fast asleep.

At first light the next morning, W.F. pushed up the shade to see where he was. From the train, which was racing along flat farmland, he could see a herd of brown and white cattle grazing.

After washing and brushing up, W.F. and Winnie enjoyed a warm breakfast of bacon and eggs, and then leisurely strolled the length of the train.

For the rest of the trip, W.F. read a score of scenarios in search of novel story ideas. He said very little. It was his practice to use train time for reading story material and he really didn't want to engage in trivial conversation. This was understood by anyone who traveled with him for extended periods of time and no one dared violate this unwritten protocol.

As it got close to noon, a waiter came through the train from the dining car sounding three musical notes on a chime announcing the last call for lunch.

Not long after the call, Winnie and W.F. were seated together in the rear of the dining car checking off their lunch orders while speaking of incidental things that had little to do with making pictures. This was one of those rare moments Winnie could remember W.F. discussing anything other than business.

After lunch, they walked back to their seats. W.F. was sitting with his left arm resting on the arm of his chair, financial statements spread over his lap as he examined a cash flow statement and questioned Winnie on several disbursements. At the center of things was cash generated from operations. That was the number that counted most. It was a matter of investing up front in making pictures versus a payback, which could take months if not years. This phenomenon was referred to as "lag time."

This lag time didn't please W.F. at all. A way had to be found to minimize, if not reverse, the situation. A serious question thus existed as to how to finance the growth of motion picture production. However, before W.F. could put that question to a real test a more lustrous roster of players had to be contracted. Motion pictures performed poorly at the box office without attractive players in leading roles.

As the train sped across more open country, Winnie observed long stretches of dried cornstalks change to barren wheat fields. Before long the fields went dry. Although the windows were dirty, they felt warmer. Late afternoon faded into dusk.

Morning dawned bright and cloudless and the air was a little warmer now. When Winnie lifted the shade to see where the train was, a range of snowcapped mountains slipped into view. Later in the day there was a patch of green dotted with vibrant orange groves, which merged into the California hills.

A forceful voice shouted through the door, "Los Angeles!"

The big steam engine spewing vapor in all directions chugged slowly into Los Angeles Central Railroad Station. The train arrived three hours late. One of the automatic block signals had failed along the way, forcing the engineer to stop the train.

Sol M. Wurtzel

The locomotive slowly crawled into the station, its iron wheels singing "clack-clack" as it approached the end of the track. Up and down the platform, red caps pushed empty luggage carts as their bright uniforms contrasted vividly against the dark mass of humanity gathered along the track.

W.F. caught sight of Sol Wurtzel nervously tramping up and down the platform hunting for W.F.'s car. Wurtzel was a large-framed man who wore thick-rimmed glasses and smoked black cigars. His face was always coiled into a funny grimace that people mistook for a smile.

At this time Sol Wurtzel was still this side of 30. He'd

grown up on the Lower East Side and had the advantages of a high school education. After a brief succession of jobs, he was employed as a bookkeeper for a cigar factory. His brother Sam recommended him to William Fox at Box Office Attractions, and within a short period of time he was promoted to stenographer for Charles Levin, secretary of the Fox organization and W.F.'s cousin. Detecting an artistic talent in Wurtzel, W.F. provided him with plays to read and solicited his opinions as to their filmworthiness. Then W.F. shipped him off to California to look around for a studio property to lease.

What W.F. most admired was Sol Wurtzel's street savvy. He was definitely slated for bigger things. He would become Fox Film's B-pictures man, producing pictures cheaply and quickly to satisfy the inexhaustible theater demand. In the course of his career he'd develop a real skill for the mass production of decent films in short spans of time, which would make him a valuable asset to the company.

.

Finally the locomotive jolted to a complete stop and a conductor dropped a small metal step to the ground. Passengers stumbled off the train. There was a slight nip in the air, but it was warm compared to the cold New York weather they'd left behind.

As W.F. and Winnie emerged from the train, Wurtzel eventually saw them. He ran forward to greet them waving a newspaper. A porter trying to keep up with his brisk pace pushed a cart closely behind him.

"How was your trip, W.F.?"

"Long and tiring, Sol."

Every muscle in W.F.'s body felt weaker now than when he'd lain down for sleep last night. But his mind was alert and he was ready to take on the day.

"I wish California was a little closer to New York, like New Jersey maybe. Where are we staying, Sol?"

"I booked you and Winnie at the Alexandria."

The Fox complement moved vigorously toward the station house followed by a tall porter pushing a baggage cart. "What's on our agenda, Sol?" "We're meeting Colonel William Selig this afternoon, W.F. I've also set up a meeting with Virginia Pearson. I think she's got potential as a player."

"Virginia comes from the stage and we think she can play parts like Theda Bara," Winnie added.

Which reminded W.F. that Frank Powell once had thought of casting dark-eyed Virginia Pearson for *A Fool There Was* but had decided against it; and for the life of him W.F. couldn't remember the reason why.

"What about Chaplin?" Winnie asked.

"His brother Sydney said no dice. He won't let us get within 10 feet of him," Wurtzel replied.

CHAPTER 4

In those early days the Alexandria Hotel at Fifth and Spring Streets was very much the place to stay, especially for big shots in the motion picture industry. The lobby was always crowded with important people—and you could get a good turkey sandwich and scotch and soda between five and six in the evening. To top it off, there was a reasonable selection of stogies at the cigar counter, which was located in the lobby.

As W.F., Winnie and Sol walked across the famous million-dollar rug that covered the floor of the lobby, W.F. noticed several reporters making their way toward them. Some were taking pictures. It was almost impossible to skirt around them.

One of the reporters, pad in hand, yelled out, "What are your plans in California, Mr. Fox?"

Pushing the guy back, Sol said, "Mr. Fox will hold a press conference later this afternoon, gentlemen. Give us some room!"

In no other industry was this symbolism taken seriously. It was part of what being in the motion picture business was all about. The keystone of the industry was publicity, keeping your name in print or up in lights. In a quick turnabout, the fast-stepping reporters accosted William S. Hart, who had just entered the hotel lobby. He had a rugged, outdoor look. Though built on a small scale, he was delicately proportioned and made a fine figure of a man. The distraction permitted W.F., Winnie and Sol to quickly disappear into an elevator.

The suite was comfortable enough and the bed was large. In the distance through a canyon of several tall buildings, W.F. could see a mountain range and deep valleys that covered most of the terrain. Los Angeles had the aura of a Mediterranean town, with palm and pepper trees everywhere. Colors from flowering shrubs and trees that covered the hillside glistened in the sunlight.

A phone rang. It was Jack Leo from New York.

"Jack, what kind of attendance did we get?"

"The theaters came in at 65 percent, W.F." Jack's voice was faint and W.F. could barely hear him.

"Tell Joe we gotta to do a lot better than that!"

"Joe" was Joe Leo, Jack's younger brother, whom W.F. had placed in the position of theaters manager.

"The weather's lousy, W.F."

"Then tell Joe to change the weather! Do something to fill those damn seats. You hear me?"

"Yeah, W.F."

"Send me a telegram every day!"

"Yeah."

"Tell Eve I'm all right."

Whatever the reason, W.F. wasn't going to sit still for mediocre ticket sales.

Making a long-distance call in 1915 required a lot of patience. Sometimes the wait took as long as five hours before getting through, but W.F. didn't care. He'd always felt that the key to his business was the number of paying customers who entered the company's theaters on a daily basis. That was the rock on which Fox Film was founded. An empty seat was lost forever. It was a perishable commodity much like a piece of fruit left to rot in the open air. Besides, an empty seat didn't buy any candy.

W.F. made it his business to know the exact number of people who had attended the performances the night before. He knew the number of people who entered each theater every hour. And as soon as one of those theaters showed the slightest inclination toward falling off in receipts, he was able to send for the executive of that theater and rearrange the policy to prevent it from making a loss. There was no better measure of how well one was doing in the motion picture theater business than the sold-seat count. He relied heavily on that statistic for making decisions on pictures, theater locations and the performance of his managers.

The sound of a doorbell momentarily interrupted his thoughts.

"I'm coming."

W.F. opened the door. He was surprised to see a young man standing there in a nice-fitting white jacket with a bowtie around his neck. He was carrying an ice bucket with a pitcher of orange juice in it.

"Yes?"

"Fresh California orange juice, Mr. Fox?"

"I didn't order any fresh California orange juice."

"Compliments of the house, Mr. Fox."

"Put it down on the table."

The waiter placed the ice bucket on the small table near the bed, poured a glass and handed it to W.F. He quickly left the room.

W.F. gulped it down. It tasted sweet. He then drew the blackout drapes, kicked off his shoes and lay on the bed for a short nap. There was still a long day ahead of him.

W.F. raised his good right arm and stood for a moment frozen at a lectern. Around him were newsmen, casual observers and several local politicos whose names he didn't care to remember. The press met movie dignitaries in accordance with a time-honored tradition. W.F. would be no exception.

"Thank you for coming, gentlemen. I am William Fox. My business is making motion pictures."

W.F. said a few words about the studio's plans in California and then ceded the podium to the chairman of the Los Angeles Chamber of Commerce. "Mr. Chairman, thank you for coming."

"We are happy you have chosen Los Angeles to make your pictures, Mr. Fox. No other city in the world offers seashore, mountains, desert and city civilization within an hour of the studios."

W.F. rose to his feet and cleared his throat. "That and a nickel will get you on the subway in New York."

The gathering crowd erupted into laughter. Many of the hotel's registered guests were standing around with nothing better to do.

W.F. pointed down at a reporter. "What's your question?"

"Will Fox Film make all of its movies in California?"

"That's why we're here, young man. You have sunshine, good scenery, sunshine and... and...let me think of something else."

Some of those around W.F. laughed at his remark while the politicos grimaced.

Signaling with his finger, W.F. acknowledged another reporter. "Yes, you. The guy with the freckles."

"What kinds of pictures will you make?"

"My favorite kind. The kind that make money!"

Sol Wurtzel was frantically signaling W.F. that it was time to go and pay a visit to Colonel Selig.

"The press conference is over," W.F. said.

Winfield Sheehan and W.F. hopped into Wurtzel's shiny new Hudson and prepared themselves for the long, boring ride to 1845 Allesandro Street in Edendale, the site of Selig's studio.

Throughout the journey, W.F. couldn't help but notice how amazingly clean and spacious it was in Los Angeles. There were ramshackle houses, to be sure, but in comparison to New York there were no slums. A few wide boulevards wound through miles of windblown trees, bright flowers and emerald-green lawns. There was plenty of dirt and an occasional strong wind whipped up a lot of dust.

Winnie sat up front with Wurtzel while W.F. stretched out on the back seat.

W.F. did not speak until they reached the outskirts of the city and Winnie, having nothing to say, was also silent.

W.F. kicked off his shoes and said, "That feels better."

It was hot and dusty and all the windows were rolled down. For most of the trip Wurtzel drove over dirt roads and past endless orchards as well as an occasional farmhouse.

"Winnie, what's that Irishman Herbert Brenon up to?"

"I put him on *Soul of Broadway*, W.F."

"That's the picture with that…that…"

"Valeska Suratt," Wurtzel interjected. "You've got to meet her. She's a dumb bunny from Indiana but she's got a real cute ass and she can dance up a storm too."

"She oughta Americanize her goddamn name, Sol."

"I'll tell her that."

W.F. thought highly of Herbert Brenon, who had directed W.F.'s first picture, *Life's Shop Window*. Brenon, a likeable Irishman, had begun his career writing scenarios.

"Winnie, what the hell is this legal problem we got with Jesse Lasky?"

"Lasky filed for a temporary injunction restraining Suratt and Fox Film from exhibiting or advertising our picture. He says she's still under contract with him."

"That rotten son of a bitch!"

"Lasky wants to settle out of court," Winnie said.

"How much does that coronet player want?"

"He wants $5,000."

"Offer him $3,000. Not a goddamn penny more!"

"What if he says no?"

"Then tell him he can have the goddamn picture and shove it up his ass!"

Lasky settled for $4,000.

As for Valeska Suratt, she pleaded total ignorance. She told Wurtzel, "I'm just a little girl from Terra Haute, I don't know a thing about contracts, Mr. Wurtzel."

"I don't care if you come from Timbuktu. Just don't sign a goddamn thing until I read it, okay?" "Yes, Mr. Wurtzel."

One of Wurtzel's reputed talents was that of storyteller and he filled the unpleasant vacuum in the car with the life story of Colonel William Selig.

Wurtzel explained that bad weather in Chicago had encouraged Selig to send a film company southwest to film scenes of *The Count of Monte Cristo,*.

In 1909 Selig had built a studio in Edendale and a couple of years later built the Selig Zoo, which was the main lot for his animal films.

"I cased the area and thought it fit the bill for what we got in mind, W.F."

"How big is it?"

"A little less than an acre."

A block down from Selig's studio was the Pathé West Coast Studio and a block below on the same side of the street was the Bison Studio.

As if to bring home a point, Wurtzel said, "There's a good supply of electricity around there."

Wurtzel had heard that Selig wasn't doing too well and needed money, which was why he was leasing the Edendale studio at such a bargain price. Such opportunities, Wurtzel insisted, didn't come along every day. Selig was either so hard up or so shortsighted that he not only failed to use good stories and modern picture-making methods, he had even fallen behind the standard practices of the industry.

Wurtzel said, "Selig is out of touch, W.F."

"I appreciate the fact that you keep your eyes and ears open, Sol."

"Don't mention it. It's part of my job."

By the time they got to Edendale, the Hudson was covered with a fine coat of dust. Wurtzel pulled up to the studio gate and a crusty old guard wearing a tattered uniform approached the car. Wurtzel rolled down his window.

"Mr. Fox to see Colonel Selig."

"Just a moment."

Sluggishly the guard made his way to the back of their motorcar and slowly jotted down the license plate number. Upon completing this task he opened the big iron gate and gestured to Wurtzel to drive up. As Wurtzel steered the Hudson along a gravel path up to the gate, the sky looked ominous and rain clouds were gathering. The smell of lemon and orange orchards drifted by.

The old guard said, "After you pass through the gate, just park in front of building number two. When you get there, walk into the building and the receptionist will escort you to the Colonel's office."

The words "Selig Studio" figured prominently over the entrance. W.F. reminded himself that constantly changing studio signs would remain the most enduring trademark of the motion picture industry. He wondered how long the "Fox Studio" sign would hang over this small lot.

The Edendale studio consisted of a large two-story, barn-like structure that was made of clapboard painted dark blue; attached to it in a makeshift manner were many small buildings. A long wooden structure that W.F. first thought was an indoor stage was in fact Selig's office. Irregularly planted lemon trees and alfalfa fields surrounded the workshops and laboratory—all located on a three-quarter-acre lot.

When they entered building number two, a white-haired elderly woman with a deep tan who was seated at an old desk greeted them. She knew who they were and why they were there.

Her crinkled eyes were dubious as she avoided looking him in the eyes. "Yes?"

"Mr. William Fox is here to see Colonel Selig," Wurtzel said. Consulting her appointments book she nodded nonchalantly, rose and casually walked toward an office located at the far end of a corridor.

Edging W.F. over to one side, Wurtzel handed him an envelope, which he slipped into his suit coat pocket. No words were exchanged. It was the cashier's check for the first month's rent and a security deposit.

The receptionist reappeared and waved them on.

A smell of fine cigar smoke was hanging in the air of the high-ceiling office. Turning slowly above them were two big-blade fans creating a gentle breeze. The cuspidors were of a traditional aspect. There to greet them was the portly 51-year-old William Selig. He looked as though he had survived a tumultuous life—a bit downtrodden, thought W.F.

Ushering them to three comfortable chairs, Selig sat down behind his desk, his brow deeply furrowed.

"So you're William Fox."

"Yes I am, Colonel Selig."

"You're a lot younger than I thought you'd be."

"This is a very difficult business Colonel, I'm getting older by the day."

Selig rose and stood by a window, which overlooked the back lot. There was a crew filming a Western and a cowboy actor was riding a dark-colored horse along a dirt street.

Selig Studio in Edendale, California

Colonel William Selig

Turning Selig said, "That's Tom Mix mounted on Old Blue. Signed him up in 1910. He's a hard-riding daredevil, this fella is. Thing is though, I spend too much money making his pictures."

Flashes of lightning illuminated the sky and then cloud cover darkened the room once more.

"I built this studio in 1909. We filmed *The Spoilers* here."

"That was a very good picture, Colonel." Wurtzel said.

"We've got two glass stages, two wooden stages and six in the open air."

"We'll need that and more," W.F. said.

"With the mild climate all year round you'll be able to film good quality photography, Mr. Fox."

"That's what everyone says about California. The weather is damn near perfect," Winnie said, as a storm was about to unleash itself from the skies. There were claps of thunder and flashes of lighting; rain seemed imminent.

During a prolonged silence W.F. heard a horse neigh across the lot. Then a heavy downpour scattered the players and the crew who were hightailing it in all directions.

"Damn," Selig said.

Looking for cover, the colorfully dressed Tom Mix rode off on Old Blue.

Selig drew a long breath and let it out slowly. Turning, he faced them.

"It's a small studio, but I'm sure you'll find everything you require to make pictures."

W.F. rose and handed Selig the envelope with the cashier's check.

Selig tore it open, glanced at the amount and slipped it into a desk drawer. He turned a key and then tucked it away in his fob.

"When will you start making pictures here, Mr. Fox?"

"Tomorrow, Colonel Selig."

They parted. W.F. knew no more of what Selig was up to than before he had arrived. He did not see the man again.

The road back to the Alexandria Hotel wound along the contour of a richly green-carpeted valley and dipped into an area covered with orange groves. The motorcar had big wheels that didn't drop into every pothole that came along, for which W.F. was thankful. The sight and smell of those groves would stick with him for the rest of his life.

Over the next few years there would be a great migration of artists and fortune seekers to the West Coast, raising the population of Los Angeles to 570,000 by 1920.

The two main driving forces that led the studios' exodus to Hollywood were Edison's Trust and poor weather in the East.

Hollywood's desire to become the film capital of America looked promising. Many studios set up in or near the city, with most clustered around the main thoroughfares. The New York Motion Picture Company settled in Edendale in 1909, while Biograph set up shop in Los Angeles; Essanay was located in Niles, California; and the Kalem Company established a studio near Glendale.

The first studio located in Hollywood was the Nestor Film Company of Bayonne, New Jersey. In 1912, Carl Laemmle acquired the company and then went on to build Universal City on the former Taylor Ranch in the San Fernando Valley. After opening Universal City, Laemmle closed Nestor Studio.

Movie pioneers Cecil B. De Mille, Jesse Lasky, Samuel Goldwyn and Arthur Friend formed the Jesse L. Lasky Feature Play Company in New York in 1913 and rented a portion of a small barn at the southeast corner of Vine and Selma to make films in California.

D.W. Griffith made movies at the Majestic Reliance Studio at 4500 Sunset Boulevard.

As a direct result of all this new economic activity, Hollywood grew to 700 people in 1903, 4,000 in 1909 and 9,000 in 1915.

To take advantage of the natural scenery, the studios shot all over Hollywood and its environs. Private homes encircled with wrought-iron fences became working sets. Local citizens served as extras and the studios roped off narrow streets for motorcar crash scenes and popular chase scenes. The studios could shoot with little interference from the public.

Sets duplicating the New York skyline and a man-made metropolis provided realistic back-drops. As dawn broke behind the mountains, lively outdoor scenes were filmed throughout the area, with many crews traipsing up and down the rugged terrain. Camera positioning was freed up to allow movement of players, which added an extra dimension to filmmaking.

It was usual when working the entire night to lay off actors and crew for the rest of the following day. In the busy life actors led, it was the only time in which they could attend to their personal lives.

To the delight of local merchants, this hearty filmmaking activity brought tourists to hotels and restaurants. The Hollywood Hotel—with its vine-covered verandas and beautiful gardens—was completed in 1903 and an additional 104 rooms were added over the following three years. Among its steady guests were players such as Dustin and William Farnum, Douglas Fairbanks, Anita Stewart, Lon Chaney, Pola Negri and Norma Shearer.

Upon taking up permanent residence in California in 1917, Sol Wurtzel's home away from home became the Hollywood Hotel. The Edendale studio was less than two miles away.

Studio craftsmen worked feverishly to modernize the Edendale studio. A wooden platform large enough to hold two or three interior settings was built, outdoor stages were constructed—all the work was done by hand. The company's payroll was bloated with carpenters and painters. Sets were developed from rough pencil sketches with only the basic measurements to guide the foreman. As the sets went up, changes were improvised to correct mistakes in proportion and design. Early sets were modest—two flimsy walls, all handmade and seldom larger than 14 by 16 feet. The hammer and saw were the principal tools of the craftsman. The lighting equipment was primitive and inadequate and consisted of a series of open arc lamps operated on alternating current. About 20 overhead arc lamps were used on a set, complemented by a series of 30 1,000-watt incandescent blue floor lamps, which were supposed to eliminate the flicker that resulted from the alternating current. Power was furnished by the Los Angeles Power Company through a series of transformers on a meter system.

A sign hoisted over the entrance read "William Fox Studio."

After giving it some thought, W.F. named Sol Wurtzel production manager of the William Fox Studio at Los Angeles, California. On paper he reported to a Mr. Carlos, the superintendent of Fox Film in California. In reality his direct boss was Winfield Sheehan.

W.F. invested a lot of his time lecturing his staff on the fundamentals of the motion picture business. The industry made a low-cost product that virtually anyone could enjoy. However, the theatergoing public had diverse taste. Unlike a five and dime store, which depended on a vast assortment of product offerings, a movie theater could offer little alternative once the customer was inside the house. So to have a successful picture a film needed to achieve broad acceptance.

W.F. insisted that no product was inherently riskier than a motion picture. The selling price was up for grabs until demand could be determined; the rental a film brought in and the length of its run depended on how the picture fared with the public, and there was no cost-effective way of insuring against an unmitigated disaster.

Theda Bara in *The Devil's Daughter,* 1915

It didn't take long for Sol Wurtzel to get down to the serious business of making pictures. Every 6:30 a.m., Monday through Saturday, Wurtzel got into his Hudson and drove to the studio. Along the way he stopped at an all-night diner to have his thermos filled with coffee. During those early days he worked hectic 15-hour shifts. Too, his home life was a little barren—his wife and family were still back East—and he was happier at work than being alone in his hotel room.

Though swamped with work, Wurtzel found time to test hundreds of actors that swarmed through his office. Their parts were mimeographed and they were told what to memorize. Wurtzel inspected every shoot for little realistic details including wardrobe, making sure it was authentic and photogenic. Everything had to be ready for the shoot so that when the directorial staff and cameramen arrived on the set to line up the technical details and the lighting, there were no snags. An energetic young man named Lewis Seiler, who was there to help him tackle a heavy production schedule, assisted him.

For lunch Wurtzel went to the studio commissary where he sat at the head of one of the long wooden tables and chatted with whoever was beside him. Back in his office, he lit a cigar and plunged into the dictation of memos, of which there were many, which he tackled with great speed and concentration.

It would be near midnight by the time he left his office for the short journey to his hotel. He carted along a briefcase filled with scenarios. For homework he read a dozen or so, marked them up with a black pencil and separated those he thought had any merit. He usually fell asleep with a scenario resting on his chest and his glasses dangling from the tip of his substantial nose. More than one broken pair found their way to the wastebasket.

Wurtzel and his men were all motivated by a single-minded resolve to bring the efficiency of mass production into the disorganized jumble of activities referred to as "filmmaking."

As 1915 drew to a close, W.F. reported to his board that Fox Film grossed $3 million, with a net profit of $523,000.

CHAPTER 5
1916

Someone once told W.F., "I'd rather be lucky than smart." He sincerely believed there was a very strong element of truth to that statement.

Leaning up against a lamppost near the entrance to the Edendale studio and wearing a garish cowboy outfit,.Tom Mix waited every morning for a week, always dressed differently. W.F.'s curiosity was finally aroused.

It was a little past noon, and W.F. was holding a production meeting in his office, which had been Selig's old place of business. Sol Wurtzel, Raoul Walsh, Jack Edwards and Winfield Sheehan were there. In stifling heat, everyone was working in shirt sleeves. The same old wooden-blade fans purred overhead, creating a light, comforting draft. Wurtzel had ordered hot sandwiches and cold sodas from one of the local eating spots in town.

About halfway into a corned beef and rye, W.F. said, "They don't make corned beef like they do in New York. Did you see that crazy cowboy outside the gate, Jack?"

Unwrapping a warm sandwich from the wax paper, Jack Edwards said, "That's Tom Mix, W.F."

The name faintly rang a bell, but W.F. couldn't remember where he'd heard it before. He just couldn't place the cowboy.

"Who in the hell is he, Sol?"

"He makes movies for Selig. He's been at that gate for the past week."

"What does the goddamn cowboy want, Raoul?"

"Tom told me he wouldn't work for any other studio until he spoke to you, W.F."

"The hell you say," Winnie jested.

Walsh laughed a little. So did Jack Edwards.

"I've seen this Mix in a picture, W.F.," Wurtzel said.

"Tell us what you saw."

"Well, he jumps from horse to horse, W.F., as if he had a pair of wings, and he can ride faster than a bat outta hell."

"Damn! That corned beef is tough!" W.F. sipped more soda pop. "Then bring the crazy bastard in here, Sol. Maybe we can buy ourselves a real cowboy for a cheap price."

From the window, W.F. saw the damnedest thing he'd ever seen—Tom Mix galloping up to the building on his dark horse, leaving Sol Wurtzel trotting up behind him, swallowing lots of dust. He watched Wurtzel come forth and wipe his sweaty brow.

Dismounting, Tom Mix tied his horse to a hitching post. Mix was a little bowlegged and had the gait of a Western star.

By the time Wurtzel and Mix entered the office, everyone was eating dessert, a yellow-frosted lemon cake that the restaurant owner's wife had freshly baked, she said, especially for them.

After dusting himself off, Wurtzel sat down, and Mix stood before W.F.

Slight of stature, Tom Mix had a good strong nose, and looked like what W.F. thought a cowboy should look like, whatever that was. Since he'd never met a real cowboy, he couldn't draw one in his mind. Clinging to his 10-gallon white Stetson, Tom Mix shifted around a little, but kept his dark eyes trained on W.F.

"Tell me about yourself, Mr. Mix."

"Well, there isn't a whole lot to tell. I've worked for Colonel Selig since 1909. Made over 200 pictures, mostly one-reelers, and I guess I'd like to work for you, Mr. Fox."

"Why do you want to work for William Fox?"

"I can't say that I really know, except, well, I do my own stunts, and I can handle a horse and a rope, and I guess you've been looking for a real cowboy, or so I've heard."

"Tell me, Mr. Mix, are you a real cowboy?"

"As real as they get out in these parts, Mr. Fox."

Everyone around the room snickered at that remark.

Easing up from his chair, W.F. lit a cigar and came around his desk. He circled Tom Mix as if he were appraising a head of livestock. Circling him once more, he stood there, facing him.

"You're not a two bit sourpuss like William S. Hart, are you, Mr. Mix?"

"No, Mr. Fox, I'm not."

"How much is Tom Mix asking for?"

"I need $500 a week, and a place for my horses."

"Horses, Sol?"

"I guess a real cowboy has got to have more than one horse, W.F."

"One cowboy, and William Fox has got to feed more than one horse? Is that what you're telling me, Sol?"

"It's smart to have more than one horse, W.F. They get camera shy, you know, get their dander up."

"They get their dander up, Sol? Is that what you're telling me?"

No matter what anybody said, Sol Wurtzel was adapting just fine to the California way of doing and saying things. It was hard to picture him as a production boss, for it wasn't that long ago that Wurtzel sat taking notes like a stenographer.

Staring directly into Tom Mix's dark eyes, W.F. countered, "Three hundred and fifty a week, and feed and stable for your *horses.* Take it or leave it, Mr. Mix."

For a moment, Tom Mix's jaw went rigid. Then his hardened face broke out into a broad smile. "You've got yourself a deal, Mr. Fox. I'll get the rest of my gear, and I'll be here as soon as I finish a couple of pictures."

Tom Mix

Tom Mix set up his base of operations in Silver Lake at the Winna Brown ranch, not too far from the Edendale studio. It soon became known as Mixville. There was a big barn, corrals for the horses, and plenty of space to ride and rope. The studio constructed a false-front Western town set and a wooden bungalow that was to be Tom Mix's office. A lot of his early pictures were shot at that site. In 1919, Mix's horse, Blue, broke a leg and had to be destroyed. It was then that Mix incorporated Tony "The Wonder Horse" as his full-time movie mount.

There was a common belief shared by those who made pictures that the moment the ink dried on an unknown player's contract, a motion picture company acquired a responsibility, a commitment to find roles that would do justice to his or her talent, and an obligation to make the investment pay off.

The day William Fox signed Tom Mix, Fox Film got very lucky.

Over time, Mix turned out to be a gold mine. He never pretended to be a great actor, but he more than made up for it with thrilling stunts. It was more fun watching him dangle from a cliff than seeing the long, distressed face of William S. Hart doing one of his famous poses. During his very profitable career at Fox Film, Tom Mix would make 85 pictures for the company and become the most popular Western star of his time.

Before leaving for New York, W.F. warned Sol Wurtzel to make sure that Theda Bara was getting as much press coverage as she possibly could. Los Angeles was becoming a city of tabloids, society columns and rotogravure sections. Reporters were in a constant search for gossip.

Photoplay got its start in 1911. Their readership bought theater tickets, so it was important to plant provocative stories about the stars who made pictures. There were scoops, where a magazine stopped its presses to reveal something tantalizing about an actor or actress—information one could not find in the newspapers. It was best to keep on the good side of the fan magazines.

Theda Bara followed *A Fool There Was* with *Kreutzer Sonata,* a Russian tragedy in which she plays the amoral woman who corrupts her sister's husband. Herbert Brenon directed the film.

Enjoying her newly found wealth, Bara moved to 500 West End Avenue in Manhattan and was living with her parents, a brother and a sister. Like many other movie people of that time, she began shuttling back and forth to the West Coast to make her pictures.

Bara next appeared in *The Clemenceau Case*, where wicked wife Theda is slain by the husband she has wronged. This film too was directed by Herbert Brenon.

W.F. got worried about the stereotypical "bad woman" role Theda played and asked Jack Edwards to tone down her brooding image a little. Edwards cast her as an orphan girl in *The Two Orphans*. The romance was filmed in Quebec and is about two beautiful orphan sisters in old France.

Bara's public was disappointed with the picture because suddenly Bara had gone virtuous. Despite her box-office success as a vampire, she kept insisting she play parts other than the stereotype "vamp role" she made famous.

Theda Bara in *Carmen*

Here was a case where the public's wish to see Theda Bara as the wrongdoer far outweighed her personal goals, at least as far as W.F. was concerned. Much as Little Mary Pickford was the archetype of innocence, Theda Bara had become a deep-felt symbol of sin.

As part of the 1915 production schedule, Fox Film featured Theda Bara in *Carmen*, a six-reel picture directed by Raoul Walsh. The picture was one of the first pre-Hollywood epics. The negative cost $200,000, with the Spanish city of Cordoba being duplicated in Fort Lee. There were 5,000 extras, a real bullfight, and daredevil Art Jarvis who leapt 83 feet with a horse from a cliff into deep water.

"The role of a seductive gypsy girl is made for her," Walsh told Sheehan.

Carpenters built half an arena on the lot so that Walsh could shoot a realistic *torero* scene. However, neither a *matador* nor a bull was to be found in the Fox prop inventory. New Jersey raised a lot of tomatoes, but very few fighting bulls.

Sheehan asked Walsh how things were going on the *Carmen* picture. "Do you need anything, Raoul?"

"I could use a fighting bull, Winnie."

"Where in the hell am I going to get a fighting bull?"

"How about trying Mexico."

"Brilliant, Raoul. Absolutely brilliant. I'll wire Sol. He'll find us a damn bull."

Upon receipt of Sheehan's wire, Wurtzel sent a contingent of Fox people to Tijuana to search for a bull and a bullfighter. He also requested proper garb and some Spanish-looking assistants for the *torero*.

It wasn't long before a flat-assed *matador* appeared on the set of *Carmen*. As part of his cortege, he brought with him a full-blown supporting cast and a selection of frilly costumes, and was looking forward to being in a *pelicula*, as he was now calling it.

To win the bullfighter's cooperation, Walsh told the *matador* he was going to be a big star. "*Hombre, vas a ser un gran actor.*"

When it came time to shoot the scene, things got a little unsettled, because Walsh was insisting the crew tie the bull's hoofs down to the ground so no one would get hurt.

"*Amare el toro!*"

"*Porque, Senor* Walsh?"

In his quaint Tex-Mex, Walsh told the *matador,* "*Para que el toro no chinge a nadie!*"

Which loosely translated into, "So nobody gets hurt!"

For the scene, Walsh was going to use a miniature French camera, *De Brie,* which he wanted strapped on the bull's back so when the camera was turned on the *matador,* it was coming toward him. That way, the cameraman could take an exceptional frontal shot of the bull's horns as he charged the bullfighter. *Ole!*

There'd be only one take for this particular scene. Walsh alerted the crew. As the minutes passed, Walsh was getting a little jumpy that they'd blow the shoot. "*Senores, si fallemos, nos va llevar a la chingada!*"

Which meant they'd all get fired if things didn't turn out the way they were supposed to.

Above the ring, on the encircling wooden structure, large advertisements for Corona beer were placed in key positions. Hundreds of dark-skinned extras were hired as *aficionados* to give the shoot a feel of authenticity.

The supporting cast wasn't quite sure what to expect next from the high-strung bull. Several crewmembers staked the bull to the ground in the tunnel, his legs bound round the ankles with black cords, literally pinning him down. Then the camera was strapped to his back. In the ring, the *matador,* a red sash tight round his considerable waist, was practicing his favorite pass, *La Veronica.*

Walsh shouted, "Roll 'em!"

For mood music, a trumpeter played the melancholic "*Virgen de la Macarena.*" Two fat-assed *picadores* on horseback rode into the ring, pranced around the arena, and took up their respective stations.

A column of four *toreadores,* including the star, marched in wearing tight uniforms with sparkling embroidery. Splitting into two groups, they went off in opposite directions around the arena, saluted the authorities, and then took up their stations on either side of the tunnel from whence the bull would join the festivities.

Suddenly, things started to unravel.

One of the crew yelled out "*Hah! Hah! Toro!*" and frightened the bull. Busting out of the ground, the animal ran off, chasing the *matador* out of the arena, off the set, and into the street.

Grasping his head in frustration, Walsh asked, "*Que chingaos pasa?*"

After the foul-up, when things cooled down, the crew had a hearty laugh and then got ready to resume the shoot, this time without Walsh's bullfight scene.

A day later, one of the grips found the bull grazing in a meadow down the road a piece. The little camera was crushed, and that was the last of Raoul Walsh's artistic frontal shot.

Cecil B. De Mille filmed another version of *Carmen* starring Geraldine Farrar, at the time one of the Metropolitan's leading opera stars. The gray-eyed, shapely diva's acting skill and her natural beauty made her much sought after as a film star.

Both versions of *Carmen* premiered on the very same night, October 31, 1915. Even though Theda Bara's adaptation received rave reviews, Farrar got most of the applause because of her fame on the stage.

The *New York Telegraph* reported, "Miss Bara's version of the emotional heroine of the Spanish story is a somewhat different one from that of Miss Farrar's, but it is quite as satisfactory in every respect. Miss Farrar's acting is more abandoned in parts than Miss Bara's, but the latter gives a strong, finished performance throughout, and the shades of emotionalism are only a matter of opinion."

Fox Film was paying Theda Bara $1,500 a week, so the studio insisted that she make herself available to a solicitous press. Sol Wurtzel was burdened with the task of transporting the image Bara had created onscreen to silly still picture shoots with fan magazines.

Because Bara still didn't own a suitable residence in California for the occasion, the studio rented a Spanish villa at 2285 La Granada, which overlooked Hollywood from all its terraces. Wurtzel was there to supervise the event.

As choreographed, Theda Bara was draped in dark silks and planted in the lavish garden of the house, posing behind a well, creating a mysterious setting. Bulbs flashed continuously.

When the cameras stopped, Bara sat at a small metal table in a high-backed rattan chair and read from a copy of *Photoplay*.

Bulbs flashed again.

"How do you feel, Miss Bara?"

Responding with her favorite catch line, she said, "It is very hot in Africa."

"Does the vampire type of woman really exist, Miss Bara?"

It was a distinct relief for Sol Wurtzel to know that Johnny Goldfrap of Fox's publicity department had prepared a list of canned answers, and Theda Bara had taken the time to memorize them all.

Displaying a sober demeanor, Bara answered, "There are such women, plenty of them. I have made a special study of the type. It is a highly interesting one."

On cue, Theda lurched out of her chair, and bulbs flashed again. In a sultry pose, she slumped into another chair and stared into space, as Goldfrap had coached her to do, as if "you are looking out a window."

"I'm delighted to have this opportunity of displaying my work to American spectators, and I hope I have succeeded in depicting the complex emotions of the panther woman as vividly as they have appealed to me."

A reporter asked, "Will you always do vampires, Miss Bara?"

Feigning deep concentration, her eyes gone misty, Theda Bara thought for a moment and then responded. "During the rest of my screen career, I am going to continue doing vampires as long as people sin. I believe humanity needs the moral lesson in repeatedly larger doses."

It was finally over. Theda Bara squeezed out a last tear into a white handkerchief scented with Lily of the Valley.

Reporters began to drift out of the house. Wurtzel hopped into his car and gladly headed back to the Edendale studio.

Endless stories were told of Jesse Lasky, Adolph Zukor and Marcus Loew, the men who with Carl Laemmle and William Fox came to dominate the motion picture industry during its silent era. They were all Jews who had become the first exhibitors of pictures because early theaters could be operated with little capital; a vacant store was filled with folding chairs, an old piano, and before you knew it, you were in business. Returns were good and soon the theater men thought of film production.

Jesse Lasky, a tall, blue-eyed vivacious Californian, started his career in vaudeville. Closely connected to his speedy rise in motion pictures were his brother-in-law, Sam Goldwyn, and a struggling producer, Cecil B. De Mille.

During the early days, De Mille collaborated with Lasky on ideas for vaudeville acts, writing a few operettas for stage presentation. Because Lasky and De Mille shared a mutual taste for adventure, they shortly became very good friends. De Mille was born in Ashville, Massachusetts in 1881. His father had collaborated on plays with David Belasco.

Over lunch one day at the Claridge Grill, De Mille vented his frustration with the way things were going. "Jesse, I'm pulling out. Broadway's all right for you; you're doing well. But I can't live on the royalties I'm getting. My debts are piling up, and I want to chuck the whole thing. Besides, there's a revolution going on in Mexico, and I'm going down and get in on it, maybe write about it. That's what I need, a stimulating and colorful change of scene."

Lasky replied, "If you want adventure, I've got an even better idea. Let's make movies!"

On the back of a menu, a partnership agreement was drafted in pencil. The company was called the Jesse L. Lasky Feature Play Company. From the very outset it was severely undercapitalized, with Lasky putting up $7,500 and Goldwyn raising a like amount. De Mille mostly offered his talent and lots of sweat. Goldwyn had a lawyer acquaintance, Arthur Friend, who also bought a position in the company. He would handle legal matters for the studio.

Since De Mille knew precious little about filmmaking, he wisely contracted Oscar Apfel, a young director who'd later work for Fox, and Alfred Gandolfi, an experienced cameraman.

What De Mille needed most was a place to make a picture. Turning off a bridle path called Hollywood Boulevard, there was a very large L-shaped barn located on Vine Street advertising space for rent. The owner, Jacob Stern, lived in a white house nearby. After some haggling over the rent, Stern let De Mille use part of the barn for cinema.

Jesse L. Lasky

Lasky hired a taxi and rode out to Hollywood to see his new studio for the first time. After going around in circles through bean fields, the driver suggested that Lasky make inquiries inside the Hollywood Hotel about where he wanted to go.

The front desk clerk thought he was a guest. "How can I help you, sir?"

"I'm the president of the Lasky Feature Play Company."

"I never heard of it."

"Perhaps I should have told you that the director-general of the company is Cecil B. De Mille."

"Never heard of him, either."

More than a little frustrated, Lasky headed for the same door he had come through a few minutes before. Still within earshot, the clerk volunteered, "Tell you who might help you."

Lasky turned around, a hopeful look in his eyes. "Yes?"

"Drive down this main road until you come to Vine Street. You can't miss it. It's a dirt road with a row of pepper trees right down the middle. Follow the pepper trees for about two blocks till you see an old barn. There's some movie folks working there that might know where your company is." When Lasky heard the clerk describe the facility as a "barn," he knew he was on the right track.

The first day of shooting was December 29, 1913. *The Squaw Man,* featuring Dustin Farnum, was released on February 15, 1914. Performing well at the box office, the picture put the Lasky Studio on an even keel a lot sooner than originally anticipated. During 1914, Lasky made 21 pictures.

Not long after *The Squaw Man* debut, Lasky and Zukor were lunching together on a regular basis while Goldwyn found himself entangled in a nasty divorce proceeding with Lasky's sister, Blanche. After a series of blowups and reconciliations with Lasky, Goldwyn became uneasy with

Adolph Zukor

him, and resentful that Lasky was getting first billing on their films. Across America, "Jesse L. Lasky Presents" introduced the studio's product.

One day Adolph Zukor called Goldwyn and Lasky, proposing a merger between Zukor's Famous Players and Lasky's company. What attracted Lasky to the merger was Zukor's fine slate of players, including Mary Pickford, who was the reason Famous Players was making more pictures than Lasky's company. Zukor, on the other hand, thought the combination would give him leverage to strike a better deal for the distribution of their pictures, particularly with Paramount.

Few would question that Adolph Zukor was the unchallenged leader of the motion picture industry throughout the period 1915 to 1930. There were a number of reasons why Zukor was at the top of the heap. He understood the importance of players who drew audiences no matter what the film story. He believed that an audience would sit through a good story, even if it ran an hour or longer. He was the first to recognize the potential cost savings of running a large, integrated organization.

Adolph Zukor formed Famous Players in Famous Plays, and went out to find a talent who'd help him test his theories.

One night after dinner at Sherry's, cameraman-turned-director Edwin S. Porter told Zukor that a French producer was going to make a four-reel picture with the famous Sarah Bernhardt playing the role she'd created on the stage, *Queen Elizabeth.*

Furthermore, Porter advised Zukor that the French producer, a man named Mercanton, was in urgent need of money to film the story, and he was amenable to selling the North American rights to Zukor.

Porter said, "I merely mention it to you because the price is prohibitive."

Zukor asked him what it was, and he said Mercanton wanted $40,000.

"All right. I will take it."

That very same day, Zukor cabled $5,000 to Mercanton. The only thing he forgot to do was inform his partner, Marcus Loew, that he was about to risk some of their hard-earned capital on a single picture.

It was common knowledge that Marcus Loew was strictly a theater man. As far as anyone knew, he had no thought of making pictures. Like so many of Hollywood's moguls, he'd grown up on the tough streets of the East Side ghetto where he'd sold newspapers when he was a kid. Dropping out of school at age nine, Loew tried his hand at odd jobs before becoming a furrier.

It wasn't long thereafter that Loew and Zukor teamed up together in nickelodeons. They owned a theater called the Automatic One-Cent Vaudeville; inside, the floor was neatly carpeted with several rows of peep show machines along each wall. The trickle of nickels was constant. There were also mechanical fortunetellers and other strange-looking devices to measure strength.

When Zukor informed Marcus Loew that he had purchased the rights to *Queen Elizabeth*, Loew felt Zukor had completely lost his mind. Arguing back and forth, they reached an impasse. They accepted that their route to the future lay in different directions. Not one to compromise, Zukor sold his shares in the theaters to Loew, who was fortunate enough to have two competent executives to run his business: Nicholas Schenck, who acted as general manager, and his brother Joseph, who scouted for talent.

With the success of *Queen Elizabeth* under his belt, Zukor set on a personal course to prove that American audiences would favor features. He wanted to make feature films in the United States, so he rented the top two floors of the Ninth Regiment Armory at 213-227 West 26th Street, where he made his first feature, *Prisoner of Zenda* with James K. Hackett, who had been a hit in the play.

Now all Zukor needed was a first-rate director. He set about talking to D.W. Griffith, who was parting company with Biograph and its restrictive policies. Indomitable Zukor wanted to select his film projects and control his budgets, for he had great disdain for those who were unwilling to follow sound business practices.

"I think I can earn more, thank you," Griffith curtly responded.

A man who hungered for action, Edwin S. Porter, was more amenable to that kind of arrangement. He'd worked for Edison, designing its motion picture equipment. His well-deserved reputation as a filmmaker dated back to 1903, when he'd directed *The Great Train Robbery* for Edison. His little company, Rex—which was the trade name of a one-reel picture released weekly—wasn't faring that well, and he was fascinated with the idea of returning to make pictures without having to worry about the business side of things. Porter was an innovator, having placed the camera at a considerable distance from the actors, thus reducing the abnormality of size. From what he had seen, Zukor thought him capable of producing feature-length adaptations from literature and the stage.

To manage the business side of the company, Zukor relied heavily on Daniel Frohman, producer of stage plays. Frohman had signed up the grand lady of the America stage, Minnie Maddern Fisk, whose first film (*Tess of the D'Urbervilles*) also starred the celebrated beauty, Lily Langtry.

Zukor later said: "I interested Daniel Frohman in the enterprise and told him what I thought could be accomplished. He used his influence with the Patents company to have this Bernhardt picture licensed, and that opened the doors and I was able to distribute the picture. I believe we had to gross $60,000 to cover expenses. We did gain the knowledge that made us absolutely certain that pictures of the right type had a great future."

Later, B.P. Schulberg, a newspaperman, joined Zukor's fledgling company in charge of stories and adaptations. Zukor added to his staff J. Searle Dawley, who had considerable experience in directing short films as well as plays. Elek John Ludvigh, a lawyer who represented many theatrical producers, was taken on as legal advisor.

Realizing that distribution was just as important as film production, Zukor hired Al Lichtman, a sales type, to place his pictures with the best exchanges throughout the country. Throughout the marketing division, Zukor could sense a new, confident, even expansive air.

During all of 1914, Famous Players produced 30 features. To cope with his new productions, Zukor put up a small studio at the corner of Sunset and Hollywood, and added Mary Pickford to his growing stable of players, which included John Barrymore, H.B. Warner, Tyrone Power and Lois Weber. He soon realized that youth and beauty were indispensable features for romance on the screen and Mary Pickford had them both.

Of all the motion picture moguls, Zukor was the first to fully understand the fundamental tenets of the business. It was imperative, he said, to let the exhibitor foot some of the cost of making pictures. What this meant was the studios had to insist on receiving a larger share of early ticket sales from the first few weeks of showings of a new film. The timing of cash expenditures and cash receipts determined whether a studio could go on making pictures. A prolonged lag time between investing in a film and recouping the investment from exhibitors proved fatal to marginal filmmakers. Eventually the studios developed a "gross receipts" formula. Under this calculation, a studio received a specified percentage of box office receipts, with the percentage declining over time. For a new picture, the percentage might be high in the first week and decline after several weeks.

It was the summer of 1916 when Zukor's Famous Players merged with the Jesse L. Lasky Feature Play Company. The combined company rented another floor over the one Lasky already occupied at 485 Fifth Avenue, and the Famous Players staff moved in.

It wouldn't take long for Sam Goldwyn to become *persona non grata* around the studio. His hair-trigger temper and dictatorial attitude soon had Zukor concluding that either he or Goldwyn had to go. Getting off to a good start was important.

Goldwyn was incorrigible.

Zukor said, "Every hour on the hour, and sometimes the half hour, Sam Goldwyn sent a shock through the organization, in the manner of those pneumatic drills which shake all buildings in a vicinity." Zukor laid his cards on the table and challenged Lasky to back him or his brother-in-law, Goldwyn.

"Jesse," Zukor said, "I have come to an unhappy conclusion which may distress you more than it does me. It is a hard thing to ask you to choose between your brother-in-law and me. But many a film company has failed because of internal dissension, and I can see it happening with us. The decision will rest with you and De Mille. You do what you think best, and I will go my way, whichever you choose, without bitter thought."

Lasky knew that Goldwyn was going to be pigheaded and capricious about it. There was no way of getting him to change his style. It was a tough decision to make. Nevertheless, Lasky made up his mind. He had infinite faith in Zukor's judgment.

Lasky made the decision alone because De Mille was in Hollywood. When he found out what had transpired, De Mille said, "I am pained by this first breach of our triumvirate. I'm glad that the other parties to the quarrel did keep me out of the controversy."

Lasky said, "We have too many stockholders and their best interests have to be considered. I know Sam will never take a back seat."

This, at any rate, was the official version of the story.

On September 14, 1916, Goldwyn resigned, but still held stock and remained on the board. Toward the end of that year, Goldwyn sold his stock for $900,000.

For the rest of his life, Sam Goldwyn never forgave Jesse Lasky for "selling him out."

Samuel Goldwyn

It became readily apparent to W.F. that the small Selig studio in Edendale was insufficient for the quantity of production Sol Wurtzel had scheduled for the 1916-17 season. W.F. authorized the purchase of the Thomas Dixon studio, a property of five and a half acres located on the west side of Western Avenue at Sunset Boulevard.

The Dixon Studio, an incoherent mass of irregular buildings, consisted of an old-fashioned frame cottage nestled in a lemon grove, a two-story laboratory, and an office building. There were outdoor sets and stages scattered all over the place. New equipment and a generating plant were installed, along with some of the equipment Fox Film was using at the Edendale Studio.

Tom Mix transferred his office and horses to the new lot, but continued to make pictures in Mixville until 1925 when he moved his operation to the Mix Rancho in West Los Angeles. In the latter part of 1916, several new stages and a series of workshops were constructed on the back lot.

Forecasts indicated that Fox's film production would outstrip its filmmaking capacity in the not-too-distant future. To prevent a serious bottleneck in production, W.F. purchased eight additional acres across Western Avenue, so that by now the total investment in the Sunset Studio amounted to $215,000.

Assembling a skilled staff of support people and supplying them with modern equipment achieved additional productivity. The mills, carpenter shops, blacksmith shops, plaster shops and miniature department were each equipped to supply a director with what he required to make a good picture.

The net result of this organized approach to making pictures was a savings in time, a reduction in the cost of sets, and an authentic look to Fox pictures.

During the period 1916 to 1925, the Fox West Coast Studio was constantly upgraded in all areas. It produced 416 dramatic films and 244 comedies, or a total of 660 Fox pictures. In addition, camera equipment expanded from six Pathé cameras to a battery of Bell & Howell speed cameras, Akeley cameras, and other equipment for trick photography.

The Fox West Coast Studio spent large sums of money renting furniture, props and costumes. It came to Eve Fox's attention that it was the common practice of studio employees in California to hire furniture and furnishings to dress the sets on which the pictures were made, and on one of her visits she had seen some of the rental bills. If a piece of furniture was brought in and valued by the owner at $1,000, the company would pay 10 percent of its value per week for its rental. Sometimes it would stay in the studio four or five weeks, so the company would pay $400 or $500, and it would be in just as good condition on the day it was returned as when it was loaned to the studio.

Eve told W.F., "You're throwing temptation in the way of the employees. In the first place, you're paying too much for the lease of the furniture. There are so many places that furniture can be leased, it occurs to me that someone is receiving graft in connection with its rental. You ought to try to eliminate that." W.F. asked, "How?"

"Commission me to buy the company $100,000 or $200,000 worth of art objects and furniture. I will spend a long time gathering it, going to every auction sale in New York of all the wealthy people, and inside of six months or a year, I will have the finest set of art objects and furniture in California."

W.F. told her to proceed. Eve spent close to a year going to auction sales two or three times a week, acquiring the best art objects.

After all the purchases were made, W.F. concluded that the furniture was far more than could be used at the studio. If it were known in California that this belonged to Fox Film, no other film company would hire it. So Fox Film created a company known as Altman Art Galleries. No employee knew it belonged to Fox Film, but all of the stock was subscribed for and owned by Fox Film as a wholly-owned subsidiary. The studio shipped the goods to California and engaged quarters on Sunset Boulevard. Eve had again contributed to the success of the company.

Those early days at the Fox West Coast Studio were exciting. Soon the lemon trees and alfalfa fields gave way to landscaped gardening and modern buildings. Many future big-screen stars worked on the Fox lots: Tom Mix, Buck Jones, Janet Gaynor, George O'Brien, John Gilbert,

Will Rogers, Shirley Temple, John Wayne, Spencer Tracy, Paul Muni, Henry Fonda, Betty Grable and Humphrey Bogart, to name a few.

Even though W.F. was making more frequent trips to California, he was reminded that Fox Film still did not own a permanent facility in New York. After initially considering a film city in Flushing, Long Island, the more practical voices in the company, including Eve Fox, convinced him that the place to be was Manhattan.

Also around this time, Eve and W.F. seriously contemplated a change of residence and decided to rent a house on Riverside Drive until they could find a more permanent abode. Eve adored the size, shape and simple elegance of the place where they planned to spend more time with their daughters. Part of it was the fact that they were spending most of their time either at work or on the road getting to work.

W.F. was quite satisfied with the way things were shaping up. He realized he had to continue to expand production capacity if Fox Film was going to become a major factor in the industry. He also understood that the studio's self-generated financial resources were limited and that, sooner or later, he'd need more capital or would have to take on debt to satisfy the ever-growing need for cash.

With costly talent its principal raw material, the process of making pictures was getting more expensive. As the stars' salaries increased, other salaries tagged along. It was only common sense that executive compensation had to be in line with what the players were earning. There were also other ways to run up the cost of a motion picture, including the cost of sets, buffalo, Indians, trains, horses and extras.

It was about this time that W.F. instructed Saul Rogers to recommend alternatives for funding the long-term demands of the company. Of the investment bankers who figured in the motion picture industry, there was none as reputable as the house of Kuhn, Loeb and Company, whose partners included Otto Kahn.

A recognized patron of the arts, Otto Kahn thoroughly enjoyed the opera, and his financial

Sporting Blood **was released in 1916 by Fox.**

support of the Metropolitan Opera House was considered indispensable. A familiar sight among New York cultural events was the Kahn waxed mustache, the Kahn *boutonniere,* and the Kahn smile. "I think we should visit Mr. Otto Kahn. He seems to know everyone in show business," Rogers recommended.

"That's bad advice, Saul," W.F. responded.

"But why, W.F.?"

"Kahn is talking to Adolph Zukor. I don't believe Kuhn, Loeb can adequately serve two competitors in the same industry."

William Fox Studio on Sunset Blvd.

It was time to tally up the results for 1916. W.F. informed the board and stockholders that production had increased to 52 pictures with gross rentals of $4,200,000. Profit was $365,000, less than 1915, but justifiable given the one-time cost of Fox Film's aggressive expansion in California.

William Farnum's *The End of the Trail* was showing at Loew's New York theater, a first-run engagement on the Great White Way.

Besides William Farnum and Theda Bara, new faces appeared on the player's roll, including Gladys Coburn, George Walsh, Virginia Pearson, June Caprice, Robert B. Martell, Valeska Suratt, Alan Hale, Vivian Martin, Dorothy Bernard, Walter Law, Ormi Hawley and Nance O'Neill.

The studio also counted on a superb group of directors, including James Vincent, Oscar C. Apfel, Richard Stanton, Kenean Buel, Raoul Walsh, Edgar Lewis, John G. Adolfi, Bertram Bracken, Will S. Davis, Frank Powell, J. Gordon Edwards, Otis Turner, Mary Murillo, Maxwell Karger, Frank Lloyd, Frank C. Griffin and Roland West.

Feature-length films were definitely the trend, and the industry produced 667 of them. The motion picture became America's favorite type of entertainment. Star recognition drew crowds to the theaters, and that was driving up their salaries, which seriously worried the moguls, except for Adolph Zukor.

Zukor countered with a simple argument. "The most effective insurance in the motion picture business is a star. Practically every studio has to bid for their services. It's part of the cost of doing business."

For the year, William S. Hart and Mary Pickford were the top draws at the box office.

CHAPTER 6
1917

Because W.F. believed he had to know what the competition was doing, he sent Johnny Goldfrap to hear Zukor and Lasky comment on their plans at a press conference they were staging at the Knickerbocker Hotel.

Zukor, in his thick Hungarian accent, responded to one of the standard questions of the day.

"What kind of pictures will you make, Mr. Zukor?"

"It's not like making shoes or automobiles, where you have a model and you follow through for the year. Every picture is an enterprise by itself."

"What makes you think this new company can make better pictures, Mr. Zukor?"

"Every Hungarian is either a peasant or an artist. I'm a little of both. I'm convinced that working with Mr. Lasky, we can produce excellent pictures."

Goldfrap said Lasky wore striped trousers and pearl-gray spats, and was leaning on a blond Malacca walking stick. Smoking a pipe, he looked like someone who'd just walked off a vaudeville stage.

"The Jesse Lasky Feature Play Company started with one barn, one truck and one camera. In this new association with Mr. Zukor, we'll become the most important film studio in the business," Lasky said.

To which W.F. told Goldfrap, "Over my dead body!"

W.F. was in New York on the occasion of Belle's birthday and the subsequent party that Eve catered in their Riverside home. When he arrived he found a slew of girls, mostly of Belle's age, laughing and chattering among the streamers, balloons and party-decorated tables and chairs.

Belle and Mona Fox

In one corner was a magician performing card tricks. Eve's organizational touch was reflected in every tiny detail. The room had a party atmosphere, yet hadn't lost its class.

Eve had invited W.F.'s mother and father, Anna and Michael Fox, his two brothers, Aaron and Maurice, and the two Leos, Jack and Joe. Also there were W.F.'s three sisters, Anna, Tina and Malvina.

Aaron Fox was the most handsome of the Fox family. He had a big head covered with a mop of thick brown hair and a high broad forehead. Effusive and spontaneous, Aaron had a mouth that was always at work.

Maurice was a plain-looking fellow who seemed to fit any mold. He had inherited the same nonchalant attitude of his father, Michael Fox, and never seemed to worry. W.F.'s oldest sister, Anna, had a pleasant face, though she was not pretty. Tina was gentle and affectionate, and took after W.F.'s mother in appearance—a bit overweight and dowdy. A diligent homemaker, she showed little interest in business. The youngest Fox sibling, Malvina, was a change-of-life baby and very close to Belle's age.

For the occasion, W.F. had purchased a special gift for Belle. After she blew out the candles on her birthday cake and made her wish, he handed her a small package.

"To my little daughter, Belle, on her 13th birthday. I love you very much."

Bending over, he kissed her and encouraged her to open the package. When she got the wrapping paper off and opened the black jewelry box, she found a diamond-studded bracelet. Eve helped Belle snap on the bracelet and the 13-year-old paraded around the room, showing it off to family and friends, excited with her first piece of expensive jewelry.

This was a particularly happy moment for W.F., because not only was he able to provide for his family, he was now able to afford some of life's finer things.

Aaron and Maurice Fox were employed by Fox Film. W.F. made Aaron a vice president and member of the board. Unfortunately, Aaron's head was always larger than his talent, and some of W.F.'s executives began to complain about his obtrusiveness. W.F.'s standard response was, "Just use your own judgment. Aaron is my brother, but he has no voice in management."

The youngest of the three male offspring, Maurice was quiet and unpretentious. He was completely content with the job he had in the printing department, where he did excellent work for the company. W.F. could truthfully say that Maurice was satisfied with his lot in life and never caused him any particular embarrassment.

When the party was over, W.F. asked his chauffeur to take his parents home. They were not evening people, and he could tell by the tired look on his mother's face that she had had enough. W.F. went quickly to the foyer to say goodbye to his parents. He kissed his mother on both cheeks and extended a warm hand to his father. There was no special show of affection on either man's part, though each believed he loved the other.

As W.F. watched his parents pick up their things and leave, he cast his mind back to an earlier time, when 13-year-old William Fox had worked for D. Cohen and Sons where he'd supervised the cutting of cloth linings. W.F. had started working there from age 11 until age 15. His highest wage had been about $8. This was how he'd made his living, leaving his house at 6 in the morning, working from 7 to noon, taking 30 minutes for lunch, then working from 12:30 to 6:30, finally making his way home for dinner at 7:30. From the time he was a kid, he vowed that one day he'd own his own business. He had reached his goal and was enjoying every minute of it.

Less comprehensible was W.F.'s father, who was perfectly happy with virtually nothing of material value. He was just as content when he worked as when he didn't work. He never worried. He was very proud of his son's success, but long before W.F. had reached that point, Michael Fox had been perfectly fine with things as they were. W.F. never heard the man complain about anything in his life. When he came home and Anna told him that the butcher and baker had refused to trust him any more during the period he'd been out of work, the old man was sure that tomorrow would be all right, or that the butcher and baker would most likely change their minds.

It was Anna Fox who'd borne the brunt of raising six children. During the early years, she had been constantly preoccupied with

Anna Fox (left), William's mother

Eve Fox

putting enough food on the table. W.F. felt good about the fact that he had been able to help so much. Good fortune had shone on the family and he was thankful for that. Earlier too, W.F. remembered his father praying from the Torah, though religion never played an important role in family life.

A hush had fallen over the room, a silence that felt thick enough to cut with a knife.

"Bill?"

He was looking out the window at a white carpet of fresh snow that blanketed the street down below. He didn't even remember how long he had been there.

"Your father said this was the most beautiful scene in Manhattan."

"I was just thinking about him. He's a strange man."

"All children think their parents are strange."

"Do you think Belle liked the bracelet, Eve?"

"Did you see the look on her face? She adored it, Bill."

"That makes me happy."

"You're so pensive. What is it?"

"When I see my father, it brings back memories."

"What kind of memories?"

"It's nothing important, Eve."

"Are you going to play golf tomorrow?"

"I wouldn't miss it for the world."

Even then, golf was W.F.'s passion. The sport combined mild exercise in the outdoors with some of the thinking that went into a chess game. His favorite golfing partner was Jacob Rubenstein, an investor who, at the drop of a hat, would meet him on the course for a game.

"Are you playing with Jacob?"

"Who else would play with a one-armed golfer?"

Toward the end of the year, W.F. appointed Sol Wurtzel general superintendent of the Sunset Studio. Two resolutions were forwarded to California authorizing him to sign checks for the Fox Film Corporation and Sunshine Comedies, Inc., on the accounts they maintained at the Hollywood National Bank. At the same time, W.F. terminated Abraham Carlos, who was planning to leave Los Angeles.

At first, Wurtzel was anxious about moving his wife and four-year-old daughter Lillian to the West Coast. Finally, Hettie Gray Baker, Fox's film editor, persuaded Wurtzel to accept the challenging assignment, so he departed New York on October 12, 1917 and five days later checked into the Hollywood Hotel. Fox's West Coast Studio had a permanent manager.

Early one morning a youthful-looking man appeared in W.F.'s New York office. He said he was a relation of one of the group who had put up the $400,000, the so-called New Jersey contingent. The young man carried in his hand a single certificate of stock for 10 shares and he wanted to know how much W.F. would give him for it.

W.F. asked him where he had gotten it, and he said Mr. Kuser had given it to him.

W.F. said, "You ought not to offer that to me. These 10 shares would give me a majority."

The man said he was aware of that and it was exactly what he wanted to achieve. He said that he had a row with "them," and wanted to get even, adding that they were a bunch of "so-and-sos." "This will upset the thing Kuser has so carefully planned. If you don't buy them, I'm going to give them to you."

W.F. didn't want the the shares given to him, so he asked him if $1,000 would do.

The man nodded and said, "That would be fine."

W.F. gave him the money, took the share certificate, and put it in his vault.

From then until 1925, no man in the New Jersey contingent ever suspected W.F. had majority control of the company. For the years that he had the majority of stock in his vault, at no time did he permit a single resolution to be passed by the board of directors that was not unanimous. Over time, as the companies went to the financial markets for additional capital, W.F. learned a lesson or two about the importance of controlling interests.

During the period 1916-17, Fox Film added several new players to its roster, including Francis Carpenter, Miriam Cooper, Violet Palmer, Gladys Brockwell, Annette Kellerman, Jewel Carmen and Dustin Farnum. Tom Mix was finishing his commitment to Selig.

With the substantial increase in production activity, there was a need to carefully control costs. Despite these controls, when so many pictures were being produced at the same time, it was relatively easy for a director to get distracted from the fact that making a picture was a business enterprise.

In his own mind, W.F. was in a business much like that of construction. One came up with a design, converted that design into a blueprint, cost out the project, and monitored the progress and cost throughout the building stage. If need be there were tradeoffs, but never a total overspend that would make the picture and its negative cost a financial impossibility.

Acutely conscious of how hard it was to make a penny, W.F. constantly preached cost control, but it was an uphill fight. The creative types always had a reason or two for spending just a little bit more to make their dream pictures, which would sink a number of otherwise very much alive studios over the years.

Upon the installation of Wurtzel at the helm of the Sunset Studio, a management practice was born within the Fox organization dealing with delegation of authority. There was to be frequent communication with W.F. by letter, telegram or phone, fortified with the visit of an occasional emissary from the head office. It was check and double check. Wurtzel had to account for every penny spent by the studio on a daily basis and he had to justify every independent decision he made. Fox admonished Wurtzel, "Making pictures is a tough game, Sol."

When Sol Wurtzel moved into the superintendent's office, he was unaware that he had just stepped into a hornet's nest. While W.F. buried him with detailed instructions on how to organize the studio, Wurtzel was uncovering a substantial raw film heist that had been going on at the studio over an extended period of time. Perhaps it was because of his persistence and desire to protect Fox Film's assets that Wurtzel quickly identified the culprits and got them to admit to their guilt in signed affidavits.

Furious that the malefactors had been able to pull the wool over his eyes for such a long time, W.F. wired Sol "to prosecute the thieves to the full extent of the law." The idea was, Wurtzel thought, to recoup as much money as he possibly could in exchange for jail time. This made more sense to him.

After resolving the great film heist, Wurtzel turned his attention to making pictures. First he decided to focus on those individuals whose job it was to turn stories into pictures—the directors.

Scottish-born Frank Lloyd came to Hollywood in 1912 and played "heavy" parts at Uncle Carl's Universal Studio, where he later began to write and direct two-reelers. Under Wurtzel's tutelage, Lloyd went on to make very good pictures for Fox, including *Les Miserables,* Tom Mix's *Riders of the Purple Sage,* and *The Tale of Two Cities.*

Another veteran director at Fox was the talented Raoul Walsh. Most of his early stuff was mediocre, but he would later blossom as a director with films like *In Old Arizona.* There was also Bertram Bracken, who made his reputation in 1916 with *East Lynne.*

When W.F. suggested that Wurtzel was letting his directors manipulate him, he shot back angrily in a letter to W.F. "Mr. Lloyd, Mr. Bracken and Mr. Le Saint don't make a move unless they first consult me."

W.F. reminded Wurtzel that "Nothing suits a director any better than to hop on a train with his company and go somewhere, no matter where it is, as long as he can get away from the studio. This is the kind of work practiced in Los Angeles, and likewise in New York by the majority of our directors."

Sol Wurtzel got off to a rather good start in a dazzling style, looking things over. If his taste in pictures was not always classically flawless, that was the only black mark against him. He was a good manager and had infinite faith in the capitalist system. There was overhead to be met and a profit to be made. Operating cost, particularly labor cost, had crept up in the last year. To counteract a certain lethargy that had set in at the studio, he instilled a spirit of back-to-the-wall aggressiveness which took hold and quickly propelled the studio to extraordinary performance, culminating in Fox joining the ranks of the better-run filmmakers.

The most important event of 1917 was the declaration of war on Germany by the United States. America joined the Allies in the battle of the Atlantic and sent an expeditionary force to Europe. Hollywood turned its eye to the Great War and cranked out movies using it as a backdrop.

1917 was a good year for Fox Film. The studio made 70 pictures and had gross rentals of $7,000,000. Profits bounced back to $500,000. The industry released 687 feature-length films in 1917. Based on a Quigley Publications' poll of exhibitors, the top male and female box office stars were Douglas Fairbanks and Anita Stewart.

CHAPTER 7
1918

Fox Film started 1918 with a New Year's bash at the West Coast studio, complete with music and circulating waiters balancing trays of food and drink.

Present were William Farnum, Valeska Suratt, Theda Bara, Tom Mix, J. Gordon Edwards, Raoul Walsh, Winnie Sheehan, Jack Leo, Sol Wurtzel and dozens of other support people. For the first time, W.F. brought Eve and the girls with him to California. The Fox girls were having great fun mingling with the stars, being kissed and treated like little princesses.

It was January 1, 1918, and Eve and W.F. celebrated the New Year, his birthday, and their 18th wedding anniversary. Deftly steering Eve away from the crowd to a secluded corner, he planted a nice little kiss on his wife.

Pressing his hand ever so slightly, she said, "What's that for, Mr. Fox?"

"For believing in our dream."

"Of course, I believe. I believe in you, William Fox. From the first day I met you. I was all of 10, do you remember?"

"How can I ever forget?"

While in California, W.F. decided to personally witness one of Theda Bara's fan magazine interviews, this one with *Motion Picture Story Magazine.*

Bara was lounging in a swing at her sprawling West Adams Tudor home in Beverly Hills; she was now residing in California most of the year. There were tiger-skin rugs, crystal balls and skulls located throughout the house. Bara used them when practicing her two hobbies, astrology and perfume distillation.

A reporter had a pad, and a photographer vigorously snapped pictures. A canary swung back and forth in a wire cage, singing something or other.

Theda Bara wore indigo makeup to emphasize her pallor.

Posing, she said, "People write me letters and ask if I am as wicked as I seem onscreen. I look at my little canary and I say: 'Dicky, am I so wicked?' And Dicky replies: 'Tweet, tweet.' That may mean 'yes, yes' or 'no, no,' may it not?"

"Are you a potent influence for good, Miss Bara?"

"Most girls are good."

Shortly before the photo shoot ended, W.F. left for the studio. He'd seen enough.

Several weeks after the interview, Theda Bara's beguiling face dominated the magazine's cover. There wasn't a line in her forehead or under her eyes, and though her skin had lost some of the freshness of early youth, its texture was fine as ever. But it wasn't the same old Theda Bara. The camera was unforgiving.

During the year Bara filmed *Cleopatra*, *The Forbidden Path*, *The She Devil*, *Soul of Buddha*, *Under the Yoke*, and *When A Woman Sins.*

Theda Bara as Cleopatra

WILLIAM FOX *PRESENTS*

Theda Bara

-IN-

CLEOPATRA

STAGED BY
J. GORDON EDWARDS

FOX FILM
CORPORATION

A THEDA BARA
SUPER
PRODUCTION

Cleopatra—a lavish spectacle in 10 parts—features a well-known actor (Fritz Leiber) as Julius Caesar. After a poor start, the film did well at the box office, registering more than $1 million in ticket sales. Bara seemed perfectly cast for the role of the serpent siren of the Nile. The censors were upset because she bared a little bit too much shoulder to their liking.

In some theaters, there was a symphony orchestra to augment the film's lavish settings.

The *New York Review* wrote a critique of *Cleopatra*, which read: "Proud, defiant, willful, emotional, sinuous by turns, Miss Bara makes a representation the most auspiciously successful of her career."

The Soul of Buddha, adapted from Bara's own story, is a tragedy about a Javanese temple priestess.

Under the Yoke was proclaimed "a volcanic drama of the Philippines."

W.F. was still holding Theda to $1,500 a week, but she protested continuously, pointing the finger at Mary Pickford. "I keep reading about 'Little Mary' and, well, so much money for such an insignificant actress."

TOM MIX in MR. LOGAN, U. S. A.

Fortunately, Fox Film had Tom Mix in its stable of players; he made six pictures for the studio in 1918, including *Ace High*, *Cupid's Roundup*, *Fame and Fortune*, *Mr. Logan USA*, *Six Shooter Lady*, and *Western Blood*.

Sheehan had Lynn Reynolds direct several Mix pictures, and he did a fine job. Mix and Lynn Reynolds seemed to understand each other, and Sheehan was reluctant to make changes when a player and director were seeing eye to eye. Dan Clark, Tom's favorite cameraman, was also on the payroll.

Continuing Fox's lucky streak, Mix recommended a big, good-looking cameraman for pictures, George O'Brien. There was something about him Wurtzel liked. Soft-spoken and sincere, he turned out to be one of the easiest players Wurtzel had to deal with, even after he hit it big.

During the year, Fox Film produced and exhibited its screen version of Victor Hugo's *Les Miserables*, starring William Farnum and directed by Frank Lloyd.

The set people created 19th-century Paris on 60 acres of farmland near Fort Lee, New Jersey, and most of the town was hired for the cast of 5,000 extras. Following its opening at the Broadway Theatre, W.F. knew the film would make money.

There were times when W.F.'s meddling turned out to be timely. He kept his ear close to the ground, cognizant of the fact that a delicate balance existed between the number of pictures produced by the industry and the ability of the theater market to absorb them. As with any commodity, overproduction led to declining sales for some of the studios, since they were all eating from the same bowl.

Around this time, because of the entrance of the United States into the Great War, many of the film studios in the East were closing down temporarily and cutting back on their payrolls. Luckily Fox was not one of them, for its films were finding a ready audience. Nevertheless, W.F. took it upon himself to warn the production people not to become complacent.

"I am looking to our directors in the East and in the West to cooperate with us in every way to carry us over this present trying period, so that we will not have to follow the lead of other producers. For it is only by cooperation of our directors, actors and technical staff that we will be able to do this."

Keeping fixed costs down was the key to survival in bad times. The slenderness of the behind-the-scenes staff was important. Labor of any kind was the largest part of Fox Film's cost of making pictures.

Around a conference table in California sat Sol Wurtzel, Jack Edwards, Raoul Walsh, Frank Powell and Frank Lloyd. They were not in high spirits.

Wurtzel read from W.F.'s letter: "I therefore wish that upon receipt of this letter you call in your directors and read this letter to them so that they will know the position we are in, and so that they will give you their help."

"What in the hell does W.F. want now, Sol?" Edwards questioned in a cynical tone.

"Let me finish reading his letter, Jack!"

"I wish you could immediately dispose of all actors who are in stock except those who are under contract."

It turned out that Wurtzel had been watching the payroll with sharp interest, and there wouldn't be the need to cut that many people.

Admonishing the group, Wurtzel said, "I want your list first thing in the morning."

"How about the horses, Sol?" Walsh quipped.

"Don't be a pain in the ass, Raoul."

"Go over your general payrolls with your technical staff, and cut wherever possible. There is to be no increase in salary to anyone until further instructions from me. Go over the company payrolls and lay off all unnecessary people; by that, I mean it may be possible for one man who doesn't have enough work to do the work of another man besides his own."

Wurtzel said, "Get the picture?"

One by one, the sullen-looking directors filed out of the room without so much as a goodbye. Under the rules of the game at Fox Film, one never questioned orders from New York.

Another classic example of W.F.'s conservative mind-set was the time when the actress Gladys Brockwell requested a loan of $500 because her mother had had a very serious operation.

W.F. wrote Wurtzel: "I don't want to grant this loan of $500. You having this situation in hand, you should be able to judge just how long we will have to retain her services. I leave it to you to decide if you want to advance her this $500 and deduct it from her salary. There might be a way of doing this and taking it out of her weekly salary, so that the entire amount will be paid before the expiration of her contract. Use your own judgment in this matter."

At the fourth annual convention of Fox Film in California, W.F. set down the program for the upcoming season. All of the bigwigs were there as well several directors. The room was shaped like a theater with a stage where a speaker's platform had been hastily constructed. To the right of the podium was a deserted bandstand that supported a piano used for mood music.

The man on the platform was William Fox. "I want 26 standard pictures to be made up as follows: eight Farnums, eight Baras, and 10 special pictures, including Raoul Walsh's completed picture. What's it called, Raoul?"

"Know Your Enemy, W.F."

"Yeah, that's it. And how about *On the Firing Line,* Raoul?"

"I haven't started it yet."

Sol Wurtzel, Winfield Sheehan, Jack Edwards, Raoul Walsh and Frank LLoyd sat near the front. W.F. continued, "If there is submitted to you any story which can be made for $50,000 or less without a star, enough to attract people to the box office, a story based on a topic that is of vital interest to the public like *The Blindness of Divorce,* I would be agreeable to make three or four such pictures a season."

"We're looking, W.F.," Lloyd said.

"Our second brand of pictures of which we intend making 26 will be the Victory brand."

"I suppose you're talking Tom Mix, George Walsh and actors like that, am I right?"

"That's right, Winnie," W.F. replied. "We have to find an actress of special merit and value, one who has a splendid reputation. We're looking in New York, and you can make a search in Los Angeles."

"I may have somebody," Jack Edwards said.

"Screen test her, Jack, and send me the rushes. Tell them about our third brand, Sol."

"Yeah, sure. It's the X-L brand where we'll feature Jewel Carmen, Gladys Brockwell and Virginia Pearson."

"Which reminds me, Sol. Is Gladys paying down that $500 loan?"

"She's right on time, W.F."

"Go on, Sol."

"Our aim is not to have the cost of these pictures run much above $15,000 to $18,000 each."

"What's the idea behind these brands?" Raoul Walsh asked.

W.F. replied, "The purpose of having these three brands is to make it possible for the stars to become popular enough in the X-L brand to advance them to the Victory brand, and those in the Victory brand to advance them to Standard Pictures, so that at all times we will be making a brand of film in which to popularize new people."

A natural-born showman, Sidney Patrick Grauman had several theaters in northern California and was about to showcase the fancy Spanish colonial Million Dollar in Los Angeles. A mighty Wurlitzer provided the accompaniment. William S. Hart in *The Silent Man* opened the theater.

The man most responsible for the development of the picture palace, Grauman was one of W.F.'s favorite people. Grauman's first theater, designed by architect William Lee Woollett, was truly a work of art. Located in downtown Los Angeles, it featured an ornate terra-cotta arch over the main entrance on Broadway.

On a trip to Los Angeles, W.F. visited the Million Dollar and observed the audience response to its comfort and beauty. It reminded him of how far behind he was in theater construction, but his funds were limited and he wasn't about to embark on speculative expansion before solidifying the production side of the business. Besides, as producers, the studios were all on equal footing in terms of exhibiting their films. None of the studios controlled an appreciable part of exhibition.

Any time the subject of penny-pinching arose, W.F. could point to past attempts by defunct competitors to try to avoid putting their studio on a "businesslike" basis. When Harry Aitken was drowning in debt, he told W.F., "The banks are pushing us to pay up our loans faster. They expect miracles in a short time. Why can't they be more patient? They just haven't got the long range view of the movie business."

Aitken pleaded with his brother, Roy, "We'll come back. It will take time, and perhaps we'll need a new company. But we can do it. We've faced tough problems before. Both of us are still young and we know the movies." Harry Aitken never came back, and W.F. was quick to remind his underlings of that fact. There was but one chance to make it in pictures. If you missed the opportunity, you were out of the game.

Mixed in with the other changes transforming the industry was sound, seen more as a technical novelty than a practical medium for pictures. The motion picture industry was employing more musicians, both for mood music during filming and accompaniment during the projection of a picture. None of the studios recognized the potential impact sound would have on the motion picture industry during the late 1920s.

Theodore Case, a young scientist who would change W.F.'s life and the industry's attitude toward sound, had been toying with sound since 1911 when he was a student at Yale. Most of his time was taken up in experimenting with a selenium cell with the idea of photographing sound waves and using the positives as records for a kind of phonograph.

Shortly thereafter, Case was saying that he had succeeded in transmitting sound by light.

Case spoke at a conference and said, "The eye could not detect the variation of the light at all, but it was registered perfectly in the varying of the resistance of the selenium. The reproduction of the voice was perfect. Next I have to set up an apparatus for very delicate photographing of the light variations."

In 1916, Earl Sponable, a chemistry student from Yale, joined Case in his research. He would play an important role in bringing Case's innovative ideas into practical use. Case's invention, the AEO light, was a light source that varied in intensity with an electrical current stimulated by sounds, thus providing the light for a variable-density sound track.

A scientist named De Forest was also very much involved in this kind of research. He leased the Case cell and by 1923 had completed eight sound-on-film shorts using Case's AEO light.

When W.F. heard about these experiments, he was concerned. For one thing, technological change not only produced new modalities of production, it also forced the reorganization of an industry around it. Furthermore, that reorganization would be costly, since all the big studios had considerable assets sunk in silent film production. Yet the lesson of the past was that the speed of innovation was uncontrollable, and the only question that remained unanswered was the magnitude of the change sound would produce.

On the face of it, this supported a view of the future that was comparatively optimistic. It implied that once sound technology was practical, there would be considerable cost savings to be realized, something dear to W.F.'s heart. Music performed live in a multitude of theaters would now uniformly be presented with the film, in some fashion, so that even the modest theater audiences in the hinterland would now be able to enjoy the classics. A suitably configured apparatus could be leased to the theaters to project talkies. No doubt, W.F. reflected, there was room in the market for both silents and talkies. Another company pursuing sound technology through its subsidiary, Western Electric, was AT&T.

As chief executive, W.F. regularly poked his nose into the creative side of the business, particularly when he thought certain topics to be questionable as to content or timing.

For example, on August 19, 1918, he wrote this letter to "My Dear Sol:"

"After I have read *The Road to Berlin,* I will write to you my opinion on doing *The Girl I Left Behind Me* at the present time. This would be a serious mistake. This play deals with the Indian question. I talked to Farnum and Lloyd about the same long before we were not in this war as deeply as we are now. With the present war conditions I do not think the public is interested in our previous Indian troubles. For that reason this story is rejected for the present and I urge that you immediately search for a vehicle to take its place. In addition to this the Charles Frohman Estate would be entitled to one percent of the gross on *The Girl I Left Behind Me,* if we made a new version of it. However, my opinion is not based on the royalty question but rather on the fact that I do not think this story is a proper one to make at this time."

Soon after President Wilson and Congress declared war on Germany, C.C. Craig and Raymond Wells organized the Hollywood Officers Training Camp, which periodically met in a garage on Hollywood Boulevard near Hudson Street. Draftees were permitted to take their basic training at the athletic field of Hollywood High School.

Lilian Gish, Robert Harron and Dorothy Gish are featured in *Hearts of the World,* a tale of war set in Britain and France; D.W. Griffith directed and produced the film. The picture premiered at Clune's Auditorium in Los Angeles. Present at the gala opening were Blanche Sweet, the Gish sisters, Charlie Chaplin, Douglas Fairbanks, Mae Murray, Mack Sennett, Fatty Arbuckle and Dustin Farnum.

Adolph Zukor was out in Hollywood, visiting sets every morning, getting to know the players and technicians. "I hope that such visits make everybody feel that the business office is more than a place where we make contracts and count money. The fact is that we keep as close tabs on the human element as on box office receipts."

By this time W.F. had built a harmonious organization that, on the surface, ran smoothly and well. Sure, there were sporadic skirmishes, and occasionally there arose a misunderstanding. But overall there was rarely much commotion on the Fox lot. Management was about organizing, making decisions, and giving direction. Through either boom times or recession, the fortunes of Fox Film reduced themselves largely to a matter of the quality of its management.

If there were any doubt about who was in charge, W.F. pointed to the sign over the entrance-way. There was a constant buzz of activity on the Fox properties. W.F. explained it in simple terms: "This enormous activity is required because of the puny sum in each transaction, the sale of a ticket or a bag of popcorn."

Some accused W.F. of being an autocrat, formulating policy and direction in the darkness of his office, often alone. On the other hand, there was virtually no politics or jockeying for position. W.F. was the unquestioned leader of his domain.

Outsiders found W.F.'s success a mystery and a source of constant bewilderment. Here was a man, relatively unknown but a few years ago, whose first venture into the industry was successful beyond belief, whose unconventional philosophy was largely misunderstood, who now found himself sitting on the top rung of the motion picture ladder.

Upon his company, W.F. lavished his fullest care. There was no other activity—save a round or two of golf—for which he had the same passion. Things were done at a brisk pace. This was achieved through a mix of browbeating, cajoling and loving kindness. At one moment W.F. could be stern and obstinate, while at another he could be understanding and giving. Whether the studio would get anywhere with its program, whether it would survive long term, these were questions that only time would answer.

It was not a rare occasion that W.F. and Eve left the headquarters building at 5:30 or 6:00 in the morning. When they were leaving, it was just about time for the job to open again. The canary in their home adjusted its hours and sang for them whatever hour they returned. Even if they took a brief vacation in Atlantic City, the rushes would be brought down to them every night, and in the morning they would sit in a theater and view them. W.F. earned what he got; in fact he earned more than he got, because the first year under contract his salary was $1,000, and for the next four years he was to get $10,000.

More than once, Eve complained, "He is a slave to his business."

W.F. responded, "My business is my life."

Since his dividend income was mounting, W.F. suggested to Eve they consider a move to a new building under construction on Park Avenue. Their residence on 91st Street no longer seemed big enough. Besides, he thought they were too far north of his business location.

W.F. had his eyes on a semi-finished building going up at 270 Park, above Grand Central's train yards. The Marguery was to be an apartment house and hotel built around a lit courtyard, with tables decked out for alfresco dining. The restaurant, cafe and lounge were to be managed by the next door neighbor, the Ritz. The building would eventually cover the block between Park and Madison from 47th to 48th Streets and a hotel would occupy an L-shaped segment at the northwest corner of the block at 47th Street. Out front, one was met by a braid-festooned doorman. It was to become a world for the privileged few, far removed from the gritty slums of the Lower East Side.

Eve and W.F. were invited to inspect several finished apartments and were met by a dignified-looking gentleman who was a real estate agent. It was W.F.'s thought at the time that he'd acquire an apartment in Manhattan and then purchase a country house on Long Island where he could play golf and occasionally relax.

The agent escorted them around the apartment. Eve stepped into a spacious living room and gave it a sweeping glance, focusing on every little detail and examining the lavish workmanship, which appeared to be first class. As to space, it had all they would ever require. Standing by one of the large windows, she gazed out over the city. She could see a strip of the East River and the flourishing Manhattan skyline. After a long length of time, she turned and said, "I think the girls will love the apartment, Bill."

There had never been such excitement in his eyes. The trek between Myrtle and Park Avenues had taken him 15 years. The minute he'd entered the apartment, he knew it was just right for the Fox family.

"It's perfect, Eve."

"I'm glad you appreciate this 17-story structure of beaux arts majesty. You'll have, Mrs. Fox, a splendid arcade courtyard with gardens, and all the convenience of living in Manhattan."

The Marguery's 108 apartments would have 1,536 rooms, 1,476 closets, 100 kitchens, 100 sculleries, and 2,000 windows fronting on the street.

"When can we move in?"

Stuttering a bit, the agent looked at W.F. with some surprise. "Within, within, six months, I suspect."

Approaching the finely groomed man with the white carnation in his lapel, W.F. said, "If we made pictures like they build in New York, we'd be out of business." A moment later, W.F. signed an option agreement.

Eventually the Foxes moved into a 32-room apartment—two apartments were combined to provide additional space—on the 9th floor of the Marguery. In due course, they displayed their fine collection of art throughout the apartment, including Gainsboroughs, Van Dycks, Tintorettos, Murillos and Peter Paul Reubenses, canvases that they'd acquired on their frequent trips to Europe.

The Marguery became their home, a place where W.F. would rarely conduct his business, where Eve and he would begin to enjoy the fruits of their labor, where their two daughters would mature into young women.

The Great War was now in full swing. The battle of the Marne signaled the approaching need for an armistice; the Allied forces crossed the Meuse river into the Argonne forest and cut through the Hindenburg line.

During this period, W.F. gave a lot of his time to the Red Cross. As it happened, he was at Sulphur Springs in Virginia with his family when he read in a New York paper that the Red Cross was starting a drive of some 20 teams. Morgan was one of the captains; Rockefeller was another, as were Schiff, George Baker, an Astor and a Gould.

It occurred to him that in the present state of emergency he would form a team to be called the Allied Theatrical Motion Pictures Team and offer to raise $750,000. The more W.F. discussed the idea with his cohorts, the more buoyant he became.

About the time the idea of this drive was advanced, he received a telephone call. The caller said, "I am Mr. Rockefeller's secretary, and he would like to know when it would be convenient to call on you."

W.F. told the man to let him know when it would be convenient for Mr. Rockefeller, and he would go to his office.

The man insisted, "No, Mr. Rockefeller says that he wants to call on you. How would 11:00 do at your office tomorrow morning?"

"That would be fine." What a thrill! The richest man in the world calling on a modest movie producer on a matter that concerned him.

Next morning, W.F. was in early to clean up his desk and work as promptly as he knew how. He left word with the girl at the desk that when Mr. Rockefeller came, to come and knock three times on his door, and then show Mr. Rockefeller in—all this so W.F. would know it was he, and so his name would not be spoken and no fuss made.

W.F. waited for Mr. Rockefeller in his office. He watched the clock and when it got within about three minutes to 11:00, he had an idea that he had made the wrong arrangements. As he opened the door, there he was, the richest man in the world, sitting among the other people and salesmen waiting in W.F.'s office. W.F. asked him to please step in.

Apologetically, he said he had come a little early and that he had a special request to make. W.F. heard him out and decided it was best that he accede to his request. When W.F. became one of the captains, he made sure the Rockefeller team came in first.

While W.F. was busy making pictures, Adolph Zukor was collecting stars. In his galaxy were Mary Pickford, Douglas Fairbanks, William S. Hart and Marguerite Clark.

It was Zukor who changed the rules by which the industry paid its players, offering a few of them a participation in the profits of their pictures, a form of compensation that the rest of the studios thought to be heresy. However, Zukor was convinced that big stars drew larger audiences and paid for themselves.

When advised that some of Famous Players' stars were now participating in profits, Richard Rowland, a distributor from Pittsburgh, said, "The lunatics have taken over the asylum!"

An important distributor of Famous Players-Lasky's films was W.W. Hodkinson's Paramount. Zukor was distributing a lot of film through Paramount's sales force, which was said to be one of the finest in the industry. In fact, Famous Players-Lasky was the backbone of the organization, supplying 80 percent of the Paramount product.

There were several reasons why Paramount excelled at salesmanship. An important one was the fact that the company agreed to advance $20,000 to $25,000 for each five-reel film and pay for the cost of prints and print advertising to get first crack at good pictures. There was yet another reason: Its salesman were trained to dress with stiff propriety and act with a certain aplomb. They knew their customers and Hodkinson insisted they develop lasting relationships with them.

Distributors Rowland and James B. Clarke were invited by Hodkinson to become one of the five owners of Paramount. Paramount entered into a five-year agreement with Zukor.

Through its control of film exchanges across the country, Paramount was now dictating policy to Zukor. Famous Players was told how many comedies they should produce, how many dramas, and how to budget them. Very early in the alliance, Zukor had cast a predatory eye on Paramount. It was his belief that he could acquire 50 percent of its stock. Distilled to the fundamentals, why would a powerful studio like Famous Players share such a large part of its margin on pictures with a mere distributor? It wasn't long before Zukor finagled control of the entire company by buying out individual stockholders. Hodkinson was out and Hiram Abrams, Zukor's man, was installed as interim president.

B.P. Schulberg described what happened at the June 13, 1916 Paramount meeting when Hiram Abrams was nominated for president. "Before the S.O.B. Hodkinson knew what hit him, there was a vote of hands and he was out of office. He was a silent, unfriendly man, cold and abrupt in his dealings with all of us, even Mr. Zukor. When he saw his control of Paramount, and therefore of Famous Players, disappear like that, he didn't say a word. He simply reached for his hat and walked out."

One effect of the Paramount episode was that Zukor was never again content with anything he didn't completely control. Keeping an eye on expenses was his most important task. At Paramount, he implemented rigorous cost control.

Before long, independents were getting a little worried over Zukor's Paramount-or-none policy, meaning if an exhibitor wanted stars and their big pictures, it had to accept Zukor's smaller pictures as well. As Paramount grew in power, so did the rental rates and ticket prices. A toughened Paramount was able to insist that prospective exhibitors interested in, say, the Pickford films, acquire them in large blocks along with a fixed quantity of less attractive titles. Paramount salesmen offered a selection of different product lines from the top-quality Artcraft releases of Pickford, Fairbanks and Hart to the more bargain-basement Realart productions, in which lesser-known players were being developed. One of the most telling changes of the old Paramount was this practice, which became known as block-booking.

In response to Zukor's block-booking practices, Thomas L. Tally of Los Angeles and Mitchell Mark formed The First National Exhibitor's Circuit with the idea of having exhibitors—one member in each principal city—join forces to produce their own films. The association was to have 25 to 30 members, each owning the franchise for his district. Jones, Linick and Schaeffer of Chicago, Turner and Dankin of San Francisco, and Jensen and Von Herburg in Seattle immediately joined. Closely behind followed Finkelstein and Rubin of Minneapolis, Stanley and Jules Mastbaum of the Stanley Company of Philadelphia, the Hulse chain in Texas, the Sanger-Jordan circuit in New Orleans, Abe Blank in Iowa, Rowland and Clarke in Pittsburgh, John Kunsky in Detroit, Nate Gordon in Boston, and the Fabian circuit in New Jersey.

If Zukor was integrating forward into exhibition, what was there to prevent exhibitors from integrating backward into production?

The leader of the movement to form an independent-producing company, Thomas Tally, was one of the significant forces in exhibition on the West Coast. His Edison Phonograph and Kinetoscope Parlor was the first exhibition space in Los Angeles in 1896. In July of that same year, Tally began offering large images as well as peep-show viewers and audio headsets for phonograph recordings. In the spring of 1902 he opened the Electric Theatre—one of the early theaters dedicated exclusively to film—in Los Angeles.

The purpose of First National was to have it act as a purchasing agent for independent productions on behalf of exhibitors in 26 key cities. First National went into production and hired well-known players, contracting Charlie Chaplin for slightly more than a million dollars; he committed to eight two-reel pictures. First National also offered Mary Pickford a million dollars for three feature pictures. Her contract with Famous Players-Lasky expired in the spring of 1918.

Zukor asked De Mille what he thought the studio should do about Mary Pickford's contract, De Mille said, "I concur heartily with your decision not to try to match First National's offer."

Frustrated, Zukor told Pickford she'd been working too hard and offered her $250,000 to take a five-year vacation from pictures. If he couldn't have her, why let her work for a competitor?

"Oh, I wouldn't do that, Mr. Zukor. I love pictures, and I'm just a girl. I couldn't quit now."

"Mary, it is too big this time. It wouldn't be sound business to pay you what you would want to stay with us."

"I'm sorry," she said. "I'm very sorry."

"Well," Zukor said, "we have nothing more to complain about, you and I."

"No. We've done the best we could for each other."

As part of a management shakeup, Zukor assigned his confidant, B.P. Schulberg, to help Hiram Abrams run Paramount, the newly minted distribution arm of Zukor's expanding motion picture empire. Gradually, as Abrams exercised his authority, bad blood developed between he and Zukor because of Abrams' tightfisted management style and Zukor's idea of wanting him to act solely as a figurehead.

Zukor warned Schulberg that there was no longer any room for Abrams in the Paramount organization. Abandoning his plan to make a career with Zukor, Schulberg identified with Abrams and was now threatening to leave with him. This wasn't an easy decision for Schulberg, since he'd admired Zukor from the day Edwin Porter brought him into Famous Players as a scenario editor. But Schulberg and Abrams seemed to have the same relish for adventure.

Tilting his head to one side, Zukor told Schulberg that it would be a grave mistake for him to leave the company. "Stay with the company you have helped to build. You've got the potential to become a big-league motion picture producer, Ben."

A determined Schulberg kept insisting, "If Hiram goes, I go with him."

"All right, Ben. I think you're being a damn fool, and I know you'll regret it. But I've said my last word about this. Come to the studio in the morning and clean out your office."

But the real motive behind Abrams and Schulberg's sudden departure from Paramount was an idea that had been whirling around in their heads for a while. If the big five of filmdom—Pickford, Griffith, Fairbanks, Chaplin and Hart—could be persuaded to unite, they could control their futures, and lots of money could be made.

Zukor purchased a thousand-acre piece of land in Rockland County up the Hudson River near the village of New City, and developed it into Mountainview Farm. Zukor spent little of his leisure time with business associates and actors. There were two exceptions to that rule: Maurice Chevalier and Thomas Meighan.

On the estate, Zukor built an 18-hole golf course, a swimming pool, and even put up a gas station so his guests could fill up for free. It was a very agreeable place in springtime, with the roses in bloom and the manicured greens in perfect shape for weekends of golf.

Investment banker Otto Kahn of Kuhn, Loeb and Company was a regular visitor to Mountainview Farm. The investment banking house's main business was the railroads. Like Zukor, Kahn was a subscriber to the opera. As part of a plan to expand Zukor's empire, Kuhn, Loeb lent him $10 million, allowing him to purchase first-run theaters in major cities.

When Forrest Dryden got wind of Zukor's theater-acquisition policy, he thought the plan nothing less than ingenious insofar as it gave Zukor a leg up on the rest of the industry. He cautioned W.F., "Keep your eye on Zukor. He wants to control theaters."

"I will, Forrest."

As part of his advice, Kahn taught Zukor how to induce theater owners into accepting Paramount's stock for their theater properties, since cash was a scarce commodity at this time. The standard stock-purchase agreement contained a clause whereby Paramount agreed to repurchase its stock from the theater owner at a fixed price without reference to Paramount's market price. In essence, Paramount was offering them guaranteed repurchases at $80 a share on a fixed date of maturity. This greatly augmented an owner's willingness to accept Paramount stock, for no matter what happened, they were assured a buy-back price, or so they believed.

It was simply more workable to acquire theaters using Paramount's overvalued stock rather than cash. Kahn's theater-acquisition policy was a clever departure from the normal way of doing business. The lure, of course, was the buy-back provision. In contrast, W.F. was reluctant to follow this course of action. The obvious reason was that Fox Film wasn't as yet a public company, and so there were no stocks to trade; also, even if the company had been publicly traded, W.F. was very concerned about dilution and losing control over the company he was building.

One didn't have to be a mind reader to understand what Zukor was planning. He'd always believed, and rightly so, that if one controlled theater seats, one could dictate what was to be shown and at what price. Because it was imprudent to attempt to control a majority of all theaters, Zukor chose to buy or lease first-run theaters that acted as bellwethers for the rest of the industry. That way, Zukor rationalized, he would be able to influence independent exhibitors in the country who quickly followed successes at first-run theaters.

On the street, American audiences were drawn to see a picture when lobby posters acclaimed: "Direct from a one-year run in New York!"

Forrest Dryden invited W.F. to meet Otto Kahn. Dryden thought it wise they talk through Fox Film's long-term investment policy with one of the country's leading investment bankers. On the way downtown Dryden gave W.F. a primer on Kuhn, Loeb.

"Kuhn, Loeb is run by Jacob Schiff, Otto Kahn, Mortimer Schiff and Felix Warburg."

"They're in bed with Zukor, Forrest."

"That's not important, Bill. Investment banking houses have a way of dealing with competitors without creating a conflict of interest."

Which didn't seem to sway W.F. in one direction or the other. He stared straight ahead.

"It was old Jacob Schiff who built up Kuhn, Loeb from a small business founded in La-fayette, Indiana."

"What's it all worth, Forrest?"

"A lot, Bill."

The Fox motorcar pulled up in front of Kuhn, Loeb's building at 52 William Street. The firm occupied four floors and rented out 16. W.F. and Dryden rode an elevator to the top floor. When they entered the reception area, a large portrait of Jacob Schiff greeted them.

Dryden and W.F. were ushered into the big white Georgian partners' room that Kahn used as an office and preferred when meeting clients. White-haired Kahn kept on with his work for a bit, then suddenly looked up. Registering great surprise and delight, he rose to meet the two august-looking men.

"Forrest, how nice of you to come."

"This is William Fox, Otto."

"It is indeed a pleasure, Mr. Fox."

"Thank you for seeing us on such short notice, Mr. Kahn."

"Please be seated, won't you?"

Never without a tea rose in his lapel, Kahn was immaculately dressed in the perfect suit with some backbone of its own. One of the first of the city's rich to own an automobile, Otto Kahn shared that piece of yesterday with the likes of John Jacob Astor, Clarence Mackay and "Diamond Jim" Brady.

A butler served tea, after which Dryden gave Kahn a brief history of Fox Film, how the studio had expanded its activities in California, and a description of the few theaters it controlled.

Dryden said, "A thorough program of modernization of the studio has been put into effect, designed to bring film quality up to a higher standard."

"It sounds like you're on the right track, gentlemen."

"Fox Film also has developed a strong roster of players and directors, Otto," Dryden added.

Twisting his small mustache with stubby white fingers, Kahn was attentive to Dryden's every word. "The company seems well established and your credit is secure, so there is no reason why you can't borrow against assets."

Kahn looked directly at W.F. "Kuhn, Loeb is prepared to recommend a financing plan for your expansion, Mr. Fox."

Abruptly, the give-and-take shifted to things like funded debentures, interest coverage, bor-rowing against assets and stock issues. Kahn's conversation was rapid, precise and lucid.

The language of high finance was not completely familiar to W.F., and Kahn, recognizing this fact, stepped in. "Kuhn, Loeb is a first-rank underwriter with nationwide distributing facili-ties, which simply means we can take on large bond and stock issues and sell them in a relatively short period of time, Mr. Fox."

"I see."

"Kuhn, Loeb invites other underwriters to participate in an issue, and bonds and stocks are allotted to the underwriting group to retail to their own customers."

"The public price of the bonds is the same everywhere, Bill," Dryden said.

"How do you determine who is to be invited to join the...the..."

"The underwriting group, Mr. Fox?"

"Yes, Mr. Kahn."

"Because of our long experience, we have identified reputable firms with a strong financial standing."

Lighting a cigar, W.F. took a long drag from it. "Fascinating."

"Of course, the Fox companies could go public and float additional stock, Mr. Fox."

"Bill is concerned about losing control of the companies, Otto."

"There are ways of dealing with that, Forrest."

"How so?" W.F. queried.

"Well, for one, Fox Film could create two classes of stock, an A class which would be nonvoting, and a B class where all of the voting rights would reside. The insiders would control the B shares, and hence the board."

"Is this legal, Forrest?"

"It's perfectly legal, Bill. It's done all the time."

A sharp negotiator, Kahn decided to confront the one burning issue he knew separated the interests of Kuhn, Loeb and Fox Film.

"I understand you may have misgivings because of Kuhn, Loeb's association with Adolph Zukor."

"That is a fact, Mr. Kahn. I don't see how you can possibly serve two masters."

"We have worked with firms in the same industry before, like railroads, and separate their affairs by assigning different partners of the firm to each client. A sort of Chinese wall."

"I see."

"If that should present a problem to you, Mr. Fox, I would be more than happy to suggest other reputable investment bankers."

"Thank you, Otto," Dryden replied. "That's very kind of you."

As they rode back to the office, Dryden could not help but ponder the distrust and suspicion displayed by the little man sitting next to him. It was important to remember William Fox's early environment, that was true, but would this character trait reassert itself over and over again?

By the end of 1918, First National controlled 190 first-run theaters, 40 subsequent-run theaters, and indirectly controlled another 366 houses through subfranchise agreements. By early 1920, they controlled 639 theaters, including 224 first-run. In the autumn of 1921, First National had 3,400 subfranchised holders.

By mid-1921, Paramount owned 303 theaters, ensuring first-run exhibition in key areas. It was Adolph Zukor pitted against First National. The theater war was now on, and in full force. There was a time, not many years before, when Zukor hadn't even figured in the theater arena. Now he was moving into a leadership position. The influence of Zukor was shaping the way the motion-picture business was to be run.

As an integrated player, Fox Film seldom distributed a picture not made in its own studio. In fact, Fox, Universal and Mutual each had organized its own national network of exchanges, and rarely handled product from competitive studios.

W.F. thought the moment still inopportune for him to take the company public and dilute his 51 percent ownership stake. There were still a lot of independent theater owners who wanted Fox pictures. Although each day it was getting more difficult to exhibit Fox product in the major cities, Zukor still didn't make enough pictures to fill his own screens. Loew's was showing Fox pictures and First National was taking them, too.

Early perceptions about the performance of Louis Burt Mayer in the role of film producer were, at best, mixed. In sharp contrast to William Fox, Mayer preferred working as a partner. He wanted someone with whom to share management and production responsibilities. W.F., on the other hand, was obsessive about where the ultimate authority resided. He wanted to dot every "i" and cross every "t." Hence, the business types who surrounded W.F. were mere flunkies, serving more as conduits of information rather than as peers in decision-making.

Mayer met Al Lichtman, former sales manager of Zukor's Famous Players, who talked about distributing films on a bigger scale. Lichtman had started his career as an usher in Tony Pastor's Theater in Manhattan, and had been a manager for C.C. Pyle before he'd joined Zukor.

Along with newspaperman Walter Hoff Seely, Mayer and Richard Rowland formed Alco, which was set up to distribute pictures made by All-Star, Popular Plays and B.A. Rolfe. Seeley claimed the company had more assets than it really did, and by October 1914, Alco was on the verge of insolvency. After it plunged into receivership, a bankruptcy court ordered the liquidation of the company.

Not long after the Alco fiasco, on March 5, 1915, Mayer and Rowland gathered up what few assets were left of Alco and incorporated Metro Pictures with Richard Rowland as president and Louis B. Mayer as secretary. Joe Engel, formerly with Universal, Famous Players and other companies, also bought into the company, as did a powerful exchange man from the western states, George Grummbacher. Joining Metro's catalogue were Columbia—then a small studio located on Hollywood's Poverty Row—Quality Pictures, Popular Plays and Players, Dyreda and Rolfe.

This was a particularly grim time for Louis B. Mayer. Most of his worldly goods were tied to the success of Metro. But Mayer was not one to rest on his laurels. He was quite aware of the need to identify good pictures before his competitors, so he kept his eye on first-run showings. It was about this time that Mayer made that fateful deal with Harry Aitken to purchase the New England distribution rights to *Birth of a Nation.* The logical next step was film production, but for his plan to work he had to contract players.

With the $500,000 Mayer made from *Birth* burning a hole in his pocket, he contracted the experienced stage actor, Francis X. Bushman, who'd started his film career playing for Essanay.

Metro showed a substantial profit from the distribution of films, but Mayer still hadn't fulfilled his unremitting desire for making pictures, so he convinced Rowland and the other stockholders to allow him to make a serial called *The Great Secret.* Starring Francis X. Bushman and Beverly Bayne, *The Great Secret* went nowhere at the box office. In fact, the most memorable scenes occurred off the set. A torrid love affair erupted between Bushman, the father of five, and his young costar.

The ever-tenacious Mayer said, "I have to have a star."

Unrelenting in his search for a major star, Mayer pursued the sixth most successful actress in America, Anita Stewart, who was part of Vitagraph's waning inventory of players. No dummy, Rowland soon realized that Mayer's impetuous quest for Anita Stewart wasn't to benefit Metro, but was for another company Mayer had formed, the Gordon-Mayer Company of Boston. Gordon was Nate Gordon, a film distributor. Gordon-Mayer had no studio, no production facility, and no national distribution system.

As Mayer was fully aware, Vitagraph had an enforceable contract for Stewart's services and wasn't about to let her go without a fight. One day their lawyer appeared in court and requested that a judge issue an injunction obligating Stewart to fulfill her end of the bargain. To Mayer's dismay, the presiding judge ruled in Vitagraph's favor and Anita Stewart was forced to work an additional 26 weeks for Vitagraph to make up for the time she had frittered away with her prolonged absences.

Not one to surrender without a fight, the implacable Mayer chose his own battery of lawyers, Dunbar, Nutter, and McLennan of New York, and Bernard and Arthur Berenson of Boston, who were ready to do battle for his side. In spite of the bitter litigation, Anita Stewart signed with Mayer. He resigned as secretary of Metro, a company to which he would return again during the length of his career.

After the brief stay at Metro, Mayer associated with the prodigal film producer, Lewis J. Selznick, and his Select Pictures. Ironically, Select was then 50 percent owned by Adolph Zukor, no friend to Mayer, but this didn't seem to faze Mayer in the least. It wasn't long before Mayer and Selznick stopped talking to each other, for Mayer thought him to be a drinker and womanizer and, more important, a lousy businessman.

In a convoluted series of events, Mayer, upon losing the Stewart case and settling the Vitagraph litigation, resumed his post at Metro as head of their New England exchange, while his partner, Selznick, was left holding the bag for Select Pictures. Former partner Selznick watched his finances go into a tailspin. By 1923 he was forced into bankruptcy, and spent the rest of his years in retirement.

During 1918, after shooting *Virtuous Wives*—featuring Anita Stewart—at Vitagraph's Brooklyn studios, Mayer began negotiating with Colonel William Selig for the purchase of the 30-acre Zoo located opposite Eastland Park on Los Angeles' Mission Road. By now, the aging Selig was in deep financial trouble and Mayer acquired the studio for a reasonable price. A deal was signed in late October. Mayer made his office in a corner of a large loft-like room where the cameramen kept their equipment.

In front of a lackluster audience, *Virtuous Wives* premiered at the Strand in December 1918. Uniformed ushers handed out theater programs that were works of art, with a picture of the very beautiful Anita Stewart on every page. On the cover were the words, "And the Wise Men Shall Secure Unto Their Houses Virtuous Wives, Sayeth the Prophet."

The critics were not impressed with Mayer's first work. In spite of Stewart's reputation, the picture was nothing out of the ordinary and performed poorly at the box office.

During the year, a handsome young Italian actor called Rudolph De Valentina earned his first Universal credit in *A Society Sensation*, playing the son of a wealthy scion of society who falls in love with a poor girl.

De Valentina's performance was good enough to earn a bigger role in *All Night*, a contrived farce, where De Valentina was brought together with Carmel Myers. In the process of making pictures for Universal, De Valentina became Rudolph Valentino. In his usual manner, Laemmle hardly took notice of the actor.

At that moment Universal's business policy was quite simple: run-of-the-mill pictures that made money. There was little interest in making epic pictures. Besides, a lot of small theaters had developed an insatiable appetite for simple, uncomplicated stories, and that was precisely what Uncle Carl Laemmle doled out to them. Universal was making a determined effort to dominate the low-end part of the market.

But for two or three exceptions, all of Universal's key employees had clawed their way up through the company, most of them having started on the lot in low-paid jobs. Laemmle had some excellent talent on his payroll, directors like John Ford, Elmer Clifton, Lynn Reynolds, and players like Mae Murray and Lon Chaney. But he was unable to fully exploit them.

On the plus side of the ledger, Universal was financing its business out of its profits. Laemmle shied away from big pictures, so he had not strapped the company with excessive debt. He'd lived long enough to realize that business cycles were an inevitable phenomenon. What went up would eventually come down.

Much like William Fox, Laemmle was a man immersed in the details of his business. He insisted upon exact daily accounts of Universal's operations. He was skilled at eliminating superfluous words from telegrams. There was a pile of suggestions on his desk from underlings on how to improve the company's performance. He gave everyone a chance, and sometimes a second chance. One thing was for sure. Laemmle did not relax, no matter how good things became, for he knew that a slight falling off in earnings would panic his stockholders.

Personal tragedy struck Carl Laemmle. In the late summer and early autumn of 1918, an influenza epidemic hit the United States with brutal force. The experts were calling it the Spanish Flu, and it darkened theaters for several months. New Yorkers wore cloth masks in a futile attempt to stymie the spread of the dreaded virus. Citizens were encouraged to stay home and out of contact with each other. Before it was over, the Spanish Flu claimed more than 12,000 victims in New York alone.

Sadly, one of those victims was Carl Laemmle's wife, Recha Stern. Married for 22 years, the Laemmles had a daughter, Rosabelle, who was 15 years old, and a son, Julius, now 11.

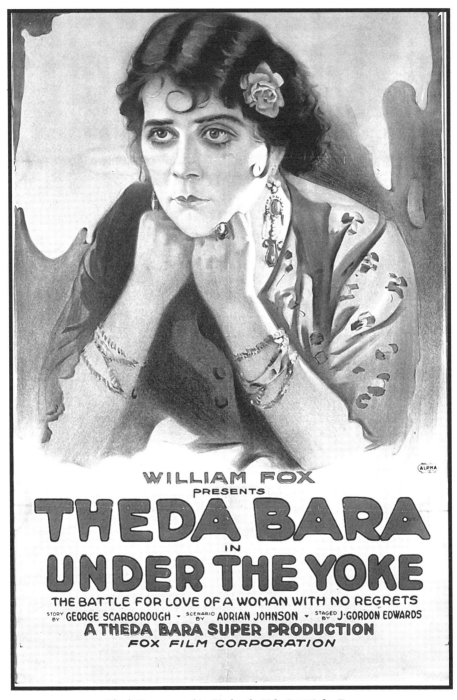

Theda Bara starred in *Under the Yoke* (1918) for Fox.

The Temple service for Mrs. Laemmle was held in New York and W.F. and Eve were there to extend their deep-felt condolences to Uncle Carl and his family. At shivah, Laemmle told them

STAGED BY
J. Gordon Edwards

WILLIAM FOX PRESENTS
THEDA BARA in SALOME
A THEDA BARA SUPER PRODUCTION

Fox Film
CORPORATION

how, during his childhood, eight of his 12 brothers and sisters had died as a result of scarlet fever. Death was something to be expected, he said. However, the death of his wife was a personal tragedy for Carl Laemmle from which he would never fully recover.

The armistice that ended the Great War was signed in November. W.F. wired Sol Wurtzel and Winnie Sheehan to toss away any war films they'd made because the public wasn't going to be in the mood for gruesome bloodshed up on the screen. With the returning military men and the slowdown in production of armament, W.F. wondered what the economy would look like in 1919.

Throughout the year, W.F. harped on his favorite topic—keeping down the cost of making pictures.

He wrote Sol Wurtzel:

> In going over the weekly payroll vouchers I notice you are paying your assistant $90 a week at this time. I am sorry that you saw fit to give your assistant two advances without first consulting me. You know that one of the grave objections that I had to Carlos was that he felt that he had reached the stage where he no longer needed to consult with me. You, however, definitely understood that you at no time would reach the stage where you were not to communicate with me before taking any definite action.

1918 was a good, if not spectacular year. Fox Film made 73 pictures, grossing over $7 million. However, earnings dropped to $275,000. Part of this unsatisfactory bottom-line performance was due to Zukor's squeeze on first-run theater showings; another part was because of the influenza pandemic, and for the first time, some exceptionally expensive features like *Les Miserables*.

The industry released 841 feature-length films. According to a Quigley Publications poll of exhibitors, the top male and female stars were Douglas Fairbanks and Mary Pickford.

CHAPTER 8
1919

Fox Film started building its new head office and eastern studio at 850 Tenth Avenue between 55th and 56th Streets. Floor space equaled 150,000 square feet, and the building would house executive offices, a laboratory and studios with approximately 5,000 employees. Construction materials included marble, brick, limestone, concrete, steel and bronze with partitions of steel and glass. The edifice would accommodate 20 sets working simultaneously.

The salient features of the planned structure comprised 12 projection rooms, restrooms, a gymnasium, a restaurant, dressing rooms, 20 darkrooms for cameramen, and a washed air system of heating and ventilation. The company invested $2.5 million and expected to occupy the building in the early part of 1920.

In the meantime, Fox Film had taken seven floors of the Leavitt building, but space was inadequate. Film work was spread all over. During the past year, the studio had occupied space in Manhattan, New Jersey, Yonkers, the Bronx and Brooklyn, and it was necessary during the past winter to send four companies to Miami, Florida.

As the days passed, W.F. filled his life with great dedication to the business. Interwoven with correspondence, meetings and telephone calls were the 101 little details of motion picture production. He kept track of every ongoing film project and assiduously studied cost reports. He pored over seat-count statistics from Fox's growing chain of theaters. Then there were the leases and titles for real property, some of which the company acquired at good prices. Every morning a production report was circulated depicting the status of all major films. It was sent to directors, producers and other department heads who affected production costs.

W.F. was looking forward to occupying the new headquarters building where he would build in additional comforts for the long days and nights he was spending at the office. W.F. decided that the 10th Avenue front of the first and second floors would be dedicated to executive offices where he'd have his office as well as Winfield Sheehan, Jack Leo, John Eisele, Herman Robbins and James E. McBride, chairman of the executive committee.

During this period of intense activity, W.F. was very much involved in the design of the walnut-paneled, cathedral-like office where he would labor for the company. First and foremost, he wanted privacy, closely followed by comfort, adequate space for conducting meetings, a subdued decor with stained-glass windows, and a secret passageway for quick escapes. There were many nasty stories floating around the industry about those deranged players who, when faced with their own mediocrity, were prone to take their frustration out on studio bosses. W.F. certainly wasn't going to let that happen to him.

The top floor of the three-story building would be used exclusively for studios. Each star would have a well-appointed dressing room and the architect made provisions for shower baths, lockers and bathrooms. W.F.'s thought was that a comfortable player was a productive player, and he wanted them to spend as little time as possible with the distractions that occurred on the busy streets of New York.

Proud that Fox Film would now become an important part of New York's bustling economy, W.F. believed that good, decent work was the best antidote for social ills. The nice thing about the picture business was that it employed all kinds of people, including tradesmen, unskilled workers, people from the arts, accountants and even a medical staff.

During the summer of 1919, Winnie and W.F. set sail for Europe to open offices in Paris, Rome, Berlin, London and Dublin to get their pictures into theaters and to facilitate filming news events. For an energetic man like W.F., travel by ship was slow and monotonous. It took forever.

While in Europe, they also looked for talent among stage performers throughout the continent. Fox Film was one of the first in the industry to understand the explosive potential of the foreign box office. There were a lot of people over there who eagerly anticipated American films. The international film industry quickly became an industry dominated by American product. In England, American pictures were occupying more than 80 percent of the playing time in all British theaters.

These were happy days for Fox Film. Tom Mix was very popular in England, introducing the stiff-upper-lip English to the excitement of the American West. Since the English never went through a similar experience as that of America's conquering of the West, the Brits could now enjoy the feeling of what it must have been like without subjecting themselves to the rigors of the real thing. W.F. was quite certain that much of the international tourism to the West was promoted by Tom Mix films being shown in English theaters.

W.F. was very proud of that fact.

The only thing he truly detested about traveling to Europe was the poor communication between the continents. W.F. relied heavily on a daily dispatch from Jack Leo to keep him apprised of what was happening in the States. The feeling of isolation was disheartening at times, and he tried to limit his trips to a month or less. He could sense Adolph Zukor taking advantage of his absences, although he justified the investment in time by recognizing that foreign rentals were growing dramatically.

When W.F. returned from Europe, he was mortified to find the great quantity of money that Jack Leo was wiring to Sol Wurtzel each week. He wrote to Wurtzel:

> I sat down to analyze, to find out why this amount was necessary, and why in spite of these large sums wired each week, you still have an indebtedness owing to merchants of approximately $70,000. Of course, $50,000 of this outstanding is the waste occasioned by the remaking of *The Coming of the Law* and *The Sneak,* but still does not account for the great tremendous sums which are wired to you each Saturday. My analysis shows me that the cause for these extraordinary amounts which you require each Saturday is as follows: First, the sets used for Excel pictures are all too large and stupendous, with too much furniture in them. Second, you know we have no desire to have Peggy Hyland or Madelaine Traverse pictures released on the Excel brand in more than 4,200 feet, titles and all. None of the pictures that you are sending in are below the 5,000-feet mark. It is hardly believable that when one analyzes the cost of Tom Mix pictures, which are large and spectacular, with many people, many horses and many other things that cause the costs to go up, that in spite of all that, it is possible to make these pictures for considerable less money than you have permitted to be expended for Peggy Hyland pictures. Reduce the size of the sets. Reduce the cost of the supporting cast. Reduce the length of the pictures and reduce the number of help to do all of the above.

While W.F. was in Europe, Zukor had taken part of Kuhn, Loeb's money and acquired a half-interest in Sid Grauman's Million Dollar Theater in Los Angeles. In May, he purchased a controlling interest in the Rialto—opened in 1916—and the Rivoli—opened in 1917—theaters, both located in New York, and in August, he took over the Black New England theaters. Zukor's theater-expansion program was a deeply planned procedure. It seemed to have two broad dimensions: theater size and location. Famous Players would make a careful study of the location and the community before signing an agreement with a theater owner. Picking good locations was a science that called for detailed information on the number of white- and blue-collar workers, payroll size, employment statistics and so on. A top Paramount executive headed up this effort.

After the Rivoli acquisition, Zukor said, "There is no building on Broadway, from the Battery to its northern end, that is more beautiful than the Rivoli Theatre."

Feeling that he might have let the horse out of the barn, W.F. told Eve there wouldn't be much left to pick over once Zukor completed his theater-acquisition program.

"Zukor has gone out of his mind!"

In her matter-of-fact manner, Eve said, "It may be time to change our policy, Bill."

"Not quite yet, Eve."

Perhaps, of course, W.F. was wrong. In the motion picture business, history had shown that one couldn't afford to be wrong more than once. As W.F. himself had once said, "One man in a deal almost always knows that he is wrong."

Was it Zukor or Fox?

After leasing the Selig Zoo, Louis B. Mayer shortly discovered that he knew precious little about making silent films. The fact was that he'd made his name distributing pictures, not making them.

The Rivoli Theatre in NYC

First National was frequently calling and asking, "Where's the product, Mayer?"

It turned out that Lois Weber, a successful director at the peak of her popularity, was available, so Mayer signed her. Work commenced on an Anita Stewart film, *A Midnight Romance.* While the picture was in the editing stage, Mayer hired yet another director, Marshall Neilan, and filmed a second Stewart feature called *Her Kingdom of Dreams.*

Things began to change when Mayer's pictures achieved a respectable level of success at the box office. For a change in scenery, Mayer traveled to New York with Margaret and his two daughters and saw a few Broadway shows. There was much unfinished business to take care of in Boston. Mayer and Nate Gordon reached an agreement to separate, and soon thereafter, the Mayers were on their way back to California. Of all the Hollywood moguls, Louis B. Mayer would be one of the first to make his primary residence in California.

Then terrible misfortune struck. There were abnormal winter rains that flooded Mayer's studio and the first floor was under water. The entire negative of his most recent picture, *The Inferior Sex,* was lost. Making the best of a bad situation and asking his investors to dip once more into their thinning pockets, Mayer arranged to have a new studio built for him in the eucalyptus grove that adjoined the Selig Zoo at 3800 Mission Road.

Realizing he had to provide something more permanent than a couple of hotel rooms for his family, the Mayers moved into a rented house on North Kenmore between Sunset and Hollywood Boulevards, a stone's throw from Fox's Sunset Studio.

On one of his many trips to New York, Lasky told Zukor that he was using up ideas as fast as they could be developed. The need for stories was at its peak. "We've got to break the bottleneck in the story department, Mr. Zukor. We can't rely any longer on simply sifting through what comes to us spontaneously. We must actively begin the creative literary processes."

At their first luncheon on Lasky's return trip to New York, Zukor said, "I bought the Charles Frohman Company for you." Shortly thereafter, Lasky returned to California with a trunk filled with plays.

The surge in picture production forced film studios to turn to professional novelists, playwrights, screenwriters and magazine writers for stories. Prior to 1919, the screen rights of novels and plays were purchasable for $1,000 to $10,000. As the demand for good stories began to exceed the supply, the price escalated.

From a theater perspective, Marcus Loew was completely attuned to what Zukor was preaching, making pictures that told stories, pictures that appealed to sophisticated audiences. Pictures longer than two or three reels, known as "features." At first blush, perhaps, it was thought that Loew's would make such pictures. But Marcus Loew kept acquiring theaters, urging his people to locate suitable properties and sign them up. By 1919, he had more than a hundred of them. Loew's Incorporated, set up to merge Marcus Loew's diverse interests, was a $25 million company listed on the New York Stock Exchange. Down on Wall Street, where they traded his stock with a high degree of enthusiasm, it was said that Loew's was a growth stock and that the theater chain would eventually control 500 theaters. On its board of directors sat Charles E. Danforth of Van Emburgh & Atterbury, Harvey Gibson, the president of Liberty National Bank, W.C. Durant, the president of General Motors, Daniel Pomeroy, vice president of Bankers Trust, James Perkins, another New York banker, and Lee Shubert, the theater impresario.

In spite of what Wall Street thought about Loew's staying focused on theaters, it was only a matter of time before the company would enter the production side of the business and make pictures. For this Marcus Loew required a creative person, someone able to transform a story into a negative, someone who understood what went on in back of a camera.

It was early morning and W.F. was still in his old office at the Leavitt building, having one of those heated discussions about players, this one related to the growing popularity of Tom Mix. A lot of ideas were bandied about the room, with everyone talking at the top of their voices.

Seated around the perimeter of the office were Winfield Sheehan, Jack Leo, Raoul Walsh and Eve. As usual, W.F. was up on his feet, pacing restlessly, puffing on what was left of a cigar. "Tom Mix is exploding at the box office. He's going to hold us up one of these days. Anybody?"

"He's passed William S. Hart in popularity, W.F.," Jack Leo said with a big smile on his face.

Brushing cigar ashes from his vest, W.F. walked over to where Eve was sitting. "What do you think, Eve?"

"Don't we have anybody else coming up on the lot, Winnie?"

"We're developing a former cameraman, George O'Brien, Mrs. Fox."

"Fox Film can't go on living off Mix, Bara, Farnum and Walsh forever," W.F. said.

"Amen," Raoul Walsh uttered.

It became apparent that Winnie's only hope in calming W.F. lay in playing what he considered to be his trump card. The rumor mill said the studio had someone with potential doing bit parts. Word spread quickly that Wurtzel had identified a hot property.

"Sol says he's got a cowboy on the lot showing some promise, W.F.."

"What's his name?"

"Charles Gebhart."

"Charles Gebhart!" Eve and W.F. said it simultaneously.

Although they didn't realize it at the time, Gebhart was going to become a major star for Fox. The studio would change his name a couple of times, first to Charles Jones and then to Buck Jones. At the beginning of his Fox career, Buck Jones doubled for and worked in films with Tom Mix and Bill Farnum. Later, when Mix and W.F. began squabbling about Mix's salary, W.F. signed Buck Jones at $400 a week to star in a series of films budgeted at less than those of Tom Mix. W.F. figured he'd keep Mix in line that way.

Unfortunately, Buck Jones' first Fox feature was an unmitigated disaster. After seeing the film, W.F. wired Sol Wurtzel and told him in no uncertain terms that he wouldn't release the picture. He said the direction was amateurish and he was sorely disappointed.

Part of the scheme between W.F. and Wurtzel was to make Mix envious with Buck Jones' first picture. After the picture's debacle, Wurtzel wisely put Jones in the hands of experienced directors like John Ford, Bernard Durning and Scott Dunlap.

In 1919 Theda Bara made several pictures for the studio, including *The She-Devil*, *The Light*, *When Men Desire*, *The Siren's Song*, *A Woman There Was*, *Kathleen Mavoureen*, *La Belle Russe* and *The Lure of Ambition*.

While filming *Kathleen Ma-voureen*, Bara fell for the director, English-born Charles J. Brabin. A tall, good-looking man, Brabin was recognized as a good director with great aesthetic faculties. He became an expert in serial direction, starring Pearl White in 10 serials in the three years she worked for Fox Film.

Bara boasted, "His mental brilliance was not the first attractive quality I noticed about Charles. It was the way he walked."

Brabin was directing *La Belle Russe,* in which Bara played twin sisters. The end of the Great War signaled a whole new generation of moviegoers, and audiences were tiring of the vamp formula.

Threading through Old World props and pieces of furniture, Wurtzel was making one of his unannounced visits on the set of *La Belle Russe.* The crew was picking up their equipment, winding up things for the day.

Bara made her way to where Wurtzel was standing. She had a strange glare in her eyes. "I am through with vamp pictures, Sol, and I am glad, for I never wanted to appear in that kind of role."

Tom Mix and Buck Jones both appeared in *The Speed Maniac* from Fox in 1919.

"What in the hell are you talking about, Theda?"

"Just this, Sol. My future plans are to present women of the world, just as you find them in any city or country town."

"Are you falling off your rocker, Theda?"

"I want more money, Sol!"

"No dice!"

"Did a Mary Pickford picture ever provoke a riot?"

"I don't give a shit about Mary Pickford. The two of you are a couple of has-beens."

Visibly annoyed, Wurtzel whirled around and marched off the set.

Bara was making $4,000 weekly and asking for $5,000. In response to her persistent requests for more money, W.F. reviewed the investment in her negatives, which were costing Fox Film $60,000 each to produce, and compared that number to her crumbling box office receipts.

"If Theda wants to go, let her go, Sol. Her numbers are lousy." Besides, Tom Mix was spectacular at the box office and Jack Edwards was prepping another *femme fatale* by the name of Betty Blythe.

The following day, during a brief *tête-à-tête*, Wurtzel informed Bara of W.F.'s decision to hold on her salary.

"Sol, you're making a big mistake."

"We all make mistakes, Theda."

Her face gone ugly, Bara said, "I refuse to vamp another single, solitary second unless Winfield Sheehan first gives me the opportunity to prove I can be as good as easily as I was bad!"

Shaking his head in amazement, Wurtzel watched Bara sashay from his office, acting a bit like an actress who didn't quite pass muster in a screen test.

As part of the construction of the new head office on 10th Avenue, W.F. insisted the builders install a well-equipped barbershop to waste as little time as possible trimming his hair and mustache. Although the company still hadn't officially inaugurated the building, executives were now installed in many of the offices and film directors were using several stages to make pictures.

Fox's publicity man, Johnny Goldfrap, kept insisting that W.F. grant an interview to the *Times*. He finally agreed on the condition the reporter come to the barbershop, which was reached through a panel from the projection room. It was 1 a.m. In the barbershop, W.F. had assembled part of his staff, including Jimmy Grainger, Jack Edwards and Winfield Sheehan.

Gus the barber hung W.F.'s suit jacket on a nearby perch. Tilting back the barber chair, he helped W.F. climb into it for a relaxing shave.

"Shave and a facial massage, Gus. Trim the hair and the mustache."

Applying a hot towel, Gus wrapped his customer's face in a twisted shape so that only the tip of his big nose was sticking out. It lay there for a few seconds before Gus removed it. Applying hot lather, he began shaving W.F. with a straight razor.

In the midst of filming a Zane Grey novel, Jack Edwards wanted to clear a few things with W.F.. "We've purchased the rights to several Zane Grey novels and—"

"Not so close, Gus!"

While stretching W.F.'s skin with one hand, Gus was shaving with the other.

"I don't like that last scenario, Jack."

"But it's practically your own, W.F."

"Very well, make it all mine. Meet me at the golf links tomorrow morning and we'll work on the train coming in. The climax needs strengthening."

Edwards wisely dropped the subject. This wasn't a good time to debate or argue with W.F. Not while he was being closely shaved.

"Any film monopoly on the horizon, Winnie?"

"Not as yet, W.F. But this battle between Zukor and First National is tying up a lot of theaters."

"Tell Saul Rogers to start a suit! This industry must be free or—"

Gus slapped more lather on his face and W.F. snorted angrily, blowing soap from his nostrils.

"Jack, where are the takes in scene 238? Should have been here already!"

"Well, there were just a few feet."

"Makes no difference! I want to see every foot, understand? Every foot."

Fox's national sales manager, Jimmy Grainger, asked, "Is my report satisfactory, W.F.?"

Gus was examining a small cut on W.F.'s face.

"Witch hazel and keep the towel out of my mouth, Gus."

"I'll try, Mr. Fox."

"You know your report isn't finished, Jimmy. You've skipped 30 theaters in the cities of Detroit, Denver and Los Angeles."

"I'll get on it right away."

"All over, gentlemen. I've got to go to work."

W.F. stood erect and let Gus powder him down.

"W.F., the *Times* wants an interview," Winnie said.

W.F. stared at the young reporter. "I dislike publicity."

"Will you merge the Fox Film Corporation?"

W.F. found one last cigar and lit up. Grainger poured him a cup of hot, steaming coffee.

William Fox poses in front of an outdoor movie screen.

"My business is making and showing pictures. I'm William Fox and always will be."

Doing an about-face, W.F. left the room.

A couple of days later the *Times* published a blurb entitled, "What kind of a fellow is Fox?"

In the article the reporter described the events he'd witnessed during the shave and facial, quoting from the dialogue. W.F. kind of enjoyed the article, which the reporter cleverly entitled, "What others say of him."

"He's a boy for play and a fiend for work."

"He can build a photoplay and a photoplay theater, every detail."

"Six out of every seven nights he is at work in his office."

"He plays golf as he works and plans, alone."

"He is the aggressive figure in the film business."

"He's a fighter."

"He takes big chances."

"He demands that business be played wide open."

"He is impetuous but clear-eyed."

Because of a palpable shift of so much of Fox Film's production to the West Coast Studio, W.F. was spending more time in California observing and attending to the cost of negatives, which were now averaging $25,000 for B pictures and $100,000 for features. The studio was in full swing and so far had come through with flying colors. The men W.F. bred as his studio management were all trained in the same tradition, making profitable pictures.

The big studio bosses, Zukor, Laemmle and Fox, lived in New York and journeyed to Los Angeles several times a year to check production and hobnob with the stars who lived in California. A fancy reception at the Los Angeles train station was a regular feature of the welcoming ceremony. When the festivities ended, the moguls immersed themselves in tedious meetings, time-consuming contract negotiations, conferences and more conferences.

Despite the long trip, and W.F. hated to admit this, he was actually getting to like California. The place was overflowing with strange people employed by the studios, and the picture business had a total payroll of $25 million a year.

Motion pictures were becoming a significant industry. But there still remained the fact that the New York offices, although responsible for film production, tightly controlled the California studios. Studio people, the moguls claimed, though brilliant and imaginative, were incapable of understanding high finance.

By 1919, Hollywood was a small town. There was Santa Monica beach and the Ocean Park Bath House and not much else. There wasn't a lot to do except for making pictures. There were a few good restaurants, but when compared to New York, Hollywood was a veritable wasteland. Other than the Hollywood Hotel there was the newly constructed Garden Courts Apartments on Hollywood Boulevard, just east of La Brea Avenue. It was a magnificent Renaissance-style structure whose interior was decorated with fine oriental carpets, grand pianos and splendid paintings. During his early days in Hollywood, L.B. Mayer called the Garden Courts his home.

In a fan magazine, Lillian Gish was quoted as saying: "What social life there was revolved around the people in the studio, for we knew no others."

During the late teens a small group of independent studios set up shop in Hollywood, primarily on Sunset Boulevard near Gower Street, an area that came to be known as Poverty Row and Gower Gulch.

Most of these companies quietly passed into history, companies like Loftus Features, L-KO Motion Picture Company, Sterling Motion Picture Company, Quality Pictures Corporation, Frances Ford Studios, Waldorf Productions, Century Film Company, Willat Studios, California Studios, Bischoff Comedies, Choice Productions, Goodwill Studios and Chadwick Pictures Company.

In 1919, several major stars joined forces as United Artists, mostly as a distribution company for their independent productions. Charlie Chaplin, for example, always wanted to manage every penny generated from his films, so he built his own studio on La Brea Avenue. Hollywood's sweethearts, Pickford and Fairbanks, purchased a studio from Jesse D. Hampton on the north side of Santa Monica Boulevard, two blocks west of La Brea. There Fairbanks filmed two of his more noteworthy swashbuckler movies, *Robin Hood* and *The Thief of Baghdad.*

The original stockholders of United Artists were Mary Pickford, Charlie Chaplin, D.W. Griffith, William S. Hart—who talked a lot but got cold feet before the papers were signed—and Douglas Fairbanks. During his Liberty Loan drives, Fairbanks had become good friends with William Gibbs McAdoo, President Woodrow Wilson's son-in-law, who had served as secretary of the treasury between 1913 and 1918. McAdoo was a lawyer and Fairbanks thought him to be the perfect candidate to run United Artists.

It seemed that the idea to form a distributing company for America's top box office draws had originated with Hiram Abrams and B.P. Schulberg. In fact, Schulberg had given up the comfort and security of a steady job with Zukor to play a role in the formation of United Artists. For their contribution, the two wheeler-dealers were asking for a big piece of the action—20 percent—and McAdoo thought two percent was more than enough. Somehow before Abrams or Schulberg could ink their names to any kind of formal agreement, they were dealt out of the game.

Douglas Fairbanks, Mary Pickford, D.W. Griffith and Charlie Chaplin—the founders of United Artists

United Artists had a lot of stars but no product, since the principals were tied down to previous commitments they had made with other studios, reminiscent of what had happened to Harry Aitken when he brought Griffith, Sennett and Ince into Triangle. Because of this, United Artists was off to a rocky start.

Pickford and Chaplin were astute business people and promptly decided that political clout alone wasn't going to turn United Artists into a profit-making venture. At this moment in its short existence, what the company needed most was an experienced hands-on manager.

The Lasky-De Mille Barn was the first Hollywood movie studio. In 1913 De Mille rented the barn and filmed *The Squaw Man.* It is now the site of the Hollywood Heritage Museum

After a relatively short stint in the company, McAdoo and his principal associate, Oscar Price, withdrew a bit frustrated when heavy-handed Hiram Abrams returned to the scene as general manager to see that the distributing company could really distribute, for that was his specialty. Like so many of Hollywood's mercenaries, he had forgotten his pact with Schulberg—all for one, one for all—and accepted the opportunity placed before him. Left in the cold, Schulberg accused Abrams of selling him out. When would he learn not to be so trusting?

Applauding the appointment, industry bigwigs said Abrams was "tough as nails and would tackle the assignment with vigor." His job was to persuade exhibitors to book United Artists pictures, and where he couldn't get bookings, Abrams rented theaters and played his pictures on extended runs.

In essence, United Artists acted as a go-between, connecting producer and distributor. It contracted with its producers to sell their product individually, without reference to any other producer.

Under the auspices of United Artists, Chaplin made many of his most memorable pictures, including *City Lights, Modern Times,* and *The Great Dictator.*

Over time, the major film stars withdrew into stately mansions behind wrought-iron gates, sequestering themselves from the eyes of curious onlookers. Fame had a price tag, and they soon became acutely aware of the fact that their privacy was gone forever, or almost forever, at least until their bright images faded from the silver screen.

In sharp contrast, W.F. could walk down any busy street in New York or Hollywood and never turn a head. Nobody ever said anything to him, even when he was formally introduced at celebrity gatherings. No one ever asked him for an autograph, except when he was signing company checks. With almost childlike delight, W.F. found this a very satisfying predicament. Although he was many times wealthier than most stars, he enjoyed the same degree of anonymity as any worker on the Fox lot.

Slowly the center of gravity shifted to what became Beverly Hills and Bel Air, although the small towns on the beach continued to draw their fair share of film stars. The number of people engaged in making motion pictures passed 25,000 and, as a consequence, new hotels and boarding houses were built to take advantage of a booming economy.

Film studios peppered the area; W.F. was never quite sure how many there actually were at any given time. The motion picture business was a lot like a revolving door, with new entrants replacing those who were forced by the local sheriff to shutter their gates.

In an attractive booklet, the Automobile Club of Southern California displayed a map of greater Los Angeles for the use of motorists driving to the city's movie studios and listed the location of Nestor, Famous Players-Lasky, National Film Corporation of America, Metro, Chaplin, Brunton, Fox, D.W. Griffith, Vitagraph, Mack Sennett, Universal, Ince and Goldwyn.

Ardent fans were clamoring to get into the studios and see the workplace of their favorite screen stars. More often than not, a visit to the studios proved a disappointment simply because there was only a hodgepodge of barn-like structures made of clapboard with many small buildings around the lot. As time passed, the studio end got more sophisticated and began to stage stunt routines for studio visitors. During difficult economic times, some of the studios would become very dependent on the studio tour business for survival.

Uncle Carl Laemmle was one of the first to open picture-making to public view. His thought was that studio visits would stimulate ticket sales. He built a grandstand from which visitors could see the director and his company at work. Later, the birth of talkies would make the practice impossible, but Uncle Carl was one of the last to give it up.

Small wonder that Goldwyn Pictures suffered a $100,000 loss in 1919. Squeezed by the inexorable battle for theaters waged by First National and Zukor, Goldwyn was finding it hard to exhibit its pictures. Initially, expectations for the studio ran high; however, by the end of 1919, Goldwyn Pictures found itself fighting an uphill battle against the emerging giants of the industry. There was a time when Sam Goldwyn thought he'd follow in the heavy footsteps of many of those who'd come before him—into oblivion. After all, he was making pictures in Harry Aitken's old Culver City studio, which he'd purchased for a song.

Was it jinxed?

In New York, W.F. summoned Winfield Sheehan into his cavernous office and ignoring the hand Sheehan offered as he entered, told him to sit down.

"There's something I want to get off my chest, Winnie."

Something was gnawing at W.F. because his good hand was shaking. "What's the matter, W.F.? What did I do?"

"It's not you. I'm talking about Sol Wurtzel. That son-of-a-bitch just doesn't want to follow company policy."

Shrugging, Winnie indicated with a gesture that he wanted to hear more.

"For example, this Mix picture."

"Which one, W.F.?"

"The Feud."

"What happened?"

"Edward Le Saint is directing the damn picture."

"I know."

"Sol writes and tells me he's spent close to $70,000 on this miserable picture. Did you know that?"

"I saw his report. Sol had to go all the way to Wyoming to find a herd of buffalo."

"Buffalo?"

"Yeah. That's what the scenario called for."

"Sol should have shut down the damn picture, Winnie!"

"Why?"

"Because we'll never get our money back, that's why!"

Sheehan sighed heavily—no point in trying to defend the indefensible. He'd just raise W.F.'s ire.

"The point is, this is a gross violation of our agreement. I've given Wurtzel total control over budgets, but once we agree on a number, he has no right to exceed that number unless I say so."

"There are times—"

"Put him on notice, Winnie. I don't want this to happen again!"

"Yes, W.F."

Upon receipt of Sheehan's scathing telegram, Wurtzel thought long and hard about how to respond to W.F.'s criticism. Experience had taught him not to fabricate answers. It was better policy to agree with him, at least, partially. "With reference to the picture *The Feud,* I have no alibi to make regarding the cost."

Wurtzel's reply went into great detail on how he had lost control of the picture's budget. Undoubtedly, part of the reason was the buffalo episode. The picture's star, Tom Mix, had insisted that it not be cut, even if it resulted in a cost overrun.

With some justification, Wurtzel wrote:

> While Mr. Sheehan was here, I took up with him the question of the costs of future Tom Mix pictures and the maximum amount of money that should be spent. Mr. Sheehan explained in detail what material to put in Mix pictures in the way of stunts, sets, characters etc., and I told him that I did not think we could make future Mix Pictures for less than $50,000. Mix is now earning $1,500 a week.

A more likely explanation was that Tom Mix was beginning to dictate how his pictures were to be made, and to hell with what it cost. That happened with a lot of the stars around Hollywood, except Chaplin, who was a sharp businessman.

Stories about W.F.'s penny-pinching ways fed lunch conversations throughout the organization; some were real while others were imagined.

For example, to reduce costs W.F. insisted that stock footage from one film be used for another, as was the case in the Mix picture, *Three Coins.* Director Cliff Smith planned to use 1,000 feet of film from *Rough Riding Romance* in the picture. W.F. lauded these cost-saving efforts at management meetings, making sure the originator of the idea got due credit.

A recent development on the *Three Coins* set upset Wurtzel. He was blaming Tom Mix for forcing Cliff Smith to spend too much on the picture. It was a five-reel film that featured Sid Jordan in the supporting cast.

That line of rationalization infuriated W.F., and when he found out about this, he called in his secretary and dictated a harsh telegram to Wurtzel:

The Lone Star Ranger (Fox, 1919)

Tom Mix captures a bad guy in *Hell Roarin' Reform* **(Fox, 1919)**

"The high-handed manner of Mix as regards the expenditure of money belonging to the Fox Film Corporation, in my opinion, is nothing short of a disgrace. You are responsible, for it began the day you loaned him $2,500 on your own account, without first receiving my sanction or the sanction of the directors of Fox Film, which I have already written you was a violation of your office. Therefore, I am warning you never to do it again. At the time you made this loan, you expected it to be returned some day. You now see that as a result of the negotiations, Fox Film is actually losing $2,500. I am of the opinion that Mix will never like you any more than you like him. You, however, are supposed to have executive ability and should be able to hide your feelings, and let come to the surface only that which will best serve the interests of Fox Film."

In spite of Zukor's expanding theater empire, W.F. was elated to report good results to his stockholders. Fox Film produced 69 pictures, a record for the studio, generating over $9 million in gross rentals, while dramatically improving its bottom line.

Most interesting was W.F.'s announcement of the formation of a news division. Fox News dispersed a news-gathering capability around the globe and began to inform theater patrons of domestic and world events. W.F. was particularly proud of this achievement. 646 feature-length pictures were released in 1919. Based on a Quigley Publications poll of exhibitors, the top male and female box office stars were Wallace Reid and Mary Pickford.

CHAPTER 9
1920

Early in 1920, W.F. purchased an estate in Woodmere on Long Island. The piece of land had a fine frontage to the bay and there was good fishing, bathing and anchorage for his yacht, the Monabelle, and a sailboat he moored in the water off the wharf.

Eve began to refer to the estate as Fox Hall, which W.F. thought sounded like a great title for a motion picture. The principal edifice was an imposing manor house constructed of wood and gray flagstone with a high turreted tower. It had more rooms than W.F. could possibly count without the help of paper and pencil. Celebrated for beautiful roses and manicured gardens, the grounds of the estate were immaculate. A separate structure housed an elaborately equipped theater with 125 seats, an orchestra pit and a Wurlitzer pipe organ where W.F., amid tapestried elegance, screened new films.

Adjoining Fox Hall was the Woodmere Golf Club. Its clubhouse was a pleasing white-shingled building with a broad porch where members would leisurely take their afternoon tea in big leather chairs, smoke cigars and discuss the news of the day. After playing nine holes, one could relax a bit and enjoy a light lunch.

For the first time in his life, W.F. was able to mix business and pleasure on a regular basis, a clear sign that he had reached a degree of financial independence in line with the big shots on Wall Street. W.F. told Eve, "I'm the luckiest man in the world."

By now, he was making enough money to afford the likes of Bobby Jones as an occasional golf companion. Jones, who was the premier golfer of his era, taught W.F. a few pointers, and one day W.F. hit a looping hole-in-one shot and became somewhat of a legend around the club. Not bad for a one-armed golfer, he thought. Everything was going well.

One morning, while playing golf with Jacob Rubenstein, W.F. said, "Jacob, you know, God is smiling on me." "Why do you say that, Bill?"

As they walked to the next hole, W.F. said, "Everything I ever wanted—it all seems to be coming true. Fox Film is a growing enterprise. I have a lovely family. But I'll have to keep a close watch on it, Jacob, lest it get away."

At that very moment, W.F. was chilled by a damp breeze coming off the water.

Looking at him in a puzzled way, Jacob said, "Are you cold, Bill?"

"It's nothing. I'll be all right."

About the time W.F. purchased Fox Hall, Mona found a beau named Douglas Nicholas Taussig. W.F. didn't think much of him, but his daughter seemed bent on marriage. This troubled him because he wasn't sure either of the girls could adjust to a lesser standard of living.

Eve and he had started their lives in a railroad flat that cost $11 a month. His daughters lived in a 32-room apartment at the Marguery and spent their weekends on nine acres in Woodmere. What bothered W.F. was that Mona was not as cunning as Belle; he felt a special obligation to get to know this "Taussig fellow," so he invited him to visit Woodmere.

A butler brought Taussig into W.F.'s study where he was going through some paperwork. There was a desk and several hard chairs. Head slightly bowed, Taussig stood there quietly, looking in his direction. He was a tall, thick-chested young man with a receding hairline. He was striking in a way. However, there wasn't a lot of vitality in him, at least that W.F. could detect.

"Please sit down, Douglas." "Thank you, Mr. Fox."

He seemed a pleasant young man, and was quite respectful in his manners.

"Douglas, if you were to marry Mona, how would you provide for her?"

A dense silence hummed in the room while Taussig thought of an appropriate answer.

At that very moment, a servant came in, pushing a tea trolley. She offered tea and hot biscuits with butter and old-fashioned English marmalade.

William Fox works outdoors at his Woodmere estate.

Politely, Taussig accepted a cup of tea, but nothing to eat. He was very tense.

Buttering a warm biscuit, W.F. spread a glob of orange marmalade on it, all the while waiting for an answer.

"I'm going to enter business for myself, Mr. Fox."

"What kind of business, Douglas?"

W.F. couldn't help but notice how Taussig tightly clutched his teacup with both hands, fearing he might spill its contents on the expensive rug. He was a nervous fellow, but under the circumstances, W.F. thought it justified.

"I'm not quite sure yet, Mr. Fox."

Taussig was silent for a minute, studying both W.F.'s face and the situation.

Finishing his biscuit, W.F. wiped his mouth clean with a finely embroidered napkin. "You know, it's best for a man to decide what he wants out of life before taking on such an enormous responsibility as marriage."

Straightening up in his chair, Taussig regarded one of the paintings on the wall.

"It's an authentic Renoir, Douglas."

"It's beautiful, Mr. Fox."

W.F. could tell young Taussig was at a loss for words, but he didn't want to antagonize him for he knew Mona would then marry him for sure, as a way of compensating for his martyrdom.

"Do you think you could—"

"Out of the question! I don't hire relatives other than my brothers and my wife's brothers. Company policy!"

Looking at W.F. for an instant like a wounded dog, Taussig said, "Oh, I see."

That night, Mona Fox and Douglas Taussig slipped away from the manor house. From up above, W.F. watched them stroll down a cobblestone path to the shore, swinging along up to the water's edge, Taussig's arm tightly wrapped around Mona's waist.

It was painfully visible to W.F. that Mona and this "Taussig fellow" were seriously contemplating marriage, and there was nothing much he could do about it.

The next morning W.F. awakened a little groggy with a severe shooting pain in one side. He knew that he was losing his dear Mona to Douglas Taussig. In spite of what he had told Taussig the night before, he realized that he would have to create a suitable position for the young man in the company. After all, it was the right thing to do for his daughter.

To relax, W.F. took a hot bath in a deep metal tub. As he soaked in the water, he thought of what he had seen the night before. For some reason, he didn't relish the thought of a wedding. On the other hand, it was comforting to know that Douglas Taussig was Jewish. That was one less thing to consider.

Over the next few months, W.F. was awfully tense about Mona and her marriage plans, so he looked for a distraction to get his mind off the whole affair.

One of W.F.'s passions in life was the fights. Aside from his work and the game of golf, he got great pleasure from watching two heavyweights exchange blows, slugging it out. Had he not entered the motion picture business with such dedication, W.F. was sure he would have made a very good boxing promoter.

W.F. offered a rich purse of $500,000 for a heavyweight championship boxing match between Jack Dempsey, the title holder, and Georges Carpentier from France. Most of the fighters whom he had known were stumblebums. Dempsey was different, a well oiled machine who could take a punch as well as deliver one.

Carpentier, a slim, engaging young man, had just won the heavyweight championship of Europe.

Part of W.F.'s scheme was to aid the Red Cross. "Forty percent of the net profits will be donated to the Red Cross, 35 percent to the winner, and 15 percent to the loser."

After a good deal of haggling, Carpentier's manager agreed to his offer, and they talked about a date for the fight. Then the manager and W.F. squabbled over rights, and the deal never came to anything. Based on this short-lived experience, W.F. decided he'd made the right choice of a business career. Boxers were an even bigger headache than movie stars.

Later, an old friend, Tex Rikard, the president of Madison Square Garden, decided to promote the fight, but it appeared that more customers were lining up at the box office than he could possibly seat in the Garden. As a result, Rikard relocated the fight to a place near Jersey City called "Boyle's Thirty Acres" where he built a makeshift stadium that would seat 100,000 spectators. On July 2, 1921, just before the fight started, Tex Rikard realized he had $1,800,000 sitting in the box office; 75,000 people had paid the price to see the fight.

W.F. was there and soon discovered that Rikard was very nervous about something. "What's wrong, Tex?"

"Bill, if Dempsey takes out Carpentier in the first few rounds, I'm gonna have a riot on my hands."

"I never thought of that."

That night, Dempsey took it easy and knocked the Frenchman out in the fourth round.

Just when the fight deal fell through, W.F. got deeply involved in putting the finishing touches on the 10th Avenue building. The opening ceremony for the headquarters and studio featured the mayor of New York, John Hyland. In a prepared speech Hyland congratulated the Fox Film Corporation for having chosen Manhattan for their facility, describing in detail his administration's unceasing effort to encourage construction that aided economic recovery in New York. Before lunch, Mayor Hyland and his companions visited the laboratory on the ground floor, presided over by vice president Jack G. Lee.

Lee explained, "The lab is one of the biggest in the world and contains every modern device. Its output capacity totals 3,000,000 feet of film weekly."

From the lab they visited W.F.'s office and study as well as a projection room, sales department, scenario department and every other branch that went toward the making of a picture.

After a hot buffet lunch served in the boardroom, a select group of prominent visitors and Mayor Hyland were escorted to one of the stages on the third floor where Charles Brabin was directing a picture.

As they ascended in an elevator, W.F. said, "The studio floor can comfortably take care of 20 film companies simultaneously." When the visit was over, Mayor Hyland thanked W.F. profusely for the invitation and departed with his staff in a convoy of motorcars.

W.F. liked Mayor Hyland, for they had a lot in common. Hyland had worked as a motorman on the elevated line while attending law school. On his way up the political ladder he had counted heavily on the backing of political stalwarts like John McCooey and William Randolph Hearst.

After the departure of Mayor Hyland, W.F. went back to his office and slumped into a comfortable chair. The most solid citizens of New York had just paid homage to William Fox, an industry mogul. It was too early to make any predictions, but he was more certain than ever that destiny had ordained his continued triumph in the motion picture business.

Sol Wurtzel's operations report had just landed on W.F.'s desk. In it Wurtzel pitched a daredevil aviator by the name of Ormun Locklear for a picture.

Unimpressed with the idea, W.F. dictated a terse reply to Wurtzel that was sent by telegram. "Sol, I cannot see on what basis Fox Film would be interested in the services of this man."

Undaunted, Wurtzel persisted and finally convinced W.F. to make an action picture with the daredevil aviator. The final stunt scenes were filmed at the Amalgamated Oil Field at Third Street and Fairfax Avenue in Los Angeles. With powerful searchlights focused on the plane, Locklear lost control and it dove vertically into the ground, bursting into a ball of flames.

In spite of the well-publicized tragedy, film critics gave the picture a thumbs-down.

Jack Leo stuck his nose in W.F.'s office. "You called me, W.F.?"

Up and pacing, W.F. turned fully around to face Leo. "Jack, see if this makes any sense to you."

"I'm listening."

Leo sat down and lit a cigarette. "What is it?"

"Carl Laemmle has made a few extraordinary pictures."

"Like what?"

"Take *The Beast of Berlin,* or *Heart of Humanity,* or *Blind Husbands,* for instance."

"I heard that *Blind Husbands* got out of hand and cost him a pretty penny."

"That's because of that Kraut bastard director who wears that stupid eyeglass. He doesn't know how to make a picture for less than a million dollars. What's his name?"

"Van Loheim or baloneyheim or something. I can't remember his goddamn name, W.F."

"It's not important."

"They say he swallows up budgets in lavish sets, costumes and props."

"Erich Von Stroheim!"

"That's it."

W.F. lit a cigar. "The thing is they were all good stories and none of the pictures had a big star, Jack."

"I didn't know that. It never crossed my mind."

Still pacing, W.F. stopped and faced Leo. "What I'm saying is, I think we should be doing the same thing, I mean, make a few big pictures without paying a fortune to a star."

"That sounds like a great idea."

"The other thing is I want to keep Sol Wurtzel away from this features program. He's got all he can do to handle Tom Mix, Buck Jones and that crowd."

W.F. relied on an innate sense of timing, and to his way of thinking, the time was ripe for this novel approach to filmmaking. Big stories with small stars.

It sounded too good to be true, Jack thought.

"We succeeded with *The Honor System.* Am I right?"

"As I remember, the returns were good."

"On the other hand, *Cheating the Public* flopped because we launched it at the wrong time."

"That's true. Unemployment was down and the story no longer made any sense."

"*Jack and the Beanstalk* would have done better if we hadn't made it into a series, isn't that so?"

"Right, W.F."

"We missed with *Woman and the Law,* and I don't know why, do you?"

"I can't even remember the damn picture."

"That's why we lost money. No one can recall the picture."

They both chuckled at W.F.'s remark.

"What's your point, W.F.?"

"The point is that from a total of 11 of these kind of pictures, listen to what I'm saying, 11 special productions without stars, only two of these were successful. *The Honor System* and *Checkers.*"

"What do you make of it?"

"I wish I knew. Look at Raoul Walsh, for instance. During the four and a half years that he has been with us, we've lost money on his pictures."

That caught Leo off guard. "Are you sure?"

W.F. fetched a piece of paper from the top of his desk and handed it to Jack Leo.

Pointing at a series of numbers, W.F. said, "Look at this. Eisele worked it up."

Casting a critical eye across the last row of numbers, Leo noticed they were all circled in red. "I'll be damned."

"To make pictures without stars is easier said than done. The only one who has been able to do this is Carl Laemmle."

"Maybe it's just a lot a good luck."

"They got somebody in their scenario department with a creative brain who watches for all timely subjects. He manages to hit the nail on the head more often than all the other companies combined."

"Yeah, they call him the boy wonder."

"What's this joker's name, Jack?"

"Irving Thalberg. He's a kid."

"Kid or no kid, we've got to double our efforts in the scenario department, Jack."

"Whatever you say."

No one in the Fox organization ever considered hiring Irving Thalberg. The golden opportunity was there, but it slipped by, totally unperceived. The thought of bringing someone in from the outside to head up the creative side of the business was alien to W.F. But there was never a better time for change. Thalberg was becoming disenchanted with Universal, and W.F. needed creative ability. On the other hand, would a young Irving Thalberg have survived very long under W.F.'s domineering management style?

"I'm worried about Edwards' next picture, Jack."

"*The Queen of Sheba?*"

"Yeah. The woman he hired is terrible. She looks like a pig!"

"Give him a chance, W.F. I haven't even closed the deal for the story."

"Remind him he's not to spend any more than we spent on making *Salome.*"

"I'll tell him."

"What about Madelaine Traverse, Jack?"

"I told Sol to tear up her contract. She's never on time for a shoot."

"That ought to get her to the studio at a decent hour."

There was trouble with Tom Mix and his new picture. W.F. screened the picture, detested what he saw, and communicated his dissatisfaction to Wurtzel.

> I have reviewed *One Quarter Apache*. There is no doubt in my mind that this picture will be accepted and rank amongst the best Tom Mix pictures that we have made. It will, however, need careful editing and cutting in order to eradicate most of the bad acting it contains. In your last letter you called attention to the fact that there are many spots in the picture where the direction is amateurish, and not up to our standard. You are right about that. Mix's acting performance is the worst I have ever seen him give. It is very evident that Jaccard knows how to create action in a picture, but he knows nothing about directing dramatic sequences.

There were many scenes in the picture that never made it to the big screen in their original form. The director, Jaccard, was put on W.F.'s watch list and would soon be out the door. As for Mix, he had a hearty laugh when he heard what W.F. thought of the picture. He had no illusions about his acting ability. On the set he was overheard asking Jaccard, "Do you want expression number one, two or three?"

Over something no one could quite recall, Wurtzel had a rift with Lynn Reynolds, one of Tom Mix's favorite directors. He stormed off the lot in a huff. W.F. pressured Wurtzel to reverse his position and take him back.

Wurtzel sent a telegram to W.F. explaining the situation.

> I have entirely forgotten my personal feeling regarding him, and if his coming back to the Fox Film Corporation to direct Buck Jones would be beneficial to the company, I would be more than pleased to have him come back. I will get in touch with him immediately and find out whether he is available, although I am still of the firm opinion that if I were permitted to handle Buck Jones and use my judgment as I see best, I will make him a big asset to Fox Film. I wish you to bear in mind that Mix still has in mind that Buck Jones is working here. Anything I do regarding the making of Buck Jones pictures must be done by me in a very diplomatic way without exciting Mix's animosity. Three weeks ago Mix came into my office and asked me if we would continue to make Buck Jones pictures. I evaded the question. Mix said that it was up to him to protect himself and protect his future. Without explaining what was on his mind, he of course meant that the continuing of making Buck Jones pictures was in opposition to him, and he would throw every obstacle in the way of making successful Buck Jones pictures.

The first regular licensed broadcast by station KDKA, operated by Western Electric on the roof of its Pittsburgh factory, was heard. KDKA was the first station to transmit presidential election results. Warren G. Harding defeated James X. Cox.

By 1920, Fox Film was harvesting the fruits of five strenuous years of labor. Tom Mix was doing well at the box office and made eight pictures. Along with Buck Jones, he became the best big-hat customer of the John B. Stetson Company, buying them by the dozen in the color white or cream.

Buck Jones, the second half of Fox's one-two punch in the field of Westerns, was coming on strong and rising in popularity. Later in the year, Fox added Pearl White to its roster as well as Peggy Hyland, Shirley Mason, Eileen Percy and Vivian Rich.

Pearl White achieved fame in silent films as a feisty risk-taking heroine.

Earlier in her career, Pearl White had achieved fame in a serial called *The Perils of Pauline*, which had been produced by Louis Gasnier for Pathé. By the time she joined Fox, she was 31 years old and not very successful in features. Pearl made *The Thief, The Tiger's Cub,* and *White Moll* in 1920, none of which fared well at the box office.

There were very few actresses on the Fox lot whom W.F. thought more highly of than Shirley Mason. He believed the petite actress showed promise. At the time, she was only 20 years old. Fox featured her in films like *Flame of Youth, Girl of my Heart, Her Elephant Man, The Little Wanderer, Merely Mary Ann,* and *Molly and I.* Although she never attained star status, Mason was a workhorse who helped pay the bills at Fox.

By wire, W.F. cautioned Wurtzel: "Shirley Mason stories should have very simple plots since her personality is so different from that of any other stars we have. I make this statement in view of the pictures I have seen with Mary Pickford and Marguerite Clark, whose types of pictures we are trying to follow with Miss Mason."

One hot afternoon, an irate Theda Bara burst into Sol Wurtzel's cluttered office, angry and frustrated, looking like someone who had been dumped for another, younger player. The studio had just wrapped *The Lure of Ambition,* which was to be her last picture under contract with Fox. Just as in many of the Westerns Wurtzel had filmed on the Sunset lot, this encounter was going to be a showdown between the forces of good and evil.

Theda Bara paraded around the office, her hands clasped tightly together, fully conscious of the fact that she was playing her last major scene at Fox. Her big round eyes wandered over every object in the room, from her film posters on the wall to the dusty shelves of books and scenarios. "Sol, I've made 39 films for this studio. I played the vamp in all of them except for six."

"So, shoot me."

"I've been vamping for five years, Sol. I'm tired."

"Take a vacation somewhere, Theda. Have you ever been to Niagara Falls?"

Bara sat on the chair opposite Wurtzel, who sat behind a desk that was from another era.

"Mr. Fox never comes to see me anymore."

"Mr. Fox is a very busy man, Theda."

"I'm only making $4,000 a week. I want more money, Sol."

"I wouldn't push my luck, Theda. Your box office has collapsed like a drunken sailor."

"I've been getting wretched stories. And I'm tired of vamping, Sol."

"Like I said, Theda, times change and so do tastes. You're not even on the most popular list anymore."

Bara was back up on her feet, hunched over Wurtzel's desk, staring down at him. "This stinking studio wouldn't exist without Theda Bara. How long do you think the public will stand your goddamn cowboys, Sol? How long?"

"The public loves to see the same damn story over and over again. They feel comfortable with it. To hell with happy endings. I hear these directors bitching about what they really want to make. Fuck 'em! What they want to make, maybe 5,000 highbrows in the whole country will pay their four bits to see. I don't give a shit about art. It's a business, Theda, and anybody who doesn't think so oughta get out of it."

"Sol, I want $5,000 a week. That's not too much to ask, is it?"

Wurtzel glanced at a wall clock. It was almost five in the afternoon and he still had to visit a couple of sets.

"Sol? Did you hear me?"

"No increase, Theda! And that's final."

Her mouth curled in anger, Bara shouted,

Tired of the vamp character, Theda Bara left Fox in 1920.

"Then I quit!"

Wurtzel quickly shoved a foolproof release across his polished desk; it was less than a page long. "I'd guessed as much. Here, just sign this release, Theda, and I'll cut a check for what we owe you." Offering her a pen, Wurtzel said, "Where I put the X."

After grasping the pen, she scribbled her name at the bottom of the release and then stormed out of Wurtzel's office, slamming the door behind her. Wurtzel edged over to a window from where he could see Theda Bara get into her chauffeured white Rolls and drive off the lot in a cloud of dust.

One of the most remarkable and significant facts about the motion-picture industry was that no star, no matter how big, was indispensable. There were hundreds of fresh faces out there, hoping for a chance at a screen test.

It wasn't until a week or so after Theda Bara's resignation that W.F. heard that Marcus Loew had made his first entry into film production by purchasing a financially impoverished independent producing and distributing company called Metro. It was still run by Richard Rowland, Mayer's former associate.

To dispel rumors of the impending purchase floating around Wall Street, Loew had sworn his management to secrecy. He went to his board of directors and tactfully offered two solid reasons for making the acquisition. Above all, the trend was definitely in the direction of integrating studios and theaters, and more ominously, Famous Players-Lasky was going to charge a percentage of the first-run theater's receipts instead of a fixed rental. In other words, the rental would be in proportion to theater receipts and this sounded like highway robbery to Marcus Loew.

It was at this time that Metro found itself overstocked with war dramas; weekly revenues had also dropped dramatically. The company needed a capital infusion to make better pictures and create an adequate distribution system. After a period of tough negotiations, Marcus Loew dished out $3 million for the studio. Metro would continue to handle films from the same independents, B.A. Rolfe, Quality Pictures and Popular Plays and Players.

When Metro was sold to Loew, Louis B. Mayer was no longer on their payroll. Mayer's Mission Road studio was busy churning out program pictures to satisfy the continuing demand for product from First National. Lois Weber had left him and he was searching for talent wherever he could find it. It was not a good time for Mayer.

Seeing all the difficulties of producing film, Marcus Loew reportedly commented, "I'm surprised to learn how many things about picture making an exhibitor doesn't know."

Even the great optimist, Marcus Loew, saw film production as a daunting task. If theater exhibition were the whole ball of wax in the film business, his stockholders would be reasonably contented. But film production? That was a whole new endeavor for which Loew needed a first-class studio head.

But who?

It just so happened that Rowland had contracted an unknown player named Guglielmi, alias Valentino, and cast him in *The Four Horsemen of the Apocalypse.* June Mathis, one of the best writers Hollywood ever produced, was assigned to compose the scenario, and she suggested to Rowland that Metro retain Rex Ingram to direct the picture. She also recommended Valentino for the principal role. From the set, the word quickly spread to the movie magazines that a leading man who had a certain innocent manner was in the making.

The Four Horsemen of the Apocalypse opened at the Lyric Theater on March 6, 1921, and was celebrated as a triumph. Valentino suddenly leapt into stardom. No one understood why Rowland failed to sign Valentino to a long-term deal. Part of the problem, though few around him realized it, was that Rowland didn't have that Midas touch for recognizing talent when he saw it.

Several weeks later, Rudolph Valentino, his shiny black hair slicked down without a part in the middle, was in Jesse Lasky's outer office requesting to see him. Lasky showed him in at once, and scarcely finished telling him how much he admired his work as the lonely, disillusioned Julio when Valentino asked him if he had a part for him.

Lasky couldn't wait to share the good news with De Mille. "I couldn't believe my ears, Cecil. Metro actually forgot to sign the guy." "It's hard to believe, Jesse."

"Metro goes and makes this very successful picture and develops one of the great box-office draws of all time in Rudolph Valentino, and doesn't bother to take an option on his future services."

Lasky told the handsome young actor not to worry, and Valentino walked out of his office with a signed contract.

To guarantee their control of Universal, Carl Laemmle and R.H. Cochrane bought out P.A. Powers, the third controlling interest in the studio, naming Laemmle as president. Cochrane had worked as a newspaperman and then had moved on to advertising.

There was little doubt in Hollywood that Carl Laemmle now controlled Universal.

Fox Film closed 1920 having produced 71 pictures grossing $12 million and reported a net profit of $1,400,000. The board of directors celebrated the company's accomplishments with champagne and a sumptuous dinner at Sherry's. At the end of the dinner, Forrest Dryden rose and offered a toast: "Well done, Bill!"

At the regular end-of-year management meeting held in the boardroom the next day, W.F. personally thanked his managers for their superb performance. However, several things were nagging at him, and W.F. decided to vent his frustration.

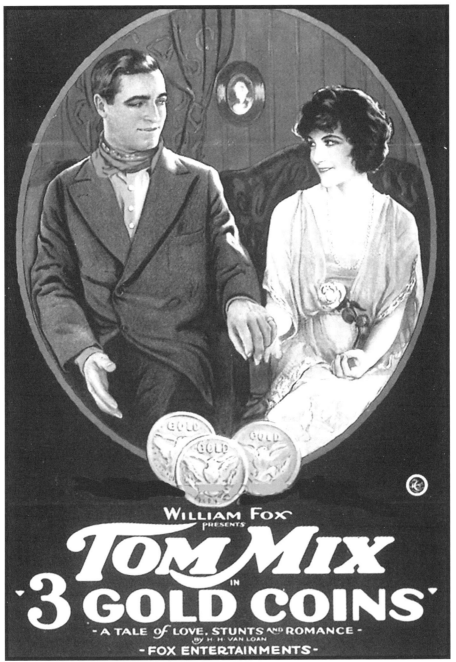

WILLIAM FOX
PRESENTS

TOM MIX
IN

'3 GOLD COINS'

- A TALE of LOVE, STUNTS AND ROMANCE -
BY H. H. VAN LOAN
- FOX ENTERTAINMENTS -

There was the affiliation of theaters with producing groups like Zukor, First National and now, he feared, Marcus Loew. W.F. told his managers to start preparing a list of available theaters for outright acquisition or some sort of alliance. Fox Film would quietly start buying small theaters to gain a foothold in certain markets.

The well-publicized concentration of first-run theaters in Zukor's camp was due, of course, to Kuhn, Loeb's particular financing plan where overinflated stock was being used to acquire undervalued theaters. As a consequence, Zukor's personal equity was being diluted with each acquisition, and soon, W.F. feared, Famous Players itself would become an acquisition target.

Fox Film had to improve the quality of its photography. W.F. insisted that it fund development work toward this end. He also requested that management be on the lookout for technical developments, no matter how obscure they appeared to be.

To a broader audience, which included Sol Wurtzel, who had come in from California for the stockholders' meeting, Winfield Sheehan, Jack Leo, Joe Leo, Eve, John Eisele, Saul Rogers and Jimmy Grainger, W.F. discussed the forthcoming season.

"What's on Edward's agenda, Winnie?"

"He left here with several stories. *The Joyous Troublemaker, The Scuttlers* and...let me think...and *The Honor of the Mounted.*"

"Be sure, Sol, that Bill Farnum and William Russell get one of these stories."

"I will, W.F."

"Winnie, checking the records I see that Farnum's salary is set to go up."

"That's right."

"Well, he's going on vacation; when he returns I want to be sure we've identified a couple of stories for him, so we don't wind up spending a lot of money for down time."

Winnie nodded affirmatively.

Removing a cigar from his jacket, W.F. lit up. "It makes good business sense."

"What about a director, W.F.?"

"I don't want Edwards on any of these pictures, Sol. Find two first class directors for Farnum. I want him to make eight pictures during this season."

"He ain't going to be happy with that."

"I don't give a damn, Winnie. We've got a good contract, right, Saul?"

"Tighter than hell, W.F."

"What else have we got on our plate, Winnie?"

"Brockwell is gone."

"Good. That last picture she made was pretty damn lousy. That son-of-a-bitch Le Saint used those extravagant sets for a picture that is a piece of crap. He's no saint as far as I'm concerned."

Wurtzel knew the jab was meant for him.

"What's wrong with you, Sol? Where does that bastard get off spending that kind of money?"

"I'm looking into it."

"Shirley Mason has got to be supported with good stories. I'm talking suspense, action, pathos and comedy. The public is tired of Mary Pickford and Marguerite Clark and their sweet namby pamby stories with no sense to them. Am I right, Jimmy?"

"You got that right, W.F. Ticket sales for those two ladies ain't what they used to be," Grainger said.

"Here's the bottom line, fellas. The real big successes of the past year were from plays that were popularized by the stage or a book: *Daddy Long Legs,* which sold millions of copies and, as a play, ran for several years; *Pollyanna;* and *Rebecca of Sunnybrook Farm,* same thing."

"I never, never looked at it that way, W.F.," Winnie said.

"I saw these three plays and saw the pictures, too. None of them had what you would call suspense, intrigue or dramatic action, and still they were the greatest motion pictures that Miss Pickford ever appeared in. Why? Because you had three great stories, great pieces of fiction written in modern times. We should not try to make a picture with Miss Mason from an unknown author or an unknown play or book. What do you think, Jimmy?"

"You're right, W.F.. If you ask the exhibitors who play Mary Pickford pictures, they'll tell you that the rest of her pictures were failures."

The industry released 797 pictures. Theater attendance exploded: 35 million spectators a week. The top stars were Wallace Reid and Marguerite Clark.

CHAPTER 10
1921

The country was suffering from something the economists were calling deflation. The motion picture industry was producing 600 to 800 features a year, and that amounted to overproduction. The strongest player in the arena was still Adolph Zukor, with his efficient distribution and increasing alliances with first-run theaters. By the end of 1921 Zukor would control more than 400 theaters.

Another phenomenon struck the industry: radio. It caught America's fancy, and a whole new set of entrepreneurs invaded the entertainment field. Impressed by the technology, W.F. carefully watched it unfold and take away some of Fox Theaters' paying customers. For the first time, an entertainment medium had been invented that permitted the user to stay in the comfort of his own home.

Mary Carr

During the year, Fox Film made a picture called *Over the Hill to the Poorhouse*, which cost $100,000 and would return a gross of $3 million over time; it was the most successful picture ever personally produced by William Fox.

It starred Mary Carr, then a 47-year-old veteran stage actress, and it seemed to touch a nerve with the paying public. Insisting the film wasn't a fluke, W.F. emphasized to his creative people the importance of having the right story at the right time.

Built to accommodate the filming activities of Fox Film, the 10th Avenue headquarters facility wasn't able to provide space for the scenario department, the paint and sign shop and various other departments that were scattered around the city. W.F. negotiated a 20-year lease for a new building at 10th Avenue and 54th Street.

An article in the January 1, 1921 edition of the *Times* said, "Mr. Fox has so rapidly developed his production and the attendant distribution of films, and found his organization still so cramped for room, that he eagerly availed himself of an opportunity to lease the Kelly-Springfield Tire Company building only one block south on 10th Avenue from the main plant."

By the early spring of 1921, W.F. finalized a deal through which Fox Film bought the rights to *Queen of Sheba*. Veteran director Jack Edwards came to him to confirm he was using Betty Blythe in the lead role. Betty was 28 years old and had made her film debut in 1918 at Vitagraph. W.F. didn't particularly like her looks, but Jack was insistent.

Examining several stills Edwards brought with him, W.F. said, "Betty Blythe is terrible. Look at this. Look at that. That could never play a queen! What are you thinking about, Jack?" "Never mind. That's my Sheba."

After months of meetings and postponements, Jack Edwards finally got his way and shot the picture. It was a complete box office disaster. When the next production schedule was announced, Edwards' name was conspicuously absent from the board. Fox Film would use him sparingly for the rest of his career at the studio.

Directors, like players, also seemed to have a time—and then that time ran out. Some of them would ride a wave of public taste and prolong their careers until that taste changed for something else. A select few, probably no more than a handful, outlived the changes in taste and found new crests to ride.

Although there were those cynics who believed otherwise, W.F. was sorry to admit that Jack Edwards had lost his touch. He was part of the Theda Bara era, and that era was over.

Taking her a little by surprise, Eve decided to celebrate Belle's 17th birthday by inviting a small group of people into W.F.'s office for cake, milk and coffee. Looking around the room, W.F. saw Winnie Sheehan, Saul Rogers, Jack Leo, Joe Leo, his brothers, Aaron and Maurice, Jimmy Grainger, John Eisele and, of course, Eve, Mona and Belle; a group that came to be known as the William Fox "family."

There were 17 candles on the three-layer cake and Belle blew them out without much difficulty. "Make a wish, Belle!" "I've already made it, Daddy."

Everyone was enjoying the moment, and when they finished W.F. decided it was a good time to quell some of the unfounded rumors that were floating around the corridors.

"We're all family here at Fox Film. We've celebrated six years as a company, and I've heard rumors in the halls that William Fox is falling behind Adolph Zukor."

In unison, everyone began hissing, "No! No!" "Let me finish!"

They were all at attention, hoping W.F. wasn't about to break bad news.

"Nothing is further from the truth. Zukor works for Otto Kahn and Wall Street. William Fox works for himself and his stockholders." A mighty round of applause erupted.

"With this group of competent managers, our players, and our knowledge of public taste, Fox Film is and will remain a significant player in the picture business."

A couple of days later, W.F. received word that the Federation for the Support of Jewish Philanthropy wanted to pay homage to him by organizing a tribute at the grand ballroom of the Hotel Astor in New York for the work he had done in a membership drive.

Members of the committee that bestowed this honor on him included some of New York's most famous faces: Edward F. Albee, Martin Beck, William E. Lewis, Arthur Brisbane, Pat Casey, George M. Cohan, Charles E. Gehring, Samuel H. Harris, Joseph Johnson, Marcus Loew, John J. Murdock, Judge Otto Rasalsky, L. Lawrence Weber, A.H. Woods, and naturally, Adolph Zukor. Several guests were accompanied by their spouses.

The most prominent guests sat at two round tables, their places marked by name cards. It turned out that W.F.'s table was

George M. Cohan

particularly jovial since George M. Cohan, A.H. Woods, Sam H. Harris and Marcus Loew were there. Cohan was in a very good mood, proudly claiming to have entered the world on the 4th of July, 1878.

W.F. had always thought his name to be Cohen, but George M. explained his real name—Keohane—was as Irish as it could possibly get, and that he was born in a $6-a-month attic of a frame house on Corkie Hill, Providence, Rhode Island. The playwright and songwriter was a little man—five-foot-six—and weighed 140 pounds. At the time, Cohan was playing at the Hudson in *The Meanest Man in the World.*

The jaunty George M. related how the Broadway theater was flourishing with 50-odd attractions available in legitimate houses.

Midtown marquees highlighted Frank Bacon in *Lightnin'*, Fay Bainter in *East Is West,* Ethel Barrymore in *Declassee,* Ina Claire in *The Gold Diggers,* John and Lionel Barrymore in *The Jest,* Edith Day in *Irene,* Helen MacKellar in *The Storm,* and Billie Burke in *Caesar's Wife.*

There was also a rumor floating around artistic circles in New York that George M. Cohan and his partner, Sam Harris, were on the verge of splitting up. By their faces, one couldn't detect any observable friction between them, but who knew? They were stage people, weren't they?

Functioning as toastmaster was Wilton Lackaye, who had acted in film without much success and had made a Fox picture back in 1915, *Children of the Ghetto.*

W.F. felt very good. The atmosphere in the room was uplifting with the stars and stripes prominently displayed above the dais. Because of a bad cold, Eve hadn't joined him that evening. Following dinner, Adolph Zukor kindly offered W.F. a ride home because he'd left his motorcar at Fox Hall on Long Island. Zukor had showed up alone, too, since Lottie Zukor wasn't one to frequent outside events, particularly if they ran much past 10 in the evening.

Ensconced in the backseat of the motorcar, Zukor and W.F. sat in complete silence. There was a persistent rumor floating around Hollywood that Zukor was in the market for another studio. Zukor spoke first. "So you're living in the Marguery, Bill?" "Yes, we are, Adolph."

Never a master of small talk, Zukor took advantage of every available moment. Of all the Hollywood moguls, he was its least edgy personality. "Bill, I'd like to buy Fox Film." As for the Zukor persistence, there it was, on full display. More than most, he was direct and to the point. Not only that, his tone of voice was surprisingly considerate.

"You know, Adolph, the other night the Prince of Wales sat next to me, William Fox, in my theater. I was so distracted I forgot my instructions to address him as 'Your Highness' and found myself saying, 'Prince, I am happy to meet you.'

"When he reached his box, I said, 'This ends my part of the performance since I've been instructed by your committee that I am to leave you here.'

"The Prince said, 'You will do nothing of the kind! Come and sit with me!'"

Zukor listened carefully and didn't know what he was expected to say to that, so he said nothing. "What I'm telling you, Adolph, is that William Fox feels he's earned the right to stay in the motion picture business."

"I understand, Bill. But if you should change your mind, call me first."

For 15 minutes, until W.F. stepped from the motorcar, a terrible silence lay between them. During that tense period W.F. realized he had but one option left for his studio. He would have to take on Zukor, Tally and Loew in the theater war. It was that or be squeezed out of the industry.

When W.F. got home he told Eve what Zukor had offered him. She was deeply offended. "Who does he think he is?"

"Adolph Zukor."

"Bill, we have to buy and build theaters."

"I know."

"What are you going to do about it?"

"I've told our people to be on the lookout for opportunities, Eve."

"That's too slow. You've got to buy a chain, darling. Before that damn Hungarian controls all the screens in this country."

In the annual search for new directorial talent and actors with striking features, Sheehan discovered a young and promising talent who was looking for a new challenge. In spite of the competitive frenzy surrounding the man, Sheehan seemed to hit it off with him. Their mutual interest in pictures and aged Irish whiskey solidified the relationship.

A little more than 26 years old, John Ford was the youngest of six children. Most of his friends called him Jack. Sometime in 1917, John Ford had begun directing pictures at Universal, mostly Westerns starring Harry Carey. A film called *The Soul Herder* had started a four-year relationship between the two men. By 1921 Ford had been at Universal for four years and had directed 39 pictures.

Now John Ford was interested in changing studios. Like so many others before and after him, he thought Laemmle wasn't thinking big enough. Budgets were tight and talent was jumping ship right and left. Behind a pair of horn-rimmed glasses was a handsome man with fine features and thick wavy hair. The only thing that detracted from his otherwise good looks was a face that was a little puffy and red. He wore a dark suit that nicely fitted his slim figure, and a white shirt with a high collar.

"I've heard good things about your work, Mr. Ford." "Thank you, Mr. Fox."

Anxious to establish Ford's impressive credentials, Winnie said, "Jack shot *Just Pals* with Buck Jones last November on the West Coast."

Besides Winnie, there were Saul Rogers, Jack Leo and Eve Fox sitting around the room.

After lighting his signature corncob pipe, Ford sat down, too. A butler brought in a pot of hot coffee. Ford took his black.

William Fox began with his now traditional line of questioning. "What do you think of Buck Jones, Mr. Ford?" "Jones can act, Mr. Fox. You've made yourself a good find." "I'm happy to hear you feel that way, Mr. Ford. What do we have here? Anybody?"

Since Winnie had struck the deal with Ford, it was his task to inform everyone of the details. "Jack has to fulfill a commitment to Universal; then he'll join us on the West Coast. We're talking $600 a week."

The price tag didn't seem to bother W.F. in the least.

"I understand you like Westerns, Mr. Ford."

"I've done other things, but I think you have two excellent players in Tom Mix and Buck Jones. I'd like to try my hand at other scenarios, Mr. Fox, if you're in agreement."

W.F. stood as if rooted to the ground, chewing the end of a dead cigar. It was time to sew up the deal.

"What's on the schedule for Mr. Ford, Winnie?"

"*The Big Punch* with Buck Jones, *Jackie* with Shirley Mason. That's as far as it goes, W.F., until he finishes his contract with Laemmle."

"How is Uncle Carl, Mr. Ford?"

"Since he lost Mrs. Laemmle in the flu epidemic, he's never been quite the same."

"That was very sad. We look forward to a long and productive relationship with you."

After finishing *Just Pals,* John Ford returned to Universal to make three final Westerns with Harry Carey—*The Freeze Out, The Wallop,* and *Desperate Trails.* Ford's salary in 1921 was $13,618.

From the very beginning of motion pictures, the Western had become a favorite silent category, with Tom Mix the most popular cowboy actor of his time. Part of Mix's appeal was that his pictures were action-packed, yet mostly nonviolent. There were fisticuffs, chases, horse tricks, rope tricks, roundups, gunfights, often with Mix performing his own stunts. Subduing villains with his fists or his lasso, he seldom fired his six-shooter. There was little bloodshed on the set. Special effects were a dormant art form at this time. Westerns were profitable, and W.F. told his directors not to toy with the formula.

Kids liked Westerns too, and they dragged their parents along to see these exciting movies, which was another powerful force in developing faithful audiences. Anything Tom Mix filmed had to be seen by certain audiences, adding spectator continuity to a sequence of pictures no matter what the story was about.

William Fox took a special interest in Mix pictures. In one of his directives he wrote Wurtzel the following:

I urge that you make a complete search and find a real, wonderful, competent director, regardless of salary, who can make real wonderful pictures with Tom Mix stories, and if you find one, advise so that we may negotiate for the purchase of it, for it seems to me that the main and principal thing is to have the foundation of a real story, and that is best developed from either a serial story running in a magazine, or from a book that contains a story which may have Tom Mix material.

Fox Film contracted a leading-man candidate, bright-eyed John Gilbert. Born in Logan, Utah, in 1895, Gilbert left the traveling stock company of his mother, Ida Adair, for a California military academy, then worked in a rubber company's Western office until his good looks and ramrod bearing landed him a job as an extra for Thomas H. Ince. One of his first good roles was in First National's *Heart O'Hills* (1919) opposite Mary Pickford.

Wurtzel wrote to W.F., "I have already selected Jack Gilbert's story. The title is *The Land of the Beginning Again.* This gives Gilbert a picturesque role. The story is laid in the Foreign Legion of Algeria. This in itself is a picturesque background, and Gilbert has a very fine and dramatic part to portray. Future stories with Gilbert will be laid along the lines and type of *Gleam O'Dawn,* where Gilbert will have a romantic, picturesque character to portray. I do not think we can make these pictures for less than $25,000."

During the early fall, W.F. made his annual trek to California and headed straight to a production meeting Wurtzel was holding with several of his directors, including John Ford, Carl Harbaugh and Lynn Reynolds. The studio had built an appropriate room for such meetings and, mercifully, it was ventilated.

When W.F. entered the room there was a short period of silence while he took his place at the head of a rectangular-shaped conference table. No one was more surprised than Sol Wurtzel to see the boss in California. Of course, over the years, it had been impossible to predict his whereabouts, and surprise visits were becoming more commonplace.

Looking down the table at John Ford, W.F. said, "I saw the *Big Punch.* It's a good picture, Jack, but there is as much difference between it and *Just Pals* as there is between cream cheese and the full moon."

"That's part of making Westerns, W.F. You're never quite sure what you've got till you project them up on the screen."

"Don't get me wrong, Jack. You've proven that if Buck Jones is properly directed he can play any part. He's daring and thrilling. I like Jones."

"I agree, W.F."

"Carl, what's on your agenda?"

Pushing up his glasses, Carl Harbaugh sighed, glanced at his notes, and recited the titles of several Eileen Percy pictures Sol Wurtzel had assigned to him. Harbaugh added, "Photographing on *Her Honor the Mayor* was finished last week. The picture will be cut and shipped next week." What Harbaugh wasn't aware of was that W.F. had told Wurtzel to dispense with his services as soon as he finished making these pictures.

In fact, W.F. had cabled Wurtzel a specific set of instructions: "With reference to *Little Miss Hawkshaw* directed by Harbaugh, I consider it the most impossible, idiotic, asinine damn picture ever made by this corporation, and if the present Harbaugh picture isn't by far a better one, he is to be dismissed immediately."

It wasn't, and Wurtzel was about to fire Harbaugh. If hard-pressed, he'd do it right there and now. Harbaugh's pictures didn't fill theaters, and that was all that really mattered.

W.F. puffed on a cigar. "By now, I'm sure you've all seen the Queen."

"I ran the picture for everybody at the studio, W.F.," Wurtzel replied.

"*The Queen of Sheba* turned out to be the whore of Hollywood." They all laughed at W.F.'s comment. Every once in a while he'd make a joke out of something serious.

"You can imagine my disappointment after the great fortune we spent on this picture. It was your duty, Sol, to have expressed your opinion, whether it be good or bad, in view of the tremendous fortune involved."

"W.F., if I could predict the outcome of every picture we make, the place would be called Wurtzel Studios." That got another big laugh out of everyone around the table, and John Ford almost spit out his pipe. W.F. was only slightly amused.

The Queen of Sheba had opened in Los Angeles at the Philharmonic Auditorium and played for six short weeks. Now it seemed a little strange that nobody noticed that ticket sales were already declining by the time *Queen* finished previewing, but the fact was that Jack Edwards had made not only a bad picture, but also a costly one. Some of that cost had to be covered by ticket sales.

"In all seriousness, the cost of everything has gone up, W.F.," Wurtzel pleaded.

"I read your report where you say the costs of sets, the costs of this, and the costs of that...Sol. I've heard that conversation so often that I'm paying no attention to it. Action is what I want to see…*now!*" That changed the mood to color red and a curious hush filled the room. Wurtzel could feel his neck tense into a knot. He took a deep breath.

"Jack, how about Shirley Mason?"

"We're finishing *Jackie*."

"What do you think of the story?"

"It's a piece of crap, but I'll spruce it up."

W.F. said, "I saw Buck Jones' *Riding with Death,* and it is without question the most disappointing film I've seen in a long time."

Buck Jones starred as Charles Jones; Jacque Jaccard directed the film.

"The direction is terrible. The story is terrible. The titles were the most amateurish I have ever seen. On the other hand, your picture, Lynn, *Trailin',* was one of the finest Mix pictures made this year."

That brought a big smile to Lynn Reynolds' face. "Thank you, W.F."

"Tom Mix warned me about this Jaccard. He's incompetent. Get rid of him, Sol!"

"I already fired him." "Good. I like a man who makes decisions!"

It was on the tip of Harbaugh's tongue to tell W.F. he could go to hell. But it occurred to him that it might be better for him to negotiate an early termination of his contract under more favorable conditions. He decided to keep his mouth shut.

"Let's talk about this lush, Jack Gilbert."

Ford tried to lighten things up. "You're not prejudiced against a man who drinks a little, are you, W.F.?"

"If you work on the screen, Jack, alcohol will eventually affect how you look. Look at that pompous ass, John Barrymore. He wears so much makeup, he looks like a clown." That got another round of laughter.

"Back to Gilbert. I previewed *Hidden Spring* out in my theater in Woodmere and invited my family and some friends. The response was uniform. The picture is junk."

Wurtzel said, "We won't release it."

"If we're going to replace Farnum with Gilbert, we can't do it with these kind of stories."

The number of industry releases in 1921 was 854. Fox Film made 65 pictures, grossed $13 million and showed a healthy net profit of $1,600,000. By this time, there were 20,000 theaters scattered throughout the country.

According to a Quigley Publications poll of exhibitors, the top male and female stars were Douglas Fairbanks and Mary Pickford.

Dynamite Allen, Footfalls and *Colorado Pluck* **were all released by Fox Films in 1921.**

CHAPTER 11
1922

An important occurrence in early 1922 for William Fox was a demonstration of Western Electric's sound-on-disc technology at Yale University's Woolsey Hall. There to make clear the technology was E.B. Craft, a vice president of the company.

Visible to the naked eye were two synchronized motors running side by side, one propelling film through a projector while the other operated a wax recording of sound. Up on the screen, there was an animated cartoon with an elementary musical score.

The next morning, W.F. called an urgent meeting of his executive staff and told them to closely monitor the progress of sound. Sooner or later, he was certain, pictures would have to talk to compete with radio, though he wasn't sure what shape the technology would take, nor at what cost to the industry. These concerns floated around in the back of his head but were not yet a high priority.

Changing technology was the filmmakers' nightmare, W.F. said. On the one hand, new inventions arose daily, inventions aimed at attracting theatergoers. On the other, the industry was reluctant to promote change since it required capital and other scarce resources, siphoning funds from more mundane things like the upkeep of studios and theater expansion.

Of all of the major players in the industry, W.F. was the first to believe that sound was inevitable. Besides, the studios were already spending tons of money to support silent productions with musical accompaniment and live shows. Silents without musical fanfare were not competitive with stage and radio. But it made the studio heads tremble to think of the conversion costs involved in modifying their studios and all the theaters for sound.

Industry leader Adolph Zukor had great disdain for the idea. He didn't want to be distracted from his steady acquisition of theater seats. Carl Laemmle, the ultimate program-picture man, thought talkies would do little for what was turning out to be a very good business.

William Fox was in no rush to force monumental change in an industry that was barely settling into being profitable. The ultimate stumbling block was that no one had resolved the technical complexity of synchronizing a sound disc with lip movement. Of one thing W.F. was sure. The sound would have to go on the film. That's why Ted Case's approach made the most sense to him.

The cataclysmic change to sound would ultimately be pushed by a smaller studio, one with very little to lose and a lot to gain, positioned in that hungry pack gathering just below the big studios, Famous Players-Lasky, Universal, Loew's and Fox.

W.F. would never have imagined it would be four brothers who were exchange men: Harry, Abe, Sam and Jack Warner.

It was a pleasant surprise for W.F. to receive a brilliantly engraved invitation to dine at Marcus Loew's elegant estate, Pembroke, at Glen Cove, Long Island. Several journalists had written articles about its enormous conservatories where all sorts of vegetation seemed to survive the cold, dank winters.

When W.F. and Eve arrived at Pembroke they were pleased to see a small and select dinner party that included their hosts, Marcus and Caroline Loew, Loew's operating head, Nicholas Schenck and his wife, Pansy, and the elder Loew son, Arthur.

Marcus Loew was a debonair man who wore a wide lapelled vest and a huge black bow tie covering most of his neck. "Thank you for joining us, Bill." "Thank you for inviting us, Marcus." Formally attired butlers circled the dinner party with trays of hors d'oeuvres and offered chilled flutes of a vintage champagne.

After a bit, Marcus Loew led his guests on a grand tour of the estate. They followed him through a large hall tiled with marble into a conservatory where Loew related how the gardens and rich vegetation had been a conception of the estate's original owner, the late Captain Joseph Raphael DeLamar, sailor, copper miner, capitalist and organist who had died in 1918, leaving $20 million and innumerable legends on Wall Street. It so happened that Loew had been able to purchase the DeLamar estate for a song.

It was apparent that Marcus Loew seemed to revel in the story of this unique well-to-do soldier of fortune. DeLamar had made a lot of money, he said, and had been solidly established; he was a true capitalist.

The main course was pheasant under glass accompanied by a fine wine. The room was lavishly decorated with flowers, and although Marcus Loew entertained frequently, each event was done with a relish for delicacy and splendor. He displayed an immense amount of dedication to make these intimate dinners agreeable to his guests. His amiability was extreme; he never minded being asked about any subject.

After dessert, Marcus Loew encouraged the gentlemen to join him in the oak-paneled smoking room where they could indulge in fine cigars and cognac and the talk would center on Adolph Zukor and his expansionist policy.

"I bought Metro and have to move Loew's deeper into film production, Bill. Adolph Zukor is tying up a lot of theaters, and I don't want to rent any of his pictures."

In addition to a formidable theater chain, Marcus Loew said he now wanted to build a formidable studio, too. Gifted with lots of money and a solid Wall Street backing, Loew was financially capable of making pictures. Loew said Zukor's campaign to control first-run theaters affected him in a peculiarly subtle and vicious way. "Zukor is purposely locating many of his East Coast theaters near ours. I won't show his pictures, if it comes to that."

Arthur Loew said, "Father, if Mr. Zukor makes good pictures, why not run them in our theaters?"

"I didn't ask for your opinion, Arthur, did I?"

"No, Father."

"Then listen, rather than speaking out of turn."

"Yes, Father."

W.F. couldn't help but notice how Nicholas Schenck kept perfectly silent during the conversation. After all, he was Loew's chief operating officer and supposedly knew more about the details of the business than anyone in the room. The problem of how far to go with integration was a delicate one for Schenck.

"What are your thoughts on the subject, Bill?"

"I understand your predicament, Marcus. But much as you speak of making pictures, I must now consider the reality of building a theater chain."

"I assure you we will continue to run Fox pictures in our theaters, Bill, no matter what happens."

"If I may intercede..."

"No, you may not! Learn to listen, Arthur. Bill, please continue."

"It seems a little ludicrous that we all go out and get ourselves deeply into debt to integrate production and exhibition, but it now appears to be necessary, since Adolph Zukor is tying up all of the first-run theaters."

"I'm afraid Zukor has set off a chain reaction of some kind," Loew said.

"I agree, Marcus."

Goldwyn's board of directors convened on March 10, 1922. The company had suffered a loss of $686,827 the preceding year, and an even bigger loss was accumulating for the current year. That night, Frank Godsol, one of Goldwyn's principal investors, said, "Goldwyn and Goldwyn Pictures are no longer synonymous."

One of the many legends of Hollywood that grew to immense proportions was the teaming up of Irving Thalberg and Louis B. Mayer.

In 1918, Thalberg worked for Universal Studios at a modest salary of $35 a week under the guardianship of Carl Laemmle. As private secretary to Laemmle, Thalberg was close to the power base and found Laemmle's disorganized approach to the business of making pictures disturbing.

On one of Carl Laemmle's return trips to New York, he charged Thalberg with keeping an eye on things. In the temporary quarters Thalberg took up in an old office building on the lot, he began to assert himself and was credited with doing away with Universal's outmoded approach to filmmaking. A perfectionist, he justified his penchant for micro-management on the grounds that his goal was to provide audiences films in which every patron could find the precise experience they wanted. His intensity, his willingness to work until the wee hours of the morning, and his eccentricities were all part of his great show. Beyond question, however, were Thalberg's innate business acumen, his vitality, and passionate belief in himself.

Upon Laemmle's return from New York, Thalberg hit him with an idea. "The first thing you should do is establish a new job of studio manager and give him responsibility of watching day-to-day operations."

After some procrastination, Laemmle acceded and gave the job to the 20-year-old Thalberg. After his appointment became widely known throughout the industry, Thalberg became the talk of the cocktail circuit that hung around the Alexandria.

The most frequently asked question was, "Who in the hell is Irving Thalberg?"

Armed with a powerful title, Thalberg wasted little time in getting down to work. Wisely, he decided to focus on studio problems first. There was a short-statured Austrian director, Erich Von Stroheim, who was consuming raw film stock as if it were going out of style in making *Merry-Go-Round.*

Erich Von Stroheim

As Von Stroheim approached thousands of dollars in negative cost, Thalberg inserted himself into the project. "I have seen all the film, and you have all you need for the picture, so I want you to stop shooting." "I'm not finished as yet," Von Stroheim pleaded, his eye frozen behind a monocle.

"Yes, you have. You have spent all the money this company can afford. I cannot allow you to spend any more."

"I am an artist," Von Stroheim roared. "I find my inspiration everywhere. I don't go by schedules prepared by lunatics with stopwatches, *dumbkopfs* counting words on a page. I embroider, I paint, red here, blue there, I compose, pianissimo, fortissimo. This is how I work. You cannot tell me, Erich Von Stroheim. What do you know? Where do you come from? An asylum, maybe?"

Quietly competent, his temper under control, Thalberg said, "If that's how you feel, I'll let you direct this film or act in it. You can't do both."

Von Stroheim boarded the first train to New York to argue his case with Laemmle. Meanwhile, Thalberg selected Rupert Julian to direct and cast Norman Kerry in the leading role. Laemmle knew that the picture was ahead of schedule and refused to change the picture around again. The news of Thalberg's victory over Von Stroheim caused a sensation around the cocktail circuit.

Irving Thalberg and Louis B. Mayer (left and center)

Rosabelle Laemmle, Carl's only daughter, was a bright, attractive young girl who had assumed the role of her late mother in the family. Thalberg came to admire her self-assurance and grace, and rumors circulated that Thalberg and Rosabelle were more than just friends. It was thought that Uncle Carl promoted the relationship until he discovered that Thalberg had suffered a childhood disease that affected his heart. At that point, Laemmle cooled on the young man and quietly pushed Thalberg to the side.

Another version of the story said Thalberg's mother, Henrietta, was barely civil to Rosabelle and was against her frail son marrying anyone. Whatever the truth in the matter, the practical-minded Thalberg realized his career at Universal was over.

While at Universal, Thalberg produced the Victor Hugo classic, *The Hunchback of Notre Dame*, and chose the multifaceted Lon Chaney to play Quasimodo. The son of deaf-mute parents, Chaney had learned to express himself through pantomime and was flawless in the role. The picture became a resounding success.

By this time, Carl Laemmle was becoming paranoid over Thalberg's obsessive control. He had never dealt with a man so young who so thoroughly comprehended the business of making pictures from a story to the finished negative.

As far as Thalberg was concerned, he thought he'd made an important contribution to Universal's fortunes and unabashedly hit Laemmle up for a raise. Laemmle insulted Thalberg when he suggested a meager $50-a-week increase and adamantly refused to negotiate further. Visibly upset, thinking his career had come to an end, Thalberg told his friends to quietly spread the word that he was in the market for another job.

In Hollywood, Jesse Lasky and Cecil B. De Mille were operating their studio on Vine Street, and De Mille, with a sharp eye for talent, was taken by Thalberg's successes. He told Lasky that they should hire the young man. Lasky asked how much Thalberg was earning at Universal and when De Mille told him Thalberg's salary was $450 a week and he wanted more, Lasky told De Mille, "We can't do it, Cecil!"

"But Jesse, this boy is a genius," De Mille protested. "I can see it! I know it!"

No matter how persuasive the argument, Lasky wouldn't budge. He had been right on Valentino, but he missed on Thalberg.

As in so many things, one man's foible became another man's good fortune.

Louis B. Mayer was at the lowest ebb of his fortunes and had to lease studio space to Benjamin P. Schulberg's Preferred Pictures. With its dirty white stucco wall and its small stages, the primitive Selig-Mayer-Schulberg Studio looked across to the Alligator Farm and Gay's Ostrich Farm. Although they were not partners in filmmaking, Mayer and Schulberg shared the fixed cost of running the studio, including such things as rent, water, power and light. Results for both sides were mediocre at best and neither studio was financially capable of making it on its own. On top of that, neither studio had a major star.

Although the Mayer-Schulberg relationship had gotten off to a good start, it would end up like most of Mayer's partnerships with he and his associates hating each other and Mayer's partner left holding the bag.

Most attempts to explain why Mayer hired the thin, frail, unassuming Thalberg, who had not as yet earned his spurs, succeeded only in perpetuating the myth that Mayer recognized talent when he saw it. There were good reasons why Mayer needed someone like Thalberg. He was sharp, recognized a good story, and had an eye for actors.

Mayer admonished Thalberg: "Find your way around. A man must crawl before he walks, walk before he runs."

Thalberg was hired for $600 a week. Much as W.F. had found Tom Mix perched on a horse by a lamp post outside his studio gate, Louis B. Mayer risked it all on a relatively unknown producer. Thalberg, he thought, had an enormous reservoir of skill.

The official party line was that Mayer first met Thalberg in 1922. According to Mayer's version of the story, their introduction and subsequent meetings occurred in the home of Edwin Loeb, the lawyer for both Mayer and Laemmle who knew Thalberg.

"Good riddance" was the word at Universal where a lot of envious older men now saw the opportunity to recreate their personae with Carl Laemmle.

Once the word got around about Laemmle's negative attitude toward his young protégé, Loeb apparently told Mayer about Thalberg, and of course, Mayer was amenable to associating with the young man and offering him a good deal. Besides, what alternative did Mayer have at this point? He had a studio, but he also had a weak roster of players and no one with the artistic sense to make commercially sound pictures.

By the end of 1922, Thalberg had directly produced or supervised the production of more than 100 pictures, reorganized a major studio, and in the process, elevated Universal's artistic prestige.

What Mayer proposed to Thalberg was setting up a separate producing company as a subsidiary of Mayer's studio, which Thalberg could run, with Mayer agreeing to give Thalberg 20 percent of the profits of the films this company produced.

With the ink on the agreement barely dry, Thalberg, at the ripe age of 23, assumed the position of vice president and production assistant of the Mayer Company under a formula many studio bosses would later employ to attract and retain talent: profit-sharing schemes.

Thinking ahead, Mayer recognized that new entrants into motion picture production were now considered merger candidates. If he and Thalberg made good pictures, one of the big four would surely come knocking at their door with a fat check.

Never put all of your eggs in one basket, Mayer often cautioned his underlings. Motion pictures were a tenuous business. Over the years, Mayer had seen many intelligent investors lose their shirts as the result of a single picture. The better course, he thought, was to use other people's money. He cleverly avoided sinking all of his money in motion-picture-related assets. Seeing diverse opportunities beyond the studio's gates, he formed the Louis B. Mayer Real Estate Company with several partners, including William Thalberg, Irving's father. Their first land

WILLIAM FOX
Presents
TOM MIX
in
CHASING THE MOON

purchase was 625 acres north of Cumberland Drive. Land was there for the asking and much of the Mayer fortune would derive from such investments.

As for Thalberg, Mayer's daughter Irene said, "My father found a son without having to raise one." Laemmle was furious over Thalberg's departure, even though he had had the opportunity to retain him on the payroll. Carl Laemmle wouldn't speak to Louis B. Mayer for a long time.

W.F. read in the *New York Clipper* that Adolph Zukor, president of Famous Players, was one of the seven "wonders of motion pictures." The article went on to say that Zukor was the very first to recognize the possibilities of producing famous plays and introducing famous players, and that "he added a tone of dignity to the film game that it had not possessed before his entrance."

Philo T. Farnsworth described an electronic television system. German engineers, Massolle and Vogt, developed a sound film system, Tri-Ergon, but didn't have the funds to perfect it. Hollywood's first synagogue, Beth-El, was organized on January 26, 1922.

During 1922, 748 pictures were released by the industry, and Douglas Fairbanks and Mary Pickford continued their reign as Hollywood's most popular stars. However, this would be the last year their popularity would dominate the screen world. The way audiences were changing did not portend well for America's most romantic couple.

For the year, Fox Film reported gross rentals of $12 million and an extraordinary profit of $2,600,000. Needless to say, there was a very short stockholders' meeting and everyone left smiling, wishing W.F. continued success in the new year.

On the whole, 1922 had been a relatively good year for Fox Film. In the debit column, the studio was falling behind in the acquisition of theaters, but its pictures were being shown because of most theaters' policy of nonalignment with the two majors, Famous Players-Lasky and First National. Marcus Loew had not yet cranked up film production at the little studio he'd purchased, Metro, and Fox Film could still count on Loew's Theaters for first-run showings.

Fox Film's performance was really quite remarkable but still hinged to a great extent on the rising popularity of Tom Mix and Buck Jones. W.F. reminded everyone of how quickly Theda Bara had faded as a vamp and told them they needed to do better in finding new stars.

CHAPTER 12
1923

There were six Warner brothers, but only four were involved in the motion picture business.

Harry Warner was a man of parts, a numbers-cruncher, the one the family relied on for important decisions. He was described as calm when faced with a problem, extremely thorough, and a tireless worker who would come to be respected by his competitors. Abe Warner was a big man and the least creative of the brothers. W.F. was never quite sure what his role was other than to serve as utility man for his brother, Harry.

Much of the credit for making sound a reality in the late 1920s would go to the inquisitive and likeable Sam Warner. His gregarious manner was contagious, and those he worked with came to adore him. Jack Warner was a dandy, a natural-born salesman, the stereotype for what became Mr. Hollywood. As he was an incorrigible loudmouth, there were those who liked Jack Warner and those who despised him.

In 1905, Sam and Abe Warner acquired a nickelodeon in Newcastle, Pennsylvania, where young Jack sang in the pit while sister Rose played the piano. It wasn't long before Harry Warner joined his brothers as business manager. By 1917, the Warners entered the distribution end of the film business.

Like many promising film men, Jack Warner was living at the Alexandria Hotel, pounding the pavement, looking for pictures to distribute from his exchange on Olive Street. Always neat and well groomed, he enjoyed playing the part of the Hollywood producer, enhanced by his ability to talk anyone to death. A mischief-maker, Jack Warner's punch lines were notorious. At any given moment, he seemed to know who was sleeping with whom.

The Warner Brothers: Harry, Jack, Sam and Albert

The next logical step for the Warners was to get into film production. To further their dream, Sam and Jack Warner scoured the streets of Los Angeles looking for a property that faintly resembled a studio. Things began to look up when they came across leasable space at Eighteenth and Main streets, the old Horsley studio, not far from downtown Los Angeles. The property had a few usable outdoor stages and an open-ended wooden shed. Not too far away was the Selig Zoo, where the brothers made a deal to use Selig's animals to film a couple of serials. Encouraged by the craze for *Perils of Pauline* serials, the Warners decided to film cliff-hanger shorts and two serials, *The Tiger's Claw* and *The Lost City*.

All that was missing was the money to make pictures. Being a Jew in a banking world dominated by Gentiles wasn't going to make it any easier. In fact, Joe Schenck told Jack Warner that he was called a kike by a bank officer who refused him a loan.

A long-running campaign of jawboning hardhearted bankers finally paid dividends when Sam Warner encountered a young executive with the Security Bank of Los Angeles, Motley Flint, a firm believer in the financial possibilities of the incipient but growing motion picture industry. One of the few Gentile bankers who was not anti-Semitic, Flint followed his instincts rather than the common prejudice of the time and turned into one of the Warners' greatest supporters, being there for them, time and again. With an unused credit line tucked in their pocket, all the Warners needed now was a good story. One day, Jack and Abe Warner ran into a couple of aspiring creative types, the Hawks brothers, Howard and Ken, and listened to their strange proposition.

"What is it?" Jack asked.

Howard Hawks said they had a story, a director, and a talented young comedian over on the Mack Sennett lot. What they needed was $3,500, and for $7,000 they'd make a comedy that would sell for $15,000.

The idea had some appeal to it. Jack could add and he realized the Hawks brothers were insinuating that the Warners could double their money. Jack and Abe Warner said they'd think about it. They went over to the nickel-and-dime gourmet emporium for a pastrami sandwich on rye and a cup of coffee, and read the story line for a slapstick picture to be called *His Night Out*. The next day the Warner brothers went to the Sennett lot and met an Italian-born comic whose real name was Mario Bianchi.

"The moniker has gotta be changed, Mario."

"Butta why, Jack?"

"Because-a we in America, *paisan, capishe*?"

Mario Bianchi transformed into Monte Banks and a relatively successful film actor.

While negotiating with the Hawks brothers, the Warners moved to Poverty Row where they leased a bigger studio that looked even worse than the first one. Jack and Sam Warner quickly converted a couple of rooms to offices and there filmed the comedy, *His Night Out.*

A couple of days after finishing the picture, Motley Flint invited Sam and Jack Warner to lunch at the Alexandria. He found them in a booth, huddling over a couple of cold beers having an animated conversation with Jack gesturing wildly with his hands.

Over beer and food, Flint told the Warners, "You're going in the right direction, fellas."

They talked about the film and Sam thanked him for his support. He said, "We want to get out of this sleazy pit, Motley."

"The studio?"

"Yeah."

"Where we gonna go that's as cheap as this place?" Jack queried.

"I've been looking at a 10-acre lot on Sunset and Bronson. It's got a building on it we can use for offices and a barn for a studio."

"I'm game, Sam," Jack said.

"Look, fellas, I don't worry about your debts; I know you'll make it," Motley assured them. As they bade farewell, Jack and Sam Warner gave Flint a bear hug and Jack thought he saw a tear in the banker's eye.

Early the next morning, with Flint's blessing, Sam and Jack Warner motored over to meet William Beesemeyer, the owner of the property. Sam did most of the haggling and the normally contentious Beesemeyer settled on $25,000, with nothing down and $1,500 a month.

Despite the change of address, the Warners' problems continued to hound them on the new lot. With very little money, no major stars, and little access to good stories, they were at a dead end.

Meanwhile, back in New York Harry and Albert Warner had taken in a new partner, Harry Rapf, who'd been Selznick's production manager. He was signed to produce several pictures. Rapf liked to invite amateur critics to express their feelings on unscreened pictures to get an idea of what the average theatergoer felt about a film.

It was Rapf who asked Jack Warner whether he wanted to make a picture with a dog.

"Why not? I've made pictures with gorillas, tigers, chimps and a lot of girls closely related to cats. You got an unemployed dog?"

"Yes. This dog's name is Rin Tin Tin. He's a police dog and he's owned by a fellow named Lee Duncan who claims he found him in a trench in France."

"So he's got a French accent?"

"I don't know, Jack. I never talked to the dog. But he can do anything. Chet Franklin,

Rin Tin Tin

you know him, he has a story called *Where the North Begins,* and he wants me to produce it."

"You like the story, Harry?"

"I think you should make it, Jack. It's got a lot of action and, believe me, the damn dog is almost human."

The first Rin Tin Tin picture was a hit, and the Warners were on their way to becoming a profitable studio. After the studio hit pay dirt, Jack Warner would always refer to Rin Tin Tin as the "mortgage lifter."

Another inventor, Dr. Lee De Forest, demonstrated Phonofilm at his studio at 318 East 48th Street. The technology purportedly reproduced sound in synchronization with the picture, with the sound recording occupying a narrow margin on the film. As part of the demonstration, instrumental musical numbers were offered to a small audience.

De Forest used a standard picture projection machine with his sound recording attachment. In recording sound, a transmitter was used that transformed the sound into electric impulses, which were then amplified and modulated using a gas-filled tube called Photion. The sound was tinny and weak and there was still a lot of work to do in perfecting the technology.

What no one understood at the time was that Phonofilm had poached technology developed by Ted Case, and there was another parallel investigation underway at General Electric. It was Case's photoelectric cell that had made it all possible.

De Forest pushed Phonofilm before perfecting the quality of the sound and publicly launched it on April 15, 1923, at the Rivoli Theatre in New York. The program consisted of shorts featuring a few name stars of the time, along with singing and some speeches. Technically, Phonofilm worked, but the sound quality was variable and tinny.

These mediocre public displays of sound-on-film systems that were not yet perfected had two immediate effects. First, they promoted sound-on-disc as being the short-term solution and encouraged Western Electric to invest in that technology. Second, the titans of the industry—Zukor, Laemmle, Loew and Lasky—believed that sound was a passing fancy without any real commercial promise. Breathing a collective sigh of relief, the titans were happy to see it fail.

Deep in its laboratories, Western Electric developed a light valve, a means of transmitting sound impulses into a photographed pattern of more or less dense horizontal bars. This became known as variable density recording. But results of this technology lagged behind the disc version, and Western Electric decided to focus heavily on the latter.

During 1923, Lasky and De Mille made several big pictures. *The Covered Wagon* was an epic Western and boosted the slumping genre. Directed by James Cruze, it starred J. Warren Kerrigan, Lois Wilson and as the villain, Alan Hale. The picture cost $782,000, but it was one of the biggest moneymakers in silent films. It played at the Criterion to standing room on a two-a-day schedule at a $1.50 for 59 weeks, breaking *Birth of a Nation's* 9-year-old record of 44 weeks.

Like so many big-budget pictures before it, *The Covered Wagon* almost didn't get made. It was a high-risk venture as far as Zukor was concerned.

When Zukor received the quarterly cash disbursement schedule he instantly phoned Lasky about a specific line item. "We've gone over your proposed pictures for the next quarter and we all agree the list is very good. But there seems to be a typographical error on your budget for a Western called *The Covered Wagon.* It says $500,000. Isn't the decimal point in the wrong place?"

"No," Lasky said. "It will cost half a million dollars to make *The Covered Wagon,* Mr. Zukor."

"But Mr. Lasky," Zukor responded, "don't you realize that Westerns are dead? Even Bill Hart's *Three Word Brand*, which we released three months ago, will hardly break even. The top boys in distribution think you've lost your mind or that you're out of touch with the changing times for wanting to make another Western at all."

"Mr. Zukor," Lasky replied anxiously, "they don't understand—but you will. This picture is more than a picture. It's an epic."

"An epic?"

"E-P-I-C."

"An epic, eh? Well, that's different. You go ahead and I'll take care of the sales department." The studio recovered its investment from two theaters alone—the Criterion and Grauman's.

De Mille's first big religious picture, *The Ten Commandments*, is two stories in one. The first half of the film is a pure biblical epic, the story of Moses and the parting of the Red Sea. The second is a melodrama of sin and religion.

When the cost sheets hit Zukor's desk in New York, he began to panic. As a matter of policy, Zukor never talked directly to De Mille. Lasky was his conduit to the California studio and its operatives. Zukor wired Lasky: "Very much concerned over Cecil B. De Mille's *The Ten Commandments.* Cost already scheduled runs over $700,000. This is a big sum to put into a picture without being absolutely sure in advance that it will be a success."

A confident Lasky wired his response:

> I fully realize the responsibility of the enormous sum of money I am spending. And as evidence of my appreciation and of my faith in this picture, I hereby waive the guarantee under my contract on this picture, other than the regular weekly payments. I believe it will be the biggest picture ever made, not only from the standpoint of spectacle but from the standpoint of humanness, dramatic power, and the great good it will do.

Elated that Jesse Lasky was throwing his full support behind the picture, Zukor wired back. "I am very pleased and appreciate your expression regarding the guarantee. You have our cooperation 100 percent."

It was an oft-repeated event for Jesse Lasky to find himself in the middle between the Hollywood types and the hardboiled Adolph Zukor. In this instance, the relationships were particularly testy because De Mille's company was producing *The Ten Commandments*, and he was financing the lion's share. Thanks to A.P. Giannini, De Mille raised $1 million in the nick of time and got back to making the picture. Once he got going, he strolled the sets, nervous and demanding, a chair boy always behind him so that the genius could sit down without looking, and a megaphone boy always beside him so that he could shout orders. A secretary followed De Mille, too, pencil in hand, ready to jot down script changes. For authenticity he read history books and sat for hours in the basement of his home, poring over reference books. Everything had to be right in a De Mille picture. And it usually was.

Famous Players premiered the film at Sid Grauman's Egyptian Theater in Hollywood on December 4, 1923, and at the George M. Cohan Theater in New York on December 21, 1923, before prestigious audiences. The final cost of what was being called an epic was $1.5 million. Its final gross would be nearly four times that.

During the year, 576 pictures were released through 15,000 theaters. Hollywood's 10 highest-paid stars were Norma Talmadge, Dorothy Dalton, Gloria Swanson, Larry Semon, Constance Talmadge, Pauline Frederick, Lillian Gish, Tom Mix, Betty Compson and Barbara La Marr. The top male star was Thomas Meighan, and the leading female star was Norma Talmadge.

In spite of all these good tidings, box office attendance plummeted, some thought as a public reaction to the frequent scandals coming to light in Hollywood.

Fox Film made 51 pictures and generated gross rentals of $11 million with a profit of $1,800,000. It was a lackluster year for Fox Film as far as major successes at the box office were concerned. W.F. told the board he was actively searching for an investment banker and considering available options for raising money, so he could buy theaters. He also warned the board that this was a particularly difficult time because Fox Film was facing new competition and alternate technologies were coming into use.

Forrest Dryden said, "We can't shy away from taking a plunge into theaters much longer, Bill."

"I am the first to agree we have to buy theaters, Forrest. Before we do, however, we must decide on whether we issue stock or take on debt."

W.F. related to Forrest Dryden that another competitor had gone bankrupt; Lewis Selznick's Select Pictures.

"What happened?"

"Bad pictures and too much poker. Selznick squandered $11 million in assets in two years."

CHAPTER 13
1924

Late in 1923, Marcus Loew made a special trip to California accompanied by J. Robert Rubin, who also represented Mayer's interests in New York. Mayer had known Rubin since the Metro days. Rubin had good connections with the Republican Party and was well established with a Wall Street law firm. Quiet and dignified, he was deeply interested in the possibilities offered by the burgeoning film industry.

Rubin led the patriarch directly to Mayer's studio where *Thy Name Is Woman*, directed by Fred Niblo and starring Ramon Novarro and Barbara La Marr, was being filmed for Metro release.

After Valentino walked, Richard Rowland quit his job as president of Metro and was replaced by Joe Engel.

The contrast between Mayer and Thalberg when compared with Joe Engel, who now ran Loew's own studio, Metro, was apparent to Marcus Loew, and he even considered at that point abandoning film production altogether. To illustrate the difference: The small Metro lot wasn't even supplying Loew's with the feature pictures it needed.

Mayer told Loew: "When you stop to think about it, all producers use the same film stock, same make of camera, same textures in the sets, same textiles in costumes, same lighting equipment. It's all the same. There's only one way a producer can be different, Mr. Loew. Brains."

Sometime after Christmas, Marcus Loew migrated to Palm Beach to recuperate from a bad cold. There he ran into Lee Shubert, a Goldwyn investor, who told him to talk to Frank Godsol, head of Goldwyn Pictures, who just happened to be in Palm Beach.

Lee and Jake Shubert owned, leased or operated 43 top-of-the-line theaters in New York, 55 theaters around the rest of the United States, and six theaters in London. They had created one of New York's most elegant music halls out of a riding ring and called it the Winter Garden.

Lee Shubert had a good nose for a deal. "Goldwyn Pictures is for sale, Marcus."

"Is there a price, Lee?"

"Discuss it with Godsol."

Tall and thin, Godsol had been managing Goldwyn Pictures since the departure of Samuel Goldwyn two years earlier. He and a syndicate of Wall Street investors had put several millions into the Goldwyn Studio, and when these had evaporated into thin air and more money was required to keep the studio afloat, Godsol had begun to think seriously about cashing out.

Frank Joseph Godsol was a theater man—he'd made deals for the Schubert organization. Godsol told an eager Marcus Loew to consider merging with Goldwyn Pictures and using its first-class studio to develop an efficient film-producing entity. "We've got a refurbished studio, a few theaters, and a good roster of players."

A deal was struck. First, Loew's would buy enough Goldwyn stock—which had dropped on the market—to take control of the company; second, Loew's Metro and Goldwyn Pictures would merge into Metro-Goldwyn.

Then a frightening thought occurred to Marcus Loew. He wasn't sure who had the necessary talent to run such a studio. It certainly wasn't Godsol, nor was it his own man, Engel. Robert Rubin had the perfect candidate, Louis B. Mayer. It was merely bringing the two men together.

Rubin arranged a meeting for Mayer with Marcus Loew and his right-hand man, Nicholas Schenck. Mayer offered his studio, a limited roster of stars, Irving Thalberg, and the man he'd just hired away from Harry Warner's studio, Harry Rapf. Mayer told Loew, "Thalberg can do the job better than anyone. If you don't take him, I'm not interested in joining you."

After quite some negotiating over profit sharing, an ironclad agreement was reached whereby Mayer would merge his studio into Metro-Goldwyn for $75,000 and become vice president and general manager at a salary of $1,500 a week. Irving Thalberg became second vice president

MGM Studio in the 1920s

and the supervisor of production. Schenck and Marcus Loew opted to keep Goldwyn's lion for the new company's logo. Included in the deal were Mayer's contracts with Fred Niblo, Reginald Barker, John Stahl, Hobart Henley and Elinor Glyn.

The rather weak roster of Goldwyn players included Huntley Gordon, Robert Frazier, Hedda Hopper, Renee Adoree, and Thalberg's future wife, Norma Shearer, a pretty Canadian who was brought to Mayer's attention through talent agent Edward Small.

The most important part of the Mayer-Loew deal was a clause specifying that 20 percent of the profits of Metro-Goldwyn would be paid to Mayer, Thalberg and Rubin under a straight-forward profit-sharing agreement Rubin had devised, the lion's share (no pun intended) going to Mayer, of course.

On April 10, 1924, a contract between Mayer and Metro-Goldwyn was signed. Marcus Loew sweetened the deal for Mayer by adding his name to the new company's name, Metro-Goldwyn-Mayer. This did a lot to inflate Mayer's already robust ego.

On a balmy Saturday morning, April 26, 1924, Mayer took command of the studio that bore his name. He shipped his equipment to the Culver City lot from the Selig Zoo. Sets were broken down into sections at Metro and hauled over to the new MGM studio where an electric sign, already being raised to the top of the tallest building, proclaimed METRO-GOLDWYN-MAYER. Mayer was installed in a bungalow office. Before he could get down to functioning in his new job, there were petty little details that had to be cleaned up; for one thing, disconnecting from his short-lived contract with First National.

As he had done with Lewis Selznick, Mayer left his current partner, this time, B.P. Schulberg, in the lurch with half a studio, half the equipment, and half the technical people they'd been sharing. It put Schulberg and his Preferred Pictures in an unsustainable position. His biggest star, Katherine MacDonald, was in steep box office decline and the fixed costs of hanging on to the Selig Studio were too high. There was still overhead to be met and a slim profit to be made.

Schulberg signed Clara Bow to a long-term contract. The "It" girl was the daughter of a Coney Island waiter who'd won a movie fan magazine contest and a role in a picture as part of the prize. Under Schulberg's watchful eye, she made a series of low-budget films.

Word got around that Schulberg's former employer, Adolph Zukor, was looking for a hands-on administrator to run the California studio. With several Clara Bow pictures under his belt and a solid contract in his hand, Schulberg decided the time was ripe to associate with a real studio again. Not one to hold a grudge, Zukor agreed to see Schulberg, who was happy meet with him.

"Well, Mr. Zukor, you sent for me."

"Yes, I remember our last talk, but what's a little pride between friends? I've been keeping my eye on you. You've made good pictures on sensible budgets. I can see you've got an eye for talent. And *The Virginian* proves to me that you can make a big Western and not just those Clara Bow wild-party movies."

"The flapper pictures gave us the money to make The *Virginian,* Mr. Zukor."

"I don't believe in grudges. A big waste of emotion. We're still the number one studio, but we've been slipping a little. That Mayer-Thalberg combination, with the Loew's theaters behind them, is getting stronger every day."

Schulberg met Zukor's eyes across the table. Zukor was smoking a cigar. Schulberg wanted to shout a profanity against Louis B. Mayer, but held his tongue. "Be careful with Mayer. He'll double-cross his own mother."

Ignoring the comment, Zukor said, "Jesse Lasky is still my partner and there's never been a bad word between us in all these years. He would never hurt anybody. He's a gentleman. But as a result, I feel some of those good people in our studio are taking advantage of him. We've got a lot of pig-headed stars and directors in the studio who think they can run everything to suit themselves. But we have to make 55 to 60 pictures a year. That needs organization and a strong hand."

"I can do it, Mr. Zukor."

"Jesse likes the idea of your coming back."

"I'm glad."

"There won't be any friction. He'll back you all the way. Go to California and talk to him."

B.P. Schulberg made his way to California and met with Jesse Lasky, who agreed to take the Clara Bow contract off his hands, giving him $25,000 for it. Little did either man know that Clara Bow was shortly to enjoy a sensational popularity totally unpredicted by Schulberg.

The Zukor-Lasky production team was now in place. Schulberg was to oversee half the studio's production filmed in the West and Hector Turnbull—Lasky's brother-in-law—was to oversee the other half. Back East, production continued at the Famous Players Studio in New York under Hugh Ford, who was assisted by Albert Kaufman, Zukor's brother-in-law.

At Loew's New York headquarters, Marcus Loew and Mayer's new boss, Nicholas Schenck, were putting the finishing touches on the formation of MGM. They quietly negotiated the purchase of Godsol's $750,000 worth of Goldwyn stock and copper magnate William Braden's $450,000. Sam Goldwyn still owned about $500,000 and was holding out for a higher bid. With his patience virtually exhausted, Loew reluctantly paid Goldwyn $1 million to get him out of the company. When it was all reduced to who contributed what to establish MGM, it came out as follows: The Goldwyn company brought in $20 million in assets; Metro, $3,100,000; and Mayer, $500,000. All this was at a time when Loew's Incorporated had a market valuation of $26 million.

The transition from the old Metro to MGM was well executed thanks to Nicholas Schenck. There was a strong contrast in tempo between the two studios, even in comparison with the rest of the industry, with MGM geared to make over 50 features. As part of the sale, MGM inherited the epic *Ben-Hur,* which was about to start shooting in Rome. Loew called in his executive staff to suggest that Mayer take control of the picture.

"Why not?" said one of the executives. "After all, Mayer knows how to salvage junk."

To represent the industry against the encroachment of censors, Will Hays agreed to serve as president of the Motion Picture Producers and Distributors of America. Overnight, he became the industry's standards czar. Formerly a prominent Republican National Chairman and then Postmaster General, he fit the profile for the job perfectly. Hays was connected, had a solid gold reputation, and was considered honorable. Most importantly, although no one mentioned it to him or anyone else, he was a Gentile.

One day Hays called W.F. and said he should listen to a man named John Golden. One of America's prominent play producers, Golden signed a contract with Fox Film giving it the right to convert some of his Broadway productions into film. The studio paid Golden $1 million with the understanding he'd supervise screen work. The whole idea was to produce clean entertainment in response to the outcry for censorship.

The plays included *Lightnin'*, which had run in New York for four years with the late Frank Bacon as its star; *Howdy Folks,* with a two-season run in New York, Boston and Chicago; *Thank-U,* a play that was popular among the clergy; *Chicken Feed,* with a season run in New York; *The Wheel; The First Year,* in which Frank Craven had been starring for five years; and *Seventh Heaven,* among the past season's biggest hits.

Fox went on to produce *Lightnin'* as a silent picture in 1925 and as a sound motion picture in 1930. The silent version starred Madge Bellamy and was directed by John Ford. The sound picture featured Will Rogers, Louise Dresser and Joel McCrea, a young man destined to become a star in talkies. The talented Henry King directed this picture.

Howdy Folks came to the screen in 1925 under the title *Thunder Mountain*, featuring Madge Bellamy. *Chicken Feed* was produced in 1925 under the title *Wages for Wives,* featuring Jacqueline Logan and directed by Frank Borzage. Fox Film produced *The Wheel* in 1925 under the same title. The picture featured Margaret Livingston and was directed by Victor Schertzinger.

None of these plays turned into box office hits except for *Seventh Heaven*, a drama written by Austin Strong, which had been published by Samuel French in 1922. It came to the screen in 1928 and featured a Fox star, Janet Gaynor. Frank Borzage directed the film.

Most film companies walked a very fine line between clean entertainment and the threat of censorship. As illustrated with the Golden plays, what turned out to be a $5 million investment in clean plays provided very little return. The definition of entertainment changed in tone and color as society's mores changed. For W.F. the question would remain: Was the film industry leading or following these changes in mores? He didn't believe anyone had been able to answer that question with any factual basis.

W.F. was proud of the cadre of directors he'd assembled at Fox Film; all well skilled craftsmen with a record of screen successes to their credit.

Another member of the Fox family, Harry Millarde, was expected to duplicate his success with *Over the Hill,* and the screen version of Channing Pollock's stage success, *The Fool.* The studio put every resource behind this film that took almost a full year to make and was released in 1925 starring Edmund Lowe. Emmett Flynn, a Fox standard bearer, made *The Man Who Came Back*, *Gerald Cranston's Lady, The Dancers* and *Everyman's Wife.*

The Man Who Came Back featured George O'Brien, someone in whom Winnie Sheehan and Sol Wurtzel had put a lot of faith. O'Brien was 24 years

Daughters of the Night (1924, Fox) with Alyce Mills and Alice Chaplin

old in 1924, a strapping, thick-chested, handsome man born in San Francisco. He was an all-around athlete and had won the heavyweight boxing championship of the Pacific Fleet during the Great War. The studio hired him as an assistant cameraman; soon he was playing bit parts. The picture that would make O'Brien a star was John Ford's *Iron Horse.*

Henry Otto, who became an expert in creating spectacular productions, directed *Inferno* and *Neptune's Romance.*

Lynn Reynolds, who had directed 17 star attractions featuring Tom Mix, started on three Zane Grey stories that were filmed as special attractions starring Tom Mix.

J.G. Blystone directed Mix in *Oh, You Tony* and *Teeth.*

Thomas Buckingham, one of the old-timers on the lot, made *Cyclone Rider.* He later also made a special, *Hunting Wild Animals in Hollywood,* and a super-special, *The Troubles of the Bride.* One of the studio's early directors, Dennison Clift, produced *Flames of Desire* from Ovida's famous novel, *Strathmore.*

Winfield Sheehan assigned John Ford to three pictures, *Hearts of Oak, The Hunted Woman* and *Damaged Souls.* J. Gordon Edwards made *It Is The Law*, his 50th picture for Fox Film. Chester Bennett directed *The Painted Lady* and also *Thorns of Passion*, an adaptation of the novel *The Roughneck,* by Robert W. Service.

Another reliable Fox director, John Conway, directed Tom Mix in the famous old romance, *Dick Turpin* and also *The Deadwood Coach.*

Included in Fox's roster of directors were Elmer Clifton, who directed *The Warrens of Virginia*; Lambert Hillyer, who made *Gold Heels* from the racetrack melodrama, *Checkers;* and Maurice Elvey, a well-known English director who had just been signed to a long-term contract and would direct *She Wolves*, a story of life in Paris.

By the mid-20s, Fox Film controlled 26 lower-quality theaters. Under a new plan of expansion, W.F. decided the studio would have to add four theaters a year in the principal cities. He acquired a site on Broadway, another in Los Angeles, and a site on Washington Street near State Street in Chicago. Fox Film's competitors were acquiring the more prominent theater chains.

In 1920, Zukor bought into the Saenger Amusement Company of New Orleans and purchased minority positions in the Stanley Company and the Black-Gray-Gordon corporations in New England. He had also taken over Black's New England Theaters Company.

By the end of 1921, Zukor controlled slightly fewer than 500 theaters and was adding new names to the list. Much more important than the size of the theater was its location and how it influenced other theaters. After the merger that joined Metro, Goldwyn and Mayer, Zukor felt compelled to speed up his theater-acquisition spree before his competition ran up the prices. The competitive battle was at present fairly matched, as far as the big studios went at least.

Zukor's former associate, Marcus Loew, was also expanding in the field of exhibition. Loew's owned and operated 40 theaters in metropolitan New York and 100 more in other American and Canadian cities.

CHAPTER 14

It was hot and dusty the day Sol Wurtzel escorted Winnie Sheehan and W.F. to take a look at a 450-acre piece of land, which was up for sale for back taxes. They'd taken off their suit coats and W.F. was perspiring because of the difficult walk up and down the hilly terrain.

"What do you think, Sol?"

"We can pick up this piece of land for back taxes, W.F."

"How much money are we talking about?"

"$23,000."

"Buy it, Sol. The site is perfect for a studio. We'll call it Fox Hills."

"I'll get on it right away."

W.F. surveyed the piece of California land one last time and said, "You know, Winnie, one day our new studio will be surrounded by a big city. I hope I'm still here to see it."

Once construction of the new studio got under way, Fox Film spent a million and a half dollars for installations and new equipment. W.F. insisted on many features nonexistent in any studio built up to that time: a way to reduce fire hazard, by equipping the building with a sprinkler system; a complete laboratory, equipped with the most modern tools available for the development and handling of negatives and for the production of positive prints; and an experimental department to conduct research for the improvement of photography, printing, toning, and the perfection of camera equipment.

Because of the range of topics being filmed, W.F. insisted the studio integrate an elaborate costume department, sufficiently supplied with costumes and accessories that Fox Film acquired all over the world. A millinery department was planned, and a complete suite of baths, dress-ing rooms, ladies hair dressing parlors, and an emergency hospital were to be included. The studio would also include a large reference library and a restaurant equipped with modern kitchen appli-ances similar to those used in the best hotels. This was going to be a state-of-the-art movie studio, a place where W.F. would make some of the best pictures in the industry.

While W.F. busied himself with plans for expansion in California, he couldn't help but note that radio was having a measurable impact on the motion picture business. After a careful analysis, he found that on rainy nights theaters were doing little or no business. He also discovered that two and a half million radios were sold during the year and there was radio music in the air, every night, everywhere. He wasn't sure of the long-term impact of radio on ticket sales, but he recognized it could only get worse.

W.F. began to pay closer attention to the experiments being attempted with talking pictures. He thought the idea of synchronizing film with a record was

- *Woman Against Woman!* -

William Fox
presents

THE IRON HORSE

Blazing the Trail of Love and Civilization

A **JOHN FORD** PRODUCTION

DIRECT FROM ONE YEAR'S RUN IN NEW YORK

doomed to failure and he wrote down 101 definitive reasons for this being so. The most obvious had to do with the fact that when film got old, the brittle part had to be cut out, and, of course, when this was done, the record and the film did not synchronize. There was no question in his mind that sound-on-film would eventually emerge as the only realistic technology.

W.F. phoned Winfield Sheehan, who was in California at this time. "Is any studio making talking pictures?"

"Not that I'm aware of, W.F."

"Keep me informed. There's a lot of experimenting going on. I went to a showing of shorts the other night and the sound was godawful, Winnie."

Fox Film finally made a "big" picture, *Iron Horse*. The picture dramatizes the building of the first coast-to-coast railroad. Out in the tough Sierra Nevada hinterland, John Ford used 5,000 extras, constructed two whole towns, built a railroad, hired Indians, buffalo, horses and cattle, and rented several locomotives. Delayed by a series of blizzards, the shooting of the picture became difficult and costly.

Ford later explained, "We nearly froze to death. We lived in a circus tent, had to dig our own latrines, build up a whole town around us."

The 49th movie directed by Ford, *Iron Horse* is 12 reels long. In the hero's role he cast bit player George O'Brien; Madge Bellamy is the heroine, and Fred Kohler plays the part of the heavy. The powerful culmination of the film is an Indian fight, with Indians circling a trapped locomotive while another train loaded with troops comes to the rescue.

Sol Wurtzel fretted and fumed that the picture was running over budget and getting out of hand. Now a well-disciplined advocate of bringing films in on budget, he was troubled with the mounting cost.

"I'm going to shut it down, W.F.!"

"Let them finish the damn picture, Sol!"

In spite of the considerable overrun, W.F. felt Ford had a roaring success on his hands, and he did. Against a negative cost of $280,000, *Iron Horse* returned over $2 million, making John Ford famous and putting a Fox picture on Broadway for the first time.

W.F. told Eve, "If I had had a son, I hope he would have been like Jack Ford."

To commemorate the conclusion of the filming of *Iron Horse*, Ford and his lovely wife Mary were invited to Woodmere. A simple lunch was served on a sunlit terrace W.F. had enclosed for such occasions, less formal than usual. There were over 10 in help on the estate most of the time.

John Ford

An elderly manservant marched off to where John Ford was sitting, carrying an unopened bottle of Jameson's Irish whiskey. "May I serve you a drink, Mr. Ford?"

Ford's face lit up with delight. "Why, yes. By all means."

Much to the man's bewilderment, Ford dumped the water in his glass into a potted plant, then held it up for the servant to fill, and didn't let him stop pouring until the glass was filled to capacity.

W.F. raised his glass of water and toasted, "To your health, Jack!"

"And to yours!"

Ford gulped down the glass of whiskey in one shot. "That's very fine whiskey."

"I'm happy you enjoy it."

Over coffee and hot strudel, Mary Ford related how on every Sunday, cowboys and navy officers would come over to the Ford house on Odin Street to drink and play cards. Tom Mix was her favorite actor, she said, even though Ford and Mix made few pictures together.

"Tom is a likeable fellow who doesn't pretend to be someone he's not," Mary said.

Mary Ford's best friend was Tom Mix's wife, Victoria Forde. No relation to the Fords, Vicky Mix had performed as a child actress with Jack's brother, Francis Ford, in his early movies. At this time, Tom and Vicky Mix were living in a four-bedroom, three-bath home with 4,000 square feet of living space. Their new address was 5845 Carrollton Way in Hollywood Hills.

There was little doubt in W.F.'s mind that the studio had acquired a brilliant director in the persona of John Ford. Unquestionably his work on *Iron Horse* had been influenced by Griffith, but one saw his own ingenuity in the film, exceptional moments created through his eyes alone, a certain longing for lost innocence. This special feeling would be expressed time and again in Ford's pictures.

Later in the year, a respected film critic ranked the best films of 1924, and W.F. was pleased to see *Iron Horse* at the top of the list.

Cecil B. De Mille made three pictures after *The Ten Commandments: Triumph, Feet of Clay,* and *The Golden Bed,* relatively low-budget stories that performed poorly at the box office.

Through most of 1924 De Mille talked about filming his next big picture with Jesse Lasky, but by early November there was still no De Mille film posted in Paramount's semi-annual announcement of forthcoming productions. Unbeknown to De Mille, the New York office had instructed Jesse Lasky to open negotiations with him and hammer out a new contract, substituting a sliding scale on gross receipts with a 50 percent share of the profits.

Persistent rumor said that De Mille was going to get the ax unless he agreed to fundamental modifications in his contract. The studio wanted more control over his pictures, and that was that.

Paramount executive Sidney Kent wired De Mille from New York: "It is not your advance we object to as much as the added expense caused by your separate unit, from which we feel we get no return commensurate with the expense it costs us. Mr. Zukor feels that this must be taken off our backs."

At first hesitant with the idea of a midlife career change, De Mille later got busy making phone calls, writing letters and talking to other studio heads. When it came to money, De Mille was no fool and knew damn well that a piece off the top was calculable, but this profit-sharing scheme? There followed a series of proposals and counter-proposals that led to an impasse. Neither side was willing to budge from their hardened position.

In the midst of floundering negotiations, De Mille's contract expired on January 9, 1925, and he reconciled himself to the fact that he would begin the year as one of Hollywood's unemployed.

Best friend Jesse Lasky was saddened by the departure of his genius director. Although he unreservedly believed in Cecil B. De Mille, the guys who held the financial reins in New York were telling him, "It's got to be run like a business."

As soon as word about De Mille's resignation hit the street, Winfield Sheehan was trying to convince W.F. that Fox Film should take a run at hiring the brilliant director. From a reliable source, W.F. had learned that De Mille didn't think much of W.F.'s way of making pictures. Looking at all the facts, W.F. thought Lasky had given De Mille too much of a free rein over production, and that was why Zukor was glad to see him go.

"Forget De Mille, Winnie!"

Against all rational argument, Mona—W.F.'s eldest daughter—decided to marry this "Taussig fellow." For the affair, W.F. and Eve would offer an exquisite wedding ceremony at Fox Hall to an exclusive guest list.

Mona and Belle in their 20s

In one busy five-day period, Eve Fox and her personal staff immersed themselves in a spate of activities dealing with the festivity. While all of this was going on, a photographer popped in for a picture of Mona that later appeared on the society page of the *Sun* over a familiar caption reading: Miss So-and-So, daughter of Mr. and Mrs. So-and-So, is to become...

Fox Hall was replete with staff and bubbly members of the wedding party bustling around in all directions. The telephone rang more times than at the office. Then there was the cost of engraving invitations, mailing them, and the work of a secretary to send them and answer any query from an invited guest. There was plenty of work to be done.

By the time the big day arrived, Woodmere's citizenry was chattering about what was to become the year's most important social affair.

Three-hundred invitations produced 250 guests at the Fox Hall theater, where the religious part of the distinctly Reform ceremony was conducted by Rabbi Goodman from Temple Emanuel. The services were performed with as much pomp and circumstance as W.F. could afford. Sprays of eucalyptus brought by plane from California banked the walls, while roses and poinsettias turned the setting into a garden.

Belle was one of the bridesmaids and she had taken great pains to look her very best. She was clutching a bouquet in her white-gloved arms and rigorously flashing a bright smile to each of the guests as they hurried into the dining room.

Food and beverage was catered by Sherry's, who brought their own china and glassware, six white towers of cake, champagne and special old shoes and paper rose petals to throw at the bride. That afternoon, there were 90 waiters serving hot bouillon, oysters and scallops, squab, breast of guinea hen, a multicolored salad, petits fours, wedding cake and coffee. The guests were offered cigarettes and cigars and there was enough mineral water to float an ocean liner. By midafternoon, 30 cases of champagne had been consumed at a cost of $3,000.

Famed society photographer Ira Hill snapped as many pictures as he could within the allotted period of time. For a wedding gift, Taussig gave Mona a gold band to wear on their wedding day. Mona gave him a pair of gold cufflinks.

During the musical part of the program, W.F. stood off to one side of the wedding party studying Mona, who was dancing closely with her new husband to the music of the Meyer Davis orchestra. The day was perfect and the environs reminded W.F. of one of his romantic pictures. He wondered whether this one would have a happy ending.

Crossing the room, Eve joined him. "Are you happy for Mona, Bill?"

He seemed to be in a trance; she thought he hardly heard her. "Bill?"

"This Taussig fellow doesn't have any ambition."

"What makes you say that?"

"He doesn't do anything but cater to Mona."

"Find a place for him in the company, Bill."

"I shouldn't, you know that, don't you?"

"Douglas is family."

"You're twisting my arm."

"What's a little twist between us?"

"I'll see what I can do, I promise."

"You're very much like my father, Bill, but very different from him, too. You have the same desire to own everything and everyone that he had. Yet you always put family first. I like that in you."

"Let's join the party, Eve."

Not long after Mona's wedding, Belle Fox married a cameraman named Milton Schwartz. He worked for a competitor. He turned out to be a philanderer, and made a lousy husband and an even worse father. W.F. never liked the man, but found a job for him, too.

Long before the girls reached puberty, W.F. had told Eve that whatever bad luck came to them in their marriages, he'd compensate by helping with their personal lives. In retrospect it was a poor decision on his part, because he'd convert his daughters into inane little socialites who were forever reliant on his good fortune.

A week after Mona's wedding, Ira Hill showed up at W.F.'s 10th Avenue office with several albums of black-and-white photographs. He spread an array of positives across a conference table, pictures of the bride and groom, Mona a little hefty but handsome in her wedding gown, and Douglas, a tall, fine figure of a man, but a trifle self-conscious in front of the camera. Eve and W.F. selected the ones they liked and told Hill to make several albums and send them a bill.

It was truly unfortunate that the Fox girls never pursued a higher education or developed their own God-given talents. W.F. insisted they let him help raise their children and demanded that their families live on the Fox properties. Eventually this would turn out to be the case, and after the marriages soured into bitter divorces, W.F. quickly moved to legally change the names of his two grandsons, William Taussig and William Schwartz, to William T. Fox and William Fox, Jr. The only thing left to remind W.F. of Mona's poor taste in men would be the "T" in her son's middle name. Once the divorces came through, the Taussig and Schwartz names were eradicated forever from family discourse and seldom spoken of.

Despite everything going on with his daughters, W.F. was happy to end the year on a high note. During 1924, Fox Film released 46 pictures and generated rentals of $10 million. Through rigorous control of production costs, profit improved to $2 million, still short of the banner year Fox Film had in 1922.

A young, brash kid with an outsized ego settled at Warners' as a writer assigned to Rin Tin Tin. His name: Darryl F. Zanuck. "He was the most brilliant bloody animal that ever lived," Zanuck said of the famous dog.

There were 579 releases in 1924 and the average ticket price was 25 cents. According to a *Film Daily* poll of exhibitors, the top box office stars were Harold Lloyd, Gloria Swanson, Tom Mix, Thomas Meighan, Norma Talmadge, Corrine Griffith, Rudolph Valentino, Douglas Fairbanks, Coleen Moore, Mary Pickford and Reginald Denny.

The *New York Times* 10 best films were *The Dramatic Life of Abraham Lincoln, The Thief of Bagdad, Beau Brummel, Merton of the Movies, The Sea Hawk, He Who Gets Slapped, The Marriage Circle, In Hollywood with Potash and Perlmutter, Peter Pan* and *Isn't Life Wonderful?*

CHAPTER 15
1925

An indignant Tom Mix was insisting upon a big salary increase. The cowboy star was at the peak of his popularity, so W.F. reluctantly agreed to increase his salary to $20,000 a week. This was a veritable fortune at a time when a stenographer earned $25 a week and schoolteachers were paid $1,000 a year.

With their inflated egos and stuffed pocketbooks, movie stars were indeed becoming an elite. The only comforting thought was that Fox Film was slowly weaning itself from its dependence on Mix pictures. Less than 10 percent of film production was Tom Mix.

W.F. wondered whether Mix, who was now 46 years old, was past his prime, perhaps doomed to early extinction along with the fading Western category. Perchance in his internal being Mix was not aware the genre was slipping, or if he were, didn't want to believe it.

Nonetheless, Mix began to enjoy his wealth and fame. As far as he was concerned, he'd make pictures forever. His oldest daughter, Ruth, was now 13 years old and lived with her mother, Olive Stokes. The baby, Thomasina, was three years old and the apple of her father's eye. Mix and Victoria Forde were thinking seriously about moving to Beverly Hills to a Spanish-Moorish two-story mansion located at 1024 Summit Drive. Tom Mix particularly liked the sweeping view of multiple canyons and rolling hills. There was plenty of room for a stable and a six-car garage, too.

At the request of W.F., Winfield Sheehan ordered that research be done with theatergoers on the subject of Mix's popularity. The technique of asking moviegoers' opinions was nothing new in the business world and was regularly practiced by consumer goods companies. When asked why they liked Tom Mix, fans simply said, "He was always the gentleman," or "He always did his own stunts."

Tom Mix's popularity was also aided by his personal appearances with Tony the Wonder Horse. Sheehan and Wurtzel kept pushing the cowboy star to attend rodeos, sports events and county and state fairs. This was another way of winning theatergoers to a more thoughtful consideration of his pictures.

True to form, Mix made seven good films for Fox in 1925 and kept the money rolling in, which was what W.F. most cared about. Fox Film still didn't have another major star that measured up to Tom Mix's stature.

It was becoming apparent to W.F. that his investors were anxious to find a way to realize their stock price gains. The typical stockholder message was short and to the point—list the company. Once or twice, it was true, W.F. had thought seriously about taking the company public. But then he had thought better of it.

Not long after Mona's wedding, Forrest Dryden proposed to W.F. that he list Fox Film. This had become a well-trodden ritual where W.F. would argue against such an action, claiming it would dilute their ownership. Another one of his concerns was the disclosure of confidential information to the competition, a requirement for publicly traded companies.

This time, W.F. surprised Dryden and said, "I'm ready to list the company, Forrest."

They sat around a conference table in W.F.'s office, the bright sun pouring in through stained-glass windows. Dryden mentioned his misgiving about Zukor's ever-widening theater chain. He said, "Talk to Otto Kahn, Bill. Let's not dillydally any longer."

In 10 flashing years, even while Fox Film was turning in a net profit that garnered the respect of its stockholders, W.F. had turned a deaf ear to the calls for going public. He was haunted by the nightmare that tormented every other movie pioneer: losing control of their companies. There

was now, however, good reason to believe that Wall Street would value Fox stock in line with the inflated price-earnings ratios of its biggest and most powerful competitors.

Fox Film's staff echoed the pressing need to open the floodgates to the capital markets. Overreliance on debt financing was beginning to concern the financial types in the company, particularly Eisele. Besides, there was no good reason why Fox Film should not tap the capital markets earlier rather than later. For the truth was that the stock market was booming.

Thanks to Saul Rogers and John Eisele, Fox Film had laid the groundwork regarding a proposed capital structure of the company and was quite prepared to go to the curb exchange. The plan was for Fox Film to authorize one million shares of stock, of which it would issue half a million. The million authorized shares would be divided into two groups: 900,000 A shares that had no vote and 100,000 B shares that carried the voting control. The original investors would control the voting stock, and W.F. would have at least 51 percent. In this manner, Fox Film would finance its expansion through equity instead of debt, and not dilute the original investors out of their controlling voting majority.

W.F. phoned Otto Kahn and asked that he recommend a reputable investment banker. Getting the right start in the market meant a lot for a company like Fox Film. From his mahogany office, Kahn suggested W.F. try Halsey, Stuart, since they were not affiliated with any competitive motion picture interests. Kahn even arranged for a lunch at the Banker's Club with Halsey's New York representative, Ernest Niver.

"One of the principals, Charles Stuart, will be at the lunch, Bill. Halsey may be one of the least known investment bankers in America, but by no means the least potent."

In a tone of lament, W.F. said, "I'm sorry we can't work with Kuhn, Loeb, Otto."

"There will come another day, Bill, I'm sure."

The truth was that W.F. had taken a real liking to the aristocratic Otto Kahn. For all their seeming differences, they were fundamentally alike. They both were enterprising businessmen and understood that the most elementary necessity of a company was growth; if it did not grow it was doomed. They also understood that there were three principal ways in which growth was accomplished: by getting more out of existing assets, adding more capacity, and creating new businesses distinct from the base business. Size of course meant power. In itself, power was neither good nor bad. The issue was how one used it. Zukor, for example, was using his muscle to control first-run theaters, which translated into more showings for his pictures.

In Kahn, W.F. saw one of the fortunate rich whose money had increased his capacity for entertainment and nourished his taste for the arts without diminishing his well-developed sense for business. He was also a Jew who was accepted by the Gentile establishment, a remarkable feat in those early days of Jewish entrepreneurship.

Ever sensitive to the importance of his reputation, Kahn was a man of his word. When he recommended a firm it was because he believed them to be of the same caliber as Kuhn, Loeb.

W.F. instructed Saul Rogers to contact Halsey, Stuart.

Rogers phoned Ernest Niver, and confirmed a lunch date. "I'd like to sit down with you, Mr. Niver, before the meeting, so we can iron out a few details."

"Shall I come to your office, Mr. Rogers?"

"No, Mr. Niver, that won't be necessary. I'll come to see you." Rogers was chauffeured to 15 Broad Street where Halsey, Stuart kept its Wall Street presence.

Niver was delighted to hear the news about Fox Film going public and offered to help Rogers arrange for an equity issue. "We should be able to float your stock without any difficulty, Mr. Rogers."

As the new financing plan gained momentum, the collaboration between Fox Film and Halsey, Stuart would result in the creation of a prosperous relationship for both parties.

Rogers sat W.F. and Jack Leo down to brief them on the subject of equity markets, a whole new world for the former garment cutter from the Lower East Side. Eisele was there, too.

W.F. was interested in the bottom line. The habits of a lifetime were hard to change. If he were to go public, then he had to be sure the studio could generate returns commensurate with the investment. Hollywood revenues and costs had snowballed in recent years. The industry was becoming capital intensive, expending a million dollars on pictures that would have cost $100,000 a few years ago.

Most importantly, who was this Halsey, Stuart?

W.F. asked a pointed question: "Who are the top originators in the business, Saul?"

Rogers glanced at Eisele, and then turned to face W.F. "From what we've been able to determine, J.P. Morgan is at the top of the list, followed by Kuhn, Loeb; Dillon, Read; Harris, Forbes; National City Company; and Lee, Higginson."

"Why in the hell are we talking to a second-rate outfit like Halsey, Stuart, Saul?" Jack Leo wanted to know.

"The big firms charge a three-point spread for underwriting, whereas I've got it from a good source that Halsey, Stuart will settle for a two-and-a-half point spread."

"Whose money stands behind Halsey?" W.F. inquired.

It was Eisele who was ready for that question. "Samuel Insull."

"The utilities man?"

"That's the one. Middle West Utilities. I'm told their relationship goes way back."

Eisele knew everything there was to know about Insull. Middle West consisted of inter-related electric power companies with interlocking boards, a virtual labyrinth that only a sharp downtown lawyer could have thought up. The seven corporations under Insull's control were Insull Utility Investments, Corporation Securities Company of Chicago, Midland United Company, Commonwealth Edison Company, Middle West Utilities Company, Peoples Gas Light & Coke Company, and Public Service Company of Northern Illinois.

"Insull's forte is said to be the reorganization of underperforming companies. He is an expert in turnarounds, W.F."

"I've read a lot about him," Leo said. "He can be one tough son-of-a-bitch, Saul."

"Halsey is Insull's investment banker," Saul added.

"What else do we know about them, Saul?"

"Well, W.F., they're into real estate bonds for office buildings, hotels and group mortgages. They've hooked up a private wire system to connect their offices in different cities."

"There's one thing that really bothers me about Halsey, Stuart, Saul."

"What's that, W.F.?"

"They're all a bunch of *goyim*."

"We'll circumcise them," Leo said. "I know a good *moyl*."

That off-the-wall suggestion drew a hollow laugh from Rogers and W.F.

At the Bankers Club, Ernest Niver and Charles Stuart waited for the Fox party in the Oak Room, where they had reserved a corner table.

A lean, towering man, chain-smoking Niver rose and greeted his guests warmly. "Mr. Fox, it is a pleasure to meet you. This is Mr. Charles Stuart."

Turning to W.F., Stuart extended a firm hand. Stuart looked exactly as W.F. had imagined him. Medium stature, spare, with a strong Nordic chin. A real *goyim*.

They all sat down.

Orders were taken and from that moment on, the discussion centered solely on finance and the reaction of Wall Street to the news that Fox Film was going public. In preparation for the meeting, Rogers had supplied Niver with three-year pro forma projections and a record of historical performance from the time the company began operations in 1915.

"What matters most to me, other than raising the money, is protecting my voting control of the company, Mr. Stuart."

"As Mr. Niver explained to Mr. Rogers, we see no problem creating two classes of stock, Mr. Fox."

"It's done every day," Niver added.

To cite a telling comparison, Niver talked about Ford Motor and how the Ford family had managed to retain control of the company even though their ownership no longer represented a majority of the stock. He said it also worked no injustice to the nonvoting stockholders, who recognized the new stock had the same call on dividends as the voting shareholders.

"If you go to debt to finance your growth," Niver emphasized, "you can't miss on operating profit because interest has got to be paid come rain or come shine." It was an attitude typical of Chicago financial institutions, which tended to be more conservative than their New York counterparts.

W.F. liked that. Besides, he didn't want to plunge the company into debt beyond its capacity to pay interest and amortize principal.

"I like your approach, Mr. Niver."

"In a business that is unique for the ruthless, cut-throat way in which your competitors compete, it's better to err on the conservative side."

"That's sound advice, Mr. Stuart," W.F. said.

"The important thing for Halsey, Stuart, Mr. Fox, is to establish a long-term relationship with Fox Film."

"I hope so, Mr. Stuart," W.F. said.

It seemed pertinent to inquire, but what was the extent of the Halsey, Stuart relationship with Insull?

"My brother is a very close friend of Mr. Insull, Mr. Fox. Very close."

With an infusion of fresh capital, Fox Film purchased 34 percent of the West Coast Theater Corporation, the interest that belonged to Adolph Ramish. Earlier, Sol Lesser and the Gore brothers had formed West Coast, absorbing Turner and Dahnken, owners of a theater circuit in and around San Francisco. Now the company owned or controlled 120 theaters throughout California. W.F. conservatively estimated the value of West Coast to be $18 million.

There remained a relatively short period of time in which W.F. had to build a theater chain large enough to compete with Zukor. As a result, W.F. would have to spend more time doing deals and less time running the studio. It was during this period that he asked his managers to think of ways to save money instead of spending it. Theater acquisitions would put a strain on the company's funds, he stressed. There was, however, good reason to believe that the theaters would soon pay for themselves, if good pictures were featured and they were well managed.

It wasn't long before Fox Film decided to buy the balance of West Coast; W.F. consulted Halsey, Stuart and bought those remaining shares through the banking firm of Hayden, Stone and Company, upon agreeing that $10 million of the purchase price should be raised by a bond issue. W.F. informed Hayden, Stone that if there were to be any bond issue in connection with this purchase, he preferred to sell the bonds through Halsey, Stuart. They were now Fox's lead investment bank and W.F. felt he should favor them with Fox Film's business. The difference between $10 million and the purchase price of the West Coast stock was to be paid from the proceeds of the sale of Fox Film stock.

There was an unpleasant controversy between Halsey, Stuart, and Hayden and Stone because the latter felt they should be permitted to issue the bonds. Rather than permit Halsey, Stuart to make this issue, Hayden and Stone exercised the option contained in their contract to underwrite the common stock, and from the proceeds paid the balance of the purchase price in cash. At the start of the negotiation, Halsey, Stuart had advanced Fox $1 million on the original signing of the contract to secure this $10 million worth of financing. When Fox Film found itself unable to sell the bonds, they returned them this advance and went to the equity market instead.

Senior partner Charles Hayden was an influential man who became even more of a power as time passed. He was chairman of the Rock Island, and had a list of directorships that read like a cross-section of industry in America. He sat on the boards of 72 corporations, including Kennecott Copper, Mavis, Coca-Cola, Mack Truck, and Shell Union Oil.

W.F. was warned by close friends not to frustrate the will of the banking community because it was a tight-knit society and word got around quickly. These friends, with more experience than he, suggested he play the game the way it was meant to be played, by the rules. One of those rules said one had to express gratitude when a banker of certain rank helped to raise money.

William Fox at work in his New York office

As a leader of a public company now seriously entertaining the idea of taking on debt to finance its theater expansion, William Fox was treading waters totally unfamiliar to him. Because of that, he relied heavily on Halsey, Stuart for their sage advice. Charles Stuart hit on an idea. "It doesn't hurt to stay on the good side of Charles Hayden. Why not go see him, Bill?"

"I'll do that, Charles."

Hayden, a long-time senior partner of Hayden, Stone and Company, was a product of the Massachusetts Tech class of 1890. W.F. was told he raised horses for competition and was very much interested in the National Horse Show. Regarding his work, it was said that practically every morning he reported to his office at nine. He judiciously divided his limited time between caring for the firm's well-heeled clientele and seeing after his multiple board responsibilities.

As for the political angle of keeping on the good side of Hayden, W.F. would explain to him that Fox Film was still young and its competitive pace was accelerated. There would be other deals to make and certainly Charles Hayden would figure in them.

In the midst of the negotiations for West Coast, Hayden had supported the deal with no strings attached. In a way, W.F. wished he had spoken to Hayden before he'd signed on the dotted line with Halsey, Stuart. But that was water over the dam.

Sitting at the far end of a highly polished mahogany table was a portly man of distinction, wearing a smartly tailored brown suit with a gold watch chain stretched across a considerable paunch.

Hayden observed W.F. for a moment, wondering whether William Fox had what it took to make it in the competitive motion picture business. "Mr. Fox, I'm sure you've read where Adolph Zukor merged his theaters with Balaban and Katz."

The Balaban part of the company was Barney and A.J. Balaban, the sons of a fish-store owner. Katz was Sam Katz, who as a boy had played the piano in Carl Laemmle's first Chicago theater. They owned a relatively large chain of theaters in Chicago.

"I read it in yesterday's paper, Mr. Hayden."

"Zukor is forming a company called Publix which will control 1,000 houses, Mr. Fox. Does this not concern you?"

"It does, Mr. Hayden."

"From the little I know about your business, all I can say is that Zukor is integrating his company and will soon control a respectable piece of the motion picture business."

"What bothers me most, Mr. Hayden, is his desire to monopolize theater seats."

The overbearing Charles Hayden rose from his chair, and towered over W.F. "Mr. Fox, that's what good business is all about. Monopoly."

The acquisition of West Coast was Fox's first major entry into theaters. The board of directors applauded the move and Wall Street thought it a wise decision. As part of its theater expansion program, Fox announced the construction of a playhouse on 14th Street with seating for 4,000, costing $850,000. Fox already operated the Academy of Music and the City Theater on the same street. The property was the site of the old Dewey Theater at 126 to 138 East 14th Street.

To design the playhouse, W.F. hired the talented Thomas Lamb. Scottish-born Lamb had built a series of Adam-style theaters throughout New England. He eventually would design more than 300 movie theaters in New York City and around the world, many for Marcus Loew, including Loew's State Theater, and the Albee Theater in downtown Brooklyn.

A theater with a seating capacity of more than 4,500 was planned on East Tremont Avenue in the Bronx, directly across the street from the Crotona Theater, which Fox also owned. Among the features of this theater was a modern refrigerating system to cool the auditorium to 20 degrees below the outside temperature. In addition, Fox was building the New Academy of Music to replace the Old Academy, which was to be demolished.

Later in 1925, W.F. formed the Fox Theaters Corporation and transferred Fox Film's theater holdings to that company. W.F. was named president of the company, which became a public corporation with 3,900,000 shares of class A nonvoting stock and 100,000 shares of class B voting stock. W.F. wound up with all the voting stock and 300,000 shares of A stock in return for his theaters, valued at $8 million dollars. The price of the stock was $22 a share; Wall Street brokers bought half a million shares at this price and sold them to the public at $25 a share.

This recapitalization netted Fox Theaters $11 million and made the company a $20 million corporation.

A complicated film-showing chart specifying when, where and how often each theater's films were to be shown was used to coordinate the activities of Fox Theaters. Most competitive theater chains were organized haphazardly. W.F. wanted no part of that. He was determined to maintain high rates of attendance and generate enough revenues to cover his fixed expenses. There was a monthly house profit and loss statement for each theater delineating operating expenses like advances for the first week's film rental, rent, water, electricity, heat, salaries (manager, organist, ushers, cashier, janitor and projectionist), advertising and depreciation.

Fox Theaters could only be profitable if each theater contributed its fair share to the whole chain.

Over dinner at the Marguery, W.F. decided to give Eve and his daughters a lecture on corporate governance. "When you create a company and own part of its shares, if all shares vote alike, your responsibility is not very much. These shares have the right to elect the board of directors, and if they haven't exerted their rights, it's their own fault. But when you own the voting shares, exactly the opposite is the case. The stockholders have no power and no rights. Their rights only come on a dishonest act. So the creator acts in a fiduciary capacity; the whole burden rests on his shoulders."

That was W.F.'s belief during the time he owned these voting shares. He felt the responsibility keenly, and at no time did he ever permit a resolution to be passed in the company without a unanimous vote. While W.F. was president of Fox Theaters Corporation, and from the time it was created in November 1925, he never received a penny of salary but gave his services to Fox Theaters without compensation.

The most significant policy change announced in 1925 was that Fox Film wouldn't produce program pictures, which meant all its features would come under the title of specials. During the 1925-26 season, Fox offered exhibitors 35 specials, seven Tom Mix, seven Buck Jones, eight two-reel pictures from O. Henry stories, eight two-reel comedies based on the Van Bibber stories by Richard Harding Davis, eight two-reel comedies based on *The Married Life of Helen and Warren,* 20 two-reel Imperial comedies, 26 Fox varieties of one reel, and 104 issues of Fox News.

The studio's dramatic schedule for 1925-26 was headed by *The Iron Horse,* recently terminating its first run at the Lyric Theater and its triumphs in Chicago and Los Angeles. Other productions on the schedule were *Havoc,* from the stage success, and *East Lynne.*

Fox's directorial staff included John Ford, Emmett Flynn, Victor Schertzinger, Rowland V. Lee, Reginald Barker, Frank Borzage, W.S. Van Dyke and Lynn Reynolds. Future Oscar winner Frank Borzage

WILLIAM FOX PRESENTS

EAST LYNNE

for Fifty Years the Greatest of all Love Stories
· EDMUND LOWE·ALMA RUBENS·LOU TELLEGEN ·
· MARJORIE DAW·FRANK KEENAN·BELLE BENNETT ·
· PAUL PANZER·LYDIA KNOTT· LESLIE FENTON ·
· ERIC MAYNE·MARTHA MATTOX· HARRY SEYMOUR ·
from the Novel and Play by Mrs.Henry Wood
SCENARIO BY LENORE J. COFFEE
EMMETT FLYNN PRODUCTION

was a welcome addition to the Fox circle of directors. When he'd arrived in Hollywood in 1913, Thomas Ince had given him a few small roles as a film actor. Later, Borzage directed pictures for Paramount's Cosmopolitan unit. From there it was on to First National where he directed two pictures featuring Norma Talmadge, *Secrets* and *The Lady.*

Because of his successful portrayal in *The Iron Horse,* George O'Brien was seen in *The Fighting Heart, Havoc* and other films. Another rising star, Edmund Lowe, was scheduled to appear in *The Johnstown Flood, East Lynne* and *The Trouble Hunter.* The handsome actor liked to play romantic leads and was becoming a leading man.

Madge Bellamy's brilliant acting in *The Iron Horse* secured for her a long-term contract with Fox Film, and she was slated to appear in *Lightnin', Havoc* and *The Dixie Merchant.* A relatively unknown actress named Alma Rubens successfully performed in two Fox specials, *Gerald Cranston's Lady* and *The Dancers.*

A versatile and unique character actor, J. Farrell MacDonald, became nationally known because of his remarkable impersonation of Casey in *The Iron Horse.* He appeared in a number of pictures in 1925-26. MacDonald's original picture work had been with Griffith in the old Biograph days on 14th Street in New York.

Studio stalwart Shirley Mason, with a record of more than 30 roles in Fox films, was featured in several pictures.

From more than 1,200 applicants and a total of 71 screen tests, Fox chose Jay Hunt to play the role of Lightnin' Bill Jones in the screen version of *Lightnin'*, the play written by Winchell Smith and Frank Bacon. At the time, Jay Hunt was 59 years old and had been connected with the theatrical profession since childhood.

In a fortuitous move, F.W. Murnau, the young German director of *The Last Laugh*, joined Fox Film.

Fox News, "Mightiest of All!" That was the tag line Fox adopted for the productive news department when studio executives realized that its semi-weekly reel of current events had attained a position no other news organization could claim. By this time, Fox had stationed cameramen all over the world. Thousands of feet of negative film arrived at the New York office every day. Whenever something important happened, it was recorded by the camera's eye. To add a dose of realism to news pictures, events were filmed in broad daylight, storms, pitch-black night, under the sea, miles above the earth, in planes, trains, ships and buildings. After screening and editing, the talented newsmen produced the most viewed newsreel in the business, thanks to an excellent staff that included Truman H. Talley, director-in-chief, and William A. White, associate director. Talley was a former reporter on the *New York Herald*.

Other members of the staff included James E. Darst, associate editor; Harvey Smith, news editor; and Harry Lawrenson, foreign editor. Because of the rapid growth of Fox News, W.F. decided to appoint Fred C. Quimby, a sales executive, to the position of sales manager of Fox News and Fox Varieties.

Pathé had pioneered the newsreel in 1910, but it was Hearst who made Ancel Wallace the first newsreel foreign correspondent by sending him to Mexico.

By the fall of 1924, Western Electric's sound-on-disc system was ready to be commercialized. A huge organization unto itself, Western Electric was a subsidiary of another behemoth, the American Telephone and Telegraph Company, more popularly known as the Telephone Company, which ranked along with U.S. Steel as one of the two largest private corporations in the world. From its birth, the Telephone Company had never scrounged for anything. It was a legal monopoly based on solid patents. With assets approaching $2 billion and revenues exceeding $600 million, the Telephone Company was indeed a force in the economy. A place where more than 100,000 girls sat before innumerable switchboards and said "thank you" nearly 50 million times a day.

The subsidiary most directly involved with the development of sound was Electrical Research Products, the research and development arm of Western Electric. Through this subsidiary the Telephone Company would carry on its non-telephone business—chiefly the distribution of talking motion picture equipment.

Along with Graybar Electric Company, these operating and research units composed what came to be known as the Bell System.

Heading up the Telephone Company was Walter Sherman Gifford. Born in Salem, Massachusetts, he graduated from Harvard along with Clarence Dillon, a financier who became a powerful force on Wall Street. The story went that after graduation Gifford asked both General Electric and Western Electric for jobs. Taking the Western Electric job, Gifford began his long and successful career earning $10 a week. Eventually he became the chief executive of the Telephone Company, keeping an office in its building on Broadway at Fulton near St. Paul's Chapel.

The Telephone Company executive most directly responsible for sound technology was John Otterson, president of Electrical Research Products, Inc., a subsidiary of Western Electric. A 1904 Annapolis (Naval Academy) graduate and a former military man, he held a Master of Science degree from Massachusetts Tech. Otterson had spent 15 years in the Navy, retiring with the rank of lieutenant in 1915.

Busy as Otterson was with running Electrical Research Products, he understood that his career depended on the success of sound-on-disc and wanted quickly to commercialize the technology, converting all the theaters he possibly could before a competitor appeared. Since the Telephone Company had a brilliant staff of patent lawyers, they immediately briefed Otterson on the importance of controlling patents that had anything to do with the reproduction of sound in talking pictures. Since Fox Film had not demonstrated its sound-on-film process, Otterson was not particularly concerned with them.

Easily the oldest and most consistent public-relations program in America was that of the Telephone Company. If a new leader was to be created or a new technology was to be given a boost, the job of putting across the desired image was that of public relations.

One early problem was the unfortunate habit of male telephone operators talking back to angry callers. Realizing that this would injure their reputation, the Telephone Company switched over to female operators. It turned out to be a successful ploy and resulted in better customer relations. Walter Gifford called his public-relations department "Information" and made it an integral part of the Telephone Company's operations. Later, when AT&T and W.F. would cross swords over patent rights to sound technology, the Telephone Company would put its public relations arm to good use and vilify William Fox.

During the spring of 1925, Harry Warner, president of Warner Bros., appointed Waddill Catchings to his board of directors. The former J.P. Morgan banker now worked for Goldman Sachs, one of Wall Street's most prestigious investment banking firms, where he'd been hired to ignite the dormant underwriting business.

A friend and Harvard classmate of Arthur Sachs, the tall, gray-headed Catchings had enormous charm and was eternally optimistic. Almost immediately, he arranged for a $3 million revolving credit line for Warner Bros. through New York's National Bank of Commerce.

With plenty of money in the bank, Warner Bros. proceeded to buy the ailing Vitagraph Corporation—which had absorbed the remains of Kalem, Selig, Lubin and Essanay—and in the process acquired its network of 50 distribution exchanges throughout the world. Along with Vitagraph's distribution, Warners inherited two small studios, a processing laboratory and a film library. Committed to the growth of Warner Bros., fledgling of the motion picture studios, the infectiously charismatic Catchings lined up another $4 million through a bond issue. He was now deeply immersed in the financial affairs of the studio. Supported by a strong balance sheet and a willing banker, Warner Bros. launched a 10-theater chain.

Warner Bros. was making a determined effort to become a major motion picture studio. Whether it would get anywhere, whether indeed it would not do better to stick to low-budget films, these were questions that the next few years would answer.

The story of how Warner Bros. was chosen to experiment with sound was told repeatedly once the technology had proven itself. Through the constant prodding of Sam Warner, the company established radio station KFWB in Hollywood to promote its films. In the process, Sam Warner became a close friend of Nathan Levinson, Western Electric's Los Angeles representative. Levinson bragged about sound-on-disc technology, which industry leaders considered underdeveloped and ill timed, both in terms of quality and more importantly, the tremendous cost it would entail to convert studios and theaters to sound.

A week or two after KFWB's debut, Levinson returned from a New York trip and burst in on Sam Warner and Frank Murphy, Warner's chief electrician.

"Sam! I've just seen something that makes the *Wizard of Oz* look like kid stuff."

"What is it, Nate? A banker with a soft heart?"

"Better than that. A talking picture!"

"No! Where?"

"In our Bell Lab in New York. Damnedest thing you ever saw. You've got to go east and take a look for yourself, Sam."

At first, Sam Warner was skeptical, but like everyone else in the industry he knew that Edison, Dr. Lee De Forest and many other inventors had attempted vainly for years to synchronize sound and motion pictures. Perhaps Western Electric had perfected the process. It was worth a look. Besides, Sam Warner wanted to meet the Bell Lab people who were tinkering around with sound.

Sam Warner traveled to New York where he saw a series of shorts in which voices and music came from a screen. The process, which Levinson explained step by step, involved the use of two synchronized motors, one propelling film through a projector, the other turning a musical and voice recording so as to coincide with the action on the screen. The sound came from two loudspeakers placed on each side of the screen. It was past two in the morning when a technician turned off the projector and Sam Warner sat there rooted in the darkness of the room. What he had just seen would change the motion picture industry forever.

"Damn!"

When Sam told his brother, Harry Warner, what he had seen, Harry was indifferent to the idea and said flatly that he had no interest in any device that had already been found useless. Knowing how stubborn his older brother could be, Sam decided not to debate the point. Patiently, he waited a few days, tricked Harry into accepting an appointment with Wall Street people, and set the meeting place at the Bell Laboratories, a location then unknown to Harry.

When he realized he had been duped, Harry Warner was surprisingly submissive and agreed to hear a sound film.

"Now that you have me here, Sam, show me what you've got."

For Harry, Sam chose a short with a symphony orchestra performing one of the classics. The music flowed out of the speakers into the tiny projection room with exceptional fidelity.

"Now, that is something!"

The first emotion that ran through the two Warners as they sat in the darkened room was dazed astonishment. It swiftly became evident to Harry Warner that this was no run-of-the-mill development. It was a technological breakthrough. There was no use in playing ostrich in light of what he had just seen and heard.

That night, Harry Warner had a change of heart about sound. "Think of the hundreds of theater guys who can't afford an orchestra or any kind of act. Or even a good piano player! What a gadget!"

Don Juan opened in 1926 and drew huge crowds.

"But don't forget you can have actors talk, too," Sam said.

"Who in the hell wants to hear actors talk? The music, that's the big plus about this."

In June 1925, Harry Warner signed an agreement that formed a partnership between Warner Bros. and Western Electric for the purpose of research on sound motion pictures. Warner Bros. was now wagering all it had and more on sound technology, but there was a lot of apprehension mixed with the excitement.

In a stern yet positive tone, Harry Warner told his brothers, "Let's do the very best we can and make good pictures."

In spite of a cold and indifferent exterior, Harry Warner was elated that Warner Bros. was the first studio to experiment with sound. "I could not believe my own ears. I walked in back of the screen to see if they did not have an orchestra there synchronizing with the picture. They all laughed at me. The whole affair was in a 10-by-12 room. There were a lot of bulbs working and things I knew nothing about, but there was not any concealed orchestra."

Two weeks later, Jack Warner started production on Warner Bros.' first sound film, *Don Juan,* which would cost the studio $110,000.

While out on the West Coast in early 1925, W.F. called a meeting to discuss what Fox Film was going to do in reference to sound.

Along with Sheehan and Wurtzel, W.F. invited Jack Ford to sit in. "Where the hell are we with sound, Winnie?"

"We've been talking to Ted Case about his sound system. It looks promising."

"Gentlemen. As sure as William Fox stands here before you, Western Electric's sound-on-disc will never work. They'll never be able to synchronize sound with lip movement. The sound has to go on the film itself. There's no other way. Case is on the right track."

Filling his pipe, Ford said, "Do you think this sound thing is gonna work, W.F.?"

"We're going to find out pretty soon, Jack."

The more he thought about it, the more W.F. realized that he was professing heresy to say that Western Electric could not surmount whatever technical obstacle was put before it. That didn't go down well with a lot of people, including some of W.F.'s own. In any case, Western Electric had talent and access to unlimited funds. In the company's laboratories engineers toiled in white coats among the subdued sounds of drills and well-oiled lathes, the activity mostly invisible and noiseless. To achieve the commercialization of their many inventions, Western Electric could call upon limitless capital and some of the finest technicians in any given specialty.

It was patently obvious that developing sound would be a different game when compared to past innovations—a game filled with lots of uncertainty. It would be like building around a dream of an idea without really knowing the eventual outcome. Something W.F. had constantly warned his management against. If successful, talking pictures would represent monumental and unpredictable change.

W.F. summarized his position thus: "The industry is going to march along with Western Electric because Western Electric is part of the Telephone Company. And no one wants to offend the Telephone Company."

During the winter of 1925, W.F. was in California; he returned to New York in early spring. The first day he arrived at his office he was greeted by his brother-in-law, Jack Leo, who said he would like to show him something in the projection room.

After the lights dimmed, the projection machine went into operation, and there was a little canary in a cage, singing. It sang beautifully from the lowest to the highest note it was possible to sing. It sang for several minutes; following that came a Chinaman with a ukulele, who sang an English song. He sang terribly and played none too well, but to W.F. it was a marvel.

At the conclusion, the lights came up.

"What do you think, W.F.?"

"I think it's marvelous, Jack!"

"I'm glad, because I spent $12,000 without your consent while you were away. Upstairs I built a temporary soundproof stage and we've been photographing soundproof pictures."

"Let's go see it."

Up on a temporary stage floor W.F. saw the soundproof room, where everything had to be done. Scattered around were microphones, mixing units and instruments.

"Jack, you're telling me talkie pictures have to be filmed in this room?"

"Ted Case says that's the only way to ensure the quality of sound-on-film."

"Where's Case now?"

"He's down in my office."

"Get him up here!"

Breathing hard, Ted Case came in and shook W.F.'s hand. W.F. couldn't get over how young he looked to be such an important inventor.

Looking him straight in the eye, W.F. said, "Mr. Case, I'm going to give you a million dollars and you can spend this million dollars in the next four months any way you like in experimenting how to make this camera photograph on the outside. Do you think you can do that?"

"I think so, Mr. Fox."

Ted Case

"Then what are we waiting for? Make sure I get a weekly report, Jack. Find a contractor who can build sound-proof stages."

"I'll get on it right away."

Several months later, Case brought to the studio various things they had photographed outside. One was a rooster crowing, which sounded exactly like a pig squealing. Another was a dog barking, which sounded like a cow. Case recognized that he didn't have it because of the confusion of sound.

About 40 days later, Case said, "Here, this time we have it."

On the screen a train photographed on the Jersey Central tracks rushed before W.F., who heard the whistle blowing and the wheels turning as though the train were with him in that room.

"Now you have it!"

In June of 1926, Case signed a contract with Fox Film for the exclusive use of his sound-on-film system. W.F. formed the Fox Case Company with its research labs and studio located on 460 West 54th Street in New York. The system was called Movietone. Courtland Smith, who was the brother-in-law of Arthur Brisbane, the featured editorial writer for William Randolph Hearst, was appointed general manager and became a key figure in the development of sound-on-film.

Case was still a long way from having a quality sound system. There were many problems facing Fox Film, including the construction of adequate sound studios, sound transmission on both the negative and positive film, and stage acoustics.

Fortunately, Fox Film had pulled through the most critical period of its growth and had appreciable earnings power to underwrite the advancement of sound-on-film. Both the risk and the profit in the financing of Ted Case's technology were underestimated. In a relatively short time Fox Film sank $6 million into research and development on sound technology.

CHAPTER 16

Under the auspices of a one-sided development agreement with Western Electric, Warner Bros. commenced its cut-and-try experimental filmmaking with sound in September 1925 at the old glass-enclosed Vitagraph studio at 15th Street and Locust Avenue in Brooklyn, near the Avenue M station of the Brighton Line. The agreement had defined milestones, fixed specifications and precise time-to-market goals. Probe-and-learn approaches were to be employed in several major technologies such as the amplification of sound.

As soon as Warners' technical people felt sure they could film talkies, Western Electric shipped its equipment to the studios in Flatbush. Noisy trains passing by at regular intervals brought experimentation to a virtual standstill. To mute the sound, technical people suspended blankets and draperies in the rafters, while Stanley Watkins, Warners' chief technical man, tramped around the floor of the stage, clapping his hands, listening with rapt attention for echoes.

Watkins admonished, "Sound on paper is one thing. Getting down to the brass tacks of making it work is quite another thing."

London-born Watkins had worked for Bell Labs through 1911, mostly doing research on hearing aids and loudspeakers. He would play a pivotal role in getting sound-on-disc up and running.

Sam Warner was complaining about "surface" noises: partly electrical and partly mechanical. Then there were "spot" noises: footsteps, coughing, sneezing and other unfortunate body sounds made by the crew. The net result, with occasional streaks of coherence, was bright confusion.

Frustrated with the subterranean rumbling of subway cars in Brooklyn, Sam Warner moved the sound experiment to Oscar Hammerstein's old Manhattan Opera House on West 34th Street and 7th Avenue, where David Mendoza, Dr. William Axt and Major Edward Bowes were hired to compose the score for *Don Juan.* In short order, important high-priced modifications to the building's interior were finished and a stage was wired for sound.

It took months to complete a sound track with a running time of one hour. The New York Philharmonic had never experienced a more challenging assignment. It was a task that required an unusual combination of talent and steadfastness. Throughout trials and tribulations, Sam Warner acted, above all, as a good salesman, personally and figuratively, plus as a technical man whose objective was simply to produce sound-on-disc.

Perturbed, Sam Warner called his brother Jack to report on the making of the sound track. "Goddamnit, Jack, things were going fine until today. There were a few explosions a block or two away, and the recording stylus jumped clear off the disc."

"What explosions?"

"Oh, those damn fool idiots around here who think they need another subway. They keep blasting rock all day long."

"Well, why in the hell don't you work at night?"

"I guess I just didn't think of it, Jack. We'll do it."

It was important for Warner Bros. to debut sound-on-disc technology with a few shorts to keep the bankers off their backs and prove the studio was on to something. Watch and wait was not acceptable to those who were putting up the money. It was a matter of concern to gain a lead over competition.

Speculation around Manhattan escalated as the day drew closer to a commercial preview of Warner Bros.' sound system.

"Are you nervous, Sam?" Harry Warner asked.

"Who's nervous?"

On the evening of Warners' debut, W.F. and Eve went to the Warner Theater to hear a man sing the introductory number of Pagliacci. Of course, they went expecting to be thrilled. This was the first person from grand opera who had consented to sing for talkies. The picture started and the actor was making all the gestures he used on stage, but the sound W.F. heard was that of a banjo, accompanied by a black man singing "I wish I was in Dixie." The operator had put on the wrong recording.

"It is almost beyond my conception that such stuff should have been passed by people of even moderate intelligence, that anyone could have tolerated for one single day the ill-fitting costumes, the incongruous action, the almost silly and typical European movements of the people; not in my wildest imagination could I have pictured anything that bad," said Irving Thalberg after screening footage of *Ben-Hur,* an epic being filmed in Italy.

The director on the *Ben-Hur* set was Theda Bara's husband, Charles Brabin. The picture featured George Walsh in the starring role, with the old silent star, Francis X. Bushman, in the role of Messala. Earlier in the year, veteran actor George Walsh had left the Fox lot under questionable circumstances and was now involved romantically with June Mathis who—besides writing the picture—had put together the cast.

It got back to Thalberg that things were out of control, with Brabin drinking too much red wine, so that he didn't realize that out on the Anzio beach were hundreds of extras doing absolutely nothing. Close to $3 million had been spent on a picture that wasn't even halfway there.

This then was the situation that Thalberg inherited from Metro. It was not pretty—yet better than it would have been had he not faced it early on. *Ben-Hur*'s plight was not unlike some of the bitter experiences Thalberg had suffered through with Erich Von Stroheim.

Naturally there was a wholesale firing. Thalberg wanted someone he could trust to get control of the budget, so he hired Carey Wilson to rewrite the story. Unimpressed by the personage of George Walsh, Thalberg wanted to replace him with Mexican-born Ramon Novarro.

To quell rumors of turmoil at MGM, Thalberg got Novarro on the phone. It was a late Sunday afternoon. "Can you come to the studio?"

"Today? Now?"

"Yes, now."

"*Pero es Domingo.*"

"*No importar.* Get over here, and *pronto!*"

A notable fact about Thalberg was that he rarely accepted no for an answer.

Novarro hopped into his car and reported to Thalberg's office, where he found the Boy Wonder sitting behind a desk piled high with scenarios. He immediately sensed Thalberg's uneasiness. The normally coolheaded Thalberg seemed quite jittery.

Thalberg didn't bother with small talk. "How would you like to play Ben-Hur?"

"Are you crazy? Of course I'd like to play Ben-Hur."

"All right. I want you to leave tomorrow. I want you to make a test today."

"No."

"Why not?"

"You know what I can do, Irving. And if you're worried about my legs—you saw them in *Where the Pavement Ends.* There's nothing wrong with them."

Novarro had real skinny legs and strutted like a peacock. There were rumors floating around Hollywood regarding his sexual liaisons.

"All right, Ramon, no test. Now listen. Tomorrow I want you to leave from the Pasadena station, not Los Angeles, where you'll be noticed. No one is to know."

The embroilment over *Ben-Hur,* despite its magnitude, drew not much more public notice than one of Chaplin's trysts, and Thalberg wanted to keep it that way. He was concerned about Schenck and that crowd getting involved with the picture.

In Rome's American Express office, Walsh read in the *Telegraph* that Novarro had signed for his part in the film. Bushman stood near him.

"Do you know anything about this, Frank?"

"First time I've heard anything about it, George."

"You know, I felt this was going to happen. But to leave me over here so long, to let me die in pictures and then to change me!"

From the Loew's New York headquarters, "The General," Nicholas Schenck, was sounding the alarm, insisting that someone with an ounce of brains go to Italy and recommend an expedient course of action.

Everyone connected with the picture was asking, "What does Nick think?"

Mayer was adamant in his response. "We'll handle it!"

Mayer soon heard from Schenck. "Go over there and fix it, L.B."

Under strain from building a studio, Thalberg said he couldn't leave the lot and felt it best to remain in California. Besides, there was that heart condition to think about. As a result, Louis B. Mayer designated his friend and counsel, Robert Rubin, to head a delegation that included Thalberg's newly designated director, Fred Niblo, J.J. Cohen, studio production manager, Ramon Novarro and Carey Wilson. Once in New York, they boarded the Cunard for Europe.

The reality of what Rubin saw in Italy horrified him; he wired Mayer that the picture was floundering and not even near completion. Niblo's wire was even more foreboding: "200 reels of film wasted. Bad photography. Terrible action."

Upon receipt of the calamitous news from Italy, Louis B. Mayer wired Nicholas Schenck. "I have no other choice. I'm leaving day after tomorrow. I'll meet you in New York before we board the Cunard."

While in New York, Mayer consulted with Schenck and several members of Loew's brass. They agreed that it was likely that the location of the picture might have to be moved to Hollywood. Then Mayer sailed for Europe with his wife, two daughters, and his family physician. He got to the location just in time to see the shooting of scenes of the galley battle between Romans and pirates off the coast of Anzio. Head down, Mayer walked around the set and noticed how flimsy the props looked.

Mayer shouted, "Who in the hell built those props?"

No one gave him a satisfactory answer and Mayer couldn't understand Italian anyway. The more he saw of what was happening, the less he liked it. A wave of disappointment rolled over him. He had inherited a mess and he knew it. He was put out by the unwieldy number of sloppily dressed men standing around, playing cards and shooting dice, while drinking red wine. They were mostly extras waiting for their next call. Their average annual earnings—if they found steady work—was under $2,000.

The next day's filming was a scene where a Roman ship is

rammed by pirates. After a fierce battle, the ship is set alight and extras vault into the water. For the long shot, the ship is bathed in oil so that it can be set afire with torches.

The part where pirates ram a Roman ship came off without any snags. However, during the torching scene, a sudden wind fanned the flames and fire spread hastily. In a state of consternation, the actors poured over the sides of the ship to save their lives.

Bushman told Niblo, "My God, Fred, they're drowning!"

"I can't help it!"

Throughout the filming of the scene, Mayer noticed a lot of waiting, reshooting, then waiting and reshooting again. A skilled smoke blower drifted smoke across the set, and to prevent things from getting completely out of hand, several able-bodied men with water hoses doused the fires.

Once things on the set quieted down, Mayer informed Niblo he was doing an about-face and moving the picture back to the more familiar terrain of Culver City. He recognized he had to get control of the picture, and his instincts told him that the only way to achieve that was by handing over *Ben-Hur* to the California studio.

Grateful that not all was lost on his European trip, Mayer gave thanks to God for an unexpected windfall. Mayer saw a Swedish picture that featured a young actress named Greta Garbo. She made a strong impression on him. There was a sensitivity there he'd rarely seen up on the screen. She was attractive, too. While in Berlin, Mayer offered the picture's director, Mauritz Stiller, a contract with MGM—as long as Garbo came as part of the package. In reality, Mayer wanted Garbo more as an actress than Stiller as a director.

Over coffee, Garbo, Stiller and Mayer met to discuss their trip to California. Mayer told an interpreter, "Tell her she has to take off weight. We don't like fat girls in my country." In heavily accented English, Garbo replied, "If that is so important, you'll see, I will be so thin like a reed when I come to America." The next day Mayer drew up a letter of agreement.

During Mayer's absence, Edgar J. Mannix arrived in Hollywood to join MGM's executive staff at the behest of Nicholas Schenck. The former bodyguard would act as Schenck's snitch in California, keeping an eye on expenditures. Mannix had landed in motion pictures when he was hired by the Schenck brothers to help them run Palisades Park.

Mayer was incensed. How dare Schenck send his informer to the studio?

"That dirty bastard!"

The moment Mannix hit the lot Mayer deliberately began to co-opt him and win him over to his side.

Once *Ben-Hur* was relocated to California, MGM craftsmen constructed a true to reality Antioch Coliseum set in an open space three miles from the studio at the intersection of Venice Boulevard and Brice Road (La Cienega). Its piece-by-piece construction was slow, but things began to take on form and shape.

As part of the action sequences Thalberg wanted a dramatic chariot race with close-ups of Ramon Novarro and Francis X. Bushman. Lifting a page from Billy Bitzer's vast catalogue of camera angles, shots were taken from a pit dug into the ground from which a cameraman could shoot the chariots lunging up and over him.

While Thalberg was recovering from a mild heart attack he had suffered at home, *Ben-Hur* premiered on December 30, 1925. Thalberg's choice for the lead role, Novarro, performed superbly as Ben-Hur. As Messala, the veteran-actor Bushman made a convincing opponent. *Ben-Hur* became one of the classics of 1926.

It would take several years for MGM to recoup its large investment in the picture.

Contrary to the popular image conjured up by the Hollywood press, Thalberg was never shy about his talent for making pictures. Mayer liked the fact that he was willing to work hard and be responsible for the entire MGM film production. But Thalberg wasn't satisfied. He wanted more money. He felt his contribution to MGM was worth a lot more than he was making.

Thalberg asked Mayer to speak to Nicholas Schenck. "Tell him that others are ready to pay me what I want."

"What?"

"Tell Schenck I want more money!"

Haughty Louis B. Mayer wasn't used to being accosted for money. "Listen to me. I'm older than you. I've always benefited from listening to older men. I'll see about getting you more money, but don't go about it this way."

Irritated, Mayer clenched his fist and raised it in Thalberg's face. "When you do this, nothing goes out! But nothing goes in, either!"

After a long sit-down with Nicholas Schenck, the contract with Mayer was favorably amended. All three members—Mayer, Thalberg and Rubin—got appreciable raises. Mayer's salary was bumped from $1,500 to $2,500 a week. Thalberg's salary increased to $2,000 and Rubin's to $1,000. More importantly, the Mayer group was guaranteed a minimum of half a million dollars in profit sharing. In return, Mayer committed to no less than 44 pictures a year, no small feat.

Shortly after the premiere of *Ben-Hur*, Thalberg contracted a former Fox player who hadn't quite fit the bill at the Sunset Studio, the dashing 24-year-old John Gilbert. With his dark looks and thick, wavy black hair, Gilbert was to become Hollywood's new heartthrob. All he really needed was a studio behind him. Thalberg had great faith in Gilbert's potential. He cast him to play the lead in *The Big Parade*, performing the role of a wealthy man who becomes a doughboy and winds up in battle. The picture cost MGM $245,000 but took in $1,500,000 in New York's Astor Theater alone. It made Gilbert a star.

During an interview for a fan magazine, Gilbert was asked why he had left Fox for MGM. "Fox doesn't have a friend in the world, because he's mean, cheap, vulgar and he's notorious for breaking his word. He's a fifth-grade dropout with an absolute contempt for education. Do you know what he said to me? 'Why should I read a book when I can buy the bum who wrote it?'"

John Gilbert

From the very outset of their on-again, off-again relationship, Gilbert and Mayer had difficulty seeing eye-to-eye on most things. In one of their infamous meetings, Gilbert mentioned that he wanted to perform in *The Widow in the Bye Street*.

Mayer asked Gilbert to describe the female character in more explicit terms. "What's she like?"

"She's a whore."

Enraged, Mayer asked, "You want me to make a film about a whore?"

"Why not? My mother was a whore."

Mayer leaped up and flattened Gilbert with a single punch to the midriff. "I ought to cut your balls off!"

"If you did, I'd still be a better man than you!"

Pundits talked effusively about Irving Thalberg and his peculiar filmmaking methodology. It was said to be infinitely more intricate than the conventional approach then in vogue in Hollywood. For one thing, Thalberg ordered retakes—the immensely expensive process of remaking pictures when they had theoretically been completed—to be an integral part of the MGM technique, instead of a last resort for correcting particularly insupportable blunders.

Industry sages were also saying that Thalberg's mind was a camera that photographed dozens of scenarios in a week and decided which of them, if any, should be turned over to MGM's many departments to be made into a motion picture.

Over time, MGM institutionalized lavish spending for pictures, spending money for an abundance of what it thought it needed to make them. Thalberg spent thousands on scenarios he never used, on writers he rarely talked to, and on actors he seldom cast, because to the very roots of his nature, he was a perfectionist. None of this sounded very much in line with Schenck's tightfisted approach to budgets, but it didn't matter as long as MGM made profitable pictures.

"We simply want to have the right horse when we need it," Thalberg insisted.

By Hollywood standards, Thalberg slept to a late hour, and it was usually not much before 10 a.m. when his black Cadillac breezed through the studio's iron grill gates, resting under the catwalk to his projection room. By this time, there were folks all over the lot who wanted to see him. High-priced writers and directors packed his anteroom, hoping to get his okay for this or that. Through the years, stories were handed down about his proclivity for keeping people waiting. It was never meant to be an insult, it was just part of his persona.

One obvious reason for his tardiness was that the studio was growing too fast. On Mayer's assurance that his authority over production would not be diluted, Thalberg reluctantly began hiring additional supervisory help. Like other successful producers, he would have to learn to delegate. Among the first to be hired was Hunt Stromberg, a one-time reporter. There followed a stream of new hires: Bernie Hyman and witty Cedric Gibbons. For the story department he found Kate Corbaley, who had spent most of her career reading for a living.

And for the production of tearjerkers there was always dependable old Harry Rapf.

W.F. convinced Tom Mix to tour Europe in support of his growing popularity overseas. The studio agreed that he should take his wife, Vicky, little Thomasina and her grandmother, as well as Tony the Wonder Horse. Tony was accompanied by Pat Christman, his handler.

While Mix was in New York, he was feted everywhere he went, including at a luncheon hosted by the mayor and another by the officers of the *Aquitania,* on which he would sail for Europe. Mix also found time to give several radio talks and rode Tony through Central Park. He had a chat with Governor Alfred E. Smith, to whom he gave one of his white Stetson hats. There were photographers wherever he went.

For the first time ever, W.F. invited Tom Mix and his family to dinner at Woodmere. Mix wore a normal suit and shiny black cowboy boots and Victoria was garbed in a floor-length gown.

W.F. and Eve were accompanied by Mona and Belle, as well as by Jack and Rose Leo. There was a lot of friendly chatter and Belle was very interested in Tom's trip. She particularly liked the cowboy star and was fascinated by his storytelling.

Eve and Tom Mix traded war stories about the difficulties of travel in Europe. "The hotels are quite nice, Tom."

Mona said, "Only drink bottled mineral water, Tom."

"The conventional wisdom is that Tom Mix will be met by royalty while you're in England," Eve said.

"That's scary, Mrs. Fox," Victoria replied.

"Don't let it be. They're people like the rest of us."

"Except they don't need to work for a living, Mrs. Fox," Tom said.

When dinner was over, W.F. escorted Mix and Leo into the comfort of his study, where they found comfortable chairs, lit Havanas and toasted Tom Mix's new picture.

"What are you shooting, Tom?"

"I just finished *The Yankee Senor,* W.F."

"Winnie said those Technicolor people were there."

"Yeah, W.F., they were. I saw a few feet and it looks good. Emmett liked it, too."

Tom Mix and Tony

"I've told you before and I'll tell you again, Tom, you've got to support your pictures with more personal appearances. The kids want to see you and Tony and they drag their mothers and fathers along with them, am I right, Jack?"

"That's what Jimmy Grainger tells us."

"Your pictures gross between $600,000 and $800,000 each, which is good, mind you, but I think we can do a lot better."

"I've been real busy on the lot."

"Why, I remember when you were a little hungrier than you are now, Tom. You'd show up just about any place and do your rope tricks."

"I'd like another drink, W.F."

A butler refilled Mix's glass with a stiff shot of bourbon, straight up.

The gilded figure of Tom Mix had sustained Fox Film for several years. He was now a high-paid luminary of Hollywood, and deservedly so, for his pictures had always produced a profit. But costs were snowballing and Mix's salary was becoming too burdensome.

"Things are going to get tough, Tom. Our competitors are getting stronger by the day. The Western is not as popular as it once was."

"I've got to pay for the spread I bought up on Summit Drive. How many more years do you think I've got, W.F.?"

"Hard to tell, Tom. Believe me, if I knew, I'd be the first to tell you."

When the Mixes disembarked from their ship in England, they were met by a contingent of 20,000 Boy Scouts, who had gathered to render a mass tribute to their cowboy hero. After visiting London, the Mix party crossed the channel by boat to arrive in Paris. Later they traveled to Berlin and finally back home.

Much as W.F. had predicted, Fox Film was inundated with requests for financial information concerning its operations. The good old days of insider board and stockholders' meetings were now

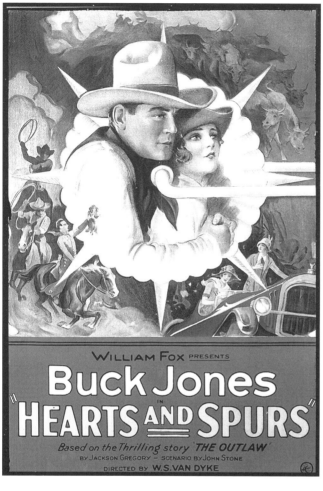

WILLIAM FOX PRESENTS

Buck Jones
in
"HEARTS AND SPURS"

Based on the Thrilling story 'THE OUTLAW'
BY JACKSON GREGORY — SCENARIO BY JOHN STONE
DIRECTED BY W.S. VAN DYKE

over. As publicly traded companies, Fox Film and Fox Theaters had to answer these formal requests or suffer the consequences in a declining stock price.

True to his belief that he was not the man to face the press, W.F. designated Jack Leo as company spokesman, since he understood the numbers and was good on his feet when it came to fielding tricky questions.

At the first such analysts' meeting, Leo informed the press that since the beginning of the new theatrical season in September, October and November, earnings had increased dramatically.

After a time, reporters made a practice of calling Jack Leo every day, and he usually reserved some new tidbit for them. He also created a room for the press in Fox Film's headquarters where they could comfortably assemble their notes and telephone stories to their desk.

Hollywood's second synagogue, Temple Israel, was founded with the backing of Sol Wurtzel. After temporarily using a private residence for services, the congregation built a magnificent temple at 7300 Hollywood Boulevard.

W.F.'s mother, Anna Fox, passed away after a short illness.

The industry made 578 pictures in 1925. Reported earnings for the major studios were:

Fox	$2,606,270
Loew's	$4,977,556
Paramount	$5,718,054
Warners	$1,101,951

Based on a Quigley Publications poll of exhibitors, the top male and female stars were Rudolph Valentino and Norma Talmadge.

The *New York Times* 10 best films were *The Big Parade; The Last Laugh; The Unholy Three; The Gold Rush; The Merry Widow; The Dark Angel; Don Q, Son of Zorro; Ben-Hur; Stella Dallas;* and *A Kiss for Cinderella.*

CHAPTER 17
1926

Early in 1926, Fox Theaters consummated a deal for the Century and Parkway theaters in Baltimore for about $1,500,000. W.F. anointed his son-in-law, Douglas Taussig, with the sonorous title of vice president of Fox Theaters, which made Mona happy. She'd given W.F. his first grandson and both Eve and he thought it appropriate that Taussig have a fitting position to go along with his new role as a father. Belle was now married to Milton Schwartz, and W.F. was wondering where he could safely put him in the organization.

The Fox siblings included W.F.'s sister Anna, who was 45 years old, Tina, now 41, his brother Aaron, 30, Maurice, 29, and the baby of the family, Malvina, 20. He was helping them financially and taking care of his father, who was living alone in a bigger apartment.

Several gossip columnists had written harshly of W.F.'s treatment of his siblings, suggesting they had been enslaved and under his thumb for everything they needed.

For good or bad, he'd decided the companies could only fully support one Fox, and that was William Fox. He discharged his family responsibility in three ways: low-level employment or a fixed amount for those incapable of working, and emergency funds when necessary. "All of my brothers and sisters had a choice. They could either accept what position or assistance I offered them or they could go out and make it on their own. It was as simple as that."

Every year a list was made up. Each sibling was to get so much in a fixed stipend, or a salary for those who were gainfully employed. W.F. insisted that he didn't want to be privy to a blow-by-blow account of his brothers and sisters' personal lives.

Around this time, the Fox Theaters Corporation had six theaters under construction with aggregate seating capacity of 26,000 patrons. W.F. had his son-in-law, Douglas Taussig, meet with the financial press to explain the company's theater-expansion policy.

Somberly dressed for the occasion, Taussig wore a white carnation in his lapel and was filled with confidence. Looking refreshed, he stood stiffly behind a lectern where a large map of the United States had been installed to one side of him.

W.F. could see Mona off in the audience, smiling brightly.

Taussig held a wooden pointer in his right hand, which he waved as he located different cities on a bright-colored map.

"Where are these theaters located, Mr. Taussig?"

"Four new super-theaters, each with 8,000 seats, will be constructed on the Pacific Coast and in the Midwest. One of the theaters will be located at Seventh and Figueroa Streets, Los Angeles; another on Market Street, San Francisco; one on Woodward and Columbia Avenues in Detroit; and on Washington and Grand Avenues in St. Louis. We've broken ground for a theater on 14th Street in Washington, D.C., and we'll also have one in operation this fall on Bedford Avenue, Brooklyn, seating another 2,500 patrons."

Taussig turned and pointed to what he believed was the final chart. Unfortunately it had fallen to the floor. A shade disconcerted, he had to stoop down and put it back on an easel.

Fox Theater in Detroit

After the presentation, Mona came up to them and kissed Douglas and then her father. "Oh, Douglas, I'm so proud of you."

W.F. thought to himself, maybe this Taussig fellow would amount to something.

Mona and Douglas Taussig walked off, arm in arm, happy as larks, for he was taking her to lunch at the Ritz.

During a press briefing, Fox Film announced further expansion of its California studios providing for construction and new equipment. The principal items were a stage, a theater, a stage lighting system, cameras and accessories. W.F. was particularly proud of the lighting system that Calvin Hoffner had designed. Lamps on all sets would be operated overhead and the studio would get rid of the unsightly "octopi" or "spiders" with their tentacles of electric wire. The lights would be under remote control with simple switches. To provide energy for the new lighting system, a 300-kilowatt generator was installed.

Compared to the old days, when all of the set work was done by hand, the Fox West Coast Studio now had a staff of specialists—woodcarvers, plaster molders with an art school education, modelers, property makers, furniture finishers, miniature men, blacksmiths, ornamental iron workers, tinsmiths, papier-mâché artists, riggers and experts in mechanical devices.

Modern sets consisted of four- or five-room apartments evolving from intricate blueprints. The so-called stage foreman of yesteryear became a construction technician, with the hammer and saw replaced by modern technical and mechanical equipment.

Meanwhile, on the Westwood lot, contractors were building the world's largest panorama and treadmill with sky backing on a steel frame.

New camera equipment was acquired for $50,000 to supplement that currently in use, 20 Bell and Howells, five Mitchells, and four Akleys with two ultra speeds. Filmmaking as a business enterprise had its own peculiar bottlenecks. One of them was the number of cameras available to crews. Without a camera, a set was an underutilized asset collecting dust.

Fox's photography expert Armin Fried, a graduate of Leipzig University, was in his 10th year of service with Fox Film in charge of the designing department. He had perfected several devices of considerable benefit to the industry in general; the latest was a gyroscopic camera car, a platform on four wheels so the camera operator could follow action from room to room, upstairs and down, indoors and out and into any location where actors had to perform.

Slowly but surely the studio was getting away from the fixed scenes that had characterized early silents. Making pictures was not magic, but a slow tedious process of cut-and-try. The good pieces survived to live another day on a theater screen, while the bad pieces were quickly discarded on the editing floor.

On May 2, 1926, Fox Film demonstrated its Movietone process at the Nemo Theater, 110th Street and Broadway. Purposely kept low profile, the spectacle turned into a relatively routine premiere. The tinny quality of the sound emanating from the deficient amplifiers had a devastating effect on the audience, and most drifted out of the theater wondering whether talkies would ever be able to duplicate real sounds and voices. The chief limiting factor for wide commercial use of sound-on-film was amplification. There were other factors, too, like the abundant background noise.

Through an emissary, Adolph Zukor asked W.F. if he could see what was going on, and W.F. told Courtland Smith to show him everything. After hearing the poor-quality sound, Zukor told Smith, "I told you that you couldn't do it."

Which was good news to Zukor. It bought his studio a respite. The thought of converting the industry to sound made him tremble. With upwards of 15,000 theaters it would be a costly and monumental task, though probably inevitable. For it was clear that if first-run theaters converted, second- and third-run houses would soon follow. The cheapest cost of sound-on-disc in a 900-seat theater was $16,000, a figure that ballooned to $25,000 for larger theaters.

One evening, Eve and W.F. sat together after dinner. They walked to his study, where W.F. sank into an upholstered chair and stretched his legs in front of him.

Eve, in a pensive mood, understood W.F.'s predicament. "What are we missing, Bill?"

"If we had those Western Electric speakers, that would be a start."

"Why don't we buy them?"

"Because they're not for sale. I expect to see them tied to a deal for their disc system."

"What are our alternatives?"

"I don't know. I need time to think."

W.F.'s mind was awhirl, wondering what he would do next.

W.F. was up at first light. Breakfast was two slices of dry toast and a cup of hot coffee, which he took black. Harold chauffeured him to his office, where he arrived punctually at 7:30 a.m. When he got to his desk, he asked his secretary to immediately call John Otterson. W.F. told him he'd like to see him. Before this, W.F. had never dealt with him in person. Otterson sounded pleasant enough, so W.F. decided to travel downtown and meet him in his office located in an impressive building—AT&T's headquarters—on Broadway and Fulton. When he got there, he found Otterson to be a heavy-set, powerful man with a long nose and a high forehead, a typically Anglo-Saxon face if he'd ever seen one.

Otterson invited him to sit down and they got right to business. "What can I do for you, Mr. Fox?"

W.F. told him that Fox owned the Case patents for sound-on-film and was in the process of testing the technology.

"How valid are those patents?"

"My lawyers tell me they're perfectly legal."

W.F. had bought the vital patents covering the photoelectric process and knew he stood on firm ground.

"I'd like to hear what you've come up with, Mr. Fox."

Several days later, W.F. invited Otterson and Walter S. Gifford to see one of his educational pictures in a school on the East Side of New York.

W.F. was pleased that Gifford came and brought his little son with him. Blond, blue-eyed Walter S. Gifford was 41 years old and was listed as one of the 59 "Rulers of America." W.F. displayed two of the silent educational pictures the studio had made to a classroom of boys and girls. Gifford was delighted and thought it a breakthrough. "The future of education is teaching with film, Mr. Fox. It's wonderful."

"If you think this is wonderful, wait until you see them when we make them in sound," W.F. said. W.F. could see that Otterson was a little perturbed that he hadn't offered to show them any of the studio's sound product.

Among Fox's recent acquisitions was the great German director, F.W. Murnau, who had directed *Nosferatu* and *The Last Laugh*, the film W.F. thought to be one of the greatest of all time. Thin and tall, he was a very meticulous man.

Fox's deal with Murnau covered four films in four years and included a salary of $125,000 for the first year, $150,000 for the second, $170,000 for the third, and $200,000 for the fourth.

Fox Film allowed Murnau to bring his cameraman, writers and other craftsmen to work with him. The studio feted the signing of Murnau with a dinner at the Ritz attended by 75 guests, where speeches were made by ex-senator Charles A. Towne and Hearst columnist Arthur Brisbane. W.F. also forced himself to say a few choice words.

As part of a fund-raising drive, W.F. gave $250,000 to the United Jewish Campaign and accepted its New York chairmanship. Members of his team met at the home of Felix M. Warburg. Their quota for the campaign was set at an ambitious $6 million.

David A. Brown, national chairman, said, "Your acceptance of the New York chairmanship and your most generous contribution will make the New York campaign the greatest in the history of New York. I congratulate all who are involved in this great humanitarian effort and am pleased that we are to have your cooperation."

W.F. replied, "I have deliberately raised the quota by $2 million because I am convinced that even if New York gives $6 million and the rest of the country exceeds the quotas that have been assigned to the various states and cities in the $15 million drive, we shall still not have a fund large enough to substantially alleviate the appalling economic tragedy that has overwhelmed the Jews in Poland, Galicia, Bessarabia, Russia and Rumania."

After the gala, W.F. had occasion to join a few industry leaders at a private dinner in the home of Carl Laemmle. Following the meal, he thought it appropriate that they toast to their good health and good fortune; he rose to say a few words to their host, Uncle Carl.

"You are the man with the greatest courage of all I know in the picture business and for you I have always had the greatest admiration, one I never expressed to you until this time."

The news from California was that Sol Wurtzel had discovered a starlet named Janet Gaynor. Petite—only five feet tall—she weighed 96 pounds and had auburn hair with brown eyes to match. One of Fox's directors, Irving Cummings, administered the screen test and was quite euphoric with what he saw. A former clerk in a San Francisco lawyer's office, Gaynor seemed to photograph well.

Sheehan instructed Cummings to send the rushes to Murnau, who was looking for a fresh face for one of the movies he was planning to shoot. After examining the test, Murnau cast Gaynor in *Sunrise.* A few days after her test, Cummings cast her in her first role for Fox, *The Johnstown Flood,* which had Janet nurturing a love for construction worker George O'Brien. She warns him of an approaching flood, but she herself drowns. Aside from being photogenic, Janet Gaynor had star quality. *Variety* reported: "Janet Gaynor, a newcomer and a corker, wins the lion's share of everything as the female Paul Revere."

The studio housed their starlet in the thatched and fairy-tale cottage once occupied by John McCormack. Gaynor became Fox's ingenuous heroine of sentimental comedy-drama.

Fox filmed the story of the tragic *Johnstown Flood,* starring George O'Brien in 1926.

"What are we gonna call this sound thing, Sam?" Abe Warner asked.

"We just closed the deal with Vitagraph. Maybe we can use something like that. Vita... something."

The Warner brothers settled on calling the new sound system Vitaphone.

An hour before the world premiere of Vitaphone, Sam and Abe Warner met in the theater to be sure everything was in order.

"What if the apparatus breaks down, Sam?"

"It won't break down."

"It could maybe crack apart some way, spoil everything."

"Nothin's gonna happen to it, Abe."

"You sure?"

"I worked my ass off for six months to make sure."

The world premiere of *Don Juan* took place at the 1,208-seat Warner Theater in New York on August 6, 1926 at prices that reached $3.30. Twenty-five cent tickets were soon to be yesterday's news.

First-nighters included William Fox, Adolph Zukor, Nicholas Schenck, Walter Gifford and other Hollywood luminaries who were intrigued with the idea of talking pictures. At 8:30 the lights dimmed and the curtains parted. On the screen, Will Hays stepped forward. His words were some of the first ever spoken on film to a theater audience.

"My friends, no story was ever written for the screen as dramatic as the story of the screen itself. Tonight we write another chapter in that story, for indeed we have advanced from that few seconds of shadow of a serpentine dancer 30 years ago when the motion picture was born—to this public demonstration of the Vitaphone synchronizing the reproduction of sound with the reproduction of action."

After the show, Harry, Sam and Abe Warner remained in the lobby, eavesdropping on theatergoers, registering their favorable comments.

"Glorious!"

"Beautiful!"

"Didn't believe it was possible."

Under a brightly lit marquee, amidst the departing theater audience, W.F. stood in a semicircle with Will Hays, Nicholas Schenck, Walter Gifford, Harry Warner and Adolph Zukor.

Harry Warner looked straight at Zukor, the only man in the industry he recognized as even more astute than he. "What do you think, Adolph?"

"It's a fad. It won't last, Harry."

It was a serious indictment, and had to be seriously considered. AT&T had gone out on a limb in the development of sound-on-disc, and wasn't about to let it die on the vine.

"Adolph, I think you're underestimating the power of sound," Gifford said.

"I may be, Walter, but trust me when I tell you that the public prefers silent pictures."

Early morning trade papers were splattered with accolades for Vitaphone.

Variety said, "Warner makes a talkie!"

The front page of *Photoplay* read: "Vitaphone bow is hailed as a marvel!"

The *Times* said: "No single word, however compounded, is quite adequate to suggest the amazing triumph which man has at last achieved in making pictures talk naturally, sing enthrallingly and play all manner of instruments as skillfully as if the living beings were present instead of their shadows...marvelous. Uncanny!"

That same night W.F. told Eve about the premiere and how tinny the orchestra had sounded. "Zukor thinks it's a fad."

"What do you think, Bill?"

"Eve, it's strange, but when I walked out of that theater, I had the same feeling in the pit of my stomach like when I first saw *Birth of A Nation*."

"We don't have much time."

"Sound will turn this industry upside down. We've got to be careful, but we have to invest in our development."

Regardless of huge press coverage for *Don Juan*, receipts were limited to one theater and in no way compensated for Warner Bros.' big stake in the picture. To put it more bluntly, the Warners had spent a lot of money preparing a picture for a single-theater release.

The reaction on Wall Street was another story. Warners' stock price shot up from $14 to $54 and this piqued the interest of the investment community.

Don Juan's first run at the Warner Theater went well into April 1927 at prices ranging from 50 cents to $2.

In spite of a remarkable stock market response, the cold reality was that the Warner brothers were spending more on sound than they could possibly recoup at the box office. The Warners faced two problems: money and time. Money and time to perfect a system that had mesmerized theater audiences wherever it was shown. And that was but the tip of the iceberg. The technical hurdles that remained were formidable, too. Splices. Skips. Synchronization. Equipping theaters, and so forth.

To compensate for a perpetual cash shortfall, Waddill Catchings taught the Warner brothers a new scheme. He suggested they form a family holding company, Renraw. Whenever the studio needed money for development, Renraw sold Warner Bros. stock on the curb. Renraw would then lend money to the studio. Trouble was, they were suffering considerable dilution in their ownership of the company.

Monte Blue cornered Jack Warner on the studio lot.

"Jack, I hear you're going to dump me when they start talking pictures."

"Look Monte, we are not making any talkies now, and don't let any of these second-rate prophets give you a bum steer."

"Oh, I know what you're thinking. You think I can't make it. But you're not going to put me out of pictures, you hear!"

Around this time, a lot of actors were sleeping poorly. There was much concern throughout Hollywood about the introduction of talkies. Silent stars were having their tonsils checked. Because of the potential for violence, Jack Warner increased security at his studio.

Overflowing with his natural exuberance, Jack Warner called a press conference at the California studio. For the affair, Warner wore a straw hat and white pants. He was playing the part of Hollywood tycoon.

Reporters barraged Warner with vague questions. The cacophony of sounds was almost unbearable. "Gentlemen! Gentlemen! One at a time. Please. I can't hear a damn thing."

Pointing to a reporter, Warner said, "Yeah, you with the goofy hat on."

"They're saying it's an impending revolution, this Vitaphone process. Do you agree, Mr. Warner?"

"Our stock is soaring; that's fine by me. Yeah, you. No, you, the fat guy with the Pancho Villa mustache."

"Do you think people will prefer talkies over silent film?"

"Kid, do men prefer good-looking broads to ugly ones?"

That got a roar of laughter out of the reporters.

"Yeah, you. No, you, the bald guy with the mutton chops."

"What about Fox Film and their Movietone process? How does it compare to Vitaphone?"

"I can't really speak for this Movietone process except to say I've not seen any features made with it. That'll be all, gentlemen."

Not bad for a beginning, he thought.

Careful estimates indicated that the Warners would have to sink $800,000 into developing Vitaphone, and none of the theaters were wired for sound. The technology was way ahead of itself. The prospects for immediate profit were unclear, and possibly less attractive than those of silent film.

To add to the intrigue of the moment, John Otterson was having clandestine meetings with Jesse Lasky about some kind of a side deal. Deep down, Otterson believed the Warners to be small fish, an obstacle to the inevitable 100 percent conversion to sound.

The one thing everyone underestimated was Harry Warner's tenacity. Once he'd seen what Sam Warner had achieved with *Don Juan*, he was convinced the technology had merit if, for nothing else, it would replace all those expensive musicians who performed in theaters.

But Harry Warner needed money, and he needed it right away, so he tried to lure his rivals to share in the development costs without Warners losing control of Vitaphone. The response was uniform. The big four—Loew's-MGM, Universal, First National, and Famous Players-Lasky—said talkies were a lot of nonsense and would pass into history with the other fads they'd seen come and go throughout the years.

Neither Warner nor Western Electric came up with an alternative and were forced, reluctantly, to go on doing business with each other. Under their contract, Harry Warner had committed to buying 2,400 complete sets of equipment from Electrical Research Products. The big studios with their wholly owned and controlled theaters erected a brick wall forcing Warner to approach the independents, who were willing to convert to sound. Harry Warner was being hounded by Otterson for not fully exploiting the market. But there was good reason for that. The price of the equipment turned out to be higher than what Warner thought he had contracted for, and this limited potential.

Incumbents were rightfully worried about taking business away from profitable silent films. They were more concerned with meeting the current needs of theaters than looking to the future.

As for Warner Bros., every drop of new money went into Vitaphone. A colossal mound of debt began tilting Warner Bros.' undercapitalized balance sheet. The Warners were now leveraged to the hilt, both in their studio and individually. Everything but the kitchen sink rode on the success of Vitaphone. Having put itself in less than a year near the top of the industry, Warner Bros., to the stunned chagrin of its competitors, went about methodically introducing sound-on-disc. There was to be no surrender. The brothers seemed to glory in the huge risk of developing sound. They were fully committed to the project.

CHAPTER 18

On Monday morning, August 23, 1926, W.F. picked up the morning paper; the headline read: "Valentino Dying."

That night, Valentino's corpse was transferred to Frank E. Campbell's funeral parlor on the Upper East Side. As befit his celebrity, the motion picture idol was laid out in the Gold Room, where a private showing was scheduled for a select group of people.

Accompanied by Winfield Sheehan, W.F. paid his personal respects to Joseph Schenck, the president of United Artists and Valentino's most recent employer. The silence inside the funeral parlor was in sharp contrast to the tumult gathering outside. The pungent aroma of freshly cut flowers permeated the room.

Because of the number of visitors, a dividing wall had been removed to combine two viewing rooms into one, with folding chairs arranged in a semicircle around the coffin. Schenck and his party sat off to one side on more comfortable armchairs and a sofa.

A little over a month before Valentino's untimely death, *The Son of the Sheik* had premiered at Grauman's Million Dollar Theater in Los Angeles, and for the event Valentino had escorted Pola Negri. She was said to be his new love interest. The picture was a strange rigmarole about a desert scion who kidnaps a dancing girl (Vilma Banky).

Schenck said the Chicago premiere had been as successful as the one in Los Angeles. In rare spirits, Valentino had departed for New York, where he had arrived on July 20 and had met with him and other executives of United Artists.

"We were all celebrating the success of his picture, Bill."

"What happened, Joe?"

"It's as if he'd been hit by a bolt of lightning."

It was a hot and stifling Sunday and most of the medical staff had left the city, Schenck related, so Valentino had not been operated on until the evening, although he had been diagnosed as suffering from an acute gastric ulcer and a ruptured appendix.

Tens of thousands of people lined up to view Valentino's body in New York and then California.

At first, it was believed that Valentino was in little danger. But then he'd taken a turn for the worse, Schenck said. "It all happened so fast."

For Joe Schenck, the conversation was a chance for him to let off steam, for now he was facing a financial problem of monumental proportions, having just lost his most important box-office star.

A man wearing a clerical collar made his way to the coffin. W.F. nudged Winnie, indicating it was time to leave. Outside Campbell's, there was a swelling crowd of people lining up to view Valentino. W.F. thought there were over a thousand onlookers, some being restrained by policemen and one of Campbell's ushers.

That night, in the late edition, W.F. read that 10,000 fans had gathered around the funeral home, wanting to see Valentino. It had taken a dozen policemen to control them. The crowd had forced the heavy door and had crashed into the parlor, temporarily disrupting the solemnity of the funeral home.

Apparently the police had sent for reinforcement and finally had regained control of the situation.

In any case, the funeral service for Valentino at St. Malachy's Chapel was scheduled for Monday, which gave Campbell's five more days for the showing. The outpouring was impressive. It again brought home to W.F. the power of the medium. How else could someone from a little village in Italy with no particular genius or high office become so well known to such a large audience?

In furtherance of the Valentino mystique, every year for a long while, on the anniversary of Valentino's death, a mysterious, thickly veiled Woman in Black was driven to the gates of the Hollywood Cemetery by a chauffeur, alighted, placed a bunch of red roses on Valentino's tomb, dabbed her eyes gently with a black-bordered handkerchief, and departed.

A theater costing $4.5 million was to be built in Dayton, Ohio, by Fox Theaters. Negotiations for the sale of the old Masonic Temple on South Main Street were almost completed.

The first Chief entered service in late November as an extra-fare premier train. It departed Dearborn Station in Chicago at 11:00 a.m. and chugged into the Los Angeles Railroad Station two days later at 5:00 p.m. The train was met by a reception committee headed by a smiling Tom Mix mounted on Tony, accompanied by 50 extras dressed in Western garb on horseback.

A multicolored banner proclaimed, "Fox Film Convention of 1926."

The train suddenly stopped. More than 200 Fox salesmen and theater managers poured off, somberly dressed, wearing different shaped hats, smoking cigars and cigarettes.

Attractive studio girls threw hard candy at the delegates as they hobbled off the train. Each delegate was personally greeted by Tom Mix, who leaned down from his horse and shook every hand. Jimmy Grainger, Fox's corpulent national sales manager, headed the group. With that famed grin on his moon-shaped face, Grainger steered the delegates over to a certain spot where the moment could be captured on film. A camera whirred and registered their broad smiles for posterity.

Following the cordial reception at the train station, the conventioneers made their way in a long caravan of open touring cars to the William Fox Studio on Sunset Boulevard. As part of the program, Sol Wurtzel arranged for a tour of the facilities, where studio personnel showed them how pictures were made. To greet the salesmen and theater managers, several stars were on the lot and many, many pictures were snapped to record the moment for the conventioneers and their friends and relatives at home. This careful planning was a tribute to Sol Wurtzel's organizational skill. No one understood better than he the importance of motivating the guys who were out there pounding the pavement, selling the films he made.

Throughout the convention, delegates were entertained and wined and dined continuously and euphorically. That same evening, the studio celebrated its good fortune with a party held in the ballroom of the grand Ambassador Hotel at 3400 Wilshire Boulevard. Everyone was formally dressed, with all of the salesmen wearing their tuxes as though they were everyday attire. Music, good food, flappers and lots of congeniality were the hallmarks of the convention.

In a spectacularly staged closing to the event, the bronzed doors of the ballroom opened to a trumpet fanfare, and a parade of Fox players, directors and producers marched in. The cavalcade was composed of cowboys on horseback, circus clowns, scantily clothed starlets and jugglers. At the head of the procession was Fox's biggest star, Tom Mix, mounted on his wonder horse, Tony.

Back on the lot the next day, W.F. stood on an improvised platform before a microphone. "I know you've heard about Warners' talkies, so let me clear up a few things. We have an instrument called Movietone, which puts the sound track right on the film. We photograph the player and at the same time on the same celluloid we photograph his voice. The Movietone or Vitaphone or whatever talking apparatus the public will ultimately adopt will be one of the greatest factors for our business that it is possible to conceive. But it may take 10 or 20 years before a good

sound product is developed. In the meantime, we have our Fox pictures to exhibit throughout this great land. We'll continue to make good pictures, you can count on that."

There was a warm round of applause. After a number of speeches, the delegates fetched their bags and hopped into the motorcars that would return them to the train station.

During the 1926 convention, it was frequently mentioned among the salesmen and theater managers that, despite the uplifting frenzy of all the talk about sound pictures, the studio's output grew less distinguishable from the other studios year by year. It was therefore a little paradoxical that now, when Fox had assembled one of the best film distribution systems in the country, its films were lacking that certain magic. In fact, on the *New York Times* Ten Best Films in 1925, there wasn't a single Fox picture.

For both Fox Film and the industry, 1926 was a good year. The studio made some fine pictures including *The Johnstown Flood* with Janet Gaynor; *Three Bad Men* with George O'Brien, directed by John Ford; *What Price Glory* with Edmund Lowe, Victor McLaglen and Dolores Del Rio; seven Tom Mix pictures; and, of course, Buck Jones films.

Few seemed willing to recognize that Tom Mix was still riding a crest of popularity. In fact, the Quigley Publications poll of exhibitors chose Tom Mix as top male star for 1926, and Colleen Moore as top female star.

Things could get out of hand during the filming of an action picture. Raoul Walsh directed a battle scene for *What Price Glory*. The shoot was mostly done after dark and one night the police were ordered to stop the noisy explosions. When the cops arrived on the set, the police chief said, "Who's directing this picture?"

Walsh cleverly pointed to one of his many assistants and they carted him off in a paddy wagon. As soon as the cops went through the studio gate, Walsh started the shoot once more. He yelled, "Roll 'em!"

The third night things got a little more complicated. A short, stocky man came running toward the camera. He looked like he had just gotten out of bed, for he was wearing a bathrobe and slippers.

"What's a-going on here? Boom. A-boom boom. All a-night long."

There was no doubt in Walsh's mind that the man was Italian and, more importantly, very angry. Walsh, who because of his height hovered over the Italian, put his arm around him and said, "What seems to be the matter, sir?"

"I'm taking a bath, the ceiling come-a down on me. What's-a going to happen here? Who's a-going to pay?"

At that moment Walsh put his hand in his pocket and retrieved a piece of paper and a pencil. "Give me your name and address and we'll take care of it."

Fox Film paid several homeowners a total of $70,000 for damages and broken windows. Incidental property damage became another line item on the production-cost sheet.

As for *What Price Glory,* it turned into a major film for the studio, ranking number three on *The New York Times* Ten Best Films list. Theater managers were delighted. They could finally point with pride to the artistic quality of a Fox picture.

Because of battle scenes, W.F. thought the studio should demonstrate its sound-on-film process with a customized musical score. Earl Sponable and Ted Case added a musical track to the sound version of the film. The first public showing of Fox's sound-on-film system was on January 21, 1927, at the Sam H. Harris Theater in New York. The public heard songs by Raquel Meller as a prelude to the nondialogue picture.

There was wide disagreement on how fast the studios would convert to sound. It was now more a question of "when" rather than "if." Earl Sponable was a little upset that Fox wasn't moving quickly enough on

Edmund Lowe and Dolores del Rio in Fox Films' ***What Price Glory?*** **(1926)**

sound. He would later confess, "Fox with his Movietone could have been ahead of Vitaphone if Fox had let us go ahead with theater demonstrations."

The truth was, W.F. kept Sponable and Case doing tests of Gertrude Lawrence, Beatrice Lilly, Ben Bernie, Chic Sale and others. He was worried about the impact sound would have on the studio's players. As in the case of any vested player, there was a considerable investment at stake, and W.F. was in no hurry to put that investment in jeopardy.

The easiest transition from silents to talkies would be one where the industry marched in lock step, installing sound equipment in response to a carefully planned timetable while making room for the thinly financed theaters that chose to delay the conversion. During the conversion the industry would continue to produce silents to satisfy that part of the market. Unfortunately, that postulation in no case reflected the bitter rivalry that characterized the industry. Relatively insignificant even a year ago, sound-on-disc had mushroomed under the sponsorship of the Telephone Company and Warner Bros. until it was on the first page of every agenda in every executive suite from New York to Hollywood.

Even with the likely prospect of bankruptcy staring them in the face, the Warners decided to make a sound picture with dialogue and singing. In Manhattan, Sam Harris and Max Gordon had a very successful semi-musical called *The Jazz Singer* running in one of the theaters. Harry Warner saw the play and liked it, so he bought the screen rights for $50,000.

Nobody said anything, but Jack Warner knew the most sensible thing to do was contact George Jessel and offer him the same part he was playing on the stage, so he did.

Hung up about the Warners' penny-pinching reputation, Jessel gave him the runaround. "I want to think about it, Jack." After a short period of give-and-take, Jessel agreed to play the lead role for $30,000. He phoned Jack Warner in California. "You know, Jack, I read the scenario your brother gave me and you made some changes."

"What changes?"

"When we set up the original contract there was nothing in it about all the extra singing and talking you now want me to do."

"I guess I don't like your attitude. You want more money, right? How much?"

"I want ten grand more."

"You've got it. It's a deal, Georgie. Come on out and I'll give you a binding letter."

"The letter first, then I come out."

"Goddamnit, Georgie. I give you my word."

"That's not enough. Your brother Harry will never go for the deal, Jack."

"Don't talk to me like a child. I'm spending millions of dollars and I don't need Harry's okay for every single buck. If you want an extra ten grand, you've got it."

"No," Jessel said flatly.

"Okay, Georgie. If you can't take my word, let's forget the whole thing."

"All right, the deal's off."

Unfazed by the temporary setback, Jack Warner went to see Eddie Cantor perform at the Orpheum Theater in Los Angeles and asked him if he was interested in taking the role.

"I can sing, right, Jack?"

"You sure can, Eddie."

"And I can dance."

"Right."

"I've had a lot of experience, and I've been around a ghetto in my day."

"You can't miss, Eddie."

"True, Jack. But I won't do it."

"Oh, for Christ's sake! Why not?"

"Because there's only man in the world who can do it, and that's Jessel."

For Jack Warner, what he was hearing just served to remind him of how little influence the Warners had in Hollywood. He went back to the studio and put on his thinking cap. He wanted a young Jewish singer who could put tears in his voice. Who could sing it with a sigh, as if he were crying out to his God.

"Wait a minute," Jack told Sam. "What about Al Jolson?" "Go find him, Jack."

America's favorite singer-entertainer was playing in *Big Boy* for one of the Schubert companies when he was contacted by one of Warners' New York executives, Morrie Safier, who hit Jolson with the idea and asked him how much it was going to cost.

"I like the part and I want $75,000, one-third down in cold cash."

"I'll get back to you, Jolie."

He swallowed hard and told Jolson he had a deal. At that moment the Warner brothers would have been willing to pay $100,000 to get their picture made.

When he found out Jolson had gotten the part, a dispirited Jessel said, "He must of put money into it."

After Courtland Smith sent his man, Joy, to Switzerland to investigate some German patents brought to his attention by

F.A. Schroeder, W.F. personally bought the North American rights to a German sound-on-film system called Tri-Ergon. He paid $60,000 out of his own pocket because he believed the trend to sound-on-film was inevitable and he wanted to control the patents and not have to go through the onerous dealings the Warners had with the Telephone Company.

The first attempts at sound-on-film, made with the selenium cell, did not work. The successful process was the photoelectric cell, and the first technicians to use that cell in the reproduction of sound were three Germans named Engl, Vogt and Massolle. They had taken out their patent in Germany, March 3, 1919, and had made their application in the United States on April 4, 1921. Under the so-called Nolan Act, the title to their patent was dated from the moment of the filing in Germany. In 1919, the inventors of this Tri-Ergon process gave private demonstrations in Germany, and in September 1922 gave in Berlin the first public demonstration in the world of the use of the photoelectric cell in the making of talking motion pictures.

They brought their invention to the United States and William Fox bought the North American rights. This established the North American Tri-Ergon Company, of which he owned 90 percent of the stock.

The United States Patent Office refused to issue the patent for the photoelectric cell. American patent laws and practices had many peculiarities. A large corporation like the Telephone Company could claim all the patents in a certain field and denounce everyone else as a bootlegger, tie them up in a tangle of lawsuits and injunctions, and go ahead and levy tribute to the extent of tens and hundreds of millions of dollars. Then, after years of litigation, it would turn out that the great corporation never had any justification for its claims, but meanwhile the inventors were ruined, and perhaps dead and buried.

The elaborate production of *Sunrise* began on September 15, 1926. W.F. ceded complete creative control to Murnau. Rochus Gliese built the complex sets and two of the best cameramen in the business, Karl Struss and Charles Rosher, filmed the picture.

Talented Karl Struss was the son of a bonnet-wire manufacturer who had studied photography at Columbia University. He had gone to Hollywood in 1919 and had been hired by Cecil B. De Mille. Struss had been one of the leading cameramen in the filming of *Ben-Hur*. Fox was lucky to get him for *Sunrise*.

Sunrise starred George O'Brien and Janet Gaynor; Hugo Riesenfeld created the synchronized musical score. Murnau finished shooting in February 1927.

Because of countless outdoor scenes with movement, Charles Rosher encountered a great degree of difficulty in shooting the film. For some scenes, such as the swamp sequence, the camera went in a complete circle, creating enormous lighting problems. Rosher built a railway line in the roof and suspended a little platform from it, which could be raised or lowered by motors. His friend and associate, Karl Struss, operated the camera on this scene. It was a big undertaking; practically every shot was on the move.

By the time the picture was finished, everyone on the set was saying Fox had a winner. W.F. thought so, too.

On the MGM lot, Thalberg produced another Garbo-Gilbert romance called *Flesh and the Devil.*

"Never before has John Gilbert been so intense in his portrayal of a man in love," reported the New York *Herald Tribune.*

The Garbo-Gilbert offscreen romance was in full bloom and that had Mayer worried. She was shacking up with Gilbert in his Beverly Hills estate, and rumors of an impending marriage filled the gossip columns. One columnist even suggested that Garbo had gone to some little Mexican town quite prepared to marry Gilbert, but at the last moment had gotten cold feet and had run away and hid until the train arrived to carry her back to Hollywood. Another version of the story had Garbo succumbing to Gilbert's pleading, but when she had gotten as far as the Santa Ana marriage bureau, she'd turned and fled, leaving Gilbert alone and distraught.

When publicly questioned on her romantic interest in Gilbert, Garbo said, "It is only a friendship; nothing more. I am very happy in pictures with Mr. Gilbert. He inspires me. With him I do not act. I live. But that is not love."

Concerned, Mayer admonished Thalberg, "He's your friend, you handle him."

There was an unpleasant encounter in Mayer's office with Mayer grabbing John Gilbert by the lapel, yelling, "Why do you have to marry her? Why don't you just go on fucking her and forget about the wedding?"

Gilbert went on the warpath, losing complete control of his temper. He took Mayer by the neck and throttled him. Before anyone could break them up, Gilbert hurled the thickset Mayer across the room, with Mayer's glasses flying off his nose, shattering as they landed on the corner of a lamp table.

Eddie Mannix finally separated the combatants and shoved Gilbert into an adjacent room. Mayer screamed, "You're through! I'll destroy you if it costs me a million dollars!"

A confident-looking Gilbert retorted, "It will cost you a million—millions! I just signed a new contract with Nicholas Schenck!"

It galled Mayer to think "The General" had signed a deal with one of his leading actors without his knowledge, passing over him.

On the other hand, Mayer wasn't about to do battle with his own money. No matter what their differences were, Mayer would continue to put up with John Gilbert until his popularity took a nosedive.

"Let them gossip," Mayer said. "MGM has America's most romantic couple."

Although gossip about the Mayer-Gilbert rift spread around town like wildfire, it was something totally different that caught W.F.'s attention. Mayer was showing interest in sound, which brought him to the office of J. Roy Pomeroy, who labored at Zukor's studio and was working with a sound-on-film process under development by RCA. Mayer ordered a blending of image and speech in a specially produced version of *Flesh and the Devil* for his own examination. This surprise event threw Thalberg into a conniption because MGM had done very little work on sound and was ill prepared at the time. To salvage the test, Mayer was compelled to ask Zukor for permission to shoot two reels at Paramount.

Predictably, Warner Bros. lost $279,000 in the five months ending August 1926. Despite this setback, Harry Warner had his banker, Waddill Catchings, arrange for a loan of $4 million, which Harry used to buy first-run theaters in Seattle, Baltimore and Cleveland.

On October 27, *Don Juan* opened at Grauman's Egyptian Theater in Los Angeles, where a celebrity crowd gathered to see the film. The theater filled with Hollywood's greatest stars, including Charlie Chaplin, Pola Negri, Harry Carey and Greta Garbo. Samuel Goldwyn and Cecil B. De Mille were also in attendance.

The next issue of *Daily Variety* hailed the picture as a triumph with the headline, "Vitaphone Thrills L.A."

The big studios, Paramount, MGM, First National, Universal and Producers Distributing Corporation, were waiting to see where sound technology would eventually settle. There were too many options out there, none of which seemed cost efficient.

Fortunately, the public knew very little about talkies: The early pictures were shown primarily in New York to elite audiences, so there was little pressure to offer talkies in other parts of the nation. Moreover, the studios were not vocal with their plans or purposes in buying sound equipment.

But choices had to be made about supporting this or that sound technology, alliances had to be formed, and qualified people had to be committed to development for practical use. This was a different game—a high-powered game replete with uncertainty. Most disconcerting was the fact that AT&T, with all its financial power, was the driving force behind the industry change. It alone acquired the rights to the components of sound systems and it alone held the key patents on those components.

In response to the uncertainty in the market, a clandestine meeting of the industry's bosses was held at Carl Laemmle's Hollywood office. Seated around a large conference table were Jesse Lasky, Louis B. Mayer, Carl Laemmle and Tom Tally. At the head of the table, wearing his trademark dark-blue suit, sat Adolph Zukor.

Zukor sat on the edge of a stiff chair. "I say we don't license anything from Harry Warner."

"Let them develop sound, if they can. Then we'll see about it," Mayer remarked.

"I agree," Tally said. "Besides, we'd have to rebuild our studios. Do you know what that would cost?"

Zukor stared at Laemmle, who had little appetite for strife. "Carl, what do you think?"

"We have too big an investment in the silent picture, Adolph."

"The effect on the overseas market would be disastrous. Only a small part of the world speaks English," Zukor noted.

"Studios would have to be entirely rebuilt," Lasky said.

"That's what I just said," Tally cynically remarked.

As the recognized leader of the industry, Zukor stood up, puffed on his cigar, and said, "Let's get down to business. We're all businessmen here and we don't have to sign any legal papers to make this deal."

Mayer studied the man he both admired and loathed. He nodded affirmatively as Zukor's eyes met his.

"I say we refuse to license Vitaphone, we—"

Tally cut in. "To hell with them both, I say! To hell with them, Adolph!"

Lowering himself into his chair, Zukor concluded, "Gentlemen! It's settled then. None of us go into sound until we all decide to do it. Is it a deal?"

Zukor looked in the direction of Louis B. Mayer. "Louis B.?"

"Agreed."

"I'm in!" Tally shouted.

"Carl?"

"Universal will respect the agreement, Adolph."

"Good!"

That evening, they all returned to their offices knowing they had bought a temporary reprieve. Relief, and the idea that they had time to consider alternatives, calmed their nerves. They had opted to watch and wait. There was a reluctance to fully commit to any given system. There was plenty to do to meet the needs of theaters showing silent films.

Mayer immediately got on the phone and reported to Nicholas Schenck. "Thalberg believes sound will be a useful adjunct to technique, but won't replace the silent film."

"What do you think, Louis B.?"

WILLIAM FOX *presents*

THE BLUE EAGLE

A Fighting Drama of Adventure, Courage, Loyalty and Strength on the High Seas

WITH

· GEORGE O'BRIEN ·

· JANET GAYNOR · MARGARET LIVINGSTON · ROBERT EDESON · WILLIAM RUSSELL ·
· DAVID BUTLER · RALPH SIPPERLY *and* JERRY THE GIANT ·

from the Story The Lord's Referee by Gerald Beaumont, scenario by L.G. Rigby

JOHN FORD PRODUCTION

"I'm not so sure, Nick. This could be bigger than I first thought."

"Who's going to pay for the expense of equipping our theaters?"

That thought left Mayer feeling clammy and cold. A heavy investment in sound equipment would reduce MGM's bottom line and his profit sharing under the agreement. Not a pleasant thought at all.

Toward the end of the year, Adolph Zukor inaugurated his New York showplace skyscraper headquarters, between 43rd and 44th Streets, a 40-story building with eight setbacks topped by a four-sided clock and a 20-foot illuminated globe signifying world conquest by the motion picture. The marquee and five-story glass arch glowed over the lobby entrance like a brilliant jewel. There was a 4,000-seat auditorium for Paramount's customers, and more than a half a million dollars went into the Italian marble trimming for the grand lobby.

The Paramount Theater was situated where the Putnam Building and the Westover Court Apartments—both Astor properties—formerly had stood on Broadway. In 1919, the Astors had sold the property for $3,845,000.

W.F. and Winfield Sheehan were there for the customary grand opening festivities and paraded around the premises visiting the various rooms—the College Room, the Chinoiserie, the Venetian Room, Peacock Alley and several others.

In Hollywood, Zukor and Lasky razed most of the old studio and spent $1 million for a 26-acre lot owned by United Studios on Marathon Street.

In 1926, 740 pictures were released and exhibited in 19,500 theaters. Average weekly attendance was 50 million.

The scorecard for the major studios' earnings read as follows:

Fox Film	$3,124,000
Fox Theaters	$ 454,000
Loew's	$6,548,244
Paramount	$5,600,815
Warners	-$1,337,826

The top 10 films as reported by the *New York Times* were *Variety, Beau Geste, What Price Glory, Potemkin, The Grand Duchess and the Waiter, The Black Pirate, Old Ironsides, Moana, La Boheme* and *So This Is Paris.*

CHAPTER 19
1927

The Radio Corporation of America, RCA, worked on a sound-on-film system much like Movietone. The system, called Photophone, previewed in February 1927 at the Rivoli Theater in New York in front of a special invitation-only audience. Two reels of MGM's *Flesh and the Devil* were accompanied by a Photophone recording of the Capitol Theater orchestra. This was the same picture that featured MGM's amorous couple, Greta Garbo and John Gilbert. Three shorts showcased the Van Curler Hotel Orchestra of Schenectady, an unknown baritone and a quartet of singers who were General Electric employees.

David Sarnoff, RCA's general manager, convinced his superiors at General Electric—the company that controlled RCA—that RCA should market their system to large movie producers, Paramount and Loew's, and forget about Fox's Movietone.

Sarnoff met W.F. at a private lunch at Fox's 10th Avenue headquarters and W.F. asked him bluntly whether he wanted to combine forces to develop and exploit sound-on-film technology.

"Let me think about it."

Much to W.F.'s displeasure, Sarnoff never got back to him. He fully understood Sarnoff was constrained by another large corporation, General Electric, and probably couldn't approve an investment over $1,000 under his own signature. W.F. decided to call off any further idea of negotiating with RCA.

Unable to arouse any interest among the major studios, Sarnoff purchased a small studio called FBO and a larger concern, the Keith-Albee-Orpheum Theater circuit, and formed R.K.O. Pictures, largely financed by Rockefeller money.

While W.F. closely watched the development of sound, Fox Film announced that $15 million would be expended in the year's program of Fox pictures. April would be the start of Fox's fiscal year and the studio estimated it already had over $5 million worth of finished pictures in the can. The studio's program included Murnau's *Sunrise*, Frank Borzage's *Seventh Heaven* and a new version of *Carmen*, produced by Raoul Walsh. Fox had no alternative but to continue its production of silent films, since theater audiences were expecting a frequent change in program in their local theaters.

Early in 1927, Jack Warner began construction on new stages for making sound pictures. He summoned one of his writers, Darryl F. Zanuck, and told him he would be the studio's executive producer with an increase in salary from $125 to $5,000 a week.

On the way out of Jack Warner's office, an inquisitive old doorman whispered to Zanuck that the incumbent production boss had just been let go, and wondered who would get the job.

An enthusiastic Zanuck replied, "Me."

The *New York Times*—February 21, 1927—reported that there were five life insurance policies that were each $4 million or more. Rodman Wanamaker and William Fox headed the list. W.F. was insured for $6 million.

The son of a kosher butcher, Alfred Cleveland Blumenthal, played an important role in the expansion of Fox Theaters. Whenever W.F. was on the coast, he used to see signs all over Los Angeles: "This property for sale. Apply to A.C. Blumenthal." Those who applied met a little man well under five feet, quite pale and feminine in appearance; he was close to 50, but could have been taken for 30. He was sharp as a steel trap and a good negotiator. If W.F. had been casting for the stereotypic unscrupulous real estate agent, he would have cast Blumenthal for the part. He looked like what he was, a sophisticated crook.

The chipmonkish Blumenthal was described as "a pint-sized financier in a suit of June-bug green, as restless as a Mexican jumping bean—and not much bigger."

Blumenthal came to New York and offered his services to Fox. The market in Los Angeles was in a deep slump and W.F. could tell he needed money. He offered W.F. a lease on a piece of land where Fox eventually built the Los Angeles Theater.

After they finished discussing the available land sites in California, they formed a company called Foxthal, with Blumenthal owning 50 percent. The company was to get the commissions that Blumenthal might earn in purchasing theaters or stocks of theatrical corporations. In fact, what this meant was that Blumenthal would act as an agent, getting half the commissions himself and giving Fox Theaters the other half.

As a result of their intimate business relationship, W.F. took a liking to him and Blumy became part of the Fox family, addressing Eve as Mother. While still in New York, the Foxes invited Blumy to dine with the family at the Marguery and, on one occasion, he joined them at Woodmere for a Sunday outing. W.F. took a fancy to him because of his street savvy, an attribute that he deeply appreciated in a businessman. But there was another side to him he disliked, and that was his proclivity for cooking up side deals for his personal benefit. W.F. warned him again and again that he was to operate aboveboard, for Fox Theaters was a public company.

Many good deals were put in Blumy's hands, and everything went well except that Blumy had a way of finding an excuse to hold out on commissions.

Somehow Blumy got wind of the fact that Herbert Lubin—no relation to Sigmund Lubin—was in financial trouble. He and his partner, Arthur H. Sawyer, had acquired a choice piece of land for $3 million and were building a theater they called the Roxy, the nickname of their showman partner, S.L. Rothapfel. The site formerly consisted of old streetcar barns that used to occupy most of the property east of 7th Avenue on 50th Street.

Blumy convinced W.F. he should call on Lubin before Zukor or Marcus Loew put a bid in on the property. It was rumored that the construction of the Roxy resulted in an overrun of $2,500,000 and Herbert Lubin was out of cash. Blumy was sure that Lubin could not raise that amount of money from the existing stockholders of the Roxy.

It was a nice day and W.F. found himself panning the outside of the theater, an exuberant mix of Renaissance, Gothic, and Moorish styles of architecture, designed by W.W. Ahlschlager.

Inside the building workmen were putting the finishing touches on the interior. A long corridor terminated in a large rotunda surrounded by green faux marble columns. Blumy and W.F. walked through the lobby, stopping, touching, examining the workmanship, which was all first class. This was to be the cathedral of the motion picture. It boasted six imperial boxes, 6,214 red plush seats monogrammed with an R, the largest oval rug in the world, bronze statues, oil paintings, a musician's gallery to serenade waiting patrons, a medical clinic, bowling alleys and three golden organ consoles.

Ahlschlager boasted of a power plant capable of lighting a city of quarter million inhabitants. The auditorium was cavernous; Ahlschlager had attempted to subdue the feeling of openness by varying the size of the architectural design in different parts of the facility.

Ahlschlager told W.F., "Each thousand is seated in its own environment, with the surrounding architecture brought down to the scale of the particular thousand. The proscenium enframement was so designed as to tie all these divisions into one architectural fantasy."

In tribute to his pomposity, Rothapfel's private box was perched above the rear of the balcony and looked as if it had been constructed for royalty. W.F. quickly surmised he'd be dealing with a degree of arrogance even greater than what he'd become accustomed to among the Hollywood types.

From a distance, W.F. could see a small man in shirtsleeves stepping up to greet him. Blumy said, "W.F., this is Herbert Lubin."

"I'm pleased to meet you, Mr. Lubin."

It was as though the man were in a trance. He didn't respond. W.F. noticed a delicate line of perspiration on his upper lip, which seemed to tremor a little.

"What seems to be the problem, Mr. Lubin?"

"I understand you're in the market for theaters, Mr. Fox."

"You're telling me the Roxy is for sale?"

"I'm afraid that's the case, Mr. Fox."

"Please, Mr. Lubin, come to my office on 10th Avenue. I'm sure we can reach an accommodation. What do you think, Blumy?"

It was time to turn Blumy's highly skilled bargaining talent to W.F.'s own good use. Blumy said, "Of course, W.F. Of course we can accommodate Mr. Lubin."

It was quite apparent that Lubin was extremely tense, and W.F. decided this wasn't the time or place to talk about money. Besides, that was Blumy's job, to determine a negotiating range acceptable to both parties.

"Until tomorrow, Mr. Fox."

"We'll expect you, Mr. Lubin."

Turning, Herbert Lubin slowly walked off.

Lubin entered W.F.'s office accompanied by an expensively clad man that he surmised was Lubin's lawyer. They drank hot tea, exchanged small talk and then got down to business.

The total cost of the site was $10 million, Lubin explained, and the Roxy was a stock company with 125,000 shares of class A stock and 350,000 common shares. Investment bankers and brokers White, Weld, who were located on the 33rd floor of number 40 Wall Street, held 176,000 common shares.

The theater had a large, sprawling space, an overbuilt lobby, a murderous debt and an appetite for consuming cash that was difficult to satisfy. Projected operating income was not robust, and its interest coverage was forecast to be two to one, i.e., two dollars in free cash flow for every dollar of interest owed to the banks.

The Roxy

This left little wiggle room. W.F. knew he would have to turn Eisele loose to work up better pro forma projections through a reduction of fixed costs. After a contentious period of negotiation, Blumy struck a satisfactory deal for Fox Theaters.

W.F. informed Jack Leo they'd need broader financing to handle the Roxy purchase and other properties they were building. A valuation was placed on the company. Fox Theaters proposed acquiring Lubin's stock plus a part of that held by White, Weld and Company to ensure Fox Theaters' control of the Roxy. Part of the purchase price would be paid in cash, but the bulk was to be financed through mortgages on the property and building.

It had come to the point where W.F. would have to use the hard assets of Fox Theaters as collateral for expansion. Rogers and Jack Leo worked feverishly on the details of the transaction and Rogers said he'd talk to Ernest Niver as soon as possible.

"Saul, I suggest we travel to Chicago to discuss all of our financing with Harold Stuart."

"I'll call them right away, W.F."

When all was said and done, the total outlay for the Roxy came to $12 million. The Roxy had current obligations of $2 million and Fox Theaters financed part of the purchase through S.W. Straus, who sold first and second mortgages totaling $6,750,000. Saul Rogers recommended a bridge loan until W.F. could meet with Halsey, Stuart for more permanent financing.

Acquisition of the Roxy gave Fox Film a Broadway playhouse for first-run showings, a feat that the studio had been unable to achieve at respectable costs. Zukor controlled the Paramount, Rialto and Rivoli. The Strand was tied to First National. MGM films had their first-run showings at the Capitol. Warner Bros. exhibited their pictures at their own theater.

The possibilities of theater expansion marched through W.F.'s head. He'd taken the first big step in a long journey to catch up with Adolph Zukor. For the moment he was encouraged; within a relatively short time, Fox Theaters had made two excellent acquisitions.

Jack Leo informed W.F. the press was demanding an interview; W.F. instructed him to arrange for the affair on the premises of the Roxy, and to be sure that his highness, S.L. Rothapfel, attended.

When the papers were signed, W.F. discovered Roxy was small potatoes even though his name adorned the marquee. Initially, Rothapfel seemed a little obstinate, but W.F. convinced him Fox would build a Roxy chain one day, and that seemed to soothe his rather ample ego.

Before an afternoon matinee, the press assembled below the Roxy's rotunda and W.F. fielded questions.

"What did you pay for the Roxy, Mr. Fox?"

"Many millions. Too many to count."

"How does it feel to own the world's largest theater?"

"Wonderful. When I bought my first theater in Brooklyn I remember that it had a second-hand piano for which I paid $30 and which had tones like a tin pan. Compare it with the magnificent organ in the Roxy Theater. To me the difference between that little old second-hand piano and the great new organ represents the forward march of the motion picture and shows what it was then and what it means to the world today."

"How about Mr. Rothapfel?"

"Roxy will continue his personal direction and supervision of the Roxy Theater in New York and will also exercise similar jurisdiction over the chain of enormous theaters to be built in New York and elsewhere by the Roxy Circuit. This entire chain of theaters will benefit through management by a man who has directed many of the large and important theaters of New York, and who has become a world figure through his radio broadcasting and his comprehensive use of the motion picture in connection with music and ballet presentations. All of the theaters will be designed by Walter W. Ahlschlager, architect of the Roxy Theater."

W.F. made a facial gesture beckoning Roxy to say something and he did.

"Hello, everybody!"

Everyone laughed. Roxy was well liked by the press and well known to millions because of his weekly radio program, which had gone off the air in 1925 after a three-year run. He had become very popular as a radio announcer and used his fame to raise money for building what he thought would be the largest and finest theater in the world.

Roxy stepped up to the microphone. "This affiliation brings to us the forceful personality of William Fox, one of the pioneers of the industry. I have known Mr. Fox intimately for 15 years and have admired his great fearlessness in building his corporation to rank as one of the great forces in the motion picture industry. He seeks an ideal which he sees exemplified in the theater we have the honor to direct."

W.F. hadn't noticed, but sometime during the press conference Herbert Lubin had worked his way through the crowd, up to the microphones.

One of the reporters saw him and fired a question. "Do you agree with that assessment, Mr. Lubin?"

A great weight lifted off his shoulders, Lubin smiled for the first time since W.F. had met him. "This affiliation is an ideal one for all concerned, as William Fox will furnish the Roxy Theater with superb attractions and Roxy will give them a most sumptuous presentation."

After closing the conference, W.F. said his goodbyes to Lubin and told Roxy he wanted to meet with him first thing in the morning to go over Fox policy with him. Roxy was seething inside, he could tell, and he immediately decided to keep an office in the Roxy Theater to keep his eye on things.

The Roxy opened March 11, 1927, just 10 days before W.F. finalized the purchase of the theater. Grauman's Chinese Theater opened on May 18, 1927, with the premiere of Cecil B. De Mille's *King of Kings.*

One of the early lessons W.F. learned about any enterprise the company acquired was that one could never really trust the guy one bought out, particularly if he were staying on for nothing more than a salary, because he had as much interest in seeing one fail as seeing one succeed. It was always better, W.F. found out, to immediately put in your own people to quickly establish authority and find out where all the skeletons were buried.

Over time, W.F. made the mistake of giving Roxy too much power, and when things got rough for W.F., Roxy quickly aligned himself with W.F.'s enemies. Having made that same mistake in a number of deals, W.F. would pay the price for his lack of judgment.

W.F. discovered that Rothapfel was equipping the theater with Vitaphone, which he agreed was the thing to do, since at the time it was the only commercially available sound system. As talkies became the norm rather than the exception, W.F. got into

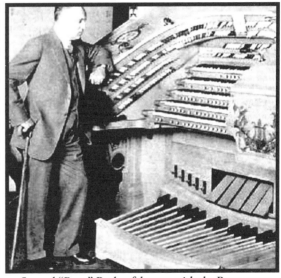

Samuel "Roxy" Rothapfel poses with the Roxy organ.

tremendous battles with Rothapfel, who kept insisting the film program interfered with the stage shows he most enjoyed planning. It got to the point where W.F. didn't want to talk with him any more, so he designated Glendon Allvine, Fox's PR man, to carry messages to Rothapfel.

In spite of frequent disagreements, W.F. came to admire Roxy's uncanny ability to organize a performance as no other person could in the industry. The motion picture was about one hour of a two-hour performance. The other hour was devoted to an overture by 110 of the finest musical artists, probably second only to those who appeared in Carnegie Hall. Then there was a ballet of 50 or 75 ballet dancers such as one would see at the Metropolitan Opera House, and a male chorus of about 60 voices. The function closed with a spectacular number in which more than 200 people were onstage at one time.

W.F. constantly warned Roxy that, although he had this stupendous program in addition to the motion picture, if the motion picture were not any good, that part of the program was spoiled and the show could not be considered a success.

"Pictures are your business, W.F. My job is to entertain our customers. If that means showing a competitor's picture, then that's what we'll have to do."

Movietone filmed Lindbergh's takeoff for Paris in 1927.

In May, Fox Film shot a piece of newsreel of Charles Lindbergh taking off for Paris; this played well for audiences, even if the sound was a little thin. In those days, there was no scripted narration. The only sounds were the natural sounds of Lindbergh, the aircraft and his ground crew.

Lindbergh mounted into the pilot's cabin, leaned out, waved, shouted a few last commands and turned a starter switch. The engine growled. The propeller turned a few stiff revolutions, the engine firing in a plume of smoke, breaking into a roar. Lindbergh guided the plane to the far end of the field and turned it around into the wind. He opened the throttle, gathering speed, flashing past awestruck spectators. At the end of 1,000 feet her wheels lifted; the Spirit of St. Louis was airborne.

Lindbergh was followed by a P. & A. news plane, which turned back when he was 100 miles at sea. Lindbergh's happy face was splattered across front pages all over America.

On the West Coast, Mayer and Thalberg were presenting MGM's most romantic couple to the Hollywood press.

The gathering was held on the rambling lawn of the Ambassador Hotel. To one side of John Gilbert stood the slight Irving Thalberg, well-appointed in a dark blue suit with a pleasing grin on his young, unlined face. Behind the lectern was positioned the stone-faced Louis B. Mayer, and next to him stood the glamorous Greta Garbo who—in awe of the admiration being bestowed upon her—looked a little nervous.

"Ladies and gentlemen! Let me introduce Greta Garbo and Jack Gilbert, MGM's most romantic couple," Mayer said.

The applause was fervent and resonated across the grounds. Most of the guests who were lodged at the hotel were now down on the lawn, taking in Hollywood and all its grandeur.

A film camera purred and bulbs flashed in true Hollywood fashion.

Stuffed-shirt Mayer looked over at a fidgety Thalberg and said, "Irving, please say a few words."

At first, Thalberg seemed a little loath to speak. A man of quiet determination, he detested personal appearances of any kind. In a business where most were arrogantly boastful, Thalberg was reputedly shy.

A reporter got in the way and Mayer shouted, "Step back! You're in front of the camera!"

In response to Mayer's command, the reporter moved back and Thalberg shuffled up behind the microphone. Flashbulbs exploded and Thalberg covered his eyes.

"We have great things planned for Garbo and Gilbert at MGM. But let Miss Garbo tell you, in her own words."

Garbo, a little wooden-faced, wearing oversized sunglasses and huge rings on her fingers, stepped up to the microphone and said, "Yacky and I will make other pictures together, won't we, Yacky?"

The reporters chuckled at her strange accent and comportment and Gilbert wrapped his arm around her waist, trying to comfort her while flashing a toothy smile for the cameras.

"Miss Garbo, your adoring public would like to know the real you."

"Ach!"

"What is your real opinion of American men?"

"Scrow!"

"What is your idea of the relative importance of love in a man's life and a woman's life?"

"I go home now."

To Mayer's delight, Gilbert and Garbo made *Love* and *A Woman of Affairs* and picked up where Fairbanks and Pickford had left off. America wanted and needed a romantic couple, and MGM was determined to give it to them.

Irving Thalberg married Norma Shearer on August 17, 1927, at 9401 Sunset Boulevard, a mansion Thalberg had rented from Pauline Frederick. For the ceremony, Cedric Gibbons constructed a flower-strewn arbor and Hollywood's most famous Rabbi, Edgar Magnin, officiated.

Irene and Edith Mayer were bridesmaids and Louis B. Mayer was best man. For the occasion, Thalberg's mother, Henrietta, wore a black velvet dress adorned with orchids. During the dinner the bride's brother, Douglas Shearer, a radio engineer, said, "Talking pictures are the coming thing."

Buried in their Auburn, New York laboratory, Case and Sponable labored diligently to perfect sound-on-film. But the one drawback of Fox's Movietone system was its speakers. The sound was weak. W.F. realized that he was compelled to make a deal with the mighty Telephone Company to obtain superior amplifiers developed by their Bell Labs. Their speakers were of the horn type and could be directed toward the most acoustically friendly areas of a theater, providing the audience with superior quality. For that, the Telephone Company insisted that Fox license them their Movietone process. Fox Film didn't have the resources or the technology to move any faster. The Telephone Company had W.F. against the wall and now they wanted the fruits of Case's work, all $6 million worth.

John Otterson called W.F. and told him things were afoot. He insinuated that the Telephone Company was considering licensing everyone in the industry with Vitaphone and "Why not throw in Movietone and let the public decide?"

As much as he wanted to go on alone, W.F. wasn't prepared to isolate himself from his competitors, who would surely jump at making deals with the Telephone Company if Warner Bros. were put back on equal footing. W.F. gave Otterson his 101 reasons why sound-on-disc was wrong. "Let the market decide, Bill."

The deal was straightforward. Otterson said the Fox Companies were to be licensed to make moving pictures on the same terms as all the other producers, but Fox was to receive the exclusive right to make sound newsreels. W.F.'s reward for all of Fox's work on sound-on-film and turning it over to the Telephone Company was that Fox was to have an exclusive newsreel license.

AT&T's sound amplification products required specialized manufacturing facilities and the use of patented know-how. Fox Film had neither. W.F. had run into a stone wall.

It was Sunday and W.F. decided to spend time with the family at Woodmere. That evening, after the family had enjoyed dinner together, W.F. invited Eve to take a stroll with him along the shoreline. There was a chilly wind and he wore a heavy jacket.

Eve wore a short coat and had buttoned it up to her chin.

In the busy life they led it was the only moment of the week in which he could be alone with her. They liked to discuss business matters while they walked.

"Otterson wants our Movietone process in exchange for their sound equipment."

"How much have we invested in Movietone?"

"$6 million."

Behind him, he could hear waves crashing up against the rocks. Off in the distance boats lay in their slips, from motor craft to various-sized yachts.

"What are they really after, Bill?"

"The Telephone Company wants to control sound technology, Vitaphone, Movietone and Otterson wants those German patents I bought."

The wind whipped up and he could see that Eve was cold. She stopped, as if he had touched a nerve. "Don't give them the Tri-Ergon patents! Those belong to us!"

"Are you sure, Eve?"

"Keep Tri-Ergon and license Movietone, Bill. We must have those speakers."

"You're right."

"When will you see Otterson?"

"I'll call him first thing tomorrow."

Although W.F. agreed to the Telephone Company's onerous conditions, Otterson put him off because he said he had to tidy up a few remaining details. It boiled down to him putting the muscle on Harry Warner, telling him the Warners were in default of the exclusive agreement, particularly with regarding the number of units Harry Warner had agreed to install in theaters.

Harry Warner was no dummy, and he quickly realized he was no match for the Telephone Company. The first thing he did was call his financial backer, Waddill Catchings, and ask for his sage advice. Catchings and Warner walked through all the possibilities and arrived at the same conclusion. The artistic quality of sound films would determine which studio would dominate the business, not the control of the underlying technology, since by its very nature the exhibitors would be forced to convert to sound and would only do so if the film producers provided an extensive catalogue of sound product.

Following an all-night session with his legal counsel, Harry Warner told Catchings he would exact a decent price for rescinding his arrangement with Electrical Research Products, and his number came to $2 million, with which Catchings agreed.

In consideration for the Telephone Company not taking Warner Bros. to court for breach of contract, Otterson negotiated a more favorable settlement of $1,300,000. With the exchange of a check for a signature, Warner Bros. gave up their exclusive license to sound-on-disc technology, and Otterson was now free to negotiate with every studio individually.

Elated at his achievement, Otterson phoned W.F. and advised him that a technical group from Bell Labs would be visiting the Fox Case laboratory and to please make available both Case and Sponable. He insisted that both the Case patents and Tri-Ergon patents were utterly worthless, but once they'd seen what Case had developed, Otterson had to admit that Case and his people had really made sound-on-film, and the telephone people now would learn to do the same.

Later in the week, W.F. was informed that the Telephone Company had reconsidered the promises made to the Fox companies, and found that they couldn't be carried out because it wouldn't be proper for the Telephone Company to show preference.

But they would in the near future find a way to compensate the Fox companies for the time, effort, money and energy that were expended. Of course, it was obvious that was not the reason they were going to violate the promises to Fox. The reason was that the other producers were able to receive a license from RCA, which had the identical system as Movietone, and had a half interest in those patents, so when the Telephone Company began competing for motion picture producers to become their licensees, they had to give them what RCA was willing to give them. It was clear, therefore, that their promises were to be broken.

CHAPTER 20

Jack Leo, Saul Rogers and W.F. boarded the Limited to Chicago to meet with Harold Stuart of the investment banking house of Halsey, Stuart. Ernest Niver, manager of their New York branch, had set up the meeting. During the trip, Rogers impressed W.F. with his intimate knowledge of the Chicago financial center. Continental Illinois Bank & Trust was the biggest Chicago bank and the fourth largest in the nation after Chase, National City and Guaranty Trust.

"Saul, what do we know about these people?"

"I called Harold Foreman, W.F." W.F. knew Foreman. He was the biggest stockholder of the Foreman-State National Bank, the last large Jewish bank in Chicago. Fox Film and Fox Theaters did a lot of their business there.

"What did Foreman have to say?"

"He vouches for Harold Stuart. He said with Insull behind the firm there was nothing much to worry about."

For the rest of the trip, Rogers briefed W.F. and Jack Leo on Harold Leonard Stuart.

Harold Leonard Stuart was born in Providence, Rhode Island and was educated at the University School for Boys of Brown University and at Lewis Institute in Chicago. He entered the investment banking business in 1901, working for N.W. Harris. A former Harris employee, Noah W. Halsey, established his own bank in New York. Stuart was manager of its Chicago office.

Halsey became an important municipal bond house and hired a staff of full-time bond salesmen. It was one of the first investment bankers to use "vigorous information" advertisements to facilitate bond selling.

The ambitious Stuart became president of the firm when banker Noah Halsey died in 1911. Now a white-haired banker of 46, he was proud of his firm's vast clientele. Quick-witted, shrewd, outspoken and genial, Stuart seemed the typical Chicago businessman. On LaSalle Street, Halsey, Stuart was considered a conservative and a well-established banking house, the most radical policy of which had been the introduction of radio advertising. Its most noticeable connection was with the utility interests of Samuel Insull. Harry Stuart and Insull were close friends who met often at the exclusive Chicago Club and traveled abroad together.

Rogers looked down at a piece of paper where he'd written copious notes. "And there's Insull, W.F."

"You already mentioned that."

"I guess I did."

The Halsey, Stuart office was situated on the southeast corner of La Salle and Adam streets, opposite the Home Insurance Building in the Rookery, which was located in the heart of Chicago's bustling financial district. The Rookery lobby was famous for Frank Lloyd Wright's work, which featured a center court at the bottom of a large interior space that brought light and air to all the offices not facing the street.

Into the flower-bedecked offices of Halsey, Stuart stepped the Fox executives.

Niver was there to greet them and escort them into the boardroom, one of the most elaborate built in Chicago within the last few years. Sunlight streamed through large windows on 30 Chippendale chairs and a long, mahogany table that dominated the room.

Sitting at the head of the table was Harold L. Stuart, who would soon become "Harry" to W.F. He was an upright, elegant-looking, clean-shaven man who took an intense interest in everything that went on around him, so it was natural that he should be interested in Fox Film. Outwardly he carried all the signs of the well-to-do investment banker: nice clothes, a perennial carnation and a quiet correctness meant to please.

Next to him sat his brother and confidant, Charles Stuart. There was a family resemblance that was apparent to everyone. The smell of fresh coffee permeated the room. Harry Stuart lit a cigarette.

Since W.F. was the client, he initiated the meeting. "Gentlemen, Mr. Niver was kind enough to call upon me offering the services of your banking house to the Fox organization."

Stamping out his cigarette, Harry Stuart said, "We're happy you have decided to do business with us, Mr. Fox. Give me some idea of what you require."

"Our immediate funding requirement is to both build and purchase theaters. I don't need to tell you of the importance of controlling first-run theaters to exhibit our studio products."

Harry Stuart glanced down at a piece of typed paper and said, "I understand you've purchased the Roxy."

"Yes, we did. We're also building in Detroit and St. Louis, and we have to refinance the Roxy purchase. Have you examined our financial statements, Mr. Stuart?"

"Ernest?"

It became apparent that Niver had gone over every number with a fine-tooth comb and was quite prepared to address any side issue. He had a well-deserved reputation for being thorough.

"Yes, we have, Mr. Fox. Halsey, Stuart will float the bonds for Detroit and St. Louis, and we believe we can raise several million dollars collateralized by the Fox Film building on 10th Avenue and your studio properties in California. We'd also be willing to take first and second mortgages against the Roxy Theater."

W.F. looked at Jack Leo and then Saul Rogers, who both nodded.

Rogers asked, "Will you draft the proper agreements, Mr. Niver?"

"I'll send you a first draft within two days, Mr. Rogers."

"I'm sure we'll be able to satisfy your every need, Mr. Fox," Harry Stuart said. "Halsey, Stuart, you'll find, will be responsive to the growth needs of Fox Films."

They rose and shook hands; Harry Stuart put his arm around W.F.'s shoulder and told him he was very pleased to have the Fox companies on his client list.

"I'm in a hurry, Harry."

"I can appreciate that, Bill. You can be sure we'll work as fast as we can."

As things developed, W.F.'s brief encounter with Harold Stuart would be one of his more productive moments, for there soon followed an avalanche of legal documents to be signed that led to filling Fox's coffers with much-needed cash.

Ever alert for meaningful relationships designed to further his career, Mayer smartly inserted himself into the political scene, a policy that W.F. was very wary of implementing because there was always a 50-50 chance of being wrong.

Back in 1924, Herbert Hoover had been Secretary of Commerce and thought about bigger things. Through Ida Koverman, a former secretary to Hoover when he'd been a self-employed engineer, Mayer had gotten to know Hoover quite intimately, almost as a friend. Mayer had campaigned actively for the Republican ticket and asked Ida Koverman to be his secretary. Because of her continuing relationship with Hoover, Mayer had advanced rapidly in party councils.

It didn't hurt that Mayer also had a good relationship with William Randolph Hearst, and eventually accommodated Marion Davies—the sweet little actress who kept the fire burning in Hearst's otherwise frigid heart—on the MGM lot.

Having hired Koverman and having decided that Hoover would be the next President of the United States, Mayer began his usual fence building and became one of the original Hoover Republicans prior to Hoover's official candidacy for the presidency.

Mayer faced a mini-uprising from his most prominent leading lady, Greta Garbo. They were alone in his office, she standing by a window in a pose, and he seated behind his noble desk.

"Greta, haven't I done everything to make you happy here?"

"No."

"What more can I do?"

"Give me more money."

"Why? Think how much better off you are since Berlin. What kind of money were you making then? Was it anywhere near the $600 a week we pay you now?"

"You are paying Jack Gilbert $10,000 a week."

"I see what you mean. I agree with you. I will make a new arrangement. How much will make you happy?"

"$5,000 a week."

"I'll give you $2,500."

"I think I go home."

Mayer knew he couldn't convince her to settle for less. And MGM couldn't afford to lose her. Mayer caved and agreed to the $5,000.

In what was to be a continuing effort to form a commercially recognizable identity, Famous Players-Lasky changed its name to Paramount-Famous-Lasky. Then it became Paramount-Publix, taking into consideration the importance of Publix Theaters, which it had acquired.

Through the acquisition of the Balaban and Katz theater chain, Sam Katz, a flamboyant showman, came as part of the package. He turned the Publix chain into a profitable, well-run entity through decoration, refrigeration, well-trained ushers and, much like Roxy, good onstage performances. The Paramount-owned theater carried the Balaban and Katz friendly touch and was soon recognized as a comfortable place to spend an afternoon or evening for entertainment.

The second half of the duo, Barney Balaban, was a numbers man, a businessman who understood the fundamentals of making money in motion pictures.

Zukor paid $13 million for two thirds of Balaban and Katz, turning Barney Balaban into one of Paramount's largest stockholders. Along with his other strengths, Zukor had an excellent eye for management talent.

On September 5, tragedy struck the industry. At age 57, Marcus Loew was dead of heart disease.

Eve and W.F., accompanied by Mona and Belle, Winnie and his wife, Kay, and Jack and Rose Leo, attended the services held on his 46-acre Long Island estate.

The Fox family was returning to Pembroke for this solemn occasion. More than 5,000 mourners joined them for the obsequies at Glen Cove. W.F. and Eve Fox extended their condolences to Caroline Loew. She was a gracious lady, though obviously distressed.

Amidst quiet murmuring, the Fox contingent followed a long line of mourners into the marble reception hall where Loew's slight body, looking like a wax figure, lay in his coffin surrounded by floral tributes. Although Loew was an Orthodox Jew, the services were Reform and mourners marched past the open coffin to pay tribute.

Off in the distance, W.F. saw Adolph and Lottie Zukor, Carl Laemmle, Rosabelle Laemmle, Nicholas Schenck and his wife Pansy, Harry Warner and Rea, Abe Warner and Bessie, Tom Tally and his wife, Harry and Roy Aitken, Will Hays and his wife, and many other dignitaries. Because of inclement

Marcus Lowe

weather, neither Louis B. Mayer nor Joseph Schenck had been able to charter a plane to fly them to the funeral.

A Rabbi paid kind tribute to Marcus Loew. "To know Marcus Loew was to love him. He was a man without an enemy."

Ten days after the death of Marcus Loew, Nicholas Schenck was named president of Loew's Incorporated and MGM. For those around the New York office, it was rumored that the notice of Schenck's ascension was quite distressing for Louis B. Mayer. It was understandable, since Mayer had lost a friend and supporter with the passing of Marcus Loew.

After shivah, Jack Leo and W.F. made their way to the State Theater at Broadway and 45th Street to meet with Nicholas Schenck. Designed by Lamb, the theater had a capacity of 3,400. Through the base of the Loew Building was a small office tower that housed Loew's sparse headquarters. They were shown into a modestly decorated meeting room where a portrait of Marcus Loew hung over them.

No more than a few minutes had elapsed when Nicholas Schenck came in and shook their hands. He was a big-headed man addicted to cigarettes, had a receding hairline and wore glasses. Though a man of common tastes, Schenck was in no sense just a high-salaried employee, for it was Schenck who had succeeded in converting a regional theater chain into a national force within the industry. He ran the business as if it were his own. To get an idea of what he had accomplished, one had to examine Loew's financial statements closely. The truth was that Nicholas Schenck had created great wealth for the Marcus Loew family, probably in the range of $50 to $60 million.

Schenck had built an organization to Marcus Loew's liking. Its theaters housed the gaudiest entertainments. He had acquired the "Mayer group," and it was clear from the beginning that the executive office would have the last word at MGM. But Thalberg required little supervision. It was Mayer that Schenck was leery about. Eddie Mannix once told Thalberg, "You're the only producer in Hollywood who never has interference from his home office."

"I'm the only producer in Hollywood who doesn't need any."

Nicholas Schenck began his career as an entrepreneur. He and his brother Joseph ran an amusement park at Fort George in upstate New York, and later acquired the Palisades Amusement Park in Ft. Lee, New Jersey, where they became associates with Marcus Loew. Loew gave them good steers on other amusement investments.

Schenck played the horses and kept a speedboat, which he used to commute between Manhattan and his large estate next to Walter Chrysler's at Great Neck.

The Loew's team consisted of Leopold Friedman, secretary, David Bernstein, vice president and treasurer, Charles C. Moskowitz, who managed some of the theaters, Robert Rubin, Mayer's ambassador in the East and general counsel, Joseph Vogel, also a theater manager, and Thomas Nelson Perkins.

"Once again, our deepest condolences, Nick."

"I will convey your respects to Mrs. Loew and the children, Bill."

"My business is pictures. I want to buy the Loew family shares."

Schenck was a calculating man who gave nothing away through useless gestures when he spoke. "So do Harry Warner and Adolph Zukor."

"Loew's and Fox can become a great studio. We have the technology, the studios. We can dominate the industry, Nick."

"The family will consider your kind offer, Bill. I'll get back to you."

W.F. knew Zukor wasn't in the running. "Marcus would turn over in his grave if you sold to Zukor, you know that."

"My compliments. The family has already instructed me not to deal with him."

"So it's Warner or Fox, is that it?"

"Or we stay as we are, Bill. That's the third possibility."

"Please let me know when we can discuss this business. I'm prepared to make a generous offer."

The day Marcus Loew died, he left behind a company that owned 200 theaters and a prosperous studio, MGM. Loew left a brother, Henry, who managed theaters, and twin sons. David worked in the office; Arthur, who sold product overseas, was married to Zukor's daughter.

Published reports said that Loew's widow inherited 400,000 shares of stock in the company, which was close to one-third of the outstanding. It was selling for $75 a share, but of course a block like that, which carried control, would require a premium price approaching $50 million.

To economically justify the acquisition, W.F. figured he would have to save a lot of money by combining things and reducing costs. There were duplicate plants, more than 130 duplicate marketing agencies, covering nearly every country in the world, and duplicate back-office administrative functions.

Once the acquisition was consummated, W.F. conservatively calculated a savings of $17 million a year just through the elimination of redundancy.

The most formidable obstacles to the acquisition were money, regulatory approval and willingness on Harry Warner's part to step back and not start a bidding war.

While the Loew's situation developed, Winfield Sheehan had just returned on the *Ile de France* from Europe, where he'd arranged for Benito Mussolini to pose twice before the Fox Case sound recording machine.

Winnie told W.F., "He delivered upon each occasion a 30-minute speech. His first speech was in English."

W.F. had bigger things on his mind.

As originally scheduled, *Sunrise* premiered at the Times Square Theater on September 23. The critics acclaimed the picture as "a brilliant achievement." It ran for 28 weeks in New York, had successful runs in Los Angeles, Philadelphia and Detroit, and was the third-highest grossing Fox film that year after *Street Angel* and John Ford's *Four Sons*.

The *Sun's* critic, John S. Cohen—used to the run-of-the-mill pictures Fox typically produced—reacted as if *Sunrise* were just another picture and caused quite a stir on 10th Avenue.

W.F. sent for his publicity agent, Glendon Allvine. "Who is this son-of-a-bitch, Cohen?"

"John S. Cohen is the reviewer on the *Sun*, a young man up from Atlanta who considers himself artistic."

"Did you read his review of *Sunrise*?"

"I certainly did."

"I'll fix that bastard. From now on the *Sun* is to get only 10 lines of advertising on any Fox picture."

"Yes, W.F."

"Until you get a memo signed by me personally authorizing more space, the *Sun* will never have more than 10 lines."

Over a period of several weeks, Sam Warner was losing weight and had a very tired look in his eyes. "I've just got a hell of a headache."

"An acute mastoid infection. We're going to operate tomorrow," his doctor said.

Unexpectedly, Sam Warner died from a cerebral hemorrhage on October 5, 1927.

Jack Warner was changing trains in Chicago, and Harry and Albert were three hours out of Los Angeles when Sam died while undergoing his second emergency surgery. He was barely 39 years old.

The curtain was scheduled to ring up for *The Jazz Singer* on October 6, 1927—just 24 hours after Sam Warner had died. A messenger hand-delivered a gold embossed invitation to Winfield Sheehan about three hours before the premiere, because Harry Warner was never quite sure *The Jazz Singer* would go on as planned, given the technical difficulties with Vitaphone and Sam's untimely death.

Charging into W.F.'s office, Sheehan said, "It's on!"

After slipping into formal wear, they hopped into W.F.'s limousine and headed to the Warner Theater on Broadway and 52nd Street, where an electrified crowd was gathering. By the time they got there it looked as if the throng was 10 deep. High above, a flashing electric sign announced: "*Opening Tonight—Al Jolson in The Jazz Singer.*"

The evening was cool and clear as W.F. slid out of the motorcar. He noticed a huge poster of Al Jolson with just his eyes, mouth, collar and white gloves outlined on a black background.

Important guests were formally dressed in tuxes and evening gowns; several invitees wore tails. Small groups had formed in the lobby, where they were sipping coffee, chatting and enjoying themselves. In one circle, W.F. saw Al Jolson, Otto Kahn and Marion Talley, who would sing part of the program. Another clique included Adolph Zukor, Nicholas Schenck and Walter Gifford. W.F. stood around with Winnie and tiny Mme. Amelita Galli-Curci, the high-nosed coloratura of Metropolitan Opera fame.

It was nearing show time and guests were encouraged to take their seats. The lights dimmed, and the motion picture world was about to change beyond its wildest imagination. Nothing would be quite the same as when they had walked into that theater.

One part of the film changed the industry forever. Onscreen, Jolson sang a chorus of "Blue Skies," then stopped and turned to his mother, actress Eugenie Besserer, and said, "You like that, Mama?"

"Yes."

"I'm glad of it. I'd rather please you than anybody I know. You know, darling, will you give me something?"

"What?"

"You'll never guess. Shut your eyes, Mama, shut 'em for little Jackie. I'm going to steal something."

Jolson kissed Besserer on the cheek and said, "Mama, darling, if I'm a success in this show, we're going to move from here."

Besserer had no idea what to say.

"Oh, yeah," Jolson continued, "we're going to move to the Bronx. Lotta nice green grass up there, whole lotta people you know, the Ginsbergs, the Wittenbergs, the Goldbergs, a whole lotta bergs."

Jolson held Besserer's hand. "I'm gonna buy you a silk dress, a nice pink dress, take you to Coney Island. I'll kiss you and hug you, you see if I don't."

Jolson went back to singing as the cantor walked in and cried, "Stop!"

Once again the synchronized background sound came up, the actor's lips moved in silence and the title cards flashed on the screen. The audience groaned, in perfect unison, at this intrusion.

The film ended with Jolson singing "Mammy."

At the end of the function, the audience stood and cheered, refusing to sit down until Jolson, who sat in a box, came onstage and took a bow.

"It's happening all over again, Winnie."

W.F. would never forget the audience's reaction to how it felt to hear a performer sing and speak for the first time on the screen. He was awed, fascinated, but on the other hand, besieged by a feeling of guilt, knowing Fox Film could have been the first to record sound dialogue.

But he'd hesitated and the Warner brothers, motivated by the raw desire to succeed, had taken a chance and seized the moment.

There was still time, W.F. thought.

The debut of *The Jazz Singer*, Oct. 6, 1927

The Jazz Singer ran 90 minutes, counting the overture and the ending music, and required 15 reels and 15 discs, putting tremendous pressure on the projectionist to be able to thread the film and cue up the discs quickly. What was going on in the projection booth seemed an insufferable task and would provide further impetus to the development of sound-on-film.

Walter Wanger, an executive with Famous Players, phoned Jesse Lasky: "Jesse, this is a revolution!"

The *New York Times* called it the "biggest ovation in a theater since the introduction of Vitaphone."

But there were still high barriers to overcome for the Warners. For one thing, a chronic shortage of cash plagued them and would continue until the receipts from *The Jazz Singer* began piling up. Also at risk was their ownership position in the studio. To finance the picture, Harry Warner had hocked his life insurance policy and the family was down to their last 60,000 shares of stock. The brothers had advanced the company $5 million and personally had endorsed another $5.5 million in borrowings.

The Jazz Singer would gross $2.6 million on a production cost of $422,000.

According to Jack Warner, Jolson's monologue was a fluke: "It is ironic, I think, that *The Jazz Singer* qualified as a talking picture only because of a freak accident. Sam was supervising the song recording when Jolson, in a burst of exuberance, cried out: 'You ain't heard nothin' yet, folks. Listen to this.'"

Director Alan Crosland told it differently. The following letter to the editor was published in the January 1931 issue of *Fortune*:

> The October issue of *Fortune* has come into my hands and, although late, I find in its leading article titled *Movies* cause for this note. The article *Color and Sound on Film* is illuminating and will probably live as a record. Great stress is laid upon the significance of the first recorded spoken dialogue in *The Jazz Singer* and that this, rather than the songs, revolutionized the industry of motion pictures. As director of *The Jazz Singer* I wish to correct an important misstatement in this otherwise authentic history. The lines spoken by Jolson were anything but accidental. They were "ad lib" lines that were rehearsed

several times before taking the scene, and instead of one line, "Come on, Ma. Listen to this," the dialogue lasted a full minute and came after Jolson sang *It All Depends on You,* accompanying himself on the piano.

Jack Warner, Sam Warner and even Jolson himself were fearful the audience would not accept the spoken voice and just as I was preparing to take the scene, they argued against it. Dialogue they claimed would sound strange and hollow after a musical number...in other words, spoken lines without a musical background, from their very novelty, might be met with derision. To overcome this I suggested that Jolson continue to play the piano with his left hand "vamping" throughout the time he was to talk. After some discussion I presented the winning argument...if the scene with the dialogue over the "vamping" music did not seem convincing when the picture was assembled, it would be a simple matter to eliminate the dialogue in the editing. Sam Warner agreed. Jack Warner consented with the reservation that we take the scene two ways, with and without the now historical dialogue.

At the end of the scene the father interrupted Jolson's second song at the piano by shouting, "Stop!," which was recorded. Certainly this was not accidental recording. So..."what took them out of their seats" and what sounded the death knell of silent pictures was not one accidental remark but a rehearsed conversation of some 60 seconds, the recording of which was the final result of an involved discussion on showmanship.

As for Al Jolson, Warner Bros. wanted him for another picture.

W.F. called for an urgent meeting of those managers most interested in the conversion to sound. Ted Case and Earl Sponable were there, as well as Jack Leo, Winfield Sheehan, Jack Lee, Courtland Smith, and of course, Eve.

W.F. was puffing on a cigar. "It's down to Movietone or Vitaphone. Those recording discs were terrible. But the audience was forgiving. We can only imagine what Jolson would have sounded like on Movietone."

"Mr. Fox, we'll need special sound studios," Sponable said.

"Aren't we rushing a little too fast?" Winnie interjected. "I mean, sound is a big investment."

There was that herd mentality once again, Sheehan's innate fear of taking big risks, his inability to recognize innovation and embrace it, his desire to maintain the status quo. But it wasn't all Sheehan's fault. After all, W.F.'s name was on the door, wasn't it?

"Too fast? Didn't you see the look on their faces when Jolson sang? Didn't you hear the applause? No, after this, I can only conclude that talkies will be the prevalent medium within a few years. From last night on, William Fox predicts the end of the silent picture. Fox Film will equip itself to make only sound pictures. Fox Theaters will be readied for only sound pictures. Movietone will dominate the industry."

"I agree, Mr. Fox," Sponable said.

"Earl, get out to California and develop a plan. I want to know what it's going to take to make good sound pictures both indoors and outdoors."

"Yes, Mr. Fox."

"You head this up, Winnie."

"Yes, W.F."

W.F. stared at Case. "Ted, can I count on your support?"

"You certainly can."

There would be chaos in the shift to sound as theaters made the necessary conversion. To install speakers and still be able to exhibit silents, the bulk of the industry's production, basically meant having parallel systems doing the same thing, expecting one or the other to eventually emerge as a clear-cut winner. There wouldn't be enough sound product to keep the theaters going, and important industry leaders were still expressing doubt about sound.

Irving Thalberg was still a nonbeliever. Thalberg reportedly told his wife, Norma Shearer, that sound was a passing fancy. Therefore, it was business as usual at MGM even though Warner Bros. was shifting its production to talkies.

Joe Schenck said, "Talking doesn't belong in pictures. I don't think people will want talking pictures long. It is my opinion that silent pictures will never be eliminated."

By the end of 1927, The Telephone Company had only equipped 159 theaters for sound, 55 of them with Vitaphone.

Industry skeptic Adolph Zukor was purposely silent on whether this was to be a catastrophe or an orderly transition of little consequence.

Paramount had an obligation to those 20,000 theaters while they were making their change-over. By the fall of 1929—a full two years after *The Jazz Singer*—only about one-fourth of them would manage it. Therefore, Zukor would continue to produce silent pictures. Often he'd make a silent film and later he'd make it over into a talkie.

Jesse Lasky was also doubtful about sound. "I thought I had flattened the arguments for sound with irrefutable logic when I pointed to Bessie's oil painting of trees blowing in the wind that hung in back of my desk and observed patronizingly, 'Do you have to hear the wind to appreciate the artist's intention?'"

Paying strict heed to W.F.'s directive, Sponable made his way to Hollywood in November and surveyed Fox's studios with the idea of adapting them for the production of talking pictures. He made a careful examination of both lots and then met with Sheehan and told him it would be difficult to make sound pictures on any of the existing stages unless he could remove the background noises that emanated from the silent productions. Since there was no experience in constructing sound stages, he contacted a Dr. Sabine, an acoustical consultant, to discuss the design of a studio that would be soundproof.

Sheehan, Sponable and Sol Wurtzel met to discuss where they thought they were, and Wurtzel sent W.F. a copy of the minutes of that meeting.

Twirling a cigarette around in his mouth, Sheehan asked, "What do we need, Earl?"

"I've surveyed both lots and it would be difficult, if not downright impossible, to make sound pictures on any of the existing stages unless we cut out the noises from the silent product work."

Sheehan padded over to a window overlooking the Westwood lot. "How in the hell are we going to do that, Earl? We gotta make silents to keep alive in the meantime."

Like a technician, Sponable gave a technical answer. "I want to hire an expert in acoustical control."

"Well, hire him, then!"

In December, Tom Mix and Tony were honored by having their names, handprints and hoof prints embedded in cement at Grauman's Chinese Theater during the showing of *Forest Ranger's Night* and *The Gaucho* with Douglas Fairbanks.

Fox Films had a sensitive matter to deal with: the renewal of Tom Mix's lucrative contract. Wurtzel was preparing the shooting schedule.

Tom Mix and Tony immortalize their foot (and hoof) prints at Grauman's.

"When is Tom Mix's contract up, Sol?"

"In March, Winnie. Why?"

"We're not renewing it."

"Tell me this is a joke."

As practically everyone knew by now, Wurtzel was no big fan of Tom Mix and they'd had their differences, but to dispense with Mix, what kind of nonsense was that?

"He wants more money!"

"I've got him scheduled for four pictures next year, Winnie."

"Make them. W.F. wants to start 1929 with sound."

For the holidays, W.F. decided to take Eve, the girls and his grandson, Billy T. to Palm Beach where he could play golf while Eve and his daughters lounged around the pool. The Taussigs were having marital problems and Belle had suffered a stillbirth. She was finding the daily routine of life to be a letdown from her former Park Avenue existence.

The family stayed at the Breakers, a comfortable hotel located on the water's edge where a few winter residents came to bathe in the warm surf. Throughout the rest of the year, Palm Beach was an empty, insect-infested strip of land where anyone with a decent income and common sense was not to be found. Come December, however, 2,000 low-paid workers removed storm shutters, aired vacant homes, requisitioned culinary supplies and prearranged the busy entertainment schedules of their rich patrons.

As was his custom, W.F. spent a few evenings at his favorite haunt, Bradley's gambling casino, playing roulette, smoking cigars and hobnobbing with old acquaintances, most of whom had little to do with motion pictures. There at the plain white clapboard house overlooking Lake Worth, he could momentarily lose himself in the excitement of the bright green tables. Besides, he was on a good run.

On their second day, Eve accompanied him to Bradley's. They were escorted through the foyer into the dining room, where the food was good and cost no more than $5 a serving. After dinner, they were ushered into the main salon where five tables of roulette and a table for dice were surrounded by formally attired patrons. There was little sound except for the mild clatter of dice, the rattle of a roulette ball searching for a lucky number, and the hushed voices of croupiers calling plays.

At the roulette table, W.F. placed $100 in chips on seven. Eve selected four. The croupier spun the wheel and then snapped the little white ball. After a couple of turns, the ball lost momentum and finally came to rest on seven. The croupier pushed several tall stacks of chips across the table to W.F. This went on for another five plays, with Eve losing on every turn of the wheel. By the time the evening was over, W.F. was up over $2,000.

Around 10 the next morning the Fox family lazed around the pool talking about nothing in particular. There was no more than a scattering of guests out at that time of day because the universal hour for rising was 11:00 a.m. Before that, nothing important ever happened in Palm Beach.

"Daddy, will this Vitaphone system cause you any problems?" Mona asked.

"We'll use Vitaphone, Movietone, whatever we can get our hands on, but we've got to please our patrons or we'll be shutting the studios down."

Belle was lying on a chaise lounge in a modish outdoor robe that she had purchased at Bergdorf's, buffing her nails.

"What's wrong, Belle?"

"I want to separate from Milton, Daddy."

There was a prolonged moment of silence where all that could be heard were the palms and the sound of soft breakers.

"Is it that bad, darling?" Eve had a pained look in her eyes.

Mona approached her sister and planted herself next to her. "Give Milton a chance, Belle. You're still upset about losing the baby, aren't you?"

Little Billy, Mona's son, was fast asleep in the beige wicker carriage Eve had given her for the trip. The top was up to protect him from the hot sun.

"Let's not make any rash decisions, darling," Eve said. "We're here so your father can rest and we all can have some fun. When we get back to New York there will be ample time to discuss Milton Schwartz. What's for lunch?"

"There's a lovely buffet, Mommy," Mona said.

"Let's go upstairs and dress for lunch, girls."

By 1:00 cocktails were served on a veranda, followed by a buffet luncheon at 2:00. The baby was now up in the room with a nanny, so after lunch, Belle and Mona had the freedom to roam the grounds, bathe in the sea and go to the spa for a hot honey bath.

Later that afternoon, the Fox girls put on summery dresses and visited friends at one of the big houses where they played bridge. For dinner they wore something spectacular they'd bought for Palm Beach.

Because of an offshore breeze, the evening had cooled off a bit. It was soothing to listen to the rustle of palms and the rhythm of pounding surf. W.F. and Eve sat on a veranda, he enjoying his cigar, she sipping a demitasse of coffee. They said nothing. One of W.F.'s character defects was his inability to discuss family problems openly, with the same gusto he dealt with business issues.

Down deep, W.F. knew Belle's marriage to Milton Schwartz wasn't going to last. He now faced the real possibility of having his two grown daughters living with him for the foreseeable future. But that didn't bother him. In a way, he liked the idea.

Later that week, Eve and W.F. were invited to the residence of one of Palm Beach's leading society figures, Mrs. Edward Townsend Stotesbury, the uncrowned "Queen of Palm Beach."

Mrs. Stotesbury was hosting one of her private dinners for a group of 20 prominent socialites that included the Jesse Laskys, who were in from California. During a typical season, it was said that Mrs. Stotesbury hosted a dozen or so regal dinners with no more than 10 to 20 select guests in attendance for each.

El Mirasol, the ornate Stotesbury estate, had been built on 42 acres of beautifully manicured gardens and was virtually hidden behind the tall row of Australian pines that lined Welles Road. It was at the time the largest single estate in Palm Beach. It was said to take 15 gardeners working summer and winter to maintain the grounds. El Mirasol had a 20-car garage and 37 chambers.

Down the road from El Mirasol was the home of Otto Kahn, where W.F. understood the Laskys were staying, the last house on the ocean before reaching the Palm Beach Country Club. Beyond that were the estates of Mrs. Hugh Dillman, Pierre L. Barbey and Joseph P. Kennedy.

To W.F.'s delight, he discovered that Otto Kahn was also attending the regal function. He was sure that Kahn had recommended him to Mrs. Stotesbury.

While still in their hotel room dressing for the dinner, Eve listened attentively to W.F. tell the story of Edward Townsend Stotesbury, a self-made man like himself.

Drummer-boy in the Civil War, E.T. Stotesbury started his career as a simple clerk in the old Philadelphia banking house of Drexel and Company and rose to be its chief executive and J.P. Morgan's principal partner in Philadelphia. Now an elder statesman, he sat on the board of a dozen banks and utility companies.

In 1912, after a shipboard romance, E.T. Stotesbury married Lucretia "Eva" Bishop Roberts Cromwell, the widow of Oliver Eaton Cromwell, a Manhattan banker, who had died two years before. Eva had three children, one of whom, James, gained a considerable degree of fame by marrying Delphine Dodge, daughter of Horace E. Dodge, in 1920. He divorced her in 1928 and married Doris "Dee-Dee" Duke in 1935. In 1940 Dee-Dee and Jimmy separated and three years later she got a Reno divorce.

From a prior marriage, Edward Stotesbury was the father of two grown daughters.

After motormaker Horace E. Dodge died, James Cromwell intervened and persuaded the widows of the two Dodge brothers to dispose of the company to an investment syndicate for $146 million—the biggest cash sale in Wall Street history.

Old and rich enough to retire in luxury, E.T. Stotesbury was probably worth $25 million. The Stotesburys spent most of the year at Whitemarsh Hall, their Philadelphia estate, with its gardens a replica of Versailles.

James "Jimmy" Cromwell was well liked and charming, a fine boxer, an erratic businessman and a writer on social and economic topics. He had ideas on birth control, libel laws, sterilization of defectives, boxing and politics. Eva's daughter, Louise Cromwell, was married to a military general named Douglas MacArthur.

Besides the Foxes, Laskys and Kahns, the guest list included Alexander Hamilton Rice (another Philadelphian) and his delightful wife, Eleanor, who was wealthy in her own right. The former Eleanor Elkins Widener inherited two respectable fortunes—one from her father, William Elkins (gas, coal, oil and street railways), and one from her late first husband, George Widener (street railways, oil, coal and gas). Widener and Eleanor's son Harry had perished on the *Titanic*. Rice, her second husband, himself a millionaire and well known as an explorer and geographer, was a lot younger than his socially prominent wife who was now 54, though she didn't look a day over 40. The Rices owned a Palm Beach estate called Palmeiral where invitations were highly solicited and difficult to come by. There was also a white stone Fifth Avenue mansion and a home in Paris.

The other guests were Mrs. Horace E. Dodge, now Mrs. Hugh Dillman, whose Palm Beach estate was even more luxurious than El Mirasol, featuring such accoutrements as gold faucets. Hugh Dillman, a former actor and the ex-husband of Marjorie Rambeau, was more than a few years younger than his wife. In fact, she was old enough to be his mother.

Mrs. Dillman was wearing something in flowered satin. Besides her Palm Beach house, there was a palace in Grosse Pointe, a yacht and some extremely precious jewels.

Of course, Mrs. Stotesbury's son, James "Jimmy" Cromwell, and his beautiful society wife and heiress to the motor fortune, Delphine Dodge, were in attendance. Delphine was the daughter of Mrs. Dillman. Later, when Cromwell absconded with Doris "Dee-Dee" Duke, Delphine would marry Raymond T. Baker, once the husband of Margaret Emerson, Bromo-Seltzer heiress, who was once the wife of Alfred Gwynne Vanderbilt. Later, she would marry French-born Mr. Godde, so that eventually she became Delphine Dodge Cromwell Baker Godde.

Only one invitee had the audacity to send her regrets, Matilda Rausch Dodge Wilson—once the secretary and later the second wife and the widow of John F. Dodge—respectfully declining the Stotesbury invitation because she said she had nothing in common with her former sister-in-law, Mrs. Dillman, except their early poverty and present wealth.

Also on the guest list was Mrs. Dorrance—the former Ethel Mallinckrodt—of the Campbell soup fortune, accompanied by two of her lovely and still unattached daughters. Mrs. Dorrance kept no yacht, nor did she adorn herself with expensive jewelry. She loved music and had a box at the Philadelphia opera. Her late husband, Dr. John T. Dorrance, left her one-fourth of his estate. Ever a businesswoman, she dutifully sat on the board of Campbell's and administered her own charities.

Edward F. Hutton and his lovely wife, Marjorie Post Close Hutton, were the guests of honor and sat near the hosts. At the time, golden-haired Marjorie was receiving an inheritance of a million dollars a year as the chief beneficiary of the Postum Company's outstanding market performance. Thirty-three years ago, Marjorie's father had taken roasted wheat bran out of an oven and created a new eating habit, breakfast cereal.

Former broker Edward F. Hutton was now chairman of the Postum Company. The Huttons' Palm Beach estate was so grand that they used extreme measures to keep intruders out. A sentry guarded the gate. A private tunnel ran from the estate to the famed Bath and Tennis Club. Both Mr. and Mrs. Hutton loved to entertain, particularly sponsoring lavish costume balls where she frequently appeared as a blonde princess.

During the seven-course gustation, topics of conversation ranged from the state of the economy to the price of emeralds.

That night, full-figured Eva Stotesbury was very grand in green satin—a gown that was sketched by her own designer—with a double-strand, diamond-studded emerald necklace hanging round her neck. She lifted the emerald necklace in one hand. "It was given centuries before by Shah Jahan to his lovely wife, Mumtaz Mahal." Mrs. Stotesbury added, "In his wife's memory, the Shah built the Taj Mahal."

W.F. said little; he had taken great pains to adopt the manner of speech as it was spoken around the enormous table. One had to have a very sensitive ear to detect his Lower East Side accent.

The courtly Mrs. Dillman wore a stunning pearl necklace that belonged to Catherine II of Russia and might have cost $800,000, which she was delighted to point out to those who could hear her.

In a true to form display of bonhomie, Hugh Dillman decided to change the train of the conversation and pepper the Hollywood types with inane questions about motion pictures, a subject about which he knew very little.

"I'm told, Mr. Lasky, that you own the largest film studio in the world, is that true?"

Elegantly tapping his lips with a cloth napkin, Lasky replied, "There are those who would disagree with that estimation, Mr. Dillman, but let me say that Mr. Adolph Zukor and I are trying to build a sizeable business enterprise."

"To which you say, Mr. Fox?"

"There is more than room enough in the picture business for all of us to grow nicely, Mr. Dillman."

"What you're saying is that we won't see an oligopoly any time soon, is that it, Mr. Fox?" Edward Stotesbury queried.

W.F. momentarily hesitated and then said, "Who knows?"

7th Heaven was released by Fox in 1927

There was no one more socially adept than the learned Otto Kahn. Sensing the *cognoscente* thought William Fox to be unsophisticated, he said, "An oligopoly is out of the question, Edward. There are over a hundred studios making moving pictures."

"Who supplies all that film?"

"Eastman Kodak, Mrs. Dillman," Jesse Lasky replied.

Mrs. Dillman glanced over at her husband, Hugh, and asked, "Do we own any stock in Kodak, darling?"

"Not that I'm aware of, dearest."

Mrs. Dillman stared across the table at E.F. Hutton. "Be a good boy, Ed, and place an order for 10,000 shares of Kodak, won't you?"

"I'm no longer a broker, Mrs. Dillman."

"Oh. Why, of course, you're in the cereal business since you married Marjorie. How silly of me."

Kahn said, "These two gentlemen represent an industry that consumes over a billion feet of motion picture film."

Mrs. Dillman fastened her eyes upon her young husband, Hugh. "On second thought, Hugh darling, buy 20,000 shares."

"I will, I promise. Very first thing Monday morning. After my doubles match, dearest. Before the market closes. I promise."

"Eva, what are your thoughts on this moving picture business?" Mrs. Rice asked. Eve Fox was caught with her mouth wide open before she realized the question wasn't meant for her.

"I think pictures are opium for the masses," Eva Stotesbury said.

Everyone seemed to be staring at William and Eve Fox.

Edward Stotesbury diplomatically interjected, "Which makes it a damn good business, Eva."

Stotesbury ushered his male guests into a commodious study, where they lit up fine cigars. Congregating to one side of the room, a butler poured a 20-year-old cognac. For a while the conversation turned on auto stocks and steel prices. Stotesbury said very little to him; W.F. had the notion that he was taking his measure.

Presently the discussion began to drift to such things as land and masterpieces of art.

In sort of a rescue mode, Jesse Lasky edged W.F. over to another part of the room.

"It's a strange world, Bill, you and I cavorting here with all these rich Gentiles."

"They still own the country, Jesse."

"At least for now."

W.F. saw Otto Kahn coming to join them; he instinctively knew something important was in the air. "I apologize for the lack of decorum at the dinner table, Bill."

"I must be honest with you, Otto. I didn't know what 'oligopoly' meant."

"It's not that important, Bill. These people like to impress those of us who grew up on the wrong side of the tracks. But take heart. Some of them were once poorer than we were."

In reality, Kahn was the scion of an eminent German banking family and had never done without.

"How do you put up with it, Otto?"

"I go to one or two of these fashionable dinner parties a season, and then I return to the real world in New York. Palm Beach is a different world, Bill. Old money likes to socialize with even older money."

At that moment Kahn got a serious look on his face and said, "I have it from a very good source that the Telephone Company is concerned about some German patents you own, Bill."

"Tri-Ergon?"

"Yes, precisely. I should tell you that they have some very expensive patent lawyers examining these filings, doubtlessly at this very moment."

"I appreciate your concern, Otto."

"If I were in your shoes, I'd try to come to terms with Mr. Gifford. He's a decent man and I'm sure you can come to an equitable arrangement. Don't try to fight them. They are too big."

"I understand. Thank you for the advice."

"I must get back to the Gentiles."

Otto Kahn disappeared into the throng at end of the room.

"If I were you, I'd listen to Otto Kahn, Bill," Lasky said.

After they parted the Stotesbury estate, W.F. knew no more of what Kahn was up to during the rest of his stay in Palm Beach, for he did not see him again.

Hollywood's 12-story Roosevelt Hotel opened across the street from Sid Grauman's Chinese Theater at Orange Drive. A syndicate of investors included Douglas Fairbanks, Mary Pickford, Louis B. Mayer, Joseph Schenck and the Marcus Loew family.

In 1927, there were 743 releases to 21,660 theaters with an average weekly attendance of 57 million patrons. According to Quigley publications, Tom Mix was the top male star and Colleen Moore the top female star.

The earnings scorecard was as follows:

Fox Theaters	$ 823,659
Fox Film	$3,120,557
Loew's	$6,737,205
Paramount	$8,057,998
Warners	$ 30,427

CHAPTER 21
1928

A theatrical district "that would rival Times Square" was to be established in Brooklyn as the result of Fox's new theater and a Paramount theater, located within a block of each other near the intersection of Flatbush Avenue and Fulton Street.

The Fox Theater, a combination office and movie palace that was being erected at a cost of $8 million, would have seating for 5,000. The theater would feature a huge foyer with art treasures, a disappearing orchestra stage, refrigeration to sterilize the air every 90 minutes and the most modern projectors. Ushers' uniforms looked much like those of a classic hotel bellhop, identifying employees by monogrammed buttons, with Fox ushers sporting innumerable microphones labeled F, and Loew's polka-dotted with lions.

Located at the corner of DeKalb and Flatbush avenues, the Paramount theater had a seating capacity of 4,500. Fashioned after an outdoor moonlit Italian garden, it was located within an 11-story commercial building. Ground floor space was occupied by stores and the Brooklyn and Manhattan Rapid Transit Company. To adorn the facility, Zukor invested nearly $3 million in sculpture, paintings, tapestries and other artifacts.

At this point in the theater war, Fox controlled more than 300 theatres, with 15 in New York, including the Roxy; the Fox in Brooklyn; the Academy of Music; and the Audubon. Seating capacity became the key statistic as the major studios continued their drive to control more theaters.

Early in January, Blumy became aware of a situation in Atlanta that, at first blush, looked like an attractive proposition. The new Shrine Mosque had run out of money and halted construction; W.F. instructed Blumy to negotiate a lease. The site was perfect for a movie theater. To achieve the latter, Fox would have to make a considerable investment in the building. W.F. consulted a reputable architect who told him it was more than feasible, so he gave the go ahead.

Meanwhile, W.F. was diligently raising money for new projects and wondering how he'd

Fox Theater in Brooklyn

come up with the payment for the Loew's shares. After consultation with several of Halsey's finance experts, a plan was developed and W.F. put it into immediate action. Halsey, Stuart sold bonds for $6.4 million for a Detroit building; $4.75 million for a St. Louis building; $4 million in debentures for a New England enterprise; $13 million in debentures for a chain of a theaters in New York; a $4 million bond issue for a new studio in California; $1.8 million for converting the New York studio to sound; and $2.5 million for refinancing the Roxy purchase—a total of $36,450,000, for which W.F. paid Harry Stuart a healthy commission of $3 million.

Another $50 million was required for the 400,000 Loew's shares. W.F. and Harry Stuart agreed W.F. should approach the Telephone Company for part of the money, since it was in their best interest to work with a strong and progressive studio for the conversion of the industry to sound.

One had to suppose that the Telephone Company didn't want those Loew's shares to fall into unfriendly hands. Gifford mulled over the proposal and then agreed to lend Fox Film $15 million for one year. He was particularly upset with Warner Bros., since it was in the midst of litigation over patent rights and licenses with the Telephone Company.

Still short of the target, W.F. also called upon the Chatham and Phoenix Bank and secured $3 million more.

Once the AT&T credit facility was in place, Harry Stuart said he'd commit to $10 million, and W.F.'s old friend, Albert Greenfield, chairman of the Bankers' Securities Company of Philadelphia, lent Fox another $10 million, accepting Loew's shares as collateral.

From its own cash reserve, Fox Film came up with $3 million. After closely examining the company's balance sheet, Jack Leo and Saul Rogers felt Fox could raise another $16 million by selling equity in Fox Theaters, which brought the total available cash pool to $57 million, leaving the companies $7 million for an emergency.

It was a lot of money, more than W.F. had ever raised before, but he was remarkably calm about the notion of taking on so much debt at one time. The memory of Harry Aitken had faded into a distant past and times had changed for the better. The economy was sound and the stock market was definitely bullish.

Armed with the knowledge he could raise the necessary money for the purchase of the Loew's stock, W.F. invited Nicholas Schenck to a round of golf at Woodmere, where he took his first pass at getting those stocks. They played the first two holes without so much as a peep about business.

W.F. wore argyle knickers and ribbed white socks that sagged a little around his thin legs. He smoked a cigar and carried an iron in preparation for his next shot. His putt missed by a fraction of an inch, so he bent over and edged the ball in with a slight tap.

As they walked off the green on the third hole, W.F. said, "What did the family say about my offer?"

"It's too low. Mrs. Loew wants $120 a share."

Handing his club to a caddy, an expression of apprehension crossed W.F.'s face. "That's way over market, Nick!"

"Harry Warner is looking for the money, Bill."

"I see."

As they walked up to the next tee his heart was pounding a mile a minute. Schenck had him over a barrel and he knew it. W.F. stopped, lit up a stogie and teed up. He drove the ball a good distance with his one good arm and Schenck smiled.

Schenck's ball sailed off the tee in a near-perfect slice.

Handing his club to the caddy, W.F. said, "Let me talk to my banker and see what he says. What's in this for you, Nick?"

"Oh, the Loew family will take care of me, Bill. Don't let that worry you."

Per the production schedule, Tom Mix would make four films for Fox Film in 1928, *Daredevil's Reward*, *A Horseman of the Plains*, *Hello Cheyenne* and *Painted Post*.

The cowboy actor was now an aging 48-year-old whose Western type of picture was declining in popularity.

Will Morrissey, the comedian, goaded Tom Mix: "Your horse Tony has a great future in the talkies. The horse can at least snort. But what can you do?"

The jibe touched a nerve; Mix punched the comedian and knocked him flat on his behind. It was no joking matter for Mix. He was facing the end of a very successful film career, and he knew it.

While in the midst of filming *Painted Post,* W.F. gave Winfield Sheehan the thankless job of telling Tom Mix the studio was going to dispense with his services. "I'm not going to renew Tom's contract, Winnie, so tell him."

"I will, W.F."

After *Painted Post*, Tom Mix rode off the Fox lot into the sunset.

Standing there much as he had that first day when he walked into the Edendale studio looking for a job, Tom Mix rocked back and forth.

Winnie liked Mix and had always felt that what he saw on the screen was pretty much the same man standing there before him. There was a genuineness about Mix that was apparent to anyone who came in contact with him. He felt sorry that he had to let Mix go because the cowboy star had done so much for the Fox studio.

"I guess we're not as popular as we once were, Winnie."

"Anything I can do for you, Tom?"

Mix scratched his head, smiled, and said, "Nope. When we finish with *Painted Post*, I guess I'll just ride out of here much like I rode in."

Coming around his desk, Winnie shook Tom's hand firmly and said, "Best of luck, Tom."

"Thanks, Winnie. Say goodbye to Mr. Fox for me."

"I will, Tom."

Film critic Chester J. Smith of the *Motion Picture News* wrote: "For the most part *Painted Post* drags while the star and the villain vie for the attention of the newly arrived girl, who has come to sketch Western types for a magazine."

The day Mix's contract expired, he signed with Keith-Albee-Orpheum for a vaudeville tour.

An agitated Earl Sponable was back in New York and asked to see W.F. By the look on Sponable's face, W.F. knew things were not going too well on the Movietone project.

"The Janet Gaynor film came in yesterday, Mr. Fox. It could not have been much worse as far as sound is concerned."

"What in the hell is going on out there, Earl?"

"I've appointed Jackson to production manager of Movietone and he's in full charge of sound production. You can expect corrective action real soon."

"Are Sol Wurtzel and Winfield Sheehan standing behind Movietone?"

"Things are in quite a jumble out there as no one knows what's what or who's who. It seems that everyone is working against everyone else and we're not accomplishing very much. I want Jackson and Schneiderman to come to New York to learn about Movietone before they get into actual production on the coast."

"Good idea, Earl."

"I suggest I remain in New York, so we can get started together and have our respective positions and activities outlined thoroughly before going back to the West Coast."

"You can count on everyone's full support."

"That's good! It seems to me this is the only way we'll get off on the right foot, as right now I am generally the last one to hear about things but the first one to be blamed if things go wrong. There is very little cooperation in evidence. It would certainly please me, as I say, if I work with these men and get off in the right direction."

"Consider it done!"

By phone, W.F. chewed off Winnie's ear for not being able to get Movietone up and running and on a fast track. He could hear Winnie breathing hard and he knew his brain was going a mile a minute, but he didn't challenge W.F.

"I've got to meet our silent film production schedule, W.F."

"You have to do both, Winnie!"

A bomb was dropped when the following article appeared in the *New York Times:*

> A deal involving the acquisition of the Stanley Company of America by the William Fox interests, which has been rumored in the financial district for some time, is well under way, and 1928 is expected to witness the unification of these two theater chains into a $300,000,000 organization maintaining control of more than 600 theaters throughout the United States.
>
> The reports of the projected deal follow by one month the acquisition by Fox of the Westco chain of theaters on the Pacific Coast, which added 250

houses to the Fox chain, making a total of 365 theaters under Fox control. The Westco properties were said by Mr. Fox to be worth $100,000,000, and these together with the Fox Theaters, and the Stanley properties numbering about 270, should the unification go through, would form a corporation valued at close to $300,000,000, exceeding in size the chains of the Paramount and Loew's interests, now Fox's chief rivals in the motion picture field.

It was also stated yesterday that the acquisition of the Stanley chain by Fox marked the final steppingstone toward control by Fox of the First National Pictures Corporation. Fox is reputed to control about 34 percent of First National while Stanley owns about 29 percent. Thus if the Fox-Stanley merger is successful, Fox would emerge with about 63 percent or control of First National.

W.F. received a surprise call from Harry Warner, who invited him to lunch at Sardi's, which was located in the Schubert Building at 234 West 44th Street.

W.F. found Harry Warner seated at a corner table, a hint of concern on his face. He had come alone. His well-tailored business suit and white shirt made his tan stand out, confirming that he had just returned from the West Coast. Harry invited W.F. to sit down. Vincent Sardi came over to take their order.

Harry rattled on about how difficult the Telephone Company was being in their dealings on Vitaphone, and how he thought sound-on-film would eventually be the technology for the industry.

In the face of so many technical impediments, progress with sound was slow. A network of agreements had been stitched together, a license here, a contract there, forming a veritable legal quagmire. As Harry saw it, there were three major challenges to overcome: uncertainty, keeping pace with technical developments and developing the right competencies.

The staggering job of sorting out who was doing what, Harry said, was becoming too much for one studio to handle. And surely, if there ever was a man who understood the future of sound by virtue of his commitment to the technology, it was William Fox.

They chatted about their children. Harry told W.F. that he planned to bring his son, Lewis, into the business as someone who would eventually succeed him.

W.F. didn't have a son and wasn't quite sure who would succeed him at the helm of Fox.

Then coffee and cheesecake arrived. Harry picked at his.

Harry Warner came directly to the point. "Bill, the price of our stock has gone up enough to give us some borrowing capacity and I've got one of two companies in mind that I'd like to buy."

"What are the two companies, Harry?"

"Loew's or the Stanley Company."

"Which would you prefer buying?"

"The Stanley Company. It fits better with what we're trying to accomplish."

W.F. raised his cup to his lips, wondering what to say next. "Fox Film owns 21,000 shares of First National, which I got when we bought West Coast, and I'm not about to part with those shares."

This was relevant because the Stanley Company owned another third of First National and the remaining third was out there in the market, bits and pieces in the hands of small stockholders.

"I understand, Bill."

"However, I'm willing to back off from Stanley if you do the same with Loew's."

"That's fine by me. Let's not run up the price of both Loew's and Stanley."

"You've got yourself a deal, Harry."

They shook hands across the table.

Harry glanced at his watch. It was time to thank W.F. and leave. He had one last question, however, that he had to get in. "Bill, have you ever thought of selling Fox Film and Fox Theaters?"

"Never once."

Several days later, the following article appeared in the *New York Times*:

> Renewed reports of negotiations for the merger of the Stanley Company of America's interests with those of the William Fox Company were met with emphatic denial here tonight from Irving D. Rossheim, president of the Stanley Company. "They are absolutely untrue and absurd," he said, adding that "there has been a concerted barrage of misinformation emanating from New York, Newark and to some extent, from Chicago, all of which is absolutely without foundation."

The moguls in New York called the shots. The Hollywood types made the pictures.

All of the talk about acquisitions and mergers began to unsettle and concern movie czar Will Hays. He leased an apartment up on the highest sleeping floor, the 37th, of the 508-foot, 39-story-high Ritz Towers in Manhattan. The view was spectacular.

It was best that he keep an eagle eye on the swift developments taking place. The death of Marcus Loew had provoked a degree of uncertainty regarding the plans of the surviving family.

Will Hays was making a substantial contribution to the industry and deserved to be made aware of anything that might affect his office. He wasn't jittery nor was he, at least outwardly, disturbed by the amusing internecine war, which had increased in severity.

By imposing self-regulatory measures in the early 1920s, Hays had won over the public and headed off censorship bills already coming up in 22 states. The reforms undertaken helped turn into allies those very public-spirited groups that were harrying the industry. Through the organization of chain telephone committees, the industry mobilized moviegoers to pull good movies out of the red. No other industry had secured such a vast army of voluntary workers to fight its battles for it.

Masterly though the execution of the public relations campaign was, the truly significant point was the way the public was carefully canvassed to bring out all the criticisms against the studios; and how, when objectionable practices were found, they were corrected by changes in films through rigorous editing.

Versed in the ways of small-town America, Will Hays understood the vagaries of local tastes and communicated them directly to studio big wheels.

Warner Bros. was about to buy one of the biggest theater chains in America, with 250 theaters in 75 cities and every state, including the Strand. All Harry Warner had to do was come up with $100 million for the Stanley purchase.

To allay their concern, Harry Warner wanted to discuss the acquisition of Stanley with his two brothers. He met with Albert and Jack in his New York office. They were fully aware of the negotiation and waited expectantly to hear what Harry had learned from William Fox. Now it would have been impolitic for Harry to say so, but it was fairly clear that whatever he decided, his brothers would rubber stamp.

"Fox wants to buy Loew's."

"That son-of-a-bitch is crazy, Harry," Jack said.

"That's none of our business, Jack. We must have theaters."

"Harry's right, Jack," Albert said.

"We know most exhibitors are..."

Albert cut off his brother, Jack. "A bunch of stubborn tightwads!"

Harry wanted to make his point. "Exactly. When it comes to spending their own money. Their refusal to put in sound equipment means we're being locked out. Since we have so few theaters equipped, we have to look to the future. With the Stanley theaters we can ensure that all our future films have nationwide distribution."

What Harry Warner was saying was that vertical integration of film production and exhibition was the only sane policy to follow given the intense rivalry in the industry.

Albert, a bit more cautious, said, "What would Sam think about all this?"

The mention of Sam's name caused a moment of silence. Jack's eyes got a little moist. "Sam dreamed about sound theaters all over the world. He'd agree with the idea."

"Let's grab them up," Albert said.

"Uh, wait a minute, Harry, let's get back to First National." Jack took a long puff from his cigar. "How are we going to get control of the company?"

"I propose to buy 42,000 of the company's 75,000 shares."

"Hell, Harry. Why not buy the whole damn mess?" Jack queried.

"I intend to buy 'the whole damn mess.' I found out that Fox West Coast Theaters owns the remaining third of the stock. No matter, we will have a controlling interest. Fox can be bought out later."

"How much is this little shopping spree going to cost us?" Jack asked.

"One...hundred...million...dollars."

Jack whistled. "That's a lot of moola, Harry. We're taking a big chance."

"That's the name of the game," Harry said.

"Yeah, and we could be out on the street again," Jack intoned.

"If we hadn't taken risks 20 years ago, Albert would still be selling soap. And Jack, you'd be crooning ballads in a speakeasy. We need a new studio to equip for sound; we need theaters to show our films..."

Jack said, "Okay, okay. I agree. But it would be nice to know what films we're going to be showing next season."

"I plan to come out to Hollywood in October. We'll map out next season's shows then—after I have this business settled."

"If we're still in business, Harry," Jack mumbled.

Ignoring the snide remark, Harry gazed at Albert, "Do we all agree on the First National and Stanley buyouts?"

"Agreed!"

Over the next few months, Harry Warner and Waddill Catchings raised the necessary funds to buy Stanley and First National. A syndicate was put together that included Goldman Sachs and Hayden, and Stone and Company. Together, they raised $100 million. In the process, Harry Warner also bought Witmark, Remick, Harms and other music publishers.

As part of his master plan to groom his son for bigger things, Harry Warner put 20-year-old Lewis Warner in charge of Warner Bros. Music. To run First National, Jack Warner chose Hal Wallis, who would work under Warner Bros.' new production chief, Darryl Zanuck. Abe Warner became head of the company's theater division.

The little studio that was risking everything on sound, Warner Bros., was now a player.

The impact of Warner talkies was immediate. A sequence of pictures like *Lights of New York*, *The Terror* and *The Singing Fool* had studios tearing down silent stages throughout the motion picture industry. Anyone who knew anything about sound found himself in great demand.

The Lights of New York was an all-talkie that made its debut at the Strand on July 6, 1928. Although it was a mediocre picture, it grossed $1.2 million. Darryl F. Zanuck said, "*The Jazz Singer* turned them to sound. *The Lights of New York* to talk."

Right after the showing of *The Lights of New York,* Adolph Zukor called a meeting of his top executives, scolding them for their slow progress on sound. The days of wait-and-see were definitely over. "Warners is making sound pictures and what have we got? You don't know a goddamn thing about sound. A lot of dumbheads and we pay you all this money."

The Warner Bros. Theater opened in Hollywood on April 26, 1928. The picture *Glorious Betsy* was premiered for the event. With a seating capacity of 2,700 people, it became the largest theater in Hollywood.

Among the independents, Sam Goldwyn went along with the rest of the industry and encouraged his United Artists partners to sign ERPI's Recording License Agreement.

Like Universal, Goldwyn wasn't going to rush to make talkies because he believed, as did Carl Laemmle, that it would take a considerable period of time to refit all the theaters for sound. Therefore, United Artists decided to continue to produce silent pictures. Besides, Thalberg convinced Goldwyn, who often picked Irving's brain at parties, that a move to sound would take time and there would always be a market for silent film.

Because an independent producer usually worked with borrowed money and naturally had to watch his costs more closely than if he had a major studio behind him, there just wasn't a lot of room for an independent like United Artists to miss totally on a film.

Many motion picture executives worried about the impact of sound on the European market, particularly the non-English speaking countries. How was Hollywood going to deal with Italian and German audiences?

American movies dominated Britain and were occupying more than 80 percent of the playing time in all British theaters. To restrict Hollywood, the British government passed film quotas, which led immediately to a scramble of fly-by-night British producers for the new market.

Before doing experimentation with sound at MGM, Eddie Mannix and Irving Thalberg walked into Louis B. Mayer's dimly lit office, looking for guidance from the boss. They could see him poring over a financial report.

Mayer lifted his eyes. "Vogel says business is way down at the Loew's theaters, Eddie."

"Yeah. They're lining up for talkies."

"What does Nick think?" Mayer asked.

Having been swayed by the dismal seat count, Nicholas Schenck reversed himself and was now insisting that MGM move forcefully into the production of talkies.

"Nick says we ought to move full speed ahead," Mannix said.

"Irving, what do we need to do to accelerate our sound program?"

"For one, we'll need more soundproof stages, Louis B. To suppress the din of the camera, we've got to build boxes for the cameramen. It's a big job."

"How about our players, Irving?"

"I hired Dr. Marafioti. He's one of the best voice teachers in the business."

"Is he going to teach Gilbert to talk like a wop?"

Thalberg wasn't amused. He was concerned that MGM would employ a hit-and-miss system to develop talkies. That would cost money and affect his bonus.

Mayer was fearful that Greta Garbo would have too strong an accent to be accepted by her fans. Other players worried him, too. Ramon Novarro's voice, for example, was not only markedly Mexican but also overtly effeminate. John Gilbert's high tenor would probably end his film career.

"Who's going to head this thing up?"

"Douglas Shearer, Louis B."

He was Thalberg's brother-in-law and knew very little about sound. But Thalberg wanted someone he could trust in the position.

"How about Marion Davies?"

"She stammers like hell."

The emergence of sound was creating turmoil with motion picture producers and film exhibitors. The larger studios had commitments to facilities, technical people and performers that restricted their capacity to adopt new technologies. As incumbents, they had a large investment in silent filmmaking that was now becoming obsolete. Silent cameras would soon become relics relegated to museums. It was a different world now.

Intelligent choices had to be made quickly. Was it to be Vitaphone? Movietone? Photophone? Alliances had to be pursued. Western Electric? RCA? All of this while managing for today and keeping pace with momentous change.

Capital had to be invested in the development of cameras, sound stages, laboratories and the like. Tunnels were dug, burying miles of wire, linking soundproof stages to a control room.

A man deeply immersed in technological change, Walter Gifford, was quick to remind industry leaders that Western Union had turned down an opportunity to buy Alexander Graham Bell's patent on the telephone, seeing it as only an improvement on the telegraph. His point: There was a price to pay for those who chose to sit on the fence. "There is no middle position," he warned.

In the case of motion pictures, the audio dimension of filmmaking was never part of an integrated process. At considerable cost, it was added at the time of exhibition with musical accompaniment and no dialogue. *The Jazz Singer* proved, once and for all, that there was a latent desire on the part of theatergoers to hear their favorite players as well as see them.

The incumbents, if they acted, could set the pace for change. They had financially sound enterprises, management talent, respected corporate names and deep pockets.

By the spring of 1928, patrons were lining up to see Warner Bros.' *Glorious Betsy.*

William De Mille, Cecil's elder brother, said, "We sat in the darkened theater and watched *Glorious Betsy* unwind herself. I shall never forget when a military officer stood in the middle of the picture and spoke."

The challenge of sound was terrifying for many players. One of them was John Gilbert. MGM decided to introduce him to sound in a film called *His Glorious Night.*

How many other livelihoods would be declared obsolete?

A short three months after having announced Paramount "might make some talking pictures," Lasky was forced to change his position and issue an order that no more silents would be made other than those already in the pipeline.

Lasky said, "The use of sound will be dramatic, and will heighten intensely the effect of the picture. The hum of crowds, the roar of an angry mob, perhaps a shouted command, the shrill of a police whistle, the bark of a dog, a knock on a door, it will heighten the suspense."

Paramount's Long Island Studio, which had been inactive for some time, was now mobilized for making talkies. Its proximity to New York meant stage actors could make pictures while performing roles on Broadway. It was all a matter of proper scheduling. This became an important economic advantage for the Eastern studios, including Fox Film, because it obviated burdensome traveling and moving expenses to California. In fact, on most nights, the players left the set to return home to their families in time for dinner. In the course of only a few months, a whole new category of players with hardy vocal chords and theatrical training surfaced, while some of the top stars of the silent era evaporated into thin air.

For instance, George Bancroft had been worth $5,000 or $6,000 a week to Paramount until he had to speak. He made a few talking pictures, but his fans weren't particularly enthralled with them. He vanished into professional anonymity.

The "It" girl, B.P. Schulberg's ingénue, Clara Bow, possessed a nasal voice so irritating that it drove dogs into fits of howling. Since the defect was a permanent part of her anatomy, she voluntarily retired. On her way out the door, she purportedly said, "I'm very glad to've meetin' yuz."

Rudy Valentino's successor as the most celebrated romantic male lead, MGM's Jack Gilbert, had to abdicate his title at the very peak of his career. His voice just didn't seem to fit his face and body. In the talkie *His Glorious Night,* critics reported that Gilbert's pitch was "microphonically wrong." The pleasant light baritone voice wasn't what John Gilbert's fans had fantasized about. MGM, under contract to pay Gilbert $250,000 per picture, was left with no alternative but to ask him to tear up his agreement for $500,000. No tears were shed since L.B. Mayer had a large stable of versatile players and didn't particularly like Gilbert anyway.

On the other hand, Greta Garbo would make a show of her appealing Swedish accent and stand out in talking pictures. *Anna Christie* went into production on October 7 and the shooting was uneventful.

Other stars who faded from the screen were Norma Talmadge—Joe Schenck's wife and Constance Talmadge's sister—Colleen Moore and Florence Vidor, while the veteran, husky-voiced Marie Dressler came out of obscurity after having played supporting roles most of her career and climbed to a new height of popularity at age 61. Canadian-born Dressler became the most valuable player in Hollywood, earning a salary of $4,000 a week and making pictures that averaged a profit of $800,000 each—far more than Garbo, Gaynor or Harlow.

Vilma Banky, Sam Goldwyn's discovery, had a strong Hungarian accent and had to retire at 25. Her screen partnership with Ronald Coleman—whose career would accelerate with the switch to sound—abruptly ended.

Greta Garbo managed to make the transition to sound.

Another example of the changing tides was the gaunt-looking Conrad Nagel. Not particularly pleasing to the eye, he hadn't done anything much in silents but was now in demand for practically every sound picture made. His deep baritone voice resonated through theater speakers and audiences forgave his unattractive, blemished face.

Where once being photogenically correct was considered a sure ticket to stardom, now it was intonation, diction, enunciation, phraseology, command of idiom, parlance, elocution and a lot of other complicated words W.F. wasn't sure he really understood. People expert in speech assisted players in the performance of their talking roles. A new budgetary line item, that of the "diction coach," was born.

There were also directors who would not survive the transition to sound. Fred Niblo (*Ben-Hur, The Mark of Zorro*), Clarence Badger (*It*), Marshall Neilan (*Stella Maris*), Rex Ingram (*The Four Horsemen of the Apocalypse*), and one of W.F.'s early directors, Herbert Brenon (*Peter Pan,*

Beau Geste) saw their careers cut short. Even big-time directors like James Cruze (*The Covered Wagon*) encountered difficulty in the new medium.

Once Adolph Zukor made up his mind to turn over a new leaf, Paramount switched to dialogue and music within six months. Both studios were retooled and converted long before all the theaters were equipped to exhibit talkies, thus necessitating the simultaneous production of silent films. Product was required for all theaters Zukor controlled, including Balaban and Katz in Illinois; A.H. Blank theaters in Iowa and Nebraska; Lucas and Jenkins in Georgia; M and P chain in New England; Sparks in Florida; Saenger circuit in the deep South; Karl Hoblitzelle's in Texas; and others.

Over lunch with Jesse Lasky, Zukor said, "Everyone is speculating what may come next from the endless puttering with sound. Our job is to satisfy our customers, for keeping customers in a good humor greatly helps ticket sales."

During 1928, Paramount released 78 silent pictures and no talkies. By 1930, Paramount would release 65 talkies and no silents.

On the Fox Movietone lot things were looking up. Foresighted directors had anticipated the conversion to sound and were routinely testing players for voice as well as appearance. Most of the studio's major stars came from the stage and their voices were cut out for sound. W.F. was particularly delighted to hear samples of Janet Gaynor's voice tests, which reflected the very innocence she portrayed on the screen.

Fox veteran Madge Bellamy said, "There was panic, bedlam and enthusiasm."

Screen idol Charles Farrell, who was from Cape Cod, had to get rid of his thick Bostonian brogue—paak da cah—through repetitive elocution lessons.

There was one more bridge to cross in Fox's move to 100 percent talkies—terminating expensive silent players whose box office was now in steep decline.

For instance, cowboy Buck Jones, who was making $3,500 a week, had starred in 62 features between 1920 and 1928, all of which made money for the studio. After eight long years, Jones said he was tired and asked Sol Wurtzel whether he objected to his taking a vacation with his wife and daughter. Wurtzel told him to go ahead and agreed to pay his salary while he was off the lot in Europe. When Jones got back, Wurtzel reneged on the salary, mostly because W.F. and Winnie Sheehan were putting so much pressure on him to control his expenses as a result of the enormous investments facing the studio because of the conversion to sound.

Livid, Buck Jones said, "I quit!"

Shortly thereafter, Jones got himself into a Wild West Show that was sort of a circus. His last picture for Fox was *The Branded Sombrero*.

The Movietone laboratory corner-stone ceremony took place on June 29, 1928 at Fox Hills.

W.F. wrote, "To the personnel and equipment of this laboratory will be entrusted the development, fixing and making permanent on a fragile, sensitized strip of celluloid the only record that exists, and the only tangible evidence of the tremendous sums now being expended daily on the adjoining stages, on the sister lot at Fox Hills and on locations in the four corners of the globe."

Fred Beetson—head of the Motion Pictures Association—was master of ceremonies and Milton Sills spoke of "Yesterday and Today."

Reacting to W.F.'s determination to get Movietone up and running, Winfield Sheehan called Sponable into his office and announced that a committee would be formed to manage the Movietone department.

This committee would consist of Quinlan, Hansen and Balsey, all operating under Jackson and Schneiderman, who would supervise the construction of sets, lighting, photography and sound recording. Quinlan would supervise all Movietone installation work.

Once each day, usually at noon, there was a technical meeting in Sheehan's big office. Sheehan was there with Sponable and his cohorts; the progress of the day was briefly discussed. Things got very complicated and a good part of the time Sheehan did not feel like being gracious. Besides, a frustrated Earl Sponable felt he was getting the runaround from Sheehan. He wired the following message to W.F.: "Almost every order I issue is countermanded. Sheehan simply does not have the mentality to understand engineering problems and won't O.K. a damned thing until he does understand them."

Things got hectic on the MGM lot. The staff worked on the transformation of Culver City to sound. In fact, Thalberg's brother-in-law, Douglas Shearer, was busier than ever. Mayer's eastern studio, Cosmopolitan Studios in New York, was also wired for talkies.

Soundproof stages were installed. Tunnels were dug for the tangled wiring that connected stages to a sound center. To muffle camera noise, cinematographers were isolated in enclosed booths. Doors were electronically controlled so that studio personnel could not barge onto sound stages during the filming of a picture.

Thalberg, under a lot of pressure to convert MGM to sound, said, "Look at it this way; no one knows any more about sound than we do."

Mayer told Thalberg that the "General" wanted them to make a sound picture.

A matter of days after Schenck gave the order to make talkies, David O. Selznick was back on the MGM lot supervising Tim McCoy Westerns. He was appointed to assist Hunt Stromberg. Selznick suggested Stromberg make *White Shadows in the South Seas,* a story of a white man in Polynesia. It was to be shot on location in Tahiti. Selznick saw the picture as an idyllic love story. Stromberg saw it differently. "Tits and sand sell tickets, David."

It was rumored that David O. was seeing Mayer's younger daughter Irene, the daughter he called "my little Margaret" because of her strong resemblance to her mother. Around this time, Mayer went to New York to pay tribute to Nicholas Schenck and the men who controlled the purse strings for the company. Wife Margaret and daughters Irene and Edith accompanied him.

Once in New York, Mayer put a question to Irene. "Have you heard from your friend Selznick lately?"

"No, I haven't."

"He's left the studio. We kicked him out. I didn't think you'd be hearing from him."

By the distraught look on his daughter's face, he wasn't sure he'd stopped her from marrying David O.

With a little help from his friend, William Wellman, David O. Selznick interviewed with B.P. Schulberg, who was now on the Paramount lot. Wellman dared Schulberg to hire a man with the name of Selznick because he felt Paramount and Adolph Zukor had helped break David O.'s father, Lewis. David O. Selznick got the job; soon he was busy making pictures at the studio.

Weary of the constant struggle to survive as an independent producer, Cecil B. De Mille signed a contract with MGM on August 2, 1928 and committed to produce three pictures.

For the rest of his career, De Mille would never accept another position that required him to be an administrator and think like a businessman. In this particular case, Mayer had personally sought out De Mille, many thought to keep the ever more influential Thalberg in line. In a deliberate show of grandiloquence, Mayer built De Mille a special bungalow and held a celebration to welcome him.

As ill luck would have it, De Mille's first picture coincided with the disorderly conversion to sound, an all-talking picture called *Dynamite,* and did so-so at the box office. A third picture, a remake of the original *The Squaw Man*, barely recouped its cost. Unyielding, Mayer pushed De Mille ahead with a busy schedule.

MGM's first sound picture was *White Shadows in the South Seas,* partially filmed in Tahiti. This was the same story that had been highly touted by David O. Selznick, who received no credit for it. Thalberg contracted Robert Flaherty, a reputable documentary filmmaker, to shoot the picture and co-direct with W.S. Van Dyke, one of Thalberg's assistants. In the past Van Dyke had worked for Fox, directing several Buck Jones pictures.

Based on Frederick O'Brien's book of the same title, it is a mushy story about an alcoholic doctor and a native woman.

Flaherty earned a reputation for his genuine portrayals of real-life beauty with his pictures *Nanook of the North* and *Moana of the South Seas.* He was the father of the documentary.

Douglas Shearer dubbed sound effects and music, but there was no dialogue in the picture. The film features Monte Blue as the doctor and Raquel Torres as the Polynesian girl.

Mayer said, "Well, boys, we finally made a talkie."

Now with a little more confidence, Mayer and Thalberg decided to launch a full talking picture, *The Broadway Melody.* Western Electric supplied the equipment for a sound stage MGM built on the lot.

Over on the Universal lot, Carl Laemmle felt his peers had abandoned him. He sat at a table, a solitary figure on an empty stage, wondering what had happened to the clandestine gentlemen's agreement to convert the industry to sound as a whole or not at all. Wasn't there a wait-and-see policy? What about, "If one goes, we all go?"

During this frenzied period, Laemmle didn't hear a peep from Mayer, Tally or Zukor.

Having done nothing to enable a sensible decision on which path to follow with sound, Laemmle hastily called director William Wyler into a conference with his new sound man, Roy Hunter, and asked them what they had in mind.

Laemmle said, "I will not be stampeded into forgetting the needs of the small exhibitors."

Throughout most of its existence, Universal had catered to the smaller independent theaters with program pictures. It was thought that these entrepreneurs would be the last to convert to sound, particularly because of the cost and scarcity of independently made sound pictures. Universal had carved out a respectable share of the mom-and-pop theaters, and since this was Universal's bread and butter, Laemmle was in no hurry to push for sound unless he was forced to.

During 1928, Electric Research Products had wired 879 theaters for sound, bringing the grand total to 1,046, so Laemmle had a point. There were still 21,000 theaters out there without sound equipment, and this represented a sizeable market for silents.

Laemmle recognized the current trend dictated that he experiment with sound. So he did. Early experimentation was amateur at best. Some elemental use of sound demeaned *Give and Take,* a part-talkie with a musical score starring Jean Hersholt and George Sidney.

William Wyler, formerly a producer of two-reel Westerns, was given a modest budget to produce *Anybody Here Seen Kelly?,* a romantic comedy set in New York. The picture was ordinary. Laemmle was fit to be tied.

The BROADWAY MELODY

—with
CHARLES KING
ANITA PAGE
BESSIE LOVE

Directed by
HARRY BEAUMONT

Story by Edmund Goulding---Continuity by Sarah Y. Mason
Music by Nacio Herb Brown----Lyrics by Arthur Freed-
Dialogue by Norman Houston and James Gleason

Metro-Goldwyn-Mayer's
TALKING
SINGING
DANCING
DRAMATIC
SENSATION

Abandoning the confining do-it-alone mentality of the past, Laemmle called W.F. requesting a loan of Fox's Movietone equipment. Because of the rising number of talkies appearing all over town, he wanted to test it out, he said. In those days the Fox studios had no equipment to spare, but W.F. advised Laemmle he'd lend him the appropriate equipment for a very short period of time.

"I'll get it back to you in less than 10 days, Bill."

"That's the most I can do, Carl."

Universal's first all-talkie was made in under 10 days with Movietone, a picture they called *Melody of Love*, which did very little at the box office.

All of the major studios were now on board with sound and there was no turning back.

Western Electric, with its Vitaphone and sound-on-film processes, was frantically wiring theaters, pricing the installation of their system at $19,800 for theaters with more than 1,750 seats, $15,300 for theaters seating between 1,000 and 1,750 patrons, and $11,300 for theaters of fewer than 1,000 seating capacity.

Fox talkie pictures were still a long way from being acceptable. W.F. had noticed background noise in almost every Fox Film that he had so far exhibited.

The deal Fox Film had struck with Western Electric when it handed over its Movietone process in exchange for their speakers was in the form of a royalty-free cross license, which basically meant both companies were free to continue developing sound-on-film but the two parties to the agreement had to share their inventions with each other. Not only did AT&T want clear rights to its patents, but in order to steer its way through a maze of technical improvements on sound, it had been wise to reach an agreement with Fox on Movietone, exchanging patent rights on certain essential parts of filmmaking and projection whose manufacture would otherwise mean mutual infringement.

At this juncture, W.F. could have stopped all development and sat back like the others, waiting for the systems to mature, but that wasn't the way his mind worked. The effect of his decision to continue development of sound-on-film was far-reaching. He would remain in the crosshairs of AT&T for an extended period of time. The immediate consequence of his decision was that he would have to personally oversee the research and development effort.

W.F. ordered Sponable back to New York. Fox's piece-by-piece approach to sound-on-film was painstakingly slow, Sponable wired. Difficult choices had to be made about initiatives to support Movietone. There were different options to choose from for just about every component of the system. For example, 41-42 type amplifiers were in great demand for theater installation because of their AC operation. Other members of the committee were recommending a different approach. It was turning into a nightmare for the nontechnical people.

Sponable argued that a visit to New York would dramatically affect the speed at which the studio was developing Movietone, and by the tone of his voice, W.F. interpreted that to mean he'd better not force the issue.

There were other things to occupy Sponable's mind right now.

In lieu of the trip, W.F. told Sponable to wire him an update because the telephone connection wasn't that good and W.F. could barely hear him at times.

W.F. saw that the technical language was beginning to sound like someone talking ancient Greek. He got on the phone with Winfield Sheehan and told him to form a committee to track the studio's progress with Movietone, and to be sure he got a copy of the minutes with a summary in basic English, telling him what the hell was going on.

When Sheehan heard that, he laughed and said, "We already have a committee. The problem is to understand what the hell they're saying."

"Keep your eye on the sound people!"

"I will, W.F."

The trouble was, in the convergence of ideas there was no simple solution to producing good talkies.

The purchase of the Stanley chain gave Warners a lot more theater seats, a first-class studio situated on the valley side of Hollywood Hills, and a roster of players that included Richard

Barthelmess, Colleen Moore, Loretta Young, Billie Dove, Constance Bennett, the Talmadge sisters, Kay Francis, Milton Sills and Harry Langdon. All in all, Harry Warner had put through a good deal for Warner Bros.

Right after the Stanley closing, Jack Warner visited First National's Burbank studio and instantly fired the production manager, placing his publicity man Hal Wallis in charge. Funds were being squandered right and left, and Jack Warner's point was not to just call attention to a new policy of sound stewardship, but to note how quickly this transformation would take place. Patience was not one of Jack Warner's virtues.

Jack Warner told Wallis, "Harry will never believe this. He squeezes nickels until they come out dimes. You got too many people, Hal. Get rid of them."

The tall, affable, dimpled Wallis was 30 years old. Raised in Chicago, he got his first job sweeping out the office of the Hughes Electric Heating Company and climbed the ladder to sales manager. From sales, he branched into advertising and later into show business. In Los Angeles he managed the old Garrick Theater, where he met Sam Warner and went to work in Warner Bros.' publicity department.

It didn't take Wallis long to discover the Burbank studio had not invested a penny in sound equipment. In response to Wallis' mandate, one of Warner Bros.' engineers connected a telephone line between the new studio and the Sunset Boulevard studio, where sound was recorded. A little improvisation here and there was definitely the order of the day.

The commonest criticism of Hal Wallis was that he was a yes-man. The fact was that he felt very much in charge, and when he wasn't being overly harassed by Jack Warner, he exuded good humor and had a fine smile. Wallis ate lunch in his office, talking business all the time, and was available to both players and directors. He was frank, direct, self-confident and tolerable, and became the archetypical Hollywood executive.

Saul Rogers barged into W.F.'s office and proceeded to lecture him on a potential antitrust problem regarding Fox's acquisition of the Loew's shares. Unless they or someone with immense clout could get the government's blessing, there would be no Fox-Loew's merger.

W.F. told him the government had made no objection to the purchase of West Coast and other theaters, and Rogers quickly reminded him that no competitors were involved in the same locality. The way Rogers saw it was that the Loew's company owned theaters in the same cities with Fox, and the Fox production unit was, of course, a direct competitor of Metro-Goldwyn-Mayer.

"Let's get an opinion on this very soon, W.F."

"I don't have a done deal yet, Saul!"

"Well, any deal you make will be subject to government approval and, as sure as I'm sitting here, we'll have a new President come November."

"I'll keep that in mind."

Fox's quest for theater capacity continued unabated. Denied the Stanley Company, Fox Theaters aimed its sights on the Poli Theater chain and made an offer. The purchase for $25 million dollars bought a chain that included 20 theaters in leading New England towns with a seating capacity of 45,000.

W.F. told the press Fox Theaters was investing a million dollars to renovate and modernize the chain, particularly with regard to the installation of Movietone projectors so these theaters could present talkies and newsreels.

The Poli chain had been founded by 68-year-old Sylvester Z. Poli, and was the largest privately owned theater chain in America. A dark, intense man, Poli had decided to sell at what he thought was the top of the market. W.F. announced that Sylvester Z. Poli would continue to own a financial interest in the business.

Poli's spokesman, O.C. Edwards, manager of Poli's Palace in New Haven, said, "Mr. Poli has not been influenced by declining health to make the sale. He believes he has earned a rest."

CHAPTER 22

Fox was into its third week of exhibiting *Street Angel* at the Roxy. The picture, starring

Janet Gaynor and Charles Farrell and directed by Frank Borzage, is the tale of a poor Italian girl who takes to the streets to earn money for her sick mother. The Roxy's income was $479,000 for four weeks of exhibition, a record run.

Gaynor demanded a pay increase to $1,500 weekly, and when she appeared in Sol Wurtzel's office with two lawyers, a new five-year agreement with annual salary increases was negotiated and settled upon. On the screen Janet Gaynor was all sweetness, but in real life she was an astute businesswoman.

Around New York, talkies were beginning to dominate screens, not totally, but the trend was apparent. At the Astor Theater, MGM was exhibiting *White Shadows in the South Seas*, which they advertised as their first sound picture. Leo the Lion roared for the first time as the picture earned back its cost several times over.

Fox Film exhibited its *Lost in the Arctic* at the Gaiety, and *The Red Dance* was showing at the Globe. The Strand featured Rod LaRocque in the Owen Davis play, *At Yale*, advertised as a sensational two-reel Vitaphone talkie. Over at the Paramount, Zukor exhibited the studio's second sound picture, *Loves of an Actress,* which starred Pola Negri.

In August, Fox signed a producer, directors, writers and players for Movietone productions. The producer was Albert Lewis, who had staged *The Jazz Singer*, *The Spider*, *The Nervous Wreck* and *Rain*. The studio assigned him to the task of assembling actors and literary material for sound pictures. The directors included Charles Judels, Earl Lewis McGill, Donald Gallaher and Marcel Silver. The writers were Eugene Walter, Tom Barry, Edwin Burke, Edmond Joseph and Dave Stamper. Actors included Chick Sale, Clark and McCullough, Lumsden Hare, Gilbert Emery, Clifford Dempsey, Sylvia Field, Ben Holmes, Arnold Lucy, Helen Twelvetrees and Paul Fung.

The producer, Albert Lewis, spoke to a trade magazine, which quoted him as saying: "I am not sure how far sound effects will be carried in screen entertainment. Voices will play an important part, but it may not be possible to carry dialogue all the way through a film entertainment. It will also," he added, "be impossible to transfer stage plays to the screen without adaptation."

There were in New York only about a dozen really outstanding theater producers. David Belasco, Lee Shubert and his brother Jake, Sam Harris, "Ziggy," the Selwyns, George M. Cohan, Winthrop Ames, William A. Brady, A.H. Woods, George White, Dillingham—most everyone who was anyone in theater recognized these names. Sound pictures would begin to compete for theater talent as never before.

Irving Berlin signed a deal with United Artists to write a musical revue based on "*Say It With Music.*"

Fox-Case offered George Gershwin tens of thousands to let them use his "*Rhapsody in Blue*" and to write incidental music for them.

Among other talents, W.F. had the forethought to comprehend the importance of technical advances. The forceful introduction of radio had caught him off guard and he swore he wouldn't let television take him by surprise. Recently, in Schenectady, the General Electric Company's technicians had put on a demonstration in which a musician was dimly seen waving his baton while conducting an orchestra whose music issued from a loud speaker—with the picture appearing on a small screen.

The one thing that would make it possible to compete with television was to use a screen 10 times larger than the present screen, a camera whose eye could see 10 times as much as at the present. For example, Roxy's picture screen was 18 feet wide, and the screen W.F. proposed was about 90 feet. He believed this "Grandeur" would come closer to the third dimension he heard scientists talking about.

One afternoon, Harley Lyman Clarke, a short, stockily built gentleman, appeared in W.F.'s office with a letter of introduction from Harry Stuart introducing Clarke as the president of the Utilities Power & Light Corporation in Chicago, saying he was a reputable financier.

As it turned out, Clarke had taken on a line of products that concerned the motion picture business and was mixed up in the International Projector Company; he was now making 85 percent of all projection machines used in America. He had just formed a company called National Theaters Supplies, and as Fox was one of his customers, he had always wanted to meet W.F.

"I am in rather a peculiar way," Clarke said.

"How so?"

"Our business is building projection machines, and if you are going to turn the style from normal size to grandeur size, we are out of business."

W.F. noticed that when Clarke talked to him, he rarely looked him in the eye. He also had a peculiar habit of snorting, as if he were suffering from an allergy. During the conversation, Clarke let it be known that he was a Christian Scientist and a Shakespeare devotee. A straitlaced man to be trusted. Or so he said.

They talked and W.F. soon recognized that Fox Grandeur could benefit from both Clarke's business and the Mitchell Camera Company of Los Angeles, which W.F. had purchased. During the discussion, W.F. realized he should merge his respective holdings in camera projection into a company to be known as Grandeur. William Fox would own 50 percent and Clarke would own the other half. To compensate W.F. for his contribution, which was worth considerably more than Clarke's, he would receive 25,000 shares in a company Clarke had organized, the General Theaters Equipment Company.

W.F. formed the Fox Grandeur Corporation and ordered the testing of a special projector at his own expense. Little did he realize how disturbing his idea would be to the leaders of the industry. The principal limiting factor of Grandeur for wide commercial use was, of course, the need to change cameras and screens.

It wasn't long thereafter that Zukor and Sarnoff, who represented the Radio Corporation of America, came to see W.F. They said he was about to make a great mistake; the industry was changing from silent to sound and a great inventory had to be wiped clean. They, as an industry, were just catching their breath, and here W.F. was trying to upset it again. W.F. called it progress; they called it destruction.

Turning to Grandeur, Zukor said that enlarging the pictures could be done at another time, when all the companies could agree on a uniform size. Each company was claiming it had a much finer development at that time, so they tried to persuade W.F. not to give the premiere performance.

W.F. described the necessity of moving forward so that television did not destroy them. Of course, he was firm in his position that his duty was to further the motion picture business, and

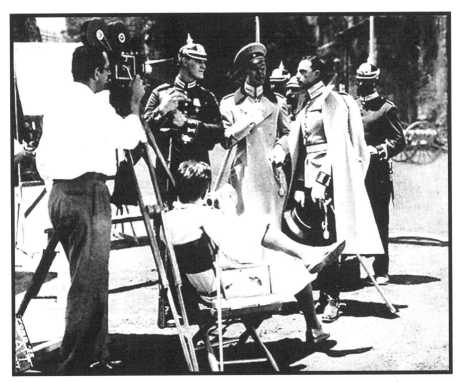

Archduke Leopold of Austria (right) had a bit part in John Ford's *Four Sons* for Fox.

he hoped it would hurt no one. W.F. was going to give his premiere, and if the public decided it was no good, that would be the end of it.

A day or two after his encounter with Clarke, W.F. got a strange call from Harry Stuart. "I'm sorry you saw Clarke before I got to you. You know, we both live in the same city, and when he asked me for this letter of introduction, I couldn't say no. I want you to watch yourself in your dealings with him—don't trust him further than you can see him. He will make every kind of promise and do nothing, so watch your step."

W.F. thought about what Stuart was trying to tell him, but passed it off as a banker's conservative advice. He went ahead with his plan to merge with Clarke's company. No other film company indulged in long-shot research of the Grandeur kind, but all the others had engineers who were just as knowledgeable as the Fox engineers, if not so numerous, and whatever Fox developed would soon be copied by the rest. It was this need for common technologies—the kinds that could be used by all studios and theaters—that forced their uniform adoption.

Winfield Sheehan reported back on the company's progress in establishing sound film units in its studios. W.F. first received word about stage construction at Westwood. The job of design was placed in the hands of Fox's architect, G.H. Muldorfer, a good architect whose sole experience in sound stage construction was limited to a one-week inspection of Fox's old stage at 54th Street.

Sponable sent W.F. a separate report, marked confidential, telling him Muldorfer had no idea what he was doing. In fact, the stage in New York was no more similar to Westwood than "a row boat was similar to an ocean liner."

"Mr. Fox," Sponable wrote, "I have made a list of all material for recording installation at Westwood in accordance with plans I submitted in the past. We have laid out a system of stages and equipment to record sound in the most economic and scientifically correct manner known to the art."

The walls of the sound stages were absolutely soundproof and each room had double partitions slightly over one foot in thickness, including an interior air space of six inches. On either side of the air space were three-inch walls of gypsum blocks, and outside each layer was an additional thickness of a cellular texture. This material was covered with heavy draperies.

Also outlined in the report were the characteristics of the ideal sound recording man, including such traits as personality, technical education, broadcast experience, even temperament, and a feeling for orchestra balance.

Scratching his head, W.F. wondered where he'd find such technicians. It wasn't going to be easy to staff Fox's sound production units.

The end result of the studio's charge into sound production was four huge sound stages covering 40 acres at Fox Hills, and with the contracting of stage players, writers and directors as well as sound experts, Fox's program for sound pictures was now taking on a life of its own. The Fox lots were busy making features, shorts and comedies. As a result of the commitment to sound, the Fox Movietone lot was littered with house fronts, gardens, Manhattan streets, Midwestern streets and a replica of Berkeley Square in London.

Meantime, Sol Wurtzel kept the ball rolling at the Western Avenue location by turning out a steady stream of good pictures. Day in day out, he was the first on the lot and the last one to go home. Confronted with a crowded production schedule, he was usually on some well-lighted stage trying to inspire a director or cajoling a player into giving a better performance. Scenery, lights and costumes were perfectly coordinated. He was proud of the accuracy of his opinions about plots, plays and scenarios, proud of his unbroken series of hits. But it was also true in the motion picture business that unusual things, and usual-unusual things, happened every day. Wurtzel was skilled enough to deal with most of them. By almost any industry standard the number and quality of films he produced was one of the most imposing in the business. W.F. knew that everything directly connected to Wurtzel was clicking. So he left him alone.

Fox Film announced eight feature pictures with dialogue and seven all-talking, two-reel comedies ready for release on January 1. Five of the full-length productions were 100 percent talkies, and three of them, which had already been completed, had talking sequences.

The three finished pictures were *Mother Knows Best* with Madge Bellamy, *Making the Grade* and *The Air Circus,* which opened on September 1, 1928 at the Gaiety Theater. The first two of these pictures were 50 percent talkies, and in *The Air Circus* Louise Dresser, Sue Carol, David Rollins and Arthur Lake spoke their lines.

The two all-dialogue features were O. Henry's *The Caballero's Way*, which Raoul Walsh was directing, with Maria Alba in the role of the Spanish girl, and *Badges*, one of Max Marcin's plays, which Lew Seller directed.

Upon completion of *Caballero's Way*, Raoul Walsh began production of the Earl Derr Biggers mystery, *Behind That Curtain*. J.G. Blystone made *Through Different Eyes*, Milton Gropper's play, in Movietone. Fox hadn't decided on the title for the fifth picture.

It was against this backdrop that Fox Theaters announced further expansion involving a plan to invest $50 million to build a chain of six or more motion picture theaters in Philadelphia.

W.F. issued the following statement to the press: "The company will start with the immediate construction of a $16 million theater which will accommodate 5,500 patrons on the southwest corner of 17th and Market streets, which Fox Theaters expects to open in September 1929."

Permits for the demolition of buildings on the theater site were to issue on the 16-story theater and office building, which was to have a 400-foot frontage. It would be the first office and theater building to have refrigerated air-cooling for every office as well as for the theater itself. The theater would have a symphony orchestra of 125 and a permanent roster of 300 performers, and would require a permanent staff of more than 600 employees.

C. Howard Crane of Detroit developed the plans. The building contract was given to the Aronberg-Fried Company of New York.

The urge to keep financing within the local banking community was uppermost in W.F.'s mind. In such circumstances, there was no one more dependable than Albert Greenfield. The relationship between W.F. and Greenfield grew over time, and not only did they invest in each other's businesses, they became best of friends.

Albert Monroe Greenfield was brought to America in 1892 from Poland at age six by his Polish parents. After attending the University of Pennsylvania for two years, he established a real estate business and married Edna Florence Kraus, whose father was a building and loan magnate. By 1920, when his father-in-law died, Albert Greenfield had accumulated 27 building and loan associations. What with these businesses and with real estate brokerage, Greenfield found himself at age 35 the owner of the largest real estate business in Pennsylvania, doing about $127 million a year. In 1925 Greenfield purchased a small bank and called it Banker's Trust Company. W.F. was one of his early investors.

When approached with the subject of a credit line, Greenfield said his bank was good for $10 million, money W.F. would use to expand his theater empire in Pennsylvania. Of course there was the matter of collateral, in this case, 250,000 shares of Loew's and $1,000,000 insurance on W.F.'s life. As a gesture of his good will and faith in W.F., Greenfield bought 100,000 shares of Fox Theaters.

Two recent developments, the opening of its Brooklyn theater and the Poli acquisition, highlighted the fact that Fox Theaters' expansion was on schedule. But there was more to do. To sell tickets seats were needed, and the more seats the greater the revenues, a lesson Adolph Zukor had taught all the moguls.

The first large theater built by Fox Theaters was in Brooklyn, erected for $9 million against which there was a bond issue of $6 million purchased by S.W. Straus and Company.

On September 8, W.F. announced his intention to acquire Walter Reade's 27 theaters in New York and New Jersey for $25 million; he expected to close within 15 to 20 days. The purchase would include the Columbia Theater in New York as well as the Astor, considered among the most valuable theater properties.

Before W.F. could finalize the deal, he had to untangle some leases Reade had negotiated since the Columbia was still being used as a burlesque house; Reade planned to convert it to a legitimate theater. The Bijou and Morosco were under lease to Shubert's. In New York, Loew's had a lease with the Astor, which played moving pictures. The deal was going to take time, because W.F. wanted to be sure he could negotiate all those leases in his favor before committing to the payment.

There were three basic ways to finance an acquisition: cash from the profits of the company, new capital from selling additional stock, or debt. Theaters were relatively easy to finance because the banks readily accepted mortgages backed by bricks and mortar, land that had an intrinsic value and first rights to the cash generated through ticket sales if things went sour.

These were good times for the motion picture industry. Average weekly attendance was high, and Fox was filling seats as soon as it could get a theater up and running. There were 22,300 theaters across the nation, with very few wired for sound. The stock market was optimistic, although there were rumblings of a possible down cycle, but who knew when.

To defray the cost of theater expansion, Fox Film decided to offer 150,000 shares of class A stock at a rate of one share for each four shares held. At this time, the company had 667,216 class A shares and 100,000 class B shares outstanding. W.F. controlled the voting B shares and hence the company, although his total interest had been severely diluted ever since he had taken the companies public.

The offering brought $12,750,000 into the Fox treasury, which the company used to pay for part of the Poli acquisition. The remainder was financed by $4 million worth of debentures issued by a company W.F. formed, Fox-New England.

Before the start of the holiday season, W.F. paid another visit to his banking friends to be sure the financing for the Loew's shares was in place. The financing he was asking for was all short term, but the bankers agreed to work with him to refinance the purchase of Loew's on longer terms once they saw how much he could save by eliminating duplication and how much operating cash W.F. could realistically count on.

That in itself was nothing to worry about; nobody expected W.F. to be anything less than fully committed to reducing the break-even point of the enormous Fox-Loew's combine. Under him labored a competent staff of industry professionals. They had statistics on every possible phase of the business. There were certain norms and ratios to match and then supersede if the merger were to succeed. W.F. never doubted that his management could achieve the goals he set for them. After all, Fox executives were stamped Fox as unmistakably as Ford motorcars were painted black. His managers were well-seasoned veterans and understood the vagaries of the motion picture industry. W.F. reminded his bankers that Fox Film and Fox Theaters had made money every year since their formation. They'd never missed a forecast.

His second job—although job numbers one and two were to be carried out simultaneously—was to modernize the studios and impose uniform production methods. And while his staff was busy reducing overhead and modernizing equipment and facilities, W.F. was to keep a close eye and an iron hand on everything from the nickels and dimes that trickled into the company's coffers to the renegotiation of short-term debt into something more permanent.

By the fall of 1928, MGM, along with the other major studios, knew that the conversion to sound was inevitable. MGM announced a production schedule that included 40 talkies, and 19 of those would have dialogue.

At Paramount, Roy Pomeroy prepared for the production of *Interference*, its first all-talking picture. He mandated that no outsiders were allowed on the set. Pomeroy was now the single most important man at Paramount.

During the year, ERPI wired 879 theaters for sound, for a total of 1,046.

As 1928 drew to a close, W.F. perused the final figures. Fox Film had a good year, releasing 55 pictures with gross rentals of $22 million. Company earnings hit an all-time high of $5,957,218. Fox Theaters earned another $1,522,079.

For Fox 1928 was an exciting year. Fox Theaters sought and closed on critical financing for theater expansion. Several theater chains were purchased or brought under the control of Fox. A merger of two industry giants was afoot. The big-screen Grandeur was in development.

Fox Film's players roster included George O'Brien, Mary Astor, Edmund Lowe, Charles Farrell, Janet Gaynor, Dolores Del Rio, Victor McLaglen, Madge Bellamy and William Russell. There were outstanding directors including Howard Hawks, Irving Cummings, John Ford, Raoul Walsh, Frank Borzage and F.W. Murnau.

The scorecard for earnings in 1928 for the major studios was as follows:

Fox Film	$5,957,218
Fox Theaters	$1,522,079
Loew's	$8,568,162
Paramount	$8,713,063
Warners	$2,044,842

On December 4, 1928, President Coolidge's optimistic State of the Union address was read to Congress. The Dow ended the day at 291.30, only four points below its all-time high.

The top male and female box office stars, based on a Quigley Publications poll of exhibitors, were Lon Chaney and Clara Bow.

820 pictures were released. There were 22,300 theaters, with very few wired for sound. Average weekly attendance was 65 million patrons.

CHAPTER 23
1929

Things were looking up for the ex-garment cutter from the Lower East Side who, like the Knopfs, Abraham Lefcourt and Saul Singer, had withdrawn from the garment trade and was now dedicating himself to other businesses and charity.

Mona and Belle were shopping for their spring clothes at Bergdorf Goodman, Hattie Carnegie, Saks Fifth Avenue and the many other swanky shops that lined Fifth Avenue. They were having their hair done regularly by Antoine Cierplikowski, who just happened to be the finest hairdresser in the city. The city was decorated for the holidays and it was a joyous time for the Fox family.

The girls surprised their father by securing an appointment with Joseph Schanz, one of America's finest tailors, who was located at 745 Fifth Avenue. One evening at the St. Regis, W.F. displayed a dark blue double-breasted suit. W.F. had invited the Greenfields, Albert and Edna, and Jack and Rose Leo to dine with the Fox family.

After dinner, Albert Greenfield rose and lifted his glass. "Health, happiness and continued prosperity, Bill Fox and family." There was something very affecting in the friendship that united W.F. with Albert Greenfield. Rising, W.F. said, "To friendship."

In January 1929, Fox Theaters announced it would erect a 52-story building and theater on the southwest corner of 47th Street and Broadway. The Central Theater on 47th Street with an entrance on Broadway, which J.J. Shubert owned, and the adjacent property to the west were situated on the site of the project.

Fox Theater in Seattle built in 1929

Blumy was the promoter of the project, so W.F. encouraged him to meet with the press. He said, "The proposed structure will be the tallest in the theater district, and the theater to be built will be comparable in size to the Roxy and Paramount."

As part of the development, Fox Theaters planned to raze the old Central Theater and was dickering with the tenants who occupied the 10-story Hanover National Bank. Part of the block front not included in the project was occupied by the Manfield Theater. Across the street were the Biltmore Theater and a wall of the Strand Theater.

This project formed part of a policy to construct Fox Theaters in big cities like Boston, Cleveland, Los Angeles, Pittsburgh, Baltimore and Chicago. The company had recently opened Fox Theaters in Brooklyn, Detroit and Washington, D.C., and was nearing completion of theaters in St Louis, San Francisco and Atlanta.

W.F. had decided that the movie-going public was ahead of the producers, and that growth and expansion, coupled with finer products, would lift the business to a higher plane. Keeping on good terms with customers often meant interpreting exactly what gave the most enjoyment. Big, elaborate theaters were part of the answer. He opted for a policy of building super-theaters in all of the principal cities of the United States, and for this purpose, in 1925, the Fox Theaters Corporation had been formed with an initial investment of $12 million.

W.F. and Jack Leo moved with a crowd entering the Fox Theater in Brooklyn.

"Jack, two years from now it would not surprise me to see our theater business do $200 million a year."

"I think you're right, W.F."

On January 10, W.F. announced the acquisition of approximately 200 motion picture theaters, which would add another 280,000 seats to Fox's capacity in the metropolitan area of New York. The company called this new group of theaters Fox Metropolitan Playhouses Inc., whose stock would be owned 100 percent by the Fox Theaters Corporation. This would make Fox Theaters the largest theater owner in New York.

A cluster of theaters in America's largest urban area made economic sense, because it was a lot cheaper to run a group of theaters in the same geographical area rather than having them scattered all across America. Contiguity kept overhead down because of reduced travel and allowed for strict supervision and the speedy exchange of film negatives, which gave Fox competitive advantage.

At this juncture, W.F. estimated Fox Theaters' national seating capacity to be 700,000, and he was aiming for the one million mark by the end of 1929. The math was pretty simple. One million seats at an average sold-seat count of 50 percent and at an average ticket price of, say, 75 cents, times 365, equaled revenues of almost $150 million annually.

Most theaters were acquired under leases having a life of more than 20 years. Later, during the depths of the Depression, the theater chains forced landlords to renegotiate fixed rents into percentage leases, almost unknown in the pre-Hoover era when the landlord received his rent mostly in the form of a percentage on all sales over a certain figure.

The annual gross business of Fox Metropolitan Playhouses was $25 million, with a net profit of $5 million.

In his now familiar role of company real estate specialist, Blumy negotiated the deal, which was prolonged over several months, whereby practically every important circuit of independent theater operators in Manhattan, Brooklyn, Queens, Kings and Westchester, and several in New Jersey and Connecticut, agreed to sell their holdings to Fox.

The important units of the acquisition were Small and Strausberg, 26 theaters, 37,000 seats; Greater M and B Circuit, 25 theaters, 31,000 seats; Joelson, 10 theaters, 15,000 seats; Greh-Knoebel, 9 theaters, 13,500 seats; Brandt, 7 theaters, 8,500 seats; Siegel, 6 theaters, 8,000 seats; Rosensweig, 7 theaters, 8,500 seats; Rachmil-Rinsler, 8 theaters, 15,000 seats; and Calderone, 5 theaters, 8,000 seats.

The average structure was three to five years old and in fairly good shape; what the trade called neighborhood houses. Under Fox's management, an organization was put into place with division managers reporting to Fox Theaters. The company proposed eliminating much of the duplication and in a short time decreased expenses by 20 percent. Also, with Fox's ability to purchase film at a lower cost, estimated at $7 million a year, and its ability to show better and newer pictures, management felt they could increase earnings for Fox Metropolitan.

In sum, through the acquisition of this circuit, Fox Theaters Corporation would now gross $100 million a year and, including the West Coast circuit, do approximately $135 million in the near-term future.

What's more, W.F. had to move expeditiously to close the deal on these theaters because independents were endeavoring to create an organization that would function as a unit in handling problems common to the exhibitors. Leading the charge was an attorney named Aaron Shapiro, but as expected, soon the exhibitors were involved in litigation over the action of some of the independents, who were adamant about buying their pictures from sources not authorized by the group as a whole.

Much of the story was familiar to W.F., and the whole affair brought back dim memories of Edison's Trust and the independents like Carl Laemmle and William Fox, who had helped bring the monopoly to its knees. In its timing, W.F.'s theater acquisition program was masterful.

Perhaps the most novel and revolutionary picture of the year was Fox's first outdoor, all-talking feature, *In Old Arizona.* It premiered at the Roxy with a guarantee: "Every Word, Every Sound Is Audible."

In Old Arizona starred Edmund Lowe, Warner Baxter and Dorothy Burgess. Baxter, portraying the Cisco Kid, won an Academy Award for his portrayal of the Mexican *bandito,* accent and all. The film has a vocal theme song, "*My Tonia,*" which plays before the credits.

Harold B. Franklin, manager of Fox West Coast Theaters, told the press:

> This film was photographed and recorded outdoors against a sweeping background of natural beauty, and in its sound recording achieved its highest artistic success up to this time. Filmed and recorded right out in the vast open spaces, the scenes and the human voice and all the accompanying sounds were reproduced with a clearness and naturalness that attracts wide attention. The Movietone process caught and reproduced with fidelity not only the voices of actors but actually the sounds of the outdoors, the whispering of the wind, and the song of the birds. The picture was notable in combining the perfected technique of the silent film with the faithful recording of music, dialogue and sound.

Janet Gaynor's first three 1929 releases were all part-talking pictures, also available in all-silent versions. *Four Devils* has a circus theme; *Christina* and *Lucky Star* are both romantic pictures.

"Major" John Zanft, husband of the fashionable couturier Hattie Carnegie, was appointed general manager of Fox Theaters.

Paramount advised Maurice Chevalier not to take voice lessons and to leave his pronounced French accent alone.

Variety reported that between June 1928 and February 1929, $24 million had been invested in the installation of sound recording equipment in the studios. As for theaters, $300 million would be required to wire them all for sound. By late February, ERPI was wiring theaters at the rate of 250 theaters per month.

MGM's *The Broadway Melody* opened at Grauman's Chinese Theater on February 1, 1929 and was an immediate sensation. It was shown at the Astor in New York on a two-a-day basis. Thalberg had decided to make the picture all-talkie and in the process shifted from Vitaphone to sound-on-film. At the time, MGM had only one sound stage.

Once the film was in the can, Thalberg asked Douglas Shearer how the production had gone.

"We had a lot of problems, Irving."

"Why?"

"Because there's no system here. Every time we need some music, we have to go out and hire musicians."

"You're talking to me like I was an office boy, Douglas."

"You're talking to me like I was an office boy!"

"What do you suggest?"

Shearer proposed that Loew's ship out to California their music library, music librarian, arranger and conductor. Thus were sown the seeds of the MGM Music Department.

The Broadway Melody grossed over $4.3 million and produced a net profit of $1.6 million.

Saul Rogers reminded W.F. that he still didn't have Justice Department approval for the acquisition of those Loew's shares, and Nicholas Schenck wasn't going to budge without a firm commitment that told him Fox would have no antitrust problems to face.

The only practical thing to do was to get on a train to Washington. Hoover had been elected early in November, but Coolidge was still President until March; consequently, they were dealing with a lame duck government.

Given the characteristics of the Loew's deal, they were told the man to see was William J. Donovan, assistant attorney general, who in the middle of January was chairman of the Boulder Dam project and was traveling out West, touring the project.

Goaded by Saul Rogers' concern, W.F. made plans to travel to Santa Fe, New Mexico, where they finally caught up with Donovan, who quickly brushed them aside, alleging his hands were more than full with the dam project. He told them to draft a letter to his secretary, Mr. Thompson, who would sit down with Rogers and "find a way to work things out."

On their way back East, Saul and W.F. drafted a detailed letter that hopefully would slide through the approval process without objection. In the letter, W.F. explained the elements of the deal and why he felt there was a responsibility to retain for America the well-earned position that it had in the making and distributing of motion pictures throughout the world. He felt that if the picture companies were deprived of a great part of their foreign revenue, they might get to a place where they could not carry on. He hoped to be able to make foreign language pictures to hold the studio's business abroad.

Copies of W.F.'s letter were sent to government officials, and Saul Rogers returned to Los Angeles to be nearer to Donovan, hoping an approval would be forthcoming.

At a late hour, Saul called W.F. from Los Angeles indicating that Thompson had approved the acquisition of the 400,000 Loew's shares and that they were free to close the deal.

"Did you get anything in writing?"

"I don't think it's wise, W.F."

"Why not?"

"Because we'll get one of their stock letters with a lot of 'ifs' and 'ors' in it, and we're better off without it. I would rather have his word than a written communication, because there are no strings attached to his word."

Since the approval was founded in a discussion where more than two people were present, W.F. let it pass. That would be the first but not the last time that he'd get poor legal advice that would have disastrous consequences for him later.

It was apparent that Nicholas Schenck was becoming impatient because Harry Warner was now back in the picture, pressing him to consider his offer. Warner put an offer of $56 million on the table. It turned out that he was feeling all the power that came from having a stock sharply rise on the market.

Schenck felt it was time to allow someone else to bid on the Loew's interest; the family was antsy. They had commissioned Schenck to sell their shares and had given him an option for their acquisition at somewhere around $100 a share. In the deal with W.F., Schenck was earning about $10 million, over and above the price he had to pay the Loew family. If Schenck could have carried out the Warner deal, he could have made $6 million more, so this began to worry W.F. He thought Schenck's word was good, but his experience of late had left him a little skeptical about things that were not put down in writing.

W.F. had carried out these negotiations for six months and had not been pressed. But one Sunday Schenck became impatient, and W.F. asked Schenck to allow him until Tuesday. He said if he didn't have the money by then, it was all off. Schenck was also worried that the news would leak to the "California people," as he called them, and W.F. guessed he was referring to Thalberg and Mayer, although he had assumed they were aware the Loew's shares were for sale because the third member of the triumvirate, the lawyer Rubin, sat in New York not far removed from Schenck. W.F. was wrong though, as he found out later, because Schenck's style was to play everything close to the vest.

W.F. went to the Telephone Company and Halsey, Stuart, making arrangements for the purchase. For the first time, Otterson suggested a condition be placed on the $15 million loan, that the Fox Companies waive all claims they had against the Telephone Company concerning promises the Telephone Company made from the beginning of the Movietone negotiations up to the time of the loan.

Otterson also proposed that William Fox give the Telephone Company the "worthless" Tri-Ergon patents, reimbursing him for what he had invested in the patents.

Things began to sour when W.F. emphatically told Otterson the Tri-Ergon patents were his personal property, and if he was so anxious to get control of them, to make him a decent offer.

A resentful Otterson stared at him, perhaps thinking to himself, "This little Jew dares stand up to the Telephone Company?"

To W.F., Otterson was nothing more than a flunky, a stooge for the Telephone Company. In fact, he doubted Otterson had the power to make him a realistic offer.

"Let's go ahead with the loan, Bill. I'll get back to you on an offer for those German patents."

"That makes more sense, John."

Certainly, things could have ended worse, W.F. thought. The Telephone Company hadn't denied him the loan and their technical exchange was proceeding nicely. As far as W.F. could see, there was no bad blood between them.

On the following morning, W.F. visited Ernest Niver in Halsey, Stuart's New York office, accompanied by Jack Leo and Saul Rogers. Niver was elated to report that Halsey, Stuart was lending the Fox companies $12 million. The investment banking house charged a discount of two and a half percent, plus interest of six percent, so that the money was supplied at a cost of 8 1/2 percent for one year.

At long last W.F. was ready to plunk down a big check for those Loew's shares.

In the *New York Times,* dated February 28, 1929, a blurb appeared on page 42 that read:

Fox-Loew's Merger Rumor

Reports that a moving picture and theater consolidation was being arranged by the Fox Film Corporation and Loew's, Inc. were received in Wall Street yesterday by activity in the stocks of the two organizations. The reports were neither confirmed nor denied at the Fox offices here, and interests identified with Loew's made no comment.

The Fox Film Corporation's Class A stock on the Stock Exchange closed with an advance of 4 1/2 points, while Loew's stock closed with an advance of 1 3/4 points at 83. The financial community has been keenly interested in reports that an outside organization would try to buy control of Loew's, Inc., but little more than a month ago, Nicholas M. Schenck, President of the Loew's organization, denied the report.

The Loew's-Fox "merger" took place on February 24, 1929, after arduous negotiations lasting six months. W.F. couldn't read any more. Everything was blurry. Over and over again, Saul Rogers had marked with an X the place on a dotted line where he had to affix his signature. So many damn papers to sign. It's all he could do, he thought. One gets to the end of a long negotiation and there is a big letdown. W.F. was very tired, exhausted in fact. But there was still more to do. That government stamp of approval was visibly absent from any piece of paper W.F. had signed. The cue to what was going on between W.F. and Schenck came with a telephone call from Eddie Hatrick, Hearst's motion picture man, to Florence Browning in New York.

"Florence, they're over at the bank right now, signing papers to sell the company to Fox."

Browning desperately wanted to relate the news to Mayer.

The Sunset Limited stopped at New Orleans on Monday, March 4, 1929. Train passenger L.B. Mayer bought a paper and read that he was now an employee of William Fox. Incensed, he tossed the paper into a wastebasket.

Irving Thalberg immediately headed east, leaving only half done Marion Davies' new film and first talkie, *Marianne.* He was calling the Fox deal an "unprincipled sell-out!"

Nicholas Schenck said he'd do everything in his power to make the transfer smooth and suggested W.F. meet with Mayer, Thalberg and Rubin as soon as possible. W.F. told Schenck that he was in complete agreement with the way he was thinking this through. "You're absolutely right, Nick."

The Loew's acquisition, which the press was calling a "merger," caused quite a stir on Wall Street. In one of his rare interviews, Schenck said, "The two organizations will continue as independent entities and Arthur and David Loew will continue as vice presidents in charge of the foreign departments as before."

Little more than a week later, Mayer, Thalberg and Rubin barged into Nicholas Schenck's office. It was humiliating to beg Schenck for more details on how the merger affected their profit-sharing agreement.

"I have been made to look like a fool," Rubin said. "This merger violates the antitrust law."

"Why, Nick? Why did you do it?" Thalberg pleaded.

In his inimitable way, Schenck tried to soothe Thalberg. "My good friend, Irving. Mr. William Fox considers your contract one of our most important assets."

Infuriated, Mayer could see they were getting nowhere with Schenck. In a controlled voice he said, "Go back to your job, Irving. Let me handle this."

On their way to Rubin's apartment, Mayer said, "There's only one way to stop this merger. I must talk to the President."

Fox Theater in Atlanta

Behind the bombast was a crafty old businessman whose rise to power was never taken for granted. If one didn't control a company, there was always vulnerability. Mayer's first big job was to impede the government's approval of the merger.

In the midst of the brouhaha over the Loew's acquisition, Fox Theaters announced it was taking a 21-year lease in the Yaarab Temple in Atlanta for the completion of which Taylor, Ewart and Company were expected to issue $1,500,000 in mortgage bonds. Besides a theater, the building would house stores, clubrooms and a ballroom.

Reporters cornered W.F., and Saul Rogers suggested, "It'd be wise to make a statement."

As much as he hated press conferences, W.F. agreed with Saul that the magnitude of the Loew's-Fox deal was such that he'd better quell any nasty rumors about firing people or closing facilities because all he would accomplish would be to incite an internal mutiny against himself.

W.F. invited reporters into the boardroom on 10th Avenue, encouraging them to fire away.

"Mr. Fox, how many additional theaters did you acquire?"

Arthur M. Loew, Marcus Loew's son, was by W.F.'s side and agreed to help respond to questions. He said, "Loew's operates 450 theaters throughout the country."

Another reporter raised his hand.

"Mr. Fox, how did you pay for the Loew's stock?"

"With American money!"

Everyone laughed, and W.F. felt the tension in the room subside a little.

"Will the board change, Mr. Fox?"

"Nicholas Schenck has agreed to remain as president of the Loew's unit and our board will stay the same. Our boards consist of Jack Leo, vice president of Fox Film Corporation and treasurer of the theaters company; Charles S. Levin, secretary of both companies; Saul Rogers, vice president and counsel of both companies; Milton J. Schwartz, assistant secretary of the film company; and Aaron Fox, treasurer of the film company and vice president of the theaters company."

During the briefing, W.F. stated that he was on the verge of closing the Fox Metropolitan Theaters Corporation acquisition and that, once in the Fox family, the group would bring Fox's theater count to 600. When added to Loew's, this gave the Fox-Loew's combine over 1,000 theaters. That number put Fox in the same league with Adolph Zukor.

That evening W.F. walked home, for he was exhausted and needed some fresh air. Too many lawyers and accountants and their foul breaths had almost asphyxiated him. More than anything in the world, he wanted his decision to purchase control of Loew's to turn out positively for him and the stockholders. It was dark and quiet on the streets by this time, though up above he could see a half moon in the sky. All the way down to 52nd Street, the street lights flickered off and on, casting a strange shadow on the faces that passed him.

For a brief moment, W.F. thought he saw Harry Aitken, but it was someone else. Had he gone too far?

On March 6, Fox Theaters announced the closing of the Reade deal and the acquisition of the Schine chain of theaters located in upstate New York, which included houses in Syracuse, Elmira, Utica, Rochester, Watertown and Auburn. Schine also operated houses in Springfield, Akron, Lima and other Ohio cities.

Several days after the Loew's purchase, W.F. got a call from Harry Stuart who said, "You've done a terrible thing!"

That comment took W.F. by surprise, and he queried, "What did I do, Harry?"

"Here is a company that has 1,350,000 shares of stock; you have 400,000, which is less than a third. What is to stop them from going into the market and buying these other shares?"

"Who is 'them,' Harry?"

"The Warners!"

"What do you want me to do now?"

"I want you to go right in the market and buy the number of shares it will take, so you will have a majority of the total number of shares outstanding."

When W.F. asked what he would buy them with, he was told he still had $7 million from the $57 million and that the brokers would carry the stock on a 50 percent margin, which would allow him to carry $14 million worth of stock. "What about government approval, Harry? Thompson only authorized the purchase of 400,000 shares."

"Buy in individual names. For goodness sake, own the majority or you will be wiped out here!"

A day or so later, W.F. got a call from John Otterson who said, "You're in a fine spot, aren't you? You had better hurry and buy those shares before someone else does!"

W.F. followed their advice and organized a syndicate of family and friends. If all went well he'd have control of Loew's before the summer began. Acting through several brokers, including Mike Meehan, a radio specialist, W.F. bought 260,900 additional shares in individual names, some in his name and some in the names of his children. This gave him more than 50 percent and made Loew's, to all intents and purposes, a subsidiary of Fox Film. He stripped the companies of all the cash they had to make this acquisition, acting entirely on the advice of his bankers and his friends in the Telephone Company. These shares were acquired between February 24 and June 1. It was W.F.'s energy and determination that had pushed through the acquisition of Loew's, despite the inherent risks.

So now the companies owed $70 million, but W.F. believed that once he could legally combine the two companies it would be a simple matter to reduce costs by $17 million a year and meet the refinanced obligations without any difficulty.

Herbert Hoover was inaugurated on March 4 and the attorney general was a man named William DeWitt Mitchell. Saul Rogers made inquiries and was told an assistant, John Lord O'Brian, was the man to see on the Loew's matter.

L.B. Mayer was the newly elected President's first dinner guest. After dinner they watched one of MGM's latest pictures. Howard D. Johnson started the picture and disappeared before the lights switched on. He was known around the White House as the vanishing operator, because the guests never saw much of him.

Mayer warned Hoover that a merger between Loew's and Fox would lead to a film oligopoly and that would be bad for the economy.

Saul Rogers and W.F. took a train to Washington and found themselves in a room with Mr. O'Brian and that same Mr. Thompson who had told Rogers that it was all right to acquire the shares. Rogers told them they were now interested in consolidating the two companies.

O'Brian looked down at a sheet of paper he was holding and said, "I see nothing in this record that indicates we have ever consented to your acquiring 400,000 shares. In fact, as I read this record, I find the opposite; we warned you against it."

A little mystified by his assessment, W.F. took comfort in the fact that the government official who had authorized the purchase was sitting just across from him. He immediately ceded him all the powers of his office but decided to bring to his attention this well-kept secret.

"Mr. O'Brian, we don't have to refer to records. You and I are fortunate to have in this room the very two men who reached this agreement. Mr. Rogers and Mr. Thompson met, and after a long drawn-out conference for a period of 30 days in which they discussed whether the department had any objections, Mr. Thompson told Mr. Rogers that the department consented to the acquisition of these shares, or that the department had no objection. Based on that word, three days later I passed a check of $50 million to the Loew family."

At that point in the conversation, W.F. turned to Thompson and said, "Won't you please talk up?"

"I will answer it another time," Thompson said, and when both he and O'Brian got up, there was nothing else to do but rise and leave.

O'Brian's reimposition of doubt caused W.F. to feel a sharp pain in the pit of his stomach, as if someone had plunged a knife into it. It felt like a double-cross and he wasn't quire sure who the two-timer was.

Two investigators from the Justice Department showed up at Fox headquarters in New York and wanted to know the complete details of the purchase of the Loew shares. Within a week of the visit, Fox got an official letter from the department asking the company to divest itself of the shares.

Because of this development, W.F. decided he'd have to go to the top. He asked Albert Greenfield to set up a meeting with Hoover. The three of them had a nice lunch in a private dining room in the White House, and after adjourning to the President's smoking room, W.F. frankly told Hoover of his embarrassment. Hoover listened to W.F. attentively; he was vitally interested. The reasons for his interest were apparent—W.F. had claimed that an injustice had been done to him by the Department of Justice.

Before leaving, Hoover requested that W.F.'s attorney, the one who had made this arrangement with the department, go back later and have another talk. W.F. suggested that perhaps he ought to engage some outstanding outside counsel, but Hoover resented that. W.F. was to incur no expense. His lawyer could do the whole thing and do it very well; in fact, that was the way Hoover wanted it done.

Accepting the word of the President, Rogers went back to Justice repeatedly, but nothing seemed to happen. The urge to keep on was diminishing. Meetings between Rogers and Justice lawyers seemed to go nowhere. The day after Rogers' arrival from his latest trip to the Capitol, Colonel Claudius Hart Huston, treasurer of the Republican National Committee, came to visit W.F.

Mr. Huston, a tall, lean man with sharp blue eyes and tight lips, inquired whether he knew a man named Louis B. Mayer.

"I do."

"He seems to be a nice sort of chap," Houston said. "Why don't you call him up some time? Why don't you ask him to come to see you?"

Paul Warburg, chairman of International Acceptance warned: "The Federal Reserve Board has lost control of the money situation by failure to take decisive action before inflation reached its present strength."

Walter S. Gifford informed the press that AT&T added 798,592 phones to the Bell system, making a total of 19,200,000.

CHAPTER 24

In the latter part of June, W.F. called Mayer. Several days later he had Mayer, Thalberg and Rubin in his office. These three gentlemen were leasing their services to MGM and were employed under a contract that still had two years to run. Under the terms of that contract, after $2 a share was paid on the common stock, these three men received 20 percent of the earnings. W.F. believed, under the contract, they would collect $3 million in 1929.

Mayer was perturbed by Fox's acquisition of the stock and said so in no uncertain terms; he told W.F. they had been improperly treated.

Up on his soapbox, Mayer said, "We built this company and made it great."

During the conversation, W.F. discovered that none of the three owned any stock.

At times losing his composure, Mayer ranted on about how he was going to use every means in his power to prevent the consolidation, legally or otherwise. To which W.F. responded, "That's your privilege, Louis B., but if we can merge these two companies, I am willing to recommend to our company to pay you and your associates $2 million. We will at that time discuss with you a new contract on an entirely different basis from the present one."

Not impressed by W.F.'s offer, Louis B. exchanged cold glances with Thalberg and Rubin and said, "You have given me a difficult task, Bill."

"What is that, Louis B.?"

"How am I going to get the government to change their opinion?"

"I think you can do it, Louis B."

Mayer's gaze wandered around the office, looking up at the windows. "That's very fine glass you have there, Bill."

"Nicola D'Ascenzo did the work."

"Expensive stuff."

Mayer, Thalberg and Rubin left in a huff. W.F. wasn't sure he had made any headway with them. Mayer was an obstinate man with an ego that filled the whole building. W.F. knew he hadn't heard the last of him.

Telegrams from Louis B. Mayer to the White House pleaded for Hoover's intervention to stop the merger. Mayer and Thalberg knew they faced an uncertain future if William Fox were to have his way. Mayer was desperate, but he had to get back to Hollywood to manage the conversion to sound and plan for the first awards ceremony.

There followed an announcement of a batch of new talking pictures from Fox Film. The Fox Film Corporation initiated a plan to establish a chain of theatrical stock companies for the purpose of discovering new actors for talkies at the Fox Palace in Hartford. Fox Film hoped that actors and dramas from the stage would furnish a steady supply of screen talent.

President Herbert Hoover found himself embroiled in the bitter fight between Fox and Mayer.

Winfield Sheehan told the press, "In finding types for such films as *Speakeasy*, in which a variety of metropolitan types were needed, and also for *In Old Arizona*, when every possibility had been canvassed for the leading woman in Hollywood and New York, it was only the chance discovery of Dorothy Burgess in a stage production that furnished the leading lady."

Will Rogers

Fox signed the satirist Will Rogers to a contract to make four talkies over 16 months for which he would be paid $600,000. Will Rogers, who called himself the contact man between politics and art, would make 20 features for Fox and become a box office draw. *They Had To See Paris* was promoted as Will Rogers' "first all-talking picture" and drew large crowds and rave reviews.

Besides Will Rogers, Fox Film signed George Jessel, William Collier and other stars, stage directors, dramatists, musical comedy producers and writers who were among 200 of Broadway's best.

In response to a stern directive from W.F., Winfield Sheehan departed for California to take charge of the company's new $10 million studio, Fox Movietone City, where 25 complete recording units were now in operation on soundproof stages at the 160-acre site.

Winnie had studio people build Will Rogers a special three-room dressing bungalow, which looked like a ranch house. He was convinced Rogers would take over where Tom Mix had left off, producing steady revenues at the box office.

The man who gave up the role of a century in *The Jazz Singer*, George Jessel, negotiated a three-year contract with Fox Film and the studio began production on a musical play with an Italian background. He would enjoy a short-lived career at Fox, since his stage delivery didn't go over well in talkies. Boasting, Jessel left Fox a free agent. "Me. I'm the only man who was ever paid $75,000 not to appear on the screen."

Other players added to Fox's roster included the singer J. Harold Murray; Edward Royce, stage director; Seymour Felix, dancer and director; Lester Lonergan, actor and director; and B.G. De Sylva, Lew Brown and Ray Henderson, musical comedy song writers.

Besides monitoring the company's effort to fully convert the studio to sound, Sheehan supervised an aggressive production program that included a musical written by Viennese operetta composer Oscar Straus; a musical comedy written by Dave Stamper, former composer of Ziegfeld shows; *Fox Movietone Follies*, which was in the editing stage and would be the first of an annual series of musical revues; *The Passing of the Third Floor Back* by Jerome K. Jerome; *Cameo Kirby* by Booth Tarkington and Harry Wilson with Warner Baxter in the title role; *Behind That Curtain* by Earl Derr Biggers, and *That Cock-Eyed World*, based on a story by Laurence Stallings and Maxwell Anderson, with dialogue by Billy K. Wells.

Among the actors whose sound tests were successful and who would play in Movietone features were Janet Gaynor, Mary Duncan, Lois Moran, Sue Carol, Mary Astor, June Collyer, Louise Dresser, Sharon Lynn, Charles Farrell, Warner Baxter, Victor McLaglen, Edmund Lowe, Nick Stuart and David Rollins.

Directors who studied the making of sound pictures and would now direct Movietone were Frank Borzage, Raoul Walsh, John Ford, F.W. Murnau, Irving Cummings, Allan Dwan, Benjamin Stoloff, David Butler, James Tinling, Alfred Werker, Berthold Viertel, Howard Hawks, George Seitz, Marcel Silver, Norman Taurog, William K. Howard and John Blystone.

Broadway playwrights who were writing dialogue at the Fox Studios included Paul Gerard Smith, Harlan Thompson, Walter Weems, Billy K. Wells, Edwin Burke and Tom Barry. Other dialogue writers at the studio included George S. Brooks, S.K. Lauren, Zoe Akins, John Hunter Booth, Gilbert Emery, Clare Kummer, George Middleton and Elliot Lester.

Throughout this period of metamorphosis, W.F. never once wavered when it came to converting the program to sound. Other producers, upon receiving the news that Fox Film would produce 100 percent talkies, said that they too were making 100 percent sound movies, supplementing them with silent versions for foreign markets.

The "General," Nicholas Schenck, when questioned about MGM's policy, said, "Our aim is to protect all the motion picture theaters which are playing our productions. We will therefore supply them with the types of pictures they can use."

The folks over at Paramount were also following the trend. Lasky said, "Within three months we will be producing 100 percent sound pictures but will also continue making silent versions of the same films. Of the 31 talking pictures in the schedule, 17 will also be supplemented with silent versions."

By March 1929, it was estimated there were about 2,000 houses equipped for sound out of thousands of theaters. Western Electric thought they could begin to wire theaters at a clip of 400 a month. More than 2,600 musicians would lose their job as theaters were wired for sound.

The instrumentality used in making Movietone pictures was Case's technique of photographing sound waves on a strip of film. The telephonic equipment that Western Electric had developed was apropos to both Vitaphone and Movietone and had been designed so that these two systems could use the same projection machine. This single feature kept the investment in fixed assets low. In a short time, the benefits for the Movietone system became plain to theaters. First and foremost, the sound and the picture were contained on the same strip of film, so that it was never possible for the two to become separated. Hence, it was not necessary for the operator to start the picture at any one spot. When the film broke and it became necessary to cut out one or more frames in order to splice the film together, there was always a proportionate loss of sound, thus preserving perfect synchronization.

There were other cost advantages, too. Movietone films were easy to ship because there was no requirement for pairing reels to discs. Another plus for Movietone in the recording process was that Movietone cameras were standard-motor driven and there were no special restrictions in the handling of the camera equipment.

Since Fox couldn't keep up with the demand of its theaters for Movietone, they ordered Vitaphone to be installed in certain Fox Theaters like the Fox in Philadelphia, the Academy of Music, the Savoy in Brooklyn, the Terminal in Newark, the American in Paterson, the Liberty in Elizabeth, N.J., the City, Japanese Garden, Nemo, Star, Audubon, Cretona, Ridgewood, all in New York, the Folly in Brooklyn, and the Jamaica in Jamaica, Long Island.

To make up for lost time, Fox's effort shifted from the battle over sound technology to equipping the studios and theaters to produce and exhibit talking pictures with whatever technology was readily available. The mathematics was simple: If one had a sound theater, the gross was dramatically higher than in those theaters that only featured silents.

It wasn't long before John Otterson showed up in W.F.'s office looking a bit out of sorts.

W.F. invited him to take a comfortable chair; a butler offered him coffee, which he readily accepted. W.F. could tell Otterson had come on a serious mission.

"What can I do for you, John?"

"Bill, we're prepared to pay you $5 million for those Tri-Ergon patents."

Bounding up from the chair, W.F. came from around his desk, puffing hard on a cigar. He thought back to what Otto Kahn had once said about the Telephone Company's patent lawyers, and he could visualize them examining filings relevant to the Tri-Ergon patents. A flame of hope flared up in W.F. Perhaps the patents were worth something after all.

Turning to face Otterson, W.F. said, "Why do you want to buy these patents if your own lawyers have said they're worthless?"

Otterson rose and said, "Putting all this aside, what I came to quarrel about is that you, William Fox, have dared to send a written communication to the Telephone Company telling them they are infringing on the Tri-Ergon patents!"

W.F. paced off in another direction, his back to Otterson. "I don't remember any such letter."

"Well, we received one."

Nicholas Schenck

"If you're violating the patents, John, then we certainly ought to claim it."

A bit calmer, Otterson sat down again and lit a cigarette. In a collected voice, he said, "All right. Let us try to dispose of this whole matter. How much do you want for these Tri-Ergon patents?"

"$25 million."

"That's out of the question!"

Otterson went out of the room, slamming the door behind him.

W.F. resolved to deal a sledgehammer blow to the Telephone Company once his patents were infringed upon. Too few entrepreneurs, he felt, knew a good thing when they saw it, and still fewer had the patience to see it through thick and thin. He had the Telephone Company over a barrel, or so he thought.

When W.F. looked back at this decisive moment in time, there was no question that he'd made a terrible mistake in not reaching a settlement with the Telephone Company. But Jack Leo had insisted that the Tri-Ergon patents might prove to be vital to the conduct of the Fox business, and he told W.F. that he owed it to the Fox Companies to offer them the right of first refusal. The flywheel was essential to the operation of sound reproduction machines.

Persuading W.F. that it was preferable to sit tight, Leo thought the patents would increase in value as the spread of talking pictures continued. History demonstrated the benefit of patent protection. Alexander Graham Bell's basic patents on telephony permitted the Bell Telephone Company to dominate the telephone industry, didn't they?

How about Fox Film's competitors? They would respond in some fashion, wouldn't they? They would be forced to band together, right?

It was William Fox who finally decided not to sell the Tri-Ergon patents to the Telephone Company; he bore that responsibility.

The following day, W.F. got an urgent call from Nicholas Schenck. "What in the hell did you say to Mayer?"

"What do you mean?"

Nicholas said Mayer had phoned him in a vile mood, screaming, 'Oh! There you are! Nick, you bastard! You dirty bastard!'

Apparently taken off guard, Schenck told W.F., "I tried to concoct a feeble excuse for not having told Mayer beforehand about the deal. Mayer said he was about to send a wire to one Herbert Hoover, the sitting President of the United States, that would read, 'Request urgent meeting to discuss Fox purchase of Loew's shares, your friend, Louis B. Mayer.' And then, the son-of-a-bitch hung up."

Mayer boarded a train to the Capitol, where he was feted with a small reception at the Hotel Carlton, organized by Mayer's dear friend, Ida Koverman. Mayer then met privately with the President. What was said, no one knew.

Isador Ostrer, the principal stockholder of a concern known as the British Gaumont Company, came to New York.

Because of an economic downturn in England, Blumy told W.F. that this chain of 300 theaters was up for sale.

W.F. calculated that if Fox Theaters were to buy Gaumont and show Fox pictures, they'd add about $5 million a year to their income. The purchase price of the shares offered was $20 million; W.F. calculated the company would get its money back in less than five years. He called Harry Stuart, who happened to be in London at the time, after which he wired him the details and asked him to check out Gaumont.

The day after his arrival W.F. invited Ostrer to dine with the Fox family in their Marguery apartment; he kindly accepted. Short and thin-bodied, Ostrer was dressed in the height of Bond Street fashion from his pointed-toe shoes and fitted shirt to the wool vest under a double-breasted frock coat. His profile reminded W.F. of D.W. Griffith, for he had a pronounced aquiline nose.

The dining room had a spirited, sophisticated scheme of decoration: A Houdon bust had for background a Boucher tapestry, little marble goddesses sat on the mantelpiece, and the Louis XV chairs had been imported from Versailles.

Following a lively dinner accompanied by an outrageously expensive Chateau Lafite, W.F. invited Ostrer and Jack Leo to join him in the smoking room. They lit expensive Havanas while a butler poured a 20-year-old cognac into antique snifters. W.F. was now ready to get down to business.

"I've discussed our purchase of your theaters with our investment bankers and we're willing to offer you $20 million dollars; $14 million in cash and $6 million in a note due in six months."

Somewhat amused at W.F.'s direct approach, Ostrer said, "Our theaters will greatly enhance the acceptance of your films in England, Mr. Fox."

"That's why I'm paying top price, Mr. Ostrer."

"Let me propose a toast to our association."

Jack and W.F. toasted.

W.F. called John Otterson and discussed the Gaumont purchase with him. Otterson knew Ostrer well, having met him in London on a recent trip. W.F. told him about the difficulty he was having in getting the government to approve the Loew's merger and how he felt a little reticent to take on this Gaumont deal unless he had the complete support of those who had lent him money.

Otterson told W.F., "I see nothing inconsistent with this deal and if necessary when the time comes, I see no problem in renewing the $15 million note, if in fact you need additional breathing space."

Across the Atlantic, Harry Stuart persuaded several London banks to lend Fox Theaters $8 million toward the purchase, and the deal was sealed. W.F. immediately signed a contract with Western Electric to install sound in those theaters, $7.5 million worth of business for the Telephone Company. He foolishly thought that this gesture would appease Otterson and erase any hard feelings he had over the Tri-Ergon patents.

In all, William Fox controlled some 1,500 theaters, and two of the largest motion picture companies in the world. Or did he?

There was always the risk of labor unions disrupting a studio's business with untenable demands. After all, the moguls were in a business without much in the way of machines except for the cameras that filmed and projected their pictures. The largest variable cost was labor, both intellectual and the more modest hourly employees. Back in November 1926, the major studios and the five labor unions had signed an agreement. The industry leaders knew labor negotiations were going to be a constant pain in their backside. Virtually everyone who labored in the motion picture industry belonged to a union or guild. There was lots of over-manning in the industry.

Mayer and three of his disciples, leading man Conrad Nagel, director Fred Niblo and Fred Beetson, head of the Association of Motion Picture Producers, met at his Santa Monica beach house to discuss the formation of an organization to mediate labor disputes. The more they talked, the more the agenda expanded; they agreed that the five branches of the industry—actors, directors, writers, technicians and producers—should form part of this organization.

Mayer was calling the organization the International Academy of Motion Picture Arts and Sciences.

Winfield Sheehan and W.F. attended a dinner and the formal meeting that followed; everyone agreed that the Academy should have a democratic makeup and represent the whole industry. It became pretty obvious that Mayer intended to control the organization he had thought up because he requested that his lawyers, Edwin Loeb and George W. Cohen, draft the by-laws and charter. The fact was, of course, that Mayer had made up his mind that he would rule over the Academy.

The organization obtained nonprofit status and became a legal corporation on May 4, 1927. In celebration, Mayer invited more than 300 people to a splendid banquet at the Biltmore Hotel. Douglas Fairbanks was appointed president of the Academy and announced, among other things, "awards of merit for distinctive achievement."

There was a lot of debate about what categories should compete for awards. The Central Board of Judges finally voted on February 15, 1929, under the supervision of King Vidor. He obviously thought that his picture, *The Crowd,* should take the "Artistic Quality of Production Award," but Mayer thought the best choice was Fox's *Sunrise,* since a Fox victory would prove that there existed no conflict of interest between the Academy and MGM. Mayer wanted no part of ruffling the feathers of Zukor, Laemmle, the Warner brothers or William Fox.

To complement the awards ceremony, Cedric Gibbons designed the statuette that became known as Oscar, a naked man plunging a sword into a reel of film. An unemployed art school graduate, George Stanley, sculpted the image in clay and Alex Smith then cast it in tin and copper and gold-plated the whole statuette.

W.F. hadn't planned to attend the first awards ceremony, and instead requested that Winfield Sheehan head the Fox party; he gladly accepted.

The ceremony was set for May 16, 1929, at 8:00 p.m. in the Blossom Room of the Hollywood Roosevelt Hotel. The hosts were Academy President Douglas Fairbanks and Chairman William C. De Mille, Cecil's brother. It was a dazzling sight, with soft lantern lights shedding rays on tailored evening gowns. Thirty-six tables were covered with fine stemware, each table bearing a likeness in waxed candy of the gold statuette award.

De Mille paraded up to the podium and inaugurated the ceremony. "Ladies and gentlemen, I want to present our master of ceremonies, the brilliant star of the silver screen, Douglas Fairbanks." Fairbanks rose from a front table, acknowledged a thunderous applause and made his way to the podium. Generally well thought of by his peers

First Academy Awards banquet

as having a business head on his shoulders, he briefly explained the voting rules and asked for brevity in acceptance speeches.

The first award was for directing. Fox's own Frank Borzage won the award for *Seventh Heaven,* and King Vidor picked up his runner-up scroll for *The Crowd.*

Fairbanks said, "I'm sorry to say that Emil Jannings is in Germany and can't be here to accept his award for best actor."

A pretty girl dressed as an usherette handed him another statuette, and Fairbanks said, "I'm happy to say Miss Janet Gaynor is here to accept her award for best actress for *Seventh Heaven*, *Street Angel* and *Sunrise*. Miss Gaynor, please."

The Fox table, which included, besides Gaynor, Winfield Sheehan, Sol Wurtzel, Frank Borzage, Benjamin Glazer, Charles Rosher, Karl Struss and Rochus Gliese, erupted in applause.

Rising, Gaynor looked like the innocent girl she'd portrayed on the screen. She wore a little dinner frock of leaf green soufflé over a satin crepe slip of the same color. The skirt was circular and the bodice and cape bertha collar were trimmed with Alencon lace.

She curtsied. "I'm so happy to accept this award. Thank you."

Fairbanks planted a little peck on her cheek.

Fairbanks said, "Tonight, since this is our first awards presentation, the Academy Board has seen fit to bestow a special award for the talkie sensation of the season, *The Jazz Singer*.

Frank Borzage

Janet Gaynor in *Seventh Heaven*

Unfortunately, Mr. Jack Warner couldn't be with us this evening, so here to accept the award is Warner Bros.' production head, Mr. Darryl F. Zanuck."

Weaving his way through the tables, the diminutive Zanuck reached the podium. He accepted the award and held it up to a sustained ovation. Then he signaled for quiet.

"This award is dedicated to the late Sam Warner, the man responsible for the successful usage of the medium."

De Mille said, "I'd like to call upon one of the Academy's oldest and staunchest supporters, and above all, one of the members of the Academy who has seen most truly its ideals and has hewn most closely to the line with the academy in trying to achieve that ideal for which the Academy stands, Mr. Louis B. Mayer."

The fact was, Mayer's windy speech was boring and self-indulgent, but it was worth noting that he paid special tribute to Herbert Hoover as "the epitome of a life dedicated to service."

Perhaps the greatest moment of levity was when Al Jolson got up and said, "I noticed they gave *The Jazz Singer* a statuette, but they didn't give me one. I could use one; they look heavy and I need another paperweight. For the life of me, I can't see what Jack Warner can do with one of them. It can't say yes." Guests laughed and applauded and insisted that Jolson sing something from the picture. Always the performer, he did.

At that first awards ceremony, Fox garnered six awards: artistic quality of production, *Sunrise;* best actress, Janet Gaynor; best director, Frank Borzage; best writer, Benjamin Glazer; best cinematography, Charles Rosher and Karl Struss for *Sunrise*; and best interior decoration, Rochus Gliese for *Sunrise.*

Discouraged by the progress of their patent lawyers, Telephone Company management put out a feeler of $10 million to buy the Tri-Ergon patents, and again W.F. refused.

Ten million dollars on a very small investment. Ten million dollars to be deposited in William Fox's personal account. It was a lot of money. Why would W.F. refuse an offer of $10 million?

There were several reasons. An obvious one, which happened to be true, was that W.F. had raised over $135 million during Fox's building period, so money was no longer an issue. The credit of the company was of the highest class and bankers were eager and seeking the privilege of underwriting or lending money to either or both companies. There was a ready market for all of the securities offered, and each time the offer was oversubscribed.

Time and again, Halsey, Stuart issued booklets, pamphlets, circulars and letters in which they described the great Fox enterprises. Again and again in their literature, they advised of the purchase of these securities, and told of the ability of William Fox; all of this they did after exhaustive and careful investigation of both companies, as well as of W.F.

Several times during the negotiations they made private loans to the companies of sums ranging from $400,000 to several millions of dollars as a result of their belief in the companies and their confidence in W.F.

Was there any pressing need to dispose of such an important asset as the Tri-Ergon patents?

At last W.F. received word from someone who understood the government approval process. Colonel Houston called him to say that everything was all right and that the only remaining stumbling block to the government approving the acquisition of the Loew's shares was a contract that existed between Loew's and Paramount. Arthur Loew had married Zukor's daughter Mildred, and the government didn't want the marriage dissolved, but they did insist on the cancellation of the alliance between Loew's and Paramount. W.F. was never privy to the document, so he couldn't respond to its details. However, if that was what was required to get the government's approval, he'd bring up the issue with Adolph Zukor himself.

CHAPTER 25

Much could be achieved by meeting with Nicholas Schenck, so W.F. made a date with him to play golf at the Lakeview Country Club on the morning of Wednesday, July 17. Perhaps a breakthrough would be possible; therefore, he also invited Adolph Zukor, who knew a lot more about the Paramount-Loew's alliance than he did. Zukor decided to bring along Thomas Meighan, one of his actors, who was also a dear friend and golfing partner.

More for support than anything else, W.F. asked Jacob Rubenstein to accompany him for a round of golf, and he was delighted to do so. They got into W.F.'s chauffeur-driven Rolls Royce and departed from Woodmere. W.F. was feeling very confident about the Loew's matter because it seemed like they were finally reaching the end to the impasse. With Zukor and Schenck speaking for the merger, he believed they could overcome any other objections raised by the Warners or anyone else.

As for Mayer, Nicholas Schenck was his boss and he could make him toe the line if necessary.

W.F.'s chauffeur, Joseph Voyes, was a recent hire and didn't know the area very well. He got lost and they found themselves on a rather obscure road with no traffic. Voyes drove moderately and carefully, feeling his way through dark shadows cast by tall trees.

When the Rolls approached the Rosyln-Old Westbury Road crossing, it was still going slowly, not much more than 20 miles an hour, Voyes uncertain which way to turn. Visibility had deteriorated. There was a hill that hid anyone coming from the left. Just as Voyes made his crossing, another vehicle came down the hill at a high rate of speed, plowing into the side of the Rolls. Suddenly, everything in W.F.'s world was topsy-turvy. Bits and pieces of glass were scattered throughout the sedan.

Dorothy Kane, the driver of the other car, later said, "I was driving slowly as I approached the intersection but the Rolls Royce, driven by Joseph Voyes, loomed up so suddenly before me that all I could do was blow my horn and try to stop, but it was too late."

Neither Mrs. Kane nor her sisters, who were the passengers in the other car, seemed to know just when the front of her motorcar hit the Rolls. It was over in an instant. The Rolls rolled over on its left side in a ditch on Old Westbury Road. The collision had caused the sedan to spin around so that, although they were being driven westward, it faced east when it turned over. The Kane car was intact and remained upright.

Rubenstein and W.F. were scrunched in the back seat of the overturned sedan, W.F. bleeding profusely from cuts. Neither Rubenstein nor W.F. were unconscious. Voyes lay beneath the sedan, his head crushed. An attorney named Reginald Moore stopped and, assisted by other motorists, pulled Rubenstein and W.F. out of the car.

W.F. stood up, kicked his right leg and said to himself, "That isn't broken." Then he kicked his left leg and discovered it was fine, too. Finally, he swung his right arm and found that it still worked; he said to himself, "Okay. I can still play golf."

In a fit of hysteria, one of the Kane sisters was standing in the middle of the road, sobbing.

Several men got out their jacks and lifted the Rolls Royce high enough to remove Voyes. There was no question in W.F.'s mind that he was dead.

Moore drove W.F. and Rubenstein five miles at high speed to the Nassau Hospital, where they were escorted to an emergency room. After a cursory physical examination, the hospital surgeon said that W.F. had fractured his skull. Rubenstein's injuries were superficial; he was patched up and taken to a room for rest and recuperation.

Adolph Zukor, Thomas Meighan and Nicholas Schenck showed up to see if W.F. was still alive. W.F. didn't remember them being in his room.

A deluge of telegrams inundated the hospital. The telephone operator was kept busy around the clock, answering inquiries about W.F. Many flowers were also delivered for him.

Upon leaving the hospital that night, Eve told a group of reporters, "Mr. Fox is resting comfortably now. I am certain that his recovery will be very rapid. He seems to have suffered chiefly from shock and needs quiet more than anything else."

A bigger impediment to recovery was W.F.'s rare blood type. It took a few hours to locate a donor, a 30-year-old actor named J. Carrol Naish, who, after hearing about the accident and the loud plea for blood, came forward and offered the appropriate blood type for a transfusion.

Jack Leo told John Zanft, vice president and general manager of Fox Theaters, to make the first official announcement concerning W.F.'s health.

"I found nothing to cause the slightest alarm in Mr. Fox's condition. It appears that he sustained only very minor injuries and voluntarily consented to remain at the hospital for observation. During the afternoon Mr. Fox talked with several executives of the company and conducted routine business with them. I feel confident that Mr. Fox will be back at his desk within the next few days."

In spite of that positive statement, there was a sharp selling movement in the shares of Fox Film Corporation. Part of the decline was recovered when W.F.'s bankers entered the market to support the price. Shares of Fox Film A stock declined from 92 3/8 to 87, but later rallied to 88 1/4. Fox Theaters dropped 1 1/2 points.

Surrounded by the press, staff physician Dr. Wilfred M. Post issued a medical report after W.F.'s transfusion. "The transfusion took place at 7:00 p.m. Mr. Fox received one pint of blood to replace the amount that he had lost during the day."

"How is he feeling, doctor?" a reporter asked.

"He suffered severe lacerations of the scalp and lost a lot of blood. We sewed him up and he's resting comfortably." Hospital surgeon Dr. Theodore Armstrong added, "Mr. Fox's condition is entirely satisfactory."

"How is Mr. Rubenstein doing?"

"He had only lacerations of the knee and other minor injuries."

During the confusion that followed the accident, Dorothy Kane and her two sisters were taken to Nassau County Police Headquarters for questioning. During the inquiry the police discovered that Dorothy Kane's driver's license had recently expired. The three ladies were released, but the district attorney, Elvin N. Edwards, ordered a grand jury investigation of the accident. Later, the case was dropped.

The day following the accident, W.F. received several long-distance telephone calls from California and a parade of visitors, including Saul Rogers, a personal friend, George Morton Levy, Jimmy Grainger, Joe Leo, the editor of *Variety,* Sime Silverman and several others.

W.F.'s brother, Maurice, also showed up. He spent several minutes at his bedside and when he left told the press, "My brother seems to be getting along fine. Among the things he said was: 'I'll be playing golf with you fellows again soon.'"

The reality was that every muscle in W.F.'s body felt weaker now than when he'd entered the hospital, as if he'd been hit by a big truck, he told Eve. His mind felt no better than his body, for as the minutes crept by, the terrible reality of what might have happened to him sent a chill down his spine. He'd come close, very close, to cashing in his chips.

W.F. was momentarily startled when Doctor Armstrong came by to take a look at him.

"How am I doing, doctor?"

"Your condition is improving and we should be able to release you in several days, Mr. Fox."

Eve smiled and grasped his hand. "I told him to eat well, doctor."

"That's very important. I'll be back to see you later today, Mr. Fox."

W.F.'s first visitors were his brother Maurice, and Jack and Joe Leo. Jack reviewed what little was going on at the office, and he thought W.F.'s attention span to be very limited.

Eve accompanied his two sisters, Anna Livingston and Tina Fried, who brought him flowers and homemade oatmeal cookies, which he passed on to his nurses who thoroughly enjoyed them.

Jack Leo confirmed his worse suspicions about his chauffeur, Joseph Voyes. "He died instantly, W.F."

W.F. told him to do something for his family. Voyes, who was single, lived in Cedarhurst. His lone survivor was his mother. Funeral services were held on Saturday morning in St. Joachim's Catholic church. The largest floral offering bore a card inscribed: "William Fox and family."

Michael, W.F.'s father, went for a few days' rest to the Rose Garden Hotel in the Catskills. He was living alone now since W.F.'s mother Anna had passed away. Michael Fox became quite nervous when he inquired about his son's whereabouts, since the family decided to keep the news of W.F.'s accident away from him. W.F. told Aaron to be sure their father got away for a rest because he had his hands full trying to get better and conduct business from his bedside.

It was a hard journey, and Michael Fox was taken ill at the hotel; the manager called the Red Cross, which immediately sent an ambulance. While on the way to the hospital, a truck sideswiped the ambulance and Michael was hurt. At the time he was 71 years old, but his condition was good. Aaron stayed with him until he was able to return home.

W.F. would find out about his father's accident after he left the Nassau hospital, since the family thought it would be too much for him. The habit of keeping bad things secret was a Fox family trait.

Following a 10-day stay in the hospital, W.F. was transported to his estate in Woodmere, on Long Island Sound, where he would spend the next three months recovering. During this period, roughly from July 27 until his return to the office in early October, W.F. felt like a piece of raw meat cast out in the desert, predators circling him from every direction. Here was an entirely unpredictable and extremely unfortunate mishap, which isolated W.F. from his work for a dangerously long period of time.

W.F. had purchased the Loew's shares in February and it was July and still no government approval. Besides not having the government's consent to consolidate Loew's and Fox, the Justice Department was still unaware he'd gone out into the market and bought additional Loew's shares on margin. In addition, there were ominous signals on the horizon concerning the stock market. The Federal Reserve Board felt that too much money was being absorbed by the stock market, and as a result, other industries were being forced to borrow money at high interest rates. What mostly bothered the Federal Reserve was over $5 billion worth of loans to brokers for margin purchases, including W.F.'s Loew's stocks.

On Friday, August 19, the *Times* headline read, "Bear Friday." The gist of the article was disconcerting. It read:

> Speculators chewed ragged cigars last week, conferred past midnight, lost their sleep. Thursday's stock market had closed strong when the Bank of England did not raise its discount rate. Late in the afternoon came an announcement that the Federal Reserve Bank of New York had raised its rate from five percent to six percent. Wall Street was caught unprepared. Tycoons rushed to telephones; brokers phoned bankers. Long after the dinner hour two Rolls still waited outside the austere House of Morgan.
>
> Detached observers were inclined to view last week's rise as an adjustment to the high rates on call money already established. But when the gong sounded on Friday, trading began with clamorous confusion. Ten thousand shares of AT&T were sold at 266, 15 points off. The *New York Times* averages showed a decline of $9.66, compared to the record May 22 decline of $8.12.

Fortunately the days passed quickly and W.F. was gaining strength. Out of his own restless mind emerged the desire to get back to the office, but the family physician told him it would be a grave mistake to rush back and risk a relapse. However, W.F. could no longer forestall the

Fox Movietone Studio in Fox Hills, Los Angeles, California

dedication of the new Fox Movietone Studio, so he told Winfield Sheehan to organize the event, which was to take place on Sunday afternoon, September 22, 1929.

The invitation read: "William Fox sends his greetings and requests the pleasure of your presence at the dedication of The Hall of Music, Fox Movietone Studio at Fox Hills, Los Angeles, California at three o'clock on Sunday afternoon, the twenty-second of September, nineteen hundred and twenty-nine."

To add stature to the inaugural, W.F. phoned Will Hays and requested that he give the keynote speech; he gladly accepted.

On August 2, a major article appeared in the *Times* titled, "Big Merger By Fox Is Reported Near," which said, "It is understood to be a general exchange of the stocks of the companies for either shares in the new company or the Fox Film Corporation, with a public offering of shares of the combined company to be made in September."

The Loew's-Fox combination was at a stalemate because the government had not sent formal notification to proceed and W.F. didn't want to anger Hoover at this stage of the game. He lamented the time that was wasted earlier in the year in unsuccessful attempts to feel out the Attorney General's department and determine if the consolidation would be permitted. But there wasn't much he could do from his home in Woodmere.

There was a spate of acquisitions in the banking field. Considerable consolidation was taking place. Bigger was better. Guaranty Trust and the National Bank of Commerce had recently combined into a $2 billion institution. Goldman Sachs Trading, headed up by Harry Warner's banker, Waddill Catchings, recorded profits of $1 million a week for the first six weeks of its existence. Blair & Company merged with Bancamerica Corporation (the security affiliate of Giannini's New York bank) and the new corporation would be known as Bancamerica-Blair Corporation, with Elisha Walker as president.

The long, hot summer set in, so W.F. decided to do something he loved and play a round of golf with Jacob Rubenstein at the Woodmere course. Several inquisitive reporters tagged along around the course with pads and still cameras, posing questions about his health, the merger and moving pictures.

On the 17th, par four, W.F. made a hole-in-one that required the spanning of a water hazard in a 150-yard drive. A reporter caught the golf shot on film and approached him. "That was a splendid shot, Mr. Fox."

"I made my first hole-in-one at the water hole at the Belleclaire Country Club in November 1924. The second occurred on the ninth hole at Woodmere in 1927. Of course, I know that all three have been a matter of luck." The crowd gathered around him laughed.

His card for 18 holes read 82 at the end of the game. Maybe his luck was about to change. Who knew?

Jack Leo and Saul Rogers came to Woodmere to review the six-month financial reports, which the companies would have to put out to the street. Glendon Allvine tagged along to see if there was anything fit to print. A former PR man at Paramount, Allvine now headed up Fox's publicity effort.

"How good are the numbers, Jack?"

"Damn good! We did in six months what we did in all of 1928!"

Saul Rogers had a big grin on his face. "We're talking $6.11 a share, W.F."

"Is there any Loew's income reported, Jack?"

"Not a dime."

"Good! Good!"

They had a light lunch out on the veranda and drank plenty of lemonade because the thermometer was pushing a sticky 90 degrees.

"Allvine, organize a press conference for early October."

"Where do you want to do this, W.F.?"

"Here in Woodmere. It's time to show the press that William Fox is alive and well and filled with ideas. Do you think they'd be willing to come way out here?"

"Certainly. You are the news."

"What'll I talk about, Allvine?"

"Tell them about your plans for the future."

After the meeting, Jack Leo got in his limousine and headed back to the office.

Saul Rogers lingered a while and said he wanted to see W.F. on a private matter. "It's important we talk."

W.F. told Rogers not to worry; his chauffeur would take him to the train station. "Let's sit out on the terrace, Saul."

Stern-faced, Rogers reminded W.F. that his contract would expire in December and he wanted to renew it. "I want to continue with Fox."

"I never imagined that you'd want to leave us, Saul, especially with all that's going on."

W.F. reminded himself that Rogers was the point man on getting the government to approve the Loew's acquisition; W.F. instinctively knew Rogers was about to hold him up.

"What salary and for what period do you want the contract, Saul?"

"I want $156,000 a year for five years."

Around this time Saul Rogers was making $60,000 a year, so this represented a hefty raise.

"That's a lot of money, Saul."

"I've earned it."

"Draw up a contract for my signature."

Upon returning to the city Rogers contacted Colonel Huston, who let him know that the government no longer objected to the merger and to please keep him informed as to how Fox planned to implement the consolidation.

Saul called W.F. immediately. "Houston says the government is ready to approve the Loew's purchase."

"It's about time."

That was a great piece of news and W.F. immediately called a meeting at Woodmere to discuss financial matters in preparation for the upcoming board meeting. Present were Saul Rogers, Jack Leo, Albert Greenfield, whose business acumen W.F. respected, and Eve Fox.

Greenfield spoke first. "I've thoroughly reviewed your financial statements, Bill, and there is no question in my mind that Fox Film must raise some equity."

"How much are we talking about, Jack?"

Jack Leo sat quietly with a serious attitude, looking down at a sheet of paper where he'd made his calculations. "We need to increase the A shares to 4,900,000, W.F."

"The B shares will remain as they are, Bill," Greenfield said.

Which meant that even if W.F. was going to be diluted by the equity increase, he'd retain his voting control, which was a comforting thought.

"What else do we have to present to the board, Saul?"

"Well, W.F., because of the Loew's thing, I suggest we increase the board from 8 to 12 and change the preference privileges and voting power vested in the B shares."

"What in the hell are you talking about, Saul?"

"You've got to share some of the voting power or we're going to wind up in court!"

Bouncing to his feet, W.F. lit a cigar, trying to collect his thoughts. What Saul was saying was inevitable, because you couldn't control a company when you owned less than 10 percent of the equity, at least not for long.

Rogers continued: "I suggest, beginning next April 15, holders of the A stock have the right to elect five directors and holders of the B stock elect seven directors. That gives you control of the board, avoids an impasse, yet gives a voice to the stockholders who own most of the company."

What Rogers said rang very true. It made him realize he'd built the company so fast that now he was paying for it dearly, a diluted interest in something he'd once controlled lock, stock and barrel. But this was the case of Zukor and the rest of the moguls, too. There just was no way to finance the rapid expansion of the big motion picture studios without raising additional equity or incurring new debt.

But Rogers wasn't finished yet. "The plan also provides, if four consecutive dividends of not less than one dollar are in default on the class A and class B common shares, that on or after the next October 15, the holders of class A shares have the right to elect nine directors and the class B shareholders three directors."

W.F. stared over at Albert Greenfield in a futile search for consolation. "Albert?"

"Bill, there is no other way to raise the amount of money you need. Unless you're willing to put up your pro rata share, there's nobody out there who's going to give you a lock on the board and the management unless you meet a certain level of financial performance."

"Is that absolutely necessary, Albert?"

"I'm afraid Mr. Rogers is right, Bill. Any new major investor is going to want representation on the board."

There was a moment of silence that seemed eternal. Rogers rose from his chair and stood facing W.F. "So what's it going to be, W.F.?"

"Draft the board proposals, Saul, and let me take a look at them."

A special board meeting was scheduled for September 17, but W.F. wasn't feeling up to making the trip to New York.

On September 19, the board approved an equity increase and the company immediately held a special stockholders meeting to ratify its action.

As originally recommended by Jack Leo, Class A shares were increased from 900,000 to 4,900,000 and the holders of A shares were entitled to elect five of the new board of directors. At the next annual meeting, Class A stockholders would have the right to elect nine of the 12 directors. This rearrangement of voting power would continue until four consecutive quarterly dividends were paid on both classes of stock. The voting privileges and the other changes in capital structure would become effective on April 15, 1930, when the annual meeting of the stockholders was scheduled.

On September 22, W.F. announced the formation of a new company, Fox-Hearst Corporation, to jointly exploit news pictures in sound. "The association with Mr. Hearst is extremely gratifying to me because of the high value he always has placed on the newsreel. I always have believed the newsreel is one of the great influences in the world, and since the development of sound pictures which enables us to present world figures and world events with all the excitement and drama of being present in person, I have placed an even higher value upon it."

An interesting article appeared in the *New York Times* on September 22 that summarized what was going on in the motion picture industry:

Contest To Divide Amusement Field

Two developments last week were significant in the movement that has been going on for two years to consolidate the theatrical amusements of the world under the control of three American companies. They were enlargements of the capitalization of the Fox Film Corporation to a point where it is capable of absorbing the numerous interests which have been reported as scheduled to be merged with the company and undetailed reports of a coalition between the Shubert Theater Corporation and the Pathé Exchange, Inc. These developments were steps in the rivalry of the Fox interests, the Radio-Keith-Orpheum interests, and the Paramount Famous-Lasky Corporation in building up complete amusement organizations.

Under these open developments are the ever-widening influences of the Western Electric Company and the General Electric Company in all parts of the amusement field. The Fox Film Corporation has risen to its position in the talking picture field, which admittedly dominates the entire amusement industry, through its license to use Western Electric's knowledge of producing talking motion pictures. The Paramount Famous-Lasky Corporation operates in the talking motion picture field under a similar license, while the third of the big companies, R.K.O., is a direct subsidiary of the Radio Corporation of America and is licensed to produce its talking pictures under the General Electric system through the RCA-Photophone Corporation, another subsidiary of the Radio Corporation.

The entrance of the two big electrical companies into the amusement field through their systems for producing talking motion pictures, brought about the present realignment by unseating two dominant companies and elevating to leadership two other companies. The Fox Film Corporation and Warner Bros. Pictures, Inc. were the two companies that pioneered with talking pictures, both under Western Electric's licenses.

Two years ago, when the talking motion picture first assumed importance, Warner Bros. and Fox started on a system of expansion. William Fox, the controlling personality in the Fox interests, obtained control of Loew's, Inc., a company which owned both Loew's theaters and Metro-Goldwyn-Mayer, one of the then dominating companies in producing and distributing motion pictures. Warner Bros., a little later, acquired First National Pictures, Inc., which, with Metro-Goldwyn-Mayer and the Paramount Famous-Lasky Corporation had been the 'big three' of the industry. The Radio Corporation of America, having placed the RCA Photophone, the General Electric's system of talking pictures, on the market, stepped in and brought Film Booking Office Pictures Corporation and the Keith-Albee-Orpheum circuit into the company under the name R.K.O., the initials of Radio Keith Orpheum.

With these three companies in the field, a race was started for theaters as outlets for products. Paramount Famous-Lasky, a leader in the theater field and also among motion picture producers, started negotiations several months ago for the acquisition of Warner Bros. These negotiations are now said to be complete and waiting only official approval from the Department of Justice to become effective.

At the same time Paramount started negotiations toward the development of an organization in the amusement field to rival in completeness that
of the Radio Corporation. It acquired a 50 percent interest in the Columbia
Broadcasting System, and Louis Sterling, managing director of the Columbia
Graphophone Company, who is now in America, is said to be here for the
purpose of completing negotiations for a large interest in the company by
Paramount.

When the present reported and confirmed negotiations are completed
the three companies will control all the vaudeville in the country, numerous
legitimate play-producing concerns, three-fourths of all the legitimate vaudeville and motion picture theaters in the country, two leading broadcasting
systems and two important phonograph companies, as well as many important
music publishing and music library houses.

Paramount and Warner Bros. announced a new combine they were calling Paramount-Vita-
phone, which would even be larger than Fox-Loew or RCA-R.K.O. A month later, the government
threatened an antitrust suit and the idea was dropped.

On October 3, from the boat landing of his estate at Woodmere, W.F. held a press conference
attended by 30 reporters. Fox's press secretary, Glendon Allvine, arrived at Fox Hall with six
limousines filled with reporters from trade associations and financial publications. W.F. began
the conference with these words: "William Fox has invited you to his home today to tell you
something of his plans for the next 25 years."

He spoke of the Tri-Ergon patents, saying, "A Movietone short just made in a Chicago
hospital was the very first recording of surgery, something that could be used for teaching." He
told them about Fox's newsreel crews, how they were at the forefront of breaking new stories,

Fox's family yacht, the *Mona-Belle*

and announced Fox would be opening the first total newsreel theater on Broadway next to the Palace.

He explained what Grandeur was and told them the studio was filming *The Big Trail* with a young actor named John Wayne, which it planned to exhibit on a large Roxy screen.

"How much will all of this cost, Mr. Fox?"

"I have no idea, but I am prepared to give one-fourth of my personal fortune to make it all come true."

The market had peaked at 382.02 on September 5. In less than three-and-a-half months, the stock market had risen more than 30 percent. What was more, within less than two years, the market had virtually doubled.

A two-bit lawyer contacted W.F.'s personal attorney, Benjamin Reass, and said he was prepared to negotiate Douglas Taussig's divorce from Mona. "Mr. Fox, for a million dollars I'll get rid of Taussig, no questions, no problems, nothing."

When Mona heard of his offer, she said, "Over my dead body. He's a son of a gun. He's an adulterer, and we're not going to give him a penny."

Unbeknown to Douglas Taussig, W.F. had hired a professional detective and had some very compromising pictures of him. A man-about-town, Taussig had been seen in some very sleazy joints, always with a different floozy hanging from his arm.

Eve told Mona "that every morning we would get the detective's report on our breakfast tray, and we were nauseous from them." Eventually the matter wound up in a bitter court dispute with Billy T., who was 5 years old at the time, up on the stand being grilled by his belligerent father. In the end, Taussig never got any money and Mona got her divorce. That was the end of Taussig, whose name was rarely mentioned in the Fox household, if at all.

The first time W.F. went to the city after the accident was on Thursday, October 24, two days after Mona had obtained a divorce from Douglas Taussig. He was there to attend a banquet in honor of his dear friend, Colonel Claudius H. Huston, recently appointed treasurer of the National Committee of the Republican Party. All the party bigwigs were there, as well as the Rockefellers, the Morgans, the Kuhn, Loeb partners and W.F.'s friends from Halsey, Stuart.

The event he took most notice of was a speech by Secretary of Commerce Lamont, who told these men that no nation could continue when its citizens refused to buy bonds and that all great nations were built on the public's willingness to buy bonds. He continued that unless a great market could be created for bonds, and this speculation in common stock were terminated, the nation was threatened. He drew a picture so bleak that W.F. trembled at the thought of what would occur the next day when these hundred bankers reached their offices and when the bell rang at 10:00 on Wall Street. No one could have listened to him that night without wanting to sell every share he owned the next morning.

At this time, W.F. had with 13 brokers approximately $20 million worth of stocks of corporations other than those he controlled, and he promptly proceeded to sell them commencing Friday morning, October 25. By Monday afternoon he had disposed of these securities, as a result of what Lamont had said on Thursday night. When the bell rang in the New York Stock Exchange on Tuesday, those $20 million worth of stock were not worth $6 million. Had W.F. not acted on his impulse as a result of what Lamont had said, not only would his companies have been embarrassed, he would have gone bankrupt.

The selling panic in late October took its toll on the Fox companies' share value. Between October 15 and November 9, Fox Film dropped from 101 to 71; Fox Theaters from 25 7/8 to 15 1/8; Loew's dropped from 64 1/4 to 49 5/8, and the Telephone Company from 300 3/4 to 229.

During all of this turmoil W.F. was still sitting on 660,900 shares of Loew's stock, for which he had paid more than $73 million; those shares had lost value. Two-thirds of the Loew's shares were in the hands of his bankers as collateral for loans that he'd drawn on for their purchase; the remaining third was held by brokers to cover his margin account.

On Black Tuesday morning W.F. was out at Woodmere, and by about 10:00 the phone started to ring. It was one of his brokers asking him to put up more money to cover the Loew's shares, which were still declining in value. W.F. called his office and asked Eisele to make out these checks and have them ready for delivery. He had no sooner hung up the phone than the broker that wanted $250,000 on his first call wanted $500,000. And soon the others began to call. The funds with which W.F. was to make these payments of additional margin were his personal funds. The telephone kept ringing, and when all of the brokers who could possibly get him on the telephone were through calling, it was clear that the amount of money would be $4 million. It was only 12:00 and the market was still to run about three hours. W.F. called his secretary and told him to tear up the checks—he would send no money to anyone.

Wearily, he went to the boathouse and took the receiver off the hook. He went up to the floor above, the room that Rubenstein occupied, and lay down on the bed and fell asleep. About 3:30 p.m. W.F. heard loud yelling, his name being called. This roused him, and when he came downstairs, Rubenstein had returned. He was agitated.

Rubenstein said there was a panic in New York—hadn't he heard him yelling?

W.F. told him that was what had awakened him. "I was half asleep."

Rubenstein said he had been yelling for a half an hour and that he was frantic. The boat was not tied up to the dock and he thought W.F. had drowned himself. W.F.'s room was on the ground floor and he said he didn't dream of looking for him upstairs. When Rubenstein found the receiver off the hook, he wasn't sure what to think.

Like it or not, W.F. knew he'd have to go to New York the next day to sort things out. He was sweating profusely. He was slowly talking to himself, organizing his thoughts, hoping that events weren't about to overwhelm him. W.F. called his new partner, Harley Clarke, and told him he was in difficulties. Of course, Clarke wouldn't lend him any money since he said he was facing short-term problems of his own.

By this time, the Loew's shares had dropped to a point where W.F. was now short $10 million on the margin account. He got Harry Stuart on the line and explained his predicament; Harry's reply was that Halsey, Stuart was in difficulties of its own and could lend him nothing.

As much as he hated to do so, W.F. then phoned John Otterson for the second time and said: "Look here, John, perhaps I had no reason to ask your company to lend me any further money, but we talked about this thing last night, and this was to be a loan without collateral. I would like to have $13 million, but I don't think I should take it without collateral. I am going to give you my personal collateral. My job is to save these companies; I am not going to think about myself in this at all."

W.F. enumerated what he owned personally and what the companies owned that was not hypothecated; the total was $50 million. He asked the Telephone Company to make a secured loan of $13 million. Otterson said that W.F. sounded different from the day before. In a few minutes he called back and told W.F. that Gifford had said no, they didn't want to lend him any more. The squeeze was on. This was no time for giving up.

CHAPTER 26

That night, W.F. had a frightful nightmare, more forceful than ever before. He could see Gifford, Otterson and Harry Stuart sitting in Gifford's opulent study, sipping wine and talking about what to do with William Fox.

The omnipotent Gifford says, "This little Jew, William Fox, talks about himself too much. He wants to own patents and control the talking picture industry, which belongs to us. He has had the insolence to notify us that we are infringing on his flywheel patent. Harry, if you will help us get those Tri-Ergon patents, you will find that the Telephone Company has more valuable financing to do than Fox."

W.F. could hear the obsequious Harry Stuart saying, "I understand, Walter. What's a flywheel?"

He could see Gifford extracting a flywheel from inside his suit coat pocket and holding it up for Stuart to see. "This little item. I've a lot of very expensive patent lawyers, Harry. They tell me this little piece of metal, if held unique by a court, could force us to pay Fox millions in royalties."

Harry Stuart says, "What makes you think Fox would do a thing like that?"

"Fox likes to sue. Remember, he sued Edison and broke the Motion Picture Patents Trust, didn't he?"

Harry Stuart nods in agreement. "You're right, Walter. He is a litigious bastard. What do you suggest we do?"

"We hold fast and stop him from borrowing any more money."

"He'll go under, Walter!"

"That's just it! Before he does, we'll bail him out, at a price. His voting shares and his patents."

"Who'll run the company, Walter?"

Gifford looks over at Otterson, who speaks for the first time. "Winfield Sheehan."

Stuart seems a little surprised. "He's real close to the Fox family, isn't he?"

Otterson says, "He's only making $145,000 a year and he'll sell his soul for the right price."

Harry Stuart asks, "Who'll approach him?"

Gifford replies, "Otterson will, at the right time, Harry. Just be sure to call your banker friends and spread the gospel: no more money for William Fox, understood?"

Harry Stuart says, "I guess no one should monopolize sound."

With a start, W.F. bounded up in bed. His nightgown was soaked with his own sweat. The endless night was over, but W.F. felt as if he'd hardly slept. He went to the windows overlooking the murky city and pushed back the curtains. He had to get control of himself. He was still in charge. As long as he controlled those voting shares, he would manage the company the way he saw fit. But he desperately needed an infusion of cash. Where? How?

There had to be somebody willing to lend money to William Fox. With the background of a bear market and the ominous signs of a pending economic recession, W.F. set about raising much-needed capital.

Time was definitely a factor. A push here and a nudge there and before you knew it, the Fox companies could wind up in a bankruptcy court. W.F. had to move fast.

First on the list was the banking firm of Hayden, Stone and Company, which had been so instrumental in the West Coast Theaters purchase back in 1926. The man in the center was Richard F. Hoyt, a partner in the firm who had tried to purchase the third interest W.F. had acquired in First National Pictures for the ridiculous price of $2 million.

Hoyt had come to W.F. and said, "You have had a streak of luck. I have just sold those 21,000 shares of First National for you. I have got you $100 a share, and this will reduce your cost price."

But W.F. had not wanted to sell those shares, because he had not wanted to help Warners merge First National.

And now it was time to summon Hoyt for assistance. This put him in a real predicament. Had Hoyt forgiven his indiscretion?

Late one evening Hoyt invited W.F. to his exquisitely furnished apartment. W.F. could tell he had been to a dinner party, for he was still dressed in evening clothes. A graduate of Harvard, Hoyt was a tall, thin man, always smiling. His natural manner was quiet and genial.

W.F. told him what had happened and that he urgently required $13 million. He had been talking for 10 minutes when he realized he might just as well be telling his troubles to a stone wall, that his words were falling on deaf ears.

"I'm sure I can read your mind, Mr. Hoyt."

"All right, if you think you can, go ahead."

From long experience, W.F. recognized that men who controlled large sums of money knew how to be hard and forbidding at times like this. Hoyt was exacting his revenge and enjoying every minute of it.

"What is running through your mind is that you figure I used the wrong method to acquire West Coast Theaters Company, two-thirds of which you sold to me for $16,500,000, and which is now worth $55 million, and that this story of trouble is music to your ears, and what you would like to do is cut out my left kidney."

"I am glad to see you did that mind-reading act so well, Mr. Fox, because when you go broke, as you will, you will be able to earn a good living doing a mind-reading act on the stage. You have made only one mistake. It isn't the left kidney that I want to cut out, but both kidneys."

Saying nothing, W.F. picked up his coat and hat and walked with a deliberate step from the room. As soon as he was gone, Hoyt picked up the phone and dialed a number from memory. "Is Mr. Otterson home?"

The panic was so severe that very few brokers went home at night. Everybody was open so that their margin clerks could figure out the amount of margin their customers had to put up the next day.

W.F. decided to summon one of these brokers, one he thought would be most friendly and with whom his account was $1 million in the red.

He told him frankly what had occurred, the position he was in, then he asked whether he thought his firm would be indulgent for a day, for 24 hours, during which time W.F. hoped to raise enough money to pay the deficiency.

He told the broker it was his plan to invite the heads of the 13 brokerage firms to his apartment the next morning at 9:00, that he was going to propose they proclaim a moratorium for 24 hours, and he wanted somebody to be there to urge it.

The broker said he would.

Jack Leo then called the brokerage firms and asked them to appear at 9:00 the next morning.

They came and W.F. told them he owed them $10 million and didn't have it. They had close to a quarter of a million shares of Loew's stock on margin, and if they sold these shares, the price would drop to nothing.

There was a long pause; finally one of the brokers said, "What are you hesitating about? If we agree not to sell these shares, he may be able to raise the money. There is a chance."

One lesson W.F. had learned early in his career was to talk to his creditors. They authorized a moratorium.

Next morning, W.F. registered for a suite at the Ambassador Hotel since he knew he'd be working around the clock and having constant meetings with lenders. Located on Park Avenue between 51st and 52nd streets, the hotel was a stone's throw from the Marguery. W.F. thought it best not to bring these problems home, since Eve was ill with a bad cold and the girls were both living at the Marguery with their children. Mona was divorced and Belle was separated from Milton Schwartz.

That night, W.F. sat alone in his suite and wrote down a list of names of everyone who could possibly help him. At the top of the list was his dear friend, Albert Greenfield, chairman of the Bankers' Securities Company of Philadelphia. Greenfield had already lent him $10 million for the Loew's purchase, and W.F. wasn't ready to admit to him the serious trouble he was in because of the Loew's purchases.

W.F. remembered, however, how Greenfield had been carrying on negotiations for his third interest in First National Pictures; he told himself that the Warners probably still wanted this stock and they were now rolling in cash. He therefore invited Greenfield to New York, and he came. W.F. had rehearsed Jacob Rubenstein, telling him that if Greenfield knew he was in trouble, the largest price he could get would be $5 or $6 million.

W.F. said to Rubenstein, "I would like to have you agree with Greenfield in whatever he says, and disagree with me." As evening fell, Greenfield called for dinner, and before they had gone halfway through the meal Greenfield referred to the First National shares.

W.F. said, "You know we have always quoted a $15 million dollar price."

Lips tightening, Greenfield went up a scale from $5 million to $10 million and finally said to Rubenstein, "Don't you think if I could sell these shares at $10 million today, that would be a fine piece of business for Fox?"

W.F. said to Greenfield, "I think you can sell these shares for $12,500,000." That night, Greenfield came back at midnight with an offer of $10 million. W.F.'s eyes twinkled as he reflected that even he was destined for a run of good luck.

The next morning the brokers reappeared and W.F. asked them for an additional 24 hours; they reluctantly agreed. Within 24 hours, Greenfield consummated the deal and brought W.F. $7,500,000 in cash and $2,500,000 in Warner Bros.' notes. W.F. called the brokers and put up a new margin, and they agreed to hold the shares until the end of the year on the basis of a margin of 35 percent of the market price. As per the agreement, Greenfield earned a commission of $500,000 and W.F. could breathe once more. He felt as if he'd just extricated his head from the mouth of a hungry lion.

Over tea, Greenfield expounded on the economy. "During the 1920s, the economy has grown at three and a half percent and inflation is below one percent. Unemployment is a low three percent and following the postwar recession we experienced in 1920-21, the economy bounced back with an astonishing growth of 30 percent in the next two years. The fundamentals are still positive, Bill." But were they?

The 1920s was the last decade in the century when the federal budget ran a surplus every year. The national debt shrank from $24 billion to $16 billion. Economic growth was driven by technology and innovation. By the decade's end, 80 percent of American households had electricity. Car ownership swelled from eight million to 24 million.

"And now the ceiling has caved in." Those were Greenfield's parting words.

Alone. W.F. was all alone, for the first time in a long time. Was it not pitiful that a grown man, wealthy beyond his wildest dreams, should lose his optimism? Maybe it was the winter. It was November and very cold. A dank, bone-penetrating cold. W.F. had the shivers. He could never seem to get warm enough. He was losing weight as if he had a terminal illness.

Perhaps he wasn't eating right. Losing weight. That had to be it. His clothes didn't seem to fit right. Shirt collars were loose fitting. Pants were baggy.

It was all so simple. The Telephone Company note for $15 million was coming due in February, and the Halsey, Stuart note for $12 million would mature on April 1, 1930.

Twenty-seven million dollars. Twenty-seven million that was nowhere to be found.

The panic had subsided on Wall Street and the whirlwind had died down. After the storm center had passed, the financial community seemed to be coming to its senses. Whoever had not jumped from a window or put a pistol to his head was behind a desk looking for solutions. It was a question of regaining confidence.

Confidence was important. Without it there was no way out of the dilemma. W.F. had to face his creditors with confidence. That had always been his forte. He was by nature optimistic.

It was time to visit Harry Stuart and try to work out their differences. What good was a bankrupt movie studio to a firm like Halsey, Stuart? Why would they not want to extricate W.F. from a temporary cash shortage? Why would Halsey, Stuart not want to extend their loan for another 24 months?

Though not a key figure in the unfolding drama, W.F. invited Jacob Rubenstein along on the trip to Chicago, more for moral support than anything else. A receptionist escorted them to Stuart's office. When they entered, Stuart had a hard look on his face. W.F. found Dr. Jekyll Stuart transformed into Mr. Hyde Stuart.

There followed a litany of accusations that made W.F. feel as if he were on trial for murder. The sale of the First National shares to Warners was a breach of their understanding, Stuart said. The firm's security interest had been jeopardized. "You've been reckless in buying Gaumont and I want nothing more to do with Fox enterprises. You can do your financing wherever you wish."

As far as Harry Stuart was concerned, Halsey, Stuart expected its $12 million on time. Or else! That was the status of their relationship.

On the way back to New York, W.F. confided to Rubenstein, "From time to time during my career I have been humiliated in one way or another, at least I thought I had been humiliated; but never in all my life have I received such humiliation as I did from Harry Stuart. He seems to gloat over the fact that I am in difficulty."

When W.F. got back to New York, he found a message to call Harley Clarke. He picked up after several rings and told W.F. that he had indirectly learned that the Telephone Company and Halsey, Stuart had merged their interest so far as concerned the Fox companies, and he thought it was a downright shame. He wished to repeat to W.F. what he had said during the summer, that he would like to acquire all of the voting shares of both companies, and if perchance W.F. couldn't see his way clear to sell all of them, he would buy a half interest in them. His banking facilities were large enough to supply all the money the companies needed. But the question was, how could he, Harley Clarke, inject himself into the picture? He didn't want to incur the animosity of the Telephone Company and Halsey, Stuart, and therefore he wanted W.F. to suggest to them that they let him make a 24-hour investigation of Fox's books to get a quick picture of the whole condition; he would then refund the debts of these companies so that Fox could repay the amounts due.

W.F. was amazed at this statement. Up to this time he hadn't known there was a merger of these two interests, and he couldn't understand why the consent of the Telephone Company and of Halsey, Stuart was necessary to raise funds for the companies.

W.F. told Clarke he would ask no such permission from Halsey, Stuart. Clarke called W.F. back, and said he had finally persuaded Halsey, Stuart to permit him to make an examination of the companies' books. If within 48 hours he couldn't make up his mind to supply the necessary funds for financing these companies, Clarke was to step aside and stay out of the picture.

Reluctantly acquiescing, W.F. let Clarke's accountants go to work on the Fox companies' books. Based on a cursory review of the financial statements, Clarke said he wasn't interested in buying anything less than all of the voting shares. This upset W.F., who told Clarke he was not interested in his proposal.

As soon as W.F. finished his business with Clarke, he began making the rounds of the banks he'd listed on a pad. He first visited Percy Johnson, president of Chemical National Bank.

W.F. showed Johnson Fox's numbers and those of Loew's; Percy Johnson said, "The timing is wrong for us."

Thinking maybe that the proposition required a bigger bank, W.F. went to see Hugo E. Scheurman, vice president of Chase National. Again, W.F. repeated the same sad story and Scheurman assured him that Chase was big enough to handle the whole deal. Albert H. Wiggin, its chairman, had a lot of interest in the motion picture industry and W.F. was to come back after lunch and get the final word.

When W.F. returned to Scheurman's office he noticed how the optimism Scheurman had shown him that same morning had been replaced by a dour look on his face.

Scheurman proceeded to tell W.F. that Chase could not take any part of the loan.

"Let me speak to Mr. Wiggin."

"That would be impossible."

"Why?"

"Mr. Wiggin is very busy these days."

"I insist!"

"I'll see what I can do, Mr. Fox."

Originally a Bostonian, 62-year-old Albert Henry Wiggin lived in New York and maintained houses in Greenwich, Connecticut and Yeaman's Hall, South Carolina. A golfer who won from a three down and four position, he played poker for the competition and loved to win. A fitting description of Wiggin included words like energetic, healthy, courageous, insensitive and intelligent. By any standard Wiggin was a rich man, with a wife and two daughters much like William Fox. He belonged to many clubs and had a modest collection of etchings.

Banking had always been Al Wiggin's specialty. The son of a Unitarian minister in Massachusetts, he had gone to work in a local bank at age 17. At 26, he had been promoted to assistant cashier. Then he had gone to New York and had become vice president of National Park Bank. Later, he joined Chase as a vice president and became its president seven years later.

It was widely recognized among the Brahmins of banking circles that Wiggin was largely responsible for creating the mammoth Chase Bank. Throughout the late 1920s the financial press had written of him in glowing terms, describing him as "one of the most vigorous and optimistic and expansive figures in the whole garden of American finance."

It had been Wiggin who by 1918 had converted Chase into the fourth largest commercial bank in the country. In the process, Wiggin had become the largest Chase stockholder.

An inveterate risk taker, Wiggin had merged several banks into Chase including Mechanics & Metals National (1926) and the National Park Bank (1929). Separately, Albert Wiggin had created and nurtured the Chase Securities Corporation, organized for the purpose of underwriting and investment banking, which had been denied to commercial banks. Wiggin let it be known up and down the Street that Chase had money to lend. The question was, would Chase lend it to William Fox?

After a lot of back and forth, Wiggin finally said yes, he'd see W.F. At this time the Fox companies owed Chase a little over $400,000, which was coming due in December.

A chauffeur deposited W.F. and Jack Leo in front of the Chase National Bank on 18 Pine Street. After getting out of the car, they stared upward at the stepped-back skyscraper, which soared into the heavens.

A doorman told them that Chase occupied 18 of 36 floors, and that Mr. Wiggin's office was on the top floor.

W.F. and Leo were ushered into the semi-circular French Renaissance boardroom where a butler placed a salver with a teapot, a sugar basin and three cups on a small table. It wasn't much more than a minute before a solid, droop-chinned man appeared at the entrance.

"Mr. Fox!" Wiggin said loudly.

"Mr. Wiggin. This is Mr. Leo, the vice-president of our company."

"Do sit down, gentlemen."

There was a deafening silence in the room. Wiggin sipped tea and kept his gaze focused on the gaunt-looking William Fox.

"Mr. Wiggin, I'm sure you are aware that the Fox companies are looking to refinance short-term debt, either through new debt instruments or an equity issue."

"Yes, Mr. Scheurman has written me on the subject, Mr. Fox."

"What can Chase National do for us?"

"These are difficult times, Mr. Fox. Mostly for bankers."

"I've been seeing quite a lot of them."

"I would expect so."

"I need your advice, Mr. Wiggin."

"Have some more tea, Mr. Fox."

A butler poured more tea. W.F. tried to retrieve a cigar but his hand shook so much that he gave up on the idea.

Wiggin's immutable composure had the effect he may have intended on W.F. and Jack Leo.

W.F. seemed to have calmed down, but he looked at Wiggin through watery eyes.

"Why didn't you come and see us when you first needed funds, Mr. Fox?"

"A mistake, Mr. Wiggin. A grave mistake."

Albert Wiggin rose from his chair and slowly paced around the room. His steps were deliberate and rather heavy.

"Mr. Fox, let me be brutally frank with you. Your company owes Chase $400,000 which will be coming due shortly. Pay that amount and we can talk again."

Silence again fell upon them. W.F. didn't know what to say. He appeared to be in a daze. The boardroom in which they sat suddenly seemed immense, with its huge Renaissance chairs twirling and the musty cigar smell becoming overwhelming.

Before W.F. could wake to the reality of Wiggin's abrupt negative response, the banker had left the room.

There flashed through W.F.'s mind the name of Dillon, Read and Company, who were investment bankers for Loew's.

W.F. sat behind his desk in his cathedral-like office. Across from him sat Jack Leo and Saul Rogers. The mood was solemn.

"What about Clarence Dillon, Saul?"

"What about him, W.F.?"

"Is he a Jew?"

"He's considered a Jew, but he doesn't acknowledge that he is."

"What do you mean?"

"His father, Samuel Lapowski, came from one of the ghettos of Poland. He migrated to Texas where he set up shop as a clothier. The old man made enough money to put Clarence through Harvard."

"So where's the Dillon from?"

"It's his mother's maiden name, W.F."

"Are you telling me that Clarence Dillon is half Jew?"

"Something like that."

"Better half a Jew than a Gentile, Saul. God knows, after Harry Stuart and John Otterson, I've had my belly full of them."

In 1924, Dillon, Read set up U.S. & Foreign Securities Corporation. It sold $25 million of preferred stock. The firm bought $5 million of second preferred. There were 1 million shares of common stock. The public got 250,000 shares as a bonus and Dillon, Read got 250,000 shares for handling the deal. The remaining 500,000 shares went to Dillon, Read partners for $100,000 or 20 cents a share, which was 20 cents more than it was worth—but with 75 percent of the common, Dillon, Read had control.

By 1929, the common hit a high of $72 a share and some Dillon, Read partners (but not Clarence Dillon) cashed in. Stock costing originally $24,110 was unloaded for $6,884,000 for a return of 28,000 percent.

Saul Rogers called on a Mr. Miller and told him W.F. wanted to have a conference with Clarence Dillon, head of the firm. A private luncheon was set up and W.F. reiterated to the lanky, good-looking Dillon the story he'd told so many times before. He'd been cautioned by an underling to be brief, for Dillon was anxious to leave the city early for a long weekend at Dunwalke, his estate in Far Hills, New Jersey.

Listening attentively, Dillon said, "We'd be happy to do your financing, Mr. Fox, but I don't think it proper that you control these companies with voting shares."

W.F. asked, "Why?"

"You'd better dissolve those voting shares and do it voluntarily, because if you don't, you might be compelled to."

Riding back to the office with Saul Rogers in the limousine, strange thoughts flowed through W.F.'s mind. A nip of cold air made his nose drip. He wiped it with his handkerchief.

"There's some sort of conspiracy going on among the bankers to dethrone William Fox by getting those class B shares, Saul."

It seemed as if W.F. had nowhere to turn except the Telephone Company. From his office, he called John Otterson and told him he was getting turned away by the bankers and needed his help. In his inimitable two-faced way, Otterson said of course he would help him.

W.F. confided that Clarence Dillon wanted those voting shares dissolved, something he wouldn't do. "There's no reason for dissolving them, Bill. Do you want the firm of Dillon, Read to do this banking?"

"Yes."

W.F. said yes because Dillon would play an important part in the consolidation of Loew's and Fox, since they were the bankers for Loew's.

"All right. I will arrange that the firm of Dillon, Read gives your matter careful consideration. We have a private opinion of that firm, but under instructions of the Telephone Company there is no danger of them doing any harm here. However, we will insure that. I am going to arrange for Mr. Bloom to lunch with Dillon Monday and tell Dillon of the interest of the Telephone Company in this matter."

Why wouldn't Otterson want to help W.F. resolve his temporary cash problem? With the motion picture industry, whose ups and downs were far more extreme than those of business in general, it was possible that the current trough would last a little longer than prior periods of financial unrest. But that's what bankers were for, weren't they? They were supposed to help their clients get over the bad times.

It turned out that Mr. Bloom was Edgar S. Bloom, president of Western Electric, Otterson's direct boss and a powerful man in the Telephone Company. This meant Otterson was really going to put things through.

Otterson informed W.F. that Dillon and Bloom had lunch, and that the firm of Dillon, Read was now prepared to give him the financial assistance he required.

W.F. met with the man Dillon had put in charge of the Fox matter, Mr. Miller, who had prepared a financial plan for the Fox enterprises involving the company issuing $75 million in preferred stocks at a price that was most attractive to the company. W.F. was met in the friendliest spirit. All his troubles had vanished. Dillon, Read was happy and proud to be the bankers for these institutions. The company gave him the memorandum that showed the type of securities they were going to have issued and sold. To W.F. it sounded like Aladdin and his wonderful lamp, and it looked as if they had consummated the transaction.

All during the time of the discussions, John Otterson was in the room. He rarely interjected a thought.

At one point in the deliberations, W.F. called Miller's attention to the fact that one of the Fox subsidiary companies had a $500,000 note falling due the next day, and that because everything had gone along so well and this plan was so wonderful, perhaps Dillon, Read could find a way to lend the company $500,000 so that its contract wouldn't go to protest. Up to this time, no obligation had fallen due and was unpaid; the record was clear from the day the company was created until the day W.F. stood in this room in the office of Dillon, Read.

In a calm voice, Miller inquired what collateral W.F. had for this loan.

There were those six notes left that the Warners had given Fox Film when the First National shares were purchased.

As further evidence of how urgent things were getting, W.F. informed Miller that the notes were in his pocket. "May I see them, Mr. Fox?"

"Of course, Mr. Miller."

The face value of two of these notes was $500,000. Miller took the six notes out of W.F.'s hand and asked what right he had to walk around the streets of New York with these notes in his pocket—didn't they belong in the vaults of the company?

A bit perturbed at Miller's tone, W.F. told Miller he was trying to sell them and raise money.

Then things got bitter.

Miller insisted W.F. leave all six notes with him and they would lend W.F. $500,000.

Miller further indicated that he needed the other four notes to raise another $1 million. "The bank will lend you $500,000 on all six notes, but not on two of them."

It was clear to W.F. this was not a friend at all; this was a foe. Miller's whole attitude toward making this loan and the questions he asked indicated clearly to W.F. that he had spent a day in vain, that the memorandum Miller had prepared was a subterfuge. Dillon had no intention of selling $75 million worth of bonds and stocks for William Fox.

W.F. asked him for a copy of the memorandum of the plan the banker had just prepared; he left and never went back. W.F. had shown a careless confidence in his dealings with Dillon. He wasn't about to let that happen again.

At their lowest quotation on the big board, the Loew's shares were close to $30. W.F. had 660,900 shares of common stock of Loew's. He had paid $125 a share for 400,000 shares, and between $70 and $80 a share for the remainder. There was a substantial margin outstanding.

Upon returning to his suite in the Ambassador, W.F. called Albert Greenfield and asked him to take the 9:00 train to New York.

It took two hours to travel from Philadelphia and two hours to get back; Greenfield told W.F. that his wife Edna was ill, and that he didn't want to spend too much time away from her. Finally, Greenfield settled on the 8:00 train. W.F. was pleased he'd accepted his invitation.

What was most noteworthy about this evening was watching Albert Greenfield, with a mouth full of food, eating very rapidly and insisting W.F. tell him what he had on his mind. When W.F. informed him the Fox companies were in serious difficulties and that there were rumors a receiver might be appointed, Greenfield became violently ill. W.F. sent for a bellboy to get all kinds of medicine.

The next morning the short, solidly built Greenfield looked much better and seemed ready to discuss alternatives. He reminded W.F. that the Warners were sitting on a mountain of cash and suggested he consider selling the West Coast Company.

"West Coast earned $5.5 million and should be worth $55 million, Albert."

That very same night Greenfield met with Harry Warner and came back to say they were very interested.

Somehow Otterson got wind of their conversations and came to see W.F. He was enraged with the thought he'd sell West Coast to the Warners, Otterson's archenemies. He immediately suggested W.F. consider a partnership with Adolph Zukor.

W.F. replied, "It's all the same to me."

Otterson said, "I want to prove our friendship. We will buy the whole thing for $55 million, and sell Zukor half of it; the Telephone Company will own the other half and will give you three years to regain it."

Again he toyed with the idea of making a deal with the devil. W.F. was desperate. When W.F. reported to Greenfield what had transpired, Greenfield's jaw dropped in astonishment.

"I think you made a mistake to authorize Otterson and Stuart to buy these shares. I have a feeling this thing is not going to come out right, and I had better keep on dealing with Warner Bros. because I think these men are stringing you. Will you please let me continue to hold on to the Warners for you? Harry Warner is now in my room upstairs and I want you to come up and talk to him." W.F. went upstairs to meet Harry Warner.

When Warner saw him, he said, "What's wrong, Bill? Are you ill?"

"I've lost a little weight is all."

Warner said he wanted to buy Fox Film and Fox Theaters. They argued back and forth and came to nothing. W.F. went back to his apartment.

A few minutes later, Otterson and Stuart showed up. Otterson lambasted W.F. for dealing with the Warners and said that Zukor no longer had any interest in the deal.

Otterson said, "Halsey, Stuart and the Telephone Company are major creditors, W.F. You're insolvent. Give us a power of attorney to run those companies."

After Otterson and Stuart departed, W.F. went to his bedroom and lay down. There was too much going on at once. His head ached and his vision was blurry. It was a case of high blood pressure; he knew that much. He felt a little nauseated and thought he would vomit, but he didn't. His heart seemed to pound in spurts and then he felt he had no pulse at all. Maybe he should go to a hospital, he thought. But that wouldn't do, for any sign of weakness and he would surely fall prey to the vultures who were now circling him.

W.F. fell into a fitful sleep and awoke at first light. He roused Albert Greenfield and told him to get dressed; they had a cup of tea at the kitchen table.

There was a dull ring at the door, and W.F. padded over to answer. "Who is it?"

There was Harry Stuart, a little more pleasant than the day before. They positioned themselves around the kitchen table and a maid served tea and toasted white bread.

Over what seemed like eternity, Stuart ranted on about how his only intention was to save the companies and how Halsey, Stuart and the Telephone Company were jointly willing to assist in any way they could, if somehow he could see fit to set up a trusteeship, a term that W.F. hadn't heard mentioned before.

"What's a trusteeship?"

Since Greenfield was acquainted with the subject, he preempted W.F. "It's a fiduciary relationship in which a trustee holds property, in this case the B shares, for your benefit, W.F."

"What does that buy me, Harry?"

"It tells the creditors we're concerned about them and we're prepared to prudently manage the assets of the companies."

"I'll think about it."

There was no apparent solution in sight, so Albert Greenfield took the afternoon train back to Philadelphia.

All that day, W.F. kept mulling over Stuart's glib reference to a trusteeship and his apparent willingness to have Halsey, Stuart fund the companies if such an agreement were entered into. Since the language of any potential solution to his problems was becoming more lawyer-like, W.F. decided he needed a first-class lawyer and told his personal attorney, Benjamin Reass, to recommend someone with a good reputation. Up to this time, he had not taken the advice of an attorney. W.F. was conceited enough to think that he could work himself out of this difficulty. But now for the first time he had been definitely confronted with a clear, precise understanding of what the Telephone Company wanted to accomplish. And at this stage he felt he must promptly be advised of his legal rights.

Bright and early the next morning, Reass and W.F. wound up in the office of Colonel Joseph M. Hartfield, a Wall Street lawyer. W.F. owed one of Hartfield's clients a couple of million dollars, so he gladly saw him. Not more than four and a half feet tall, Hartfield was a Jew from the Deep South who used the expression "you all" throughout his speech. Hartfield earned his living on Wall Street and was close friends with the bankers who were trying to break W.F.

Benjamin Reass insisted W.F. hear him out. It was soon apparent that Hartfield was distinctly a Wall Street lawyer, for every once in a while he would make some sort of suggestion that would appear as if he were fighting with the Telephone Company and Halsey, Stuart.

W.F. pointed this out to Reass but he said not to pay any attention to it. He said that it was a habit Hartfield had of rehearsing things in his mind and that Hartfield was a man who would stand by him. Hartfield had great influence and entree and was general counsel for the Morgan bank known as the Bankers Trust Company, one of W.F.'s large banking creditors.

Several sessions were involved in laying out all the facts for Hartfield. He let no conference go without commenting on his popularity with the ladies. Each conference would end with the same statement; if it was afternoon, he was going to have tea with charming ladies; if evening, he was going to have dinner with charming ladies.

Uncomfortable being represented by someone whose client was the Bankers Trust Company, W.F. advised Reass to find someone else.

It was time, perhaps, to get the best lawyer in the city or the country, so he asked Reass, "Who is the greatest lawyer in America?" He thought for a moment and said, "Charles Evans Hughes."

This was about two months prior to Hughes' appointment as Chief Justice of the Supreme Court. W.F. knew that Hughes had served as a Supreme Court justice for six years, up to 1916, when he'd resigned to become the Republican candidate for president against Woodrow Wilson. He had also served as Secretary of State in the cabinets of Harding and Coolidge. There was no doubt that Hughes had one of the most impressive pedigrees he had ever seen.

On the morning of Monday, November 25, W.F. called on Hughes and gave him a complete recital of everything that involved his companies, the episodes beginning with seeking the approval of the Department of Justice and acquiring the Loew's shares until the day he appeared before him. W.F. was confined with him in his room for more than three hours. Hughes was as vitally interested in this recital as anyone W.F. had ever spoken to. When W.F. concluded, Hughes extended his hand, the palm of which was wet with perspiration. W.F. felt a grip of friendship. Hughes asked him to dismiss the matter from his mind; he indicated that he had broad shoulders and was willing to have this burden placed upon those shoulders.

W.F. said, "Mr. Hughes, from October 28 until today, I have had an average of no more than two hours sleep a night. My brain is so tired, I can't think any more. I don't seem to be able to go any further."

"Don't worry, Mr. Fox. Let me think for you."

Not only did W.F. have business troubles to deal with, but he had illness at home. Eve was confined to her bed at their country home throughout the whole ordeal. He couldn't go to that home and he didn't dare talk over the telephone because he believed that every word he uttered was being listened to.

If W.F. was within 100 miles of New York, at no previous time during his career did he fail to take the train and sleep in his own home. But now W.F. couldn't go. He was felt like a pathetic old man and was sure that if his health were spared until he was a century old, he would never feel as old as he felt then.

It was a time of constant surprise. His life was totally unpredictable and unforeseen events seemed to have become the norm.

When W.F. arrived back at his office, he found a very perturbed Jack Leo waiting for him. They entered and sat down. He lit up a cigar and drew a long puff.

"Did you see the ticker this morning, W.F.?"

"No, what did it say?"

"The government has begun an action against you and the companies."

"For what?"

"They want you to divest those shares."

There it was again, like some recurring migraine that never seemed to go away.

"Where did you hear that, Jack?"

"It came across the Jones ticker."

"Jack, you were there. Colonel Huston said, 'Once the Paramount-Loew's contract is rescinded, the government would be satisfied.' Didn't he say that?"

"That's exactly what he said."

And all of this after visiting Hughes. Later he discovered, much to his surprise, that the name of the solicitor general of the United States government was Charles Evans Hughes, Junior.

The campaign to find a friendly banker had to continue, so W.F. decided to write a little note to the next man on his list, the infamous John D. Rockefeller.

The Chase Bank was in discussions with Rockefeller, so he thought he might get Mr. Rockefeller's support and convince him to write a note telling Albert H. Wiggin to assist him.

With the pending merger of Rockefeller's Equitable Trust with Chase National, Rockefeller moved his son-in-law Winthrop Aldrich into the position of president. But Aldrich was only the fifth-ranking officer, Albert Wiggin now being called chairman.

Through Rockefeller's personal secretary, W.F. was directed to consult Aldrich. W.F. immediately contacted his lawyer, Hughes, who said he should not keep the appointment. Hughes said, "You know Rockefeller is a Baptist and so am I, and we Baptists stick together and understand each other. If he wanted to help you, he would have sent you to Mr. Wiggin. He is a 'yes' man. But Rockefeller has sent you to the 'no' man. You will just be wasting your time."

After the Dillon incident, W.F. promised himself that he would not waste his time. He accepted Hughes' sage advice and didn't pursue the matter further.

Here he was, living on the edge. The English notes were coming due and the brokers were hounding him for more margin on the Loew's shares. He was unable to spend any time at all running the business. In spite of everything, the companies were performing well. Loew's was sitting on more than $10 million cash and earned $10 million in the last fiscal year.

All W.F. needed was a bridge loan to meet the companies' immediate obligations until he could issue new equity in them.

There was always Kuhn, Loeb. Otto Kahn was tied up with Paramount's problems, so W.F. visited Felix Warburg, one of the senior partners at the firm. W.F. had met him during war drives, and they enjoyed the acquaintance of mutual friends. Warburg listened for a short while and then excused himself.

The next port of call was the Eastman Kodak Company, whose business it was to make thin, flexible, translucent nitrocellulose base and coat it with light-sensitive silver bromide. Its principal competitor in the film trade was DuPont, which was building up its sales at a rapid pace. The motion picture industry consumed 90 million feet of negative motion-picture film in cinema studios and 1,200,000,000 feet of positive motion-picture film in theaters. Kodak sold two-thirds of Hollywood's positive film and more than one-half of its negative film.

Who should W.F. talk to?

There was no Mr. Eastman to talk to anymore. Nobody owned much Eastman stock and Mr. Eastman had given most of his fortune away. He owned 17,000 shares at the time of his death.

Kodak was managed by a group of seven senior executives who met every Tuesday morning in a conference room next to the office of Frank W. Lovejoy. Tall and soft-spoken, Lovejoy was in charge of operations and had personally called on W.F. on several occasions. He was very much a gentleman of the old school. W.F. instructed Jack Leo to arrange for a meeting with Mr. Lovejoy.

While waiting for a reply from Kodak, W.F. had a surprise visit from Will Hays.

The elephant-eared Hays was escorted into his office; W.F. immediately ordered coffee, which Hays gratefully accepted.

"W.F., I'm very sorry about all this."

Will Hays

"Thank you, Will. I'll get through this somehow."

"If you ever decide to sell your shares, W.F., I know a man who might be interested."

It took a while, but W.F. finally guessed who the mysterious suitor was, none other than Harley Clarke.

"Let me give you a price, Will. For the sake of conversation."

"I understand."

"Before my troubles, I would have told you that my price was $100 million. Now, I'd take a third of that amount."

"I'll get the message back, W.F."

A roguish smile on his face, Hays got up and left. W.F. still didn't know what Will Hays was after. Later he discovered that Hays and Clarke had a mutual friend, Senator Watson, a politician from Hays' home state of Indiana. Clarke's name was appearing in the strangest places.

CHAPTER 27

The next day was Saturday, and Clarke telephoned W.F. from Chicago. He said the price W.F. had mentioned to Hays was all right; he would pay him $33 million.

"I'll come to New York on Monday and consummate the transaction with you, W.F."

"I'm in more serious trouble than you know, Harley."

"What kind of trouble?"

"I'm told there's going to be a raid on the Loew's shares on Monday morning at 10:00, and I need enough money to lift these Loew's shares out of the hands of the brokers."

"All right. I'll have an official of Chase Bank call you tomorrow, Sunday, and give you a written communication indicating that there will be $6,500,000 to your credit on Monday morning when the bank opens."

It happened that Richard Dwight, Judge Hughes' law partner, was sitting alongside of him while he was having this conversation with Clarke. He asked Clarke to repeat to Dwight what he had just said. Clarke did so, and the next day, Sunday, Dwight called again at W.F.'s apartment in the hopes of meeting this executive of Chase Bank.

The telephone rang. It was Clarke on the phone from Chicago. He had changed his mind about doing it this way. Instead, he would take an early train out of Chicago, be at W.F.'s suite at 9:15, and bring with him a certified check for $6,500,000.

There still was no word from Rochester, New York, Kodak's headquarters. This was now Sunday morning. W.F. had told no one about the Kodak deal. There was no Chase Bank check for $6,500,000 from Clarke either.

Everybody W.F. knew to whom he could possibly go for financial aid was exhausted.

Monday morning at 9:15 Richard Dwight joined W.F., and still no Harley Clarke.

W.F. phoned the New York Central Station to see if the train was late. No, it was on time. It had arrived about 8:45. Clarke could have walked to his office and have been there 20 minutes ago. What was Clarke's purpose in calling him on the phone at all? What had been Hays' purpose? Were they delay tactics designed to force Fox Film into bankruptcy?

Maybe W.F. made a terrible mistake when he told Clarke there would be a raid on these Loew's shares. Closing his eyes, he could see the New York Stock Exchange, with brokers hustling and bustling, taking their positions at their various posts.

The phone rang at exactly 9:55 a.m., and it was the agent of the Eastman Kodak Company. "There is placed to your credit $6,500,000 at the Bankers Trust in New York," he said.

There he was! There was this God Almighty of his, saving him again!

Now it was necessary to phone 13 brokers. A half dozen of Fox's staff people who had phones took a couple of names each and got busy. By 10:15 a.m., the majority of the brokers knew that they were to take these shares out of the banks where they had hypothecated them and deliver them to Bankers Trust to receive cash for them.

At 10:30 a.m., Clarke arrived. Dwight informed him of what had just transpired with the Loew's shares. It didn't seem to surprise him. "I am prepared to buy the voting shares of Fox Film and Fox Theaters for $33 million," Clarke said. He handed W.F. several sheets of paper and added, "I have here a memorandum containing my proposal."

Slipping on his reading glasses, W.F. read its contents and quickly decided against the sale. Clarke's plan required him to authorize the board of directors of Fox Theaters to sell to Clarke the 660,900 shares of Loew's stock at a price of $33,045,000, which was $40 million less than the company paid for them. The amount he was to pay the Fox companies, $33,045,000, plus the $33 million he was to pay W.F. would be $7 million less than the price W.F. paid for the Loew's shares.

It looked like a simple proposition to carry out this plan with Clarke, because at this time the market price for Loew's was $40 a share and Clarke was proposing to buy them at $50 a share.

"My answer is no," W.F. told him. He wasn't going to milk the companies.

It was W.F.'s guess that Clarke had more than this one memorandum in his pocket. Had the stock market raid taken place, the other memorandum would probably have contained an offer of $1 million for his voting shares.

Tired and not thinking straight, W.F. went for a long walk on Park Avenue, trying to clear his head and hoping a new idea would occur to him while he strolled along the wide avenue. W.F. got in a cab and found himself in a theater whose name he couldn't recall; he saw a picture that left no impression on his mind. It was as if he were in a trance because he could see, yet he saw nothing. He could hear, yet he heard very little.

When he left the theater he headed back to the Ambassador, collapsing into bed and a deep sleep.

There was white-crested Bernard M. Baruch. Master of markets, patron of senators, confidant of presidents. The wise man who knew when to buy and when to sell. In the past, W.F. had business dealings with the Wall Street wonder, and he considered Baruch a good friend. W.F. referred to him as Bernie, a gesture he reserved for more than just acquaintances. His reputation amongst the cognoscente was huge, and his intuition admired. It would be Baruch who would persuade the Democrats not to block the Senatorial confirmation of Chief Justice Hughes. It would be Baruch who would encourage Hoover to appoint Eugene Meyer, publisher of the *Washington Post*, as Governor of the Federal Reserve Board.

Baruch's judgment about an investment was highly respected by everyone on Wall Street. The fact he would even take the time to go over the Fox situation was received as a good omen.

Baruch called upon W.F. at the Ambassador Hotel and examined the financial statements of the Fox companies. After two or three hours of poring over figures, he became wildly enthusiastic about the whole enterprise. Baruch could readily see that the common stock was selling on the basis of one year's earnings. It was customary at the time for common stocks to sell at 10 times earnings, and therefore he thought W.F. was sitting on a pot of gold.

Baruch explained to W.F. that during the entire panic he was the confidential advisor to Albert Wiggin; Wiggin was his personal friend, and both Wiggin of Chase and Mitchell of National City rested on his advice. The matter that now confronted W.F. was insignificant, and there would be no problem in straightening it out promptly.

W.F. was not to worry, Baruch said. W.F. was naturally filled with hope.

The Stuart brothers called upon Baruch, and that made W.F. very nervous.

Baruch insisted that their attitude made no difference. He was entirely focused on the results of the company, which were undeniably good. He said he wanted to hear Halsey, Stuart's side of the story before committing himself to any specific course of action.

What transpired at the conference W.F. would never know, but he did understand that from that time on Baruch was longer available for his phone calls. He could readily see that when Baruch had to decide between Wiggin, Gifford, Stuart and Fox, there was no contest.

During the month of November it was common to read in the newspapers of men who had met with reverses during these 30 days, resorting to every known means to bring life to an end. During this period there were suicides daily, and in each instance there was a Wall Street record behind it. W.F. was reminded that Wall Street wound crookedly, with a river at one end and a cemetery at the other, and now this became a reality to him. During these 30 days he had exactly 60 hours of sleep. He was mentally tired and physically worn out.

Why not appeal to Henry Ford? In the past, Ford had tangled with his own bankers, and he knew how it felt to be stabbed in the back. Certainly the world's greatest industrialist would understand W.F.'s predicament?

Could Colonel Huston arrange a meeting, perhaps? Unfortunately, no.

Then someone came up with the idea of David A. Brown, a Jewish banker and philanthropist, whose brother was Ford's architect. It was said that Ford threw Brown's request for a meeting into a wastebasket the minute he saw the name William Fox referenced.

And then it all came back to W.F. Ford had started a weekly paper, the *Dearborn Independent*, bought and read mainly by people who were unfriendly to Jews. When Ford had been in the midst of his Jew-baiting campaign, he'd selected William Fox as a victim. In response, W.F. had made up his mind to throw a searchlight on Ford and see if he had a weak spot. Fox News had hundreds of cameras and cameramen from coast to coast take moving pictures of all wrecks where Ford autos were involved, record the grisly details, then get from experts affidavits stating that Ford defects were the cause of the accidents.

In spite of the stock market crash, theater receipts were strong. The United States industrial production index reached a peak in the middle of 1929. There was no inkling that the economy was about to turn sour in a big way. Up to mid-1930 there would be a business cycle similar to most business cycles. Throughout the course of the Fox struggle, the furthest thing from W.F.'s mind was the thought of a great recession. It was another bump in a long road, and things would eventually work themselves out.

Unfortunately, enormous mistakes in judgment would be made. The Federal Reserve would fail to increase the quantity of money in a low-inflation economy still experiencing substantial real growth.

On June 17, 1930, one of the largest increases in tariff history was signed into law, the infamous Hawley-Smoot Tariff, dealing a lethal blow to international business confidence and the worldwide economy. The financial system eventually collapsed in the first semester of 1933.

The Kodak loan kept a few wolves away from the door, but others began to gather. There was the Gaumont note and other creditors were threatening foreclosure.

Hughes and his partner, Richard Dwight, were talking about a trusteeship they said would bring Halsey, Stuart and the Telephone Company into a nonadversarial position.

"I put myself entirely in your hands," W.F. told Hughes.

He had the best lawyer in the land to look out for his interests, didn't he?

If Hughes wanted W.F. to sign a trusteeship, why would he not? In this way, perhaps, W.F. would gain the unfaltering support of his two biggest creditors.

The issue at stake was 150,101 shares of voting stock in W.F.'s name, which represented the controlling interest in the Fox companies. Whoever owned these shares had the power to elect the board of directors and appoint management. Whoever owned these shares had the final say on any important decision.

Deposit these shares in a trust, Dwight insisted.

Show your good faith, Hughes said.

Let us help you refinance these companies, Otterson encouraged.

To do that, let's create a trusteeship where we all participate in the difficult decisions facing the companies, Stuart said.

It's only a temporary arrangement, Dwight said.

Something to convince the creditors that we all have the interest of the companies uppermost in our minds, Stuart said.

W.F.'s head ached terribly, and he wasn't sure what any of this talk really meant. He was physically debilitated.

Trust us, they all said.

He had the finest lawyer in the land, didn't he?

The following day W.F. received a transatlantic call from Winfield Sheehan, who was in London on business. W.F. had not talked to Sheehan about the financial difficulties of the companies, since he believed there was very little Sheehan could contribute other than to keep his mind on running the business.

By this time, Sheehan had stepped up in life. He owned a large Mediterranean house in Beverly Hills at 1197 Angelo Drive, a fitting mansion for a Hollywood kingpin. It had a sunken garden and a library ceiling imported from Spain. It was said the house required 33 servants to maintain the level of good living to which Sheehan had become accustomed. The front entrance was protected by an iron gate; to one side was a row of trees and beyond them a fleet of cars.

At this particular moment in his life Winfield Sheehan was between wives, having divorced the Ziegfeld beauty Kay Laurel and not yet married the soprano Maria Jeritza.

Through press releases, Sheehan read that the financial collapse of the market had produced a near insolvency in the Fox empire. In an unsettled voice Sheehan asked, "What is wrong and how wrong is it?"

"Nothing is wrong," W.F. replied. "There is no danger and everything will be all right."

Sensing Sheehan was left with a bad taste in his mouth, W.F. wondered how much he knew and how much he was trying to get out of him. That afternoon, Sheehan decided to wrap up things and return to New York. Whenever he was in Manhattan, he usually stayed at his suite at the Savoy-Plaza.

W.F.'s guess was that both Otterson and Stuart were getting ready for his dethronement and the assumption of power by their stooge, Winfield Sheehan. Call it premonition or just the fact that W.F. could read people, but there was no doubt in his mind that Winfield Sheehan would be the first to jump ship. Later that same day Sheehan wired that he'd arrive in New York on December 3 and come straight to W.F.'s apartment. W.F. wired back telling him he was looking forward to seeing him.

Charles Evans Hughes

Charles Evans Hughes sent for W.F. and said, "Now that the agreement is ready for signature, you have to make a choice. Shall I continue to be your lawyer, or do you wish my firm to become the attorneys for the voting trusteeship?"

Unaware of the implications of what Hughes was saying, W.F. insisted Hughes decide whatever he thought best for the companies. As he had told Hughes the day before, he couldn't think and he didn't know what to say.

Hughes said no, W.F. must decide whether he wanted him to remain his attorney, or whether he wanted his firm to be attorneys for the trusteeship. Without giving it any real thought, W.F. released him as his attorney, thinking that what he needed most was to have Hughes be attorney for the trustees, to see that no trouble came to him. Hughes gave W.F.'s shoulder a lingering squeeze and said, "I'll have the papers for you to sign in the morning, Mr. Fox."

The negotiations concerning the trust agreement took place in the presence of Hughes, Dwight, Reass, Hartfield, Otterson, Stuart and several other minor-league lawyers. In a positive tone, Harry Stuart carefully laid the groundwork for the trusteeship, explaining his firm's willingness and desire to be of great service to the Fox companies.

One of the self-styled lawyers made a motion: "As trustees I suggest we name John Otterson, Harry Stuart and William Fox."

Harry Stuart said Halsey, Stuart wanted to make little or no change in the present running of the organization and that W.F. had no right to suspect that this was anything else but a friendly gesture. To prove how friendly it was, it was the intention of the Telephone Company that when it had received its $15 million back, it would surrender the trusteeship of Otterson, at which time his brother, Charles Stuart, would become trustee.

W.F. told Stuart he saw no difficulty in the whole matter. He said, "You have expressed to me in the most friendly terms the wish to help my enterprise."

There was also the little-discussed issue of management. W.F. reminded Stuart of their most friendly relationship until the crash. He was perfectly willing to create this trusteeship, with the distinct understanding there was to be little or no change in the set-up of these organizations, and that he had no objection to the firm of Halsey, Stuart having two of the trustees after the Telephone Company received its money. There had never been a time when W.F. was more proud of his frontline managers, he told them.

To be sure, Stuart implied, there was no change in management even contemplated. Furthermore, none was ever discussed.

There was, of course, no written agreement to this effect, as it was not insisted upon by W.F.'s counsel.

As part of the bargain, W.F. agreed to turn over to the trusteeship the voting shares of Fox Film Corporation, 50,101 shares out of 100,000 class B shares as well as 100,000 class B shares of the Fox Theaters Corporation, which was 100 percent of the voting stock. These shares would be turned over to Bankers Trust accompanied by an escrow letter.

W.F. also agreed to deliver to the trustees the resignations of all the directors of the companies, and of such officers of the companies "as the trustees might request, with the exception of the president."

In W.F.'s mind, the third paragraph of the agreement was the whole reason for the trusteeship: "The trustees will endeavor to prepare a plan of reorganization and refinancing of the companies and in the meantime will undertake negotiations with a view to preventing the sacrifice of the assets of the companies, including particularly securities pledged. The trustees will also undertake to negotiate with creditors and other persons interested in the situation with the view of obtaining their forbearance and co-operation during the period of the preparation and submission and adoption of any such plan."

Partially out of a mixture of fatigue and hopelessness, and partially on a feeling that things couldn't be worse, W.F. decided to go along with the trusteeship. In a totally debilitated state of mind, W.F. picked up a pen and signed his name to a document whose import he didn't fully comprehend. In essence, he was delivering control of the companies to his two greatest adversaries, hoping they would find it in their best interest to save them and William Fox in the process. For the moment, he thought he was safe. He'd been spared the ordeal of continuing litigation. He could return to making motion pictures at last. He was secure inside the confines of the trusteeship agreement. Or so he thought. In any case, he signed the trust agreement.

At 7:30 that same night, December 3, 1929, Winfield Sheehan hastened off his steamship, hailed a taxi and headed for W.F.'s apartment at 270 Park Avenue.

With the ink barely dry on the trusteeship agreement, W.F. told Winnie that Fox Film's troubles were over because Harold Stuart and John Otterson were busy coming up with a plan to refinance the companies. Sheehan stood by a window and stared blankly at the distant lights. He lit a cigarette and squeezed it tightly between his fingers. "I hope you didn't bite off more than you can chew, W.F."

It was no secret that Winfield Sheehan was now in the market for a new job. It was difficult for W.F. to understand how Fox Film could do more than it already had to foster his career. Even Sheehan, the high priest of high pressure, who occasionally traveled on company time and expense, had to accept the fact that but for W.F. he might have wound up pounding a beat as a New York City policeman. No, there was no question about it. Sheehan would lead the mutineers and try to take over the studio that bore W.F.'s name.

The minute William Fox signed the trusteeship, he became a minority representative on what became, *de facto,* a new board of directors. It was the stupidest thing he'd ever done, and now at age 51, he was regretting the day he'd first met Justice Hughes.

He was, however, as had been demonstrated throughout his career, a man of iron will. He wasn't about to give up.

The reaction on much of Wall Street to the signing of the trusteeship was mixed.

On the day after signing the trusteeship agreement, Otterson invited the Fox Companies' bankers to the offices of the Telephone Company, where he begged their indulgence until such time as a refinancing plan could be submitted for their approval. Since Otterson waved a big stick, everyone quickly agreed.

The one open question about the trusteeship was whether W.F. would be permitted to exercise his powers. On the other hand, what precise use Otterson would exploit under the agreement remained to be seen. By the end of the first meeting it became readily apparent that W.F. would be outvoted on every issue presented to the trustees.

Through a number of reliable sources, W.F. determined that Winfield Sheehan and Nathaniel King were secretly meeting with Otterson; he confronted Hartfield about this. W.F. told Hartfield of the agreement to keep Jack Leo, Sheehan and King on the board, but now Otterson and Stuart were preparing to remove Leo. "That would be all wrong, Colonel! Mr. Leo must be retained because his executive position is about on a par with a carburetor of an automobile."

"What's your point, Bill?"

"I didn't know that Otterson and Stuart were to run the companies. It was only to enable them to do the necessary financing, that's what the voting trust was for!"

"Bill, I don't know any more of what they have on their minds than that they don't want Leo for a director—he's too close to you."

That evening, W.F. went home ill. He stayed in bed for five or six days, and in that period of time the two trustees were able to hold meetings without him to interfere. It was at this point that W.F. began to seriously consider hiring a top-notch litigator, a man unafraid to take on the Gentile establishment, a legal practitioner with spotless credentials. But who?

One of the things Otterson did was summon Harold B. Franklin, president of West Coast Theaters, a wholly owned subsidiary of Fox Film. A hands-on manager, Franklin had increased earnings to $5,500,000 and was about to earn close to $700,000 under his profit-sharing agreement.

Otterson told him they wanted to make him president of Fox Theaters, a post W.F. held.

Harold B. Franklin

There was a split second of hesitation and then Franklin happily accepted the position.

There was no love lost between W.F. and Franklin. As profits went in the theater-end of the business, Westco was a good performer. Fiercely competitive, Franklin gave more thought to his theater chain than anyone else in the division. To determine how things should be done, he let his theater managers talk things over among themselves. His purpose was immediate profits, and his managers were answerable for tangible results.

As for loyalty to W.F.? Franklin didn't even bother to call W.F. when Otterson made him the offer. It was just too good to pass by.

It didn't take long for W.F. to clearly realize that he had made a terrible mistake. His one good card, the control of the voting shares, had been played in the wrong game with the wrong players for the wrong reasons. Too much of his time was spent regretting his unfortunate decision and that began to cloud his thought process.

W.F. held a trustee meeting at the offices of the Telephone Company. When W.F. arrived, Richard Dwight, Charles Stuart and a lawyer to act as secretary were present. Otterson came in and took the chair at the head of the table. "You are occupying the chairman's seat and I presume you are to be the chairman?" Dwight asked.

"These stocks don't belong to us; it strikes me it would be more appropriate to have Mr. Fox as the chairman of the trustees for his own stock," Charles Stuart said.

After Hartfield showed up, the meeting started. Hartfield said, "Before the meeting can go forward, I believe Mr. Fox should give us a statement of the assets and liabilities of William Fox."

W.F. found this demand a little surprising, since both of the companies were stock companies and his personal net worth had nothing to do with their financial status unless he had personally guaranteed some of the debt. He vehemently objected and the committee went on to the next point, the Gaumont purchase.

It became necessary to call London, which Otterson did from the Telephone Company's offices, and carry on quite a lengthy conversation with his representative in London who was handling English creditors, all of whom he knew. The Telephone Company representative's suggestion was that $1 million was necessary to temporarily tide over the requirements in England.

The trustees then collectively returned to the subject of W.F.'s personal wealth, with their tone of voice more hostile. He had seen scenes portrayed in pictures of a prisoner receiving the third degree in an effort to make him break down and confess. Here he was getting the third degree as hard as it was possible. By whom? A sheriff's posse. Otterson representing the Telephone Company, Charles Stuart of Halsey, Stuart, and Dwight of the firm of Hughes, Schurman. Dwight, who only a short time before was his personal attorney. To their consternation, W.F. gave them nothing and Otterson adjourned the meeting.

Through W.F.'s sense of preoccupation ran defiance. He wasn't about to accede to the unreasonable demands of what amounted to a kangaroo court. But there was a price to pay, a continuous and unending strain with which he hoped he could cope.

Several more trustee meetings were held; most of the time was spent discussing protocol. From that point on, it seemed that no matter what the subject, the vote was always the same, 2 to 1. It was clear to W.F. that he was better off spending the remainder of his time running the affairs of Fox Film and Fox Theaters.

W.F. went back to Woodmere and his family. He consulted his personal lawyer and good friend, Benjamin Reass, who came to Fox Hall with Hartfield. The conference included Reass, Jack Leo, Colonel Hartfield, Eve Fox and his daughter Mona.

In the course of their conversation Hartfield told him it was important that he meet with Dwight. One of the things that W.F.'s lawyers had failed to include in the voting trust agreement was a definite understanding that when the Telephone Company was reimbursed for the $15 million they had lent the company, Otterson would resign as a trustee.

One of the thoughts in W.F.'s mind was that he wanted the Telephone Company out of his business as soon as he could get it out. He didn't want the Telephone Company running his business—particularly in view of the long-standing controversy over the Tri-Ergon patents. Hartfield had failed to include that in the voting trust agreement. W.F. told Hartfield he thought he would be well enough to come to New York on Sunday to have the conference he suggested. W.F. did go to New York that Sunday evening to hold a conference with Reass, Newman, Rubenstein, Hartfield and Dwight. "The trustees are doing things behind my back!"

"They are doing what they are supposed to be doing, Bill," Dwight replied.

Numbed though he was, W.F. told Dwight that when this trust agreement was drawn, his firm had failed to include that Otterson was to resign as a trustee as soon as the Telephone Company had received its $15 million.

"There never was such an understanding, and if you think there is, then we'll call the whole deal off, Bill."

Knowing full well Dwight's client would never agree to that modification, after a short period of haggling, W.F. got up and left. It was an inauspicious start to what was on the whole a rotten deal.

It wasn't long before the lawyer playboy, Hartfield, phoned W.F. and reminded him that his firm, White and Case, was also counsel for Bankers Trust, which could present a conflict of interest.

"I understand, Colonel Hartfield."

Hartfield said he wanted to level with him. Something few seemed willing to do.

"What do you mean?"

"They have no intention of electing Jack Leo as a director. They don't want you to remain as president either, Bill."

Few seemed willing to consider the whole matter a brazen scheme to usurp his power and abscond with his voting shares. Under the trust agreement, if it became necessary to dissolve the B shares, they were to give W.F. 1 1/2 shares of A stock for each share of B stock. Had they done that they would have given him 75,000 shares of Fox Film at the market price of $20 a share, and 150,000 shares of Fox Theaters at $8 a share, so he would have shares with a market value of $2,700,000, a mere pittance for a controlling block of shares.

During this difficult period one of the editors of the *New York Times* constantly kept in touch with him and insisted W.F. tell him all he could as the case progressed.

An article appeared in the paper insinuating a new holding company and their dissolution of the B shares. W.F. said, "I always thought you were my friend, but you played a dirty trick. Who gave you that story about a new holding company?"

"It was given to me by your bankers."

Since signing the voting trust agreement on December 3, everything had gone against W.F. Otterson and Stuart sold a million dollars of Warner notes, something he could have done for himself, and they requested an additional $5 million of collateral from him. They had gone behind his back to entice Winfield Sheehan and others to join their cause, and they brought Franklin in from California, naming him president of Fox Theaters. They removed Jack Leo from the boards, and they wanted to remove W.F. from the presidency of the companies.

Hardly two weeks after Sheehan had returned to the States, W.F. became convinced that he had betrayed his trust and gone over to the other side, now openly conspiring against him. He had never been able to confirm where or when Sheehan sold his loyalty, but having read hundreds of scenarios, he always imagined it must have gone something like this:

We first see the outside of the University Club. Standing seven stories tall behind a three-story facade, the Renaissance palazzo at 1 West 54th Street was the place where the wealthy and powerful Gentiles met to talk business.

The camera moves inside, passing through a mostly male lunch crowd, landing on the table of Winfield Sheehan and John Otterson. They are conversing between mouthfuls.

Winnie says, "I can remember when we started, John. Did you ever see Theda Bara?"

It's important to make small talk and show you're human, Sheehan tells himself.

Otterson replies, "Who didn't!"

"Those were the days," Sheehan says. He sips a fine red wine.

Otterson gets that icy look on his face and says, "I'm going to come right to the point, Winnie. We're going to take over the Fox Companies. We don't intend to sell any assets. We want the companies to function and continue as before."

"We?" Sheehan says in an innocent tone. He doesn't want Otterson to think he makes a habit of turning on his superiors.

"The Telephone Company and Halsey, Stuart. We'll need someone with experience to run the company and that someone is you."

"What about W.F.?"

Got to be sure where the old man stands, Sheehan thinks to himself. Don't want any unpleasant surprises here.

"Fox will be out of the picture."

"But how? Who?"

"You leave that to us," Otterson says.

Much like a silent film villain, Sheehan gets that avaricious look in his eyes and Otterson can read him like a book. Sheehan wants to know how many pieces of gold he is to receive for the assassination of his leader.

Sheehan says, "Have you thought about—"

Otterson interrupts. "Money?"

"Yeah, money."

Otterson lays his cards on the table, and its a full deck. "In the first year, a quarter of a million dollars, $300,000 the second year, $350,000 the third, and $500,000 the fourth year."

As the organist plays Wagner's *Tannhauser*, Sheehan smiles, telling himself, "I'm rich! I'm rich!"

"By your eyes, Winnie, do I understand that to be a yes?"

"Yes."

CHAPTER 28

Under the watchful eye of the Telephone Company's legal counsel, Otterson instructed Sheehan to assemble a group of executives and draft a round-robin letter accusing William Fox of mismanagement. Winnie thought for a while and then ticked off five names for Otterson: Saul Rogers; James Grainger, national sales manager and Winnie's confidant; C.P. Sheehan, Winnie's brother; John Zanft, a vice president of theaters; and Courtland Smith, from Movietone news, a former aide to Will Hays who owed what little he had attained in life to the faith W.F. had put in him.

Six traitors in all. Sheehan, Rogers, Grainger, Sheehan, Zanft and Smith. Ready to betray William Fox and everything for which he stood. There was nothing more to say. The only thing left to do was affix their signatures to the accusatory letter.

Who actually composed the inflammatory letter was not clear to W.F. and remains a mystery to this day. He didn't know if Otterson's lawyers drafted the document so that the devious Sheehan could fill in the blanks, or whether they'd hired a professional scenarist to fabricate the preposterous lies the letter embodied.

One thing was for sure. W.F. knew Sheehan could not have written it by himself; he wasn't that creative.

In the interim, W.F. decided to run things from Fox Hall where he could surround himself with family and the few remaining friends he could still count on. From that moment on, it seemed that no matter where she was, Eve was no longer her confident self.

That first evening was a solemn occasion. He embraced Eve and held her tightly. A spasm of pain forced Eve to cough. She pretended it was his cigar smoke, but he knew she'd been ill with a pulmonary condition for some time now. They stood before a warm, crackling fireplace and the firelight was reflected in her tired eyes. Eve was feeling low-spirited and it was written all over her face.

Around the darkened room W.F. saw Mona, Belle, Jack Leo and Benjamin Reass. The fire was not bright enough for them to see each other's faces clearly, and that's the way W.F. wanted it. He was a very thin replica of the William Fox of six months ago.

W.F. sat in his favorite chair, a blanket draped over his lap to protect him from the chilly breeze that seemed to penetrate his body and mind and cause him to shiver uncontrollably. He looked more like a hospital patient than a businessman.

"I've made a terrible mistake, Benjamin. I've taken that which I earned by the sweat of my brow, over 25 years of hard labor, and parted with it."

"Now, as your lawyer, let me say the trusteeship agreement is poorly drafted, Bill."

"Charles Evans Hughes wrote it. No better lawyer in the land, they told us."

"Rotten son-of-a-bitch!" Leo interjected.

Realizing that this line of conversation would never do, Reass switched over to more pleasant things. "I understand the studio is doing very well, Bill."

"That would be one piece of good news, if I only knew who owned it."

Head bowed, Elsa shuffled in from the kitchen and refilled their teacups. Freshly baked oatmeal and raisin cookies were spread on a silver platter.

Reass smiled and accepted a cookie. "Thank you, Elsa." He took a bite. "These are delicious."

"I've got to get back to the city," W.F. insisted.

Feebly, W.F. made an attempt to get up, but quickly collapsed into his chair.

Padding over to where her father was sitting, Belle gently tucked the wool blanket around his thin legs. She had never seen her father this way; he had always been a pillar of strength for the family. It frightened her.

"Not until the doctor says you can go, Bill," Eve whispered in a hoarse voice.

"Please take more time, Daddy," Mona pleaded.

There wasn't any more time. He wanted to say it loudly, but he couldn't. Everyone was under unbearable pressure and he didn't want to add to an already grim state of affairs. One of the bitterest tragedies of the whole affair was the thought of handing over his shares to the likes of Otterson, Stuart and whoever else was behind the plot to remove him from his companies.

Jack Leo had brought a copy of Winnie's denunciatory letter with him, what was now being referred to as the "round-robin" letter.

"Where is it? Give me this damn letter?"

Jack extricated a multi-page document from his pocket and handed it to W.F.

"Where are my reading glasses?"

Mona brought a pair of glasses to her father, who tried to slip them on. He had developed a severe case of the shakes in his one good arm.

Eve adjusted the glasses on his nose. "There."

As he started to read the text to himself, he slowly became nauseated, for the voice in his head was that of his Brutus, Winfield Sheehan.

Sheehan wrote: "The undersigned, executives of the above companies, having in mind and in heart the preservation and rehabilitation of the properties of the above companies and the maintenance of the high morale of the executive and administrative forces of the companies, as well as the general employee body of the companies, and the interests of the shareholders and creditors, have deemed it necessary, after careful deliberation to direct this message to you in the hope that you will give it the prompt consideration and action thereon that it requires."

W.F. set the letter down for a moment; a great pain began to grip the back of his neck, as if someone were squeezing it with all their might. He peered down at the letter but only read bits and pieces of it. "The trustees under the trust agreement should be permitted to function in accordance with the terms...you have committed yourself to it...any endeavor on your part...to recede from that position would be contrary to the best interests...we wish you to know..."

As he was about to say something, his words faltered when he read a part that was insufferable, the mutineers telling him that they stood by him as they pretended to save the ship. "We wish you to know that there is not the slightest desire on our part to have you feel that we are reflecting on you nor receding in our personal loyalty to you, but we in turn feel that after the disinterested efforts we have put into the companies, we are entitled from you a loyalty to us, to our reputations and our positions that we confidently believe you will reciprocate."

Reciprocate? The word stuck in his craw. He had lifted Winfield Sheehan from a nobody and turned him into a movie producer. The ungrateful bastard was now plotting against him, working openly with his enemies.

And then there was that two-timing son-of-a-bitch, Saul Rogers. Wasn't he supposed to get the government to sign a waiver for the Loew's purchase? Wasn't he supposed to read the trusteeship agreement and warn W.F. against signing it? Wasn't he supposed to look out for the best interests of the companies?

At the end of the road they were all a bunch of traitors. They'd sold themselves out to his adversaries. Reciprocate? In a raised voice, W.F. shouted it: "Reciprocate?"

Startled, Mona rushed to his side. "What's wrong, Daddy?"

"I'm going to bed," was all W.F. could articulate.

W.F. summoned Saul Rogers to his estate. Rogers arrived around lunchtime and W.F. invited him to his office, where Elsa had prepared a spread that included chicken noodle soup and cold roast beef sandwiches.

There was to be no preamble. Festering inside, W.F. got straight to the point. "You've been my personal counsel for 25 years. I expected more from you, Saul."

Nobody who has not lived through a treachery like this could possibly understand how wounded W.F. felt at that moment. He had gone out on a limb time and again for Rogers. He knew it and W.F. knew it. Without William Fox, Saul Rogers was a nebbish.

"How do you expect to get out of this mess, W.F.?"

W.F. went on to tell him of at least six different methods.

"You're in difficulty, W.F., and the only people who can possibly save the situation are the Telephone Company and Halsey, Stuart, and you ought to go along with any proposal they make."

"Otterson doesn't like you, Saul. He stills remembers the patent infringement notice you sent him."

Rogers thought it typical of W.F. to use that line of reasoning rather than admitting he was in over his head. Rogers had nothing to fear. He was on the right side of the issue, he thought.

"How can you now tell me that these are the people I must ally myself with; how can you possibly sell your soul, Saul, which you have done?" Rogers fetched his hat and coat and left.

W.F. felt tears stinging in the back of his eyes. The more W.F. thought about the wording in the round-robin letter, the more he believed Saul Rogers had written it.

A door opened and W.F. made out the fragile shape of his wife, Eve Fox. He looked again and saw what he hadn't noticed the first time. Eve had lost a lot of weight, just as he had, and she appeared emaciated.

"You heard what Rogers, just said, Eve?"

"Every word of it."

"They'll all turn on me before this is over."

"All the others that you have faith in may double-cross you, but never Blumy."

Her words echoed in his mind. Never Blumy. Never Blumy. Never Blumy.

At the time of his return from London, Blumy owed the Foxthal Company close to $3 million, money he'd generated on the Loew's purchase and the Gaumont acquisition.

W.F. requested he come to Woodmere, and after giving him a lot of feeble excuses, Blumy finally showed up.

W.F. invited him into his study. "Sit down, Blumy."

As he sat in his favorite armchair, W.F. could tell Blumy was a little taken back by the way he looked. W.F. appeared to be years older than he was and his face was thin and drawn.

"You know the trouble I'm having."

"Yes, I've heard."

"You owe me money, Blumy, and I desperately need it now."

"I can't, W.F. They've asked me to join the new management team."

"Sheehan?"

"Yes."

At that precise moment, W.F. heard a sound from behind the door, and guessing who it was, he pushed hard against the arm of his chair and once upright, left the study.

There was Eve, looking very angry, standing there with a bottle of vitriol in her hand.

"I'm going to blind him! This dog who has called me mother! If he is going to destroy you, I am going to destroy him!"

Pushing her into another room, W.F. locked the door and then went and got rid of Blumy. Blumy never knew how close he had come to losing his sight.

Blumy hit the one spot that had put Eve in a fit of anger. He was disloyal. She thought she knew Blumy well enough to believe he was incapable of turning on the man who had lifted him from the gutter. Moreover, her intuition had seemingly failed her, and this left her distressed and in a state of despair.

They returned to W.F.'s study; he lit a cigar, and for a moment kept silent. He realized she was shaken and did not know quite what to say.

"Get a good lawyer, Bill. All these men you have called your friends and collaborators will turn on you sooner or later."

"I promise you that I will, Eve."

That night, W.F. had a change of heart. Enough of those white-shoed *goyim* lawyers. What he needed was a fierce litigator, someone with enough courage to take on the Gentile establishment. A Jew with balls.

By this time, W.F. had run out of names, or so it seemed. Benjamin Reass chose Clarence J. Shearn, who had been an appellate judge, to accompany them to a meeting of the bankers scheduled for December 23 at the office of the Telephone Company.

Right up front Shearn made the case that W.F. had no intention to go on with the trusteeship agreement and asked that they extend some $6,800,000 unsecured.

W.F. told the bankers, "Gentlemen, doesn't it seem peculiar to find a man with $20 million worth of valuable property, and not able to raise any money? I would like to make you a proposal. Since the voting trust agreement has been abrogated, the only interest you can possibly have is for these companies to return the money that is due you. We can't give it to you in cash; we haven't got it. What we have got is $20 million worth of property unencumbered. You form a committee among yourselves, and you have that committee pick out of it $2 worth of collateral for every dollar we owe you. We will make you a secured creditor. Instead of your bank's money being in jeopardy, we want to guarantee that we are going to pay it."

A Chase vice president, Sherill Smith, acted as leader of the group. He kept looking for reasons the bankers could not accept W.F.'s proposal. Smith had come to the bank in 1921, having been a national bank examiner for over 11 years. Across his pitiless face was indelibly impressed the mark of a dyed-in-the-wool auditor.

There were two species of the human race that W.F. came to loathe. Lawyers and auditors. Smith fit the mold of auditor to perfection.

How could W.F. give his properties as collateral when Fox Film and Fox Theaters owed Halsey, Stuart $12 million? Smith asked. Dwight raised his voice to catch everyone's attention, "Since Mr. Fox will not respect the terms of the trusteeship agreement, I shall withdraw." The meeting was over.

To further his common sense argument that a bird in the hand was worth two in the bush, W.F. wrote a concise letter to the 13 banks that were the companies' creditors, offering again collateral for their loans. He received no reply. The first thing he learned was there were no ordinary rules for negotiating a settlement, and so no reason for them to want to compromise. There was no attempt on the bankers' parts to provide him explanations, and none sought to justify their dilatory actions. What he did understand was that they were playing a game of all or nothing at all, and he, William Fox, was destined to lose no matter how much effort he expended in this game.

With all that was going on, W.F. had almost forgotten it was December 30 and he hadn't been home since the middle of the month. Plus, there was the triple anniversary to celebrate—his birthday, his wedding and New Year's Eve—right around the corner.

Physically spent, W.F. found Eve feeling under the weather, too. All they could manage was a quiet dinner at home with their two daughters. A butler uncorked a bottle of champagne and W.F. toasted his girls. "To our health." There was a prolonged moment of silence.

Married in Hollywood was one of Fox's 1929 films

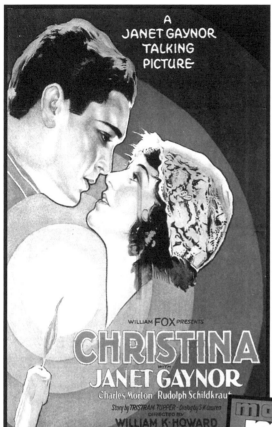

Then Eve spoke. "We can sell the art collection, Bill."

In their Park Avenue home they had a truly remarkable assortment of art, one of the best collections of paintings ever seen in one apartment, a collection they had begun the third week after their marriage. Eve's comment was in response to what a lady friend had said one evening as W.F. sat lamenting his situation. "All these things are going to end up in the public auction room; you know they are going to strip your home."

"The only thing I want to take along with me is the little picture you bought me three weeks after we were married," Eve said, choking back her tears.

Belle and Mona were sobbing and W.F. had great difficulty restraining himself. He suddenly felt a wave of affection for them come over him. But it was getting late and he needed rest, enough rest to be able to continue the battle to save Fox Film and Fox Theaters. Kissing his daughters

tenderly, he said goodnight and he and Eve went to their room.

In spite of all the turmoil in W.F.'s life, Fox Film and Fox Theaters enjoyed a record year in 1929, which made the bankers' position with William Fox seem even more ludicrous.

The earnings scorecard for 1929 read:

Fox Film	$11,848,275
Fox Theaters	$2,660,261
Loew's	$11,756,956
Paramount	$15,500,000
Warners	$17,271,805

CHAPTER 29
1930

The *New Movie* magazine reported: If you want our selection of the most interesting film events for 1930 that are scheduled, here they are:

Maurice Chevalier and Claudette Colbert in *The Big Pond*
The coming Paramount-Famous-Lasky revue, *Paramount on Parade*
The Vagabond King with Dennis King and Jeanette MacDonald
John Boles' appearance in *La Marseillaise* with Laura La Plante
Lilian Gish in *The Swan*
Carmen with Bebe Daniels as the cigarette girl
Richard Barthelmess once again as an Oriental in *Son of the Gods*
Broad Minded, another sequel to *The Cock-eyed World* with Victor McLaglen
and Edmund Lowe together again
Greta Garbo in *Anna Christie* and *Romance*
The three coming war plays: *The Case of Sergeant Grischa, All Quiet on the Western Front* and *Journey's End*
The appearance of John McCormack, the tenor, in *I Hear You Calling Me*
And D.W. Griffith's production of the life of Lincoln

The stock market crash and the consequent loss of investor confidence partially destroyed the consumer psyche. There was a slight curtailment in payrolls, a noticeable drop in retail sales, and a sharp reduction in automobile production. Remarkably, motion picture theater receipts were still holding strong.

Impervious to what was happening in the motion picture business, Fox's bankers gathered on January 2, 1930 in W.F.'s office on 10th Avenue; W.F. reiterated his offer to give them $2 worth of collateral for each dollar's worth of loans. In return, all they gave him was a cold shoulder.

An article entitled "Receivership Hint Brings Stock Break" appeared in the January 3 edition of the *Times.* This was in reaction to an announcement by the Lazarus Class A stockholders' committee who told the press they regarded a receivership as "inevitable."

At the time, W.F. didn't know how many shares they represented, but they were formed by Farrar Lazarus, 1 Madison Avenue, and chaired by Allan I. Cole, said to be a former president of the Pennsylvania Exchange Bank. As W.F. had suspected, no one could locate Lazarus as a holder of record.

He issued the following:

In connection with statements which have been made by counsel for the so-called stockholders' committee, I wish to say that the assets of Fox Film Corporation, over and above all liabilities, are in excess of $73 million, and the earnings for the year 1929 are over $13 million with a special nonrecurring profit of $6 million, or a total for the year 1929 of more than $19 million. From all appearances, the year 1930 will be the greatest in every respect in the history of the company.

On January 5, W.F. called for another meeting and offered personal collateral, which was again turned down by the bankers. One of the bank presidents went so far as to tell him that he'd like to do something for him, but that his hands were tied.

"What do you mean?"

"Chase is the lead bank and I'm compelled to follow their instructions."

"Lead bank?"

"They're heading the creditor's committee, Bill."

There he was again, Albert H. Wiggin, the poker-playing banker who always had a marked card up his sleeve. What was he up to? What did he want?

It was not a matter of common knowledge that W.F. personally owed the Bank of United States $1 million secured. In fact, the fiduciary relationship that existed between banker and client dictated extreme discretion when revealing anything to do with the status of a personal loan.

What was known was that Fox Film owed another $1,600,000 unsecured to the same bank. The president of the bank, Bernard Marcus, related to W.F. that he couldn't help him with the Fox Film loan, but that he should not worry about the personal loan.

Within days rather than weeks, Chase discovered W.F. had a sizeable personal loan with Bank of United States. W.F. was called on the carpet by Marcus and told that for reasons he was unable to comment on, it was now necessary for W.F. to supply additional collateral for the personal loan. This came as no great surprise to W.F., given the web work in which he now found himself operating.

For collateral, there were two valuable pieces of property that W.F. owned. In one he had an equity interest of $600,000, and the other was a piece of property for which Rockefeller had offered $1,450,000; they had mortgages of a little less than $625,000.

"Take your pick, Mr. Marcus."

Per bank protocol, Marcus called in Mr. Day, a prominent real estate man in New York, to appraise the two pieces of property. Based on his assessment, there was no more than a $500,000 equity interest, which impressed W.F. as a low-ball figure. However, given the circumstances, W.F. put up both pieces of property as collateral.

It turned out that Mr. Day was Joseph P. Day, a man who had created for himself a real-estate fortune—one big enough to stand next to the Astor fortune. Day had invested with Albert H. Wiggin in the Corbin land development company. Day owned the white spots on the shore of Coney Island's boardwalk, the site of Brighton, Manhattan and Oriental beaches. Day sold subdivisions, office building sites, industrial and chain store sites.

Besides his real estate activities, Day was a member of the board of the Metropolitan Life Insurance Company. He also served as a trustee of the Union Dime Savings Bank of New York. During his daily life, he shuttled between an expansive home at Short Hills, New Jersey and his town house on Gramercy Park, then to his office on Liberty Street, three blocks above Wall.

Because of his considerable wealth, Day socialized with all the politicians and was intimate with Jimmy Walker. He went everywhere with him: to horseraces, the fights and football games.

Day was on a mission. The Rockefellers wanted that sliver of land on Sixth Avenue. Day would get it for them.

In the spring of 1931, W.F. met Mr. Day after the Bank of United States had closed its doors.

"When I was in difficulty you had a chance to serve me and you didn't do it. You were elected as an appraiser of two pieces of property I had."

Day replied, "I knew all about them. I will frankly tell you about it. I had business arrangements with Bernie Marcus in every real estate enterprise. When he asked me to make these appraisals, he told me the exact amount he wanted the appraisals for."

"You must have known their real value," W.F. said, "because Rockefeller had already announced that he was building the Rockefeller Center, and that I owned the only 110 feet of property that was not included in his purchase."

W.F.'s property was on Sixth Avenue, a row of small buildings running between 48th and 49th Streets, and would be included in three square blocks bought by Rockefeller on which the new Radio City, or Rockefeller Center, would be built.

On the mergers and acquisitions front, rumors abounded; one said that R.K.O. had acquired a part of the Loew's shares, specifically those held by Chase National Bank as collateral for a loan to the Fox Film Corporation.

Hiram Brown, president of R.K.O., said, "Never heard of such a transaction, and it couldn't possibly take place."

Another rumor floating around was that Kodak would become interested in the management of the Fox companies. That was also denied, this time by Lewis D. Jones, a vice president of Eastman Kodak.

On January 11, 1930, W.F. announced the January 15 dividend would be paid in scrip instead of cash. To be able to meet its obligations in a timely manner, the Fox companies had to conserve cash.

The following day, W.F. received an unexpected visit from Colonel Claudius C. Huston at his 10th Avenue office. Huston told him he brought the regrets of President Hoover, and he wanted to be of help if he possibly could.

What W.F. didn't need was more advice. There was a conspiracy to drive him out of the motion picture business, and one of the conspirators was Albert H. Wiggin of the Chase Bank.

"Tell Mr. Wiggin to stop, Colonel!"

Soon thereafter, Huston visited Wiggin and was told in no uncertain terms that Wiggin resented the White House interfering in the business of his bank, and that Huston "had better go home and mind his own business."

What W.F. wanted more than anything in the world was a lawyer who was willing to take on the intransigent Telephone Company.

Things were getting very complicated and it looked as though nothing was quite so simple as it once seemed. The people that William Fox knew best were no longer to be trusted and he wasn't quite sure who was in whose camp. The fact was, he needed a lawyer with a clear and impartial mind who had no ax to grind with either side.

Reass got an idea of who William Fox's lead counsel should be. "How about Samuel Untermyer?"

Untermyer was a superbly qualified litigator. He had been born in 1858, educated at the Columbia Law School and was now a senior partner at Guggenheim, Untermyer & Marshall. As counsel for the Pujo Committee, Untermyer had investigated the Money Trust in 1913 and was said to have been the only lawyer who had ever cross-examined J.P. Morgan and George F. Baker. He was also reported to be the personal attorney for the Guggenheims.

According to Reass's sources, Untermyer unquestionably ranked as one of the best trial lawyers in the land and quite recently had successfully argued a case for a five-cent fare on New York subways. He'd also represented Warner Bros. in a long, drawn-out struggle with the Telephone Company. He was reputed to be a man of great professional learning and dignity. His judgment was valued not merely because it encompassed an expertly drawn and brilliantly conceived legal opinion, but because it was *his* judgment.

"He can plead a difficult case, Bill."

"Where do we find Mr. Untermyer, Benjamin?"

"He's resting in Atlantic City. He's got a bad case of asthma."

"Do you think he can do the job?"

"He's the one man the gang downtown is afraid of, Bill. He's a respected litigator."

"Call him, Benjamin."

"I already have."

"What did he say?"

"He wants us to send our case over to his office."

"What did you tell him?"

"I sent him the whole file."

"Let's go see him right away. Make an appointment."

"He'll see us the day after tomorrow."

W.F. and Reass boarded a train to Atlantic City and found the President Hotel, where Untermyer was said to occupy a penthouse suite. A servant ushered them in, and before long a small figure crowned with a mane of silvery white hair and sporting a gray mustache entered the room. He was holding a rather long pipe. W.F. guessed him to be a man in his early 70s.

Untermyer greeted W.F. pleasantly, "Mr. Fox, I presume."

It was a delightful room, white-carpeted and filled with colorful furnishings.

"Mr. Untermyer. This is Benjamin Reass, my personal attorney."

"Of Hirsh, Newman, Reass and Becker?"

"Why, yes, Mr. Untermyer."

"A very fine firm, Mr. Reass. Can I offer you gentlemen something to drink?" Upon their answer, the servant was back in a jiffy with three large glasses of cold water.

They were sitting around a white wicker table. W.F. smoked what was left of a cigar while Untermyer toiled with his pipe. There were periods when he coughed a lot.

"Have you read everything we've sent you, Mr. Untermyer?"

"Most of it, Mr. Fox. There are three large file folders bulging with documents sitting on my desk."

"What do you think?"

"You've got yourself one helluva legal struggle going on."

"Will you represent me?"

"Of course I will."

"The bankers are driving me to the wall. I've built the greatest moving picture enterprise in the world—and that's why they want it."

"Who drew up that convoluted trusteeship agreement, Mr. Reass?"

"Hughes."

"Stands to reason. They always protect their own."

"What do you mean, Mr. Untermyer?"

"It's not important, Mr. Fox. Just an observation from an old lawyer who, over the length of his career, has seen just about everything."

W.F. reached for a fresh cigar and unwrapped it. The servant flicked a match and lit it.

"Mr. Untermyer, this has been my business since 1904. I couldn't believe when I gave the certificate for my voting shares to Bankers Trust that I was handing over my business to the bankers. That certificate is my heart—I must get it back. That voting trust agreement is a dagger at my heart—I must get away from it."

Untermyer crossed the room to a window and ran his fingers idly down the slats of the Venetian blinds. He pinched the rubbery skin of his throat between thumb and forefinger, turned and looked at W.F.

"You are right in the appraisal of the dangers of your position, Mr. Fox. One—I can't promise you there is any way to break out of the voting trust agreement. Two—your companies are in debt over their ears, and without bankers to refinance you, the court will certainly throw you into receivership—and in a receivership your stock will be wiped out. Three—it's going to be next to impossible to persuade any other bankers to finance your companies."

Untermyer approached W.F. His bony hand closed on his shoulder, as if to signal that in spite of what he had just said, all was not lost.

"That trusteeship agreement, I wish you hadn't signed it. How much time do we have, Mr. Fox?"

"Not much, I'm afraid, Mr. Untermyer. Notes are coming due next week."

Untermyer filled his pipe from a half-pound tin. He lit it. "There's the matter of my fee, Mr. Fox. Our firm requires a $100,000 retainer. If I can salvage something for you, so you are not completely wiped out, I'll expect a total of a million dollars. Bring me a certified check for the retainer and the company statements for the last five years."

"You'll have everything you've requested in short order."

"God speed and we'll see each other in New York."

There was nothing more to discuss. Untermyer guided them to the door. He took a step toward W.F. with his hands open. "I'd be happy to have my driver drop you off at the train station, Mr. Fox." "That won't be necessary, Mr. Untermyer. There's a car waiting for us downstairs." Reass and W.F. went to the train station and were soon back in New York.

On the ride back, W.F. kept thinking about that voting-trust agreement. But it wasn't really a trusteeship agreement. The title was entirely wrong. Stuart and Otterson never intended to be trustees—they intended to be destroyers of what he had built up. They didn't intend to protect him. They intended to wreck him and take his property. And when Hughes helped to draw up this paper, no one knew better than he that he had prepared an agreement that would not act in the interest of William Fox, that he was not protecting him and that these men were receiving powers not accorded to trustees.

W.F.'s mind was working a mile a minute as he examined every possible way to raise money short of holding up a bank.

In search of a realistic alternative for financing the companies, W.F. consulted Professor John T. Madden of New York University's School of Commerce, whose specialty was accounting and finance, and together they worked out a plan for a $35 million bond issue that they would sell to the exhibitors. If each of the 16,000 exhibitors were to take $2,000 worth of Fox bonds, Fox's problem would be solved.

David A. Brown, president of the Broadway National Bank, would become president of the Fox Securities Corporation and would mail circulars explaining the plan to theater owners.

The press found Harry Stuart in Otterson's office and questioned him about the new financial scheme W.F. had put forth. Stuart said, "We have not been consulted and have no comment."

The government action to declare the Fox purchase of Loew's stock a violation of antitrust law had legs of its own. On a separate front, the companies' attorneys filed a motion averring that Fox Theaters Corporation was not engaged in interstate commerce and therefore not subject to the Clayton Act.

The newspapers disclosed that "William Fox, president of both corporations, owns only a trifle more than 5 percent of the outstanding stock of Fox Film Corporation and just 10 percent of that of Fox Theaters Corporation."

Another mighty name on W.F.'s prospect list was that of A.P. Giannini, the California banker who had supported the motion picture industry since its infancy, and in the process had become a legend in California.

In response to W.F.'s query, Giannini's New York representative, Elisha Walker, president of Bancamerica-Blair, made a date with him at the 10th Avenue offices.

Before the meeting, Reass briefed W.F. on Bancamerica-Blair. "Walker became a Salomon partner in 1910. In 1920, Blair and Company absorbed the Salomon firm. In March 1929, Blair and Company merged with Bancamerica Corporation."

"What kind of man is Elisha Walker, Benjamin?"

"A practical type...good with numbers, they say."

At the start of the meeting, Walker told W.F., "We want to do your financing, Mr. Fox."

REORGANIZATION CONSENT ASKED BY FILM CHIEF

Fox Seeks Approval of Plan From Stockholders and Creditors

NEW YORK, Jan. 28. —(AP) — William Fox today sought the consent of creditors and stockholders to a reorganization plan by which he hopes to stave off receivership for the Fox Film Corporation and the Fox Theatres Corporations, which he heads.

His proposal advanced by his counsel, Samuel Untermyer, at a federal court hearing on three or the four receivership petitions pending, calls for the resignation of all officers and directors of the Fox Film Corporation, and the appointment of Bernard M. Baruch, Edward Delafield, president of the Bank of America, and Herbert F. Howell, president of the Commercial National bank, as trustees of the voting stock.

Creditors expressed opposition to the plan thru their counsel, Morton Bogue, who said, "we would rather have a receivership."

The Fox proposal stipulated that the resignations of the officers and directors would be deposited with the court to become effective when Harry L. Stuart and John E. Otterson, resigned from the trusteeship which was formed under an agreement last December.

The proposal also designated six of seven names for a new board of directors which included Fox and Winfield Sheehan, his general manager.

Keepers from the office of Sheriff Farley took possession of all buildings and contents owned by the Fox Film Corporation in New York on after the sheriff's

Elisha Walker had a talent for keeping things simple. There were no expensive charts or time-consuming explanations. What Fox needed most was an unprecedented amount of cash, and it could either be injected as equity or debt. Thankfully, the meeting was short, for the directive from California was to develop a sound recapitalization plan for Fox.

Once again the accountants and lawyers—58 accountants from the prestigious firm of Price, Waterhouse & Company, and 22 lawyers—invaded Fox's offices for 30 days and nights, studying every transaction, every resolution, looking for misdeeds on W.F.'s part.

The Fox Securities plan floundered because so much of its success depended on those same executives who'd signed the round-robin letter. Pat Powers had promised to buy $1 million in bonds, but then Sheehan learned about Pat Powers and from then on W.F. no longer had the $1 million subscription.

There was no way to control the eventual cannon shots fired by stockholders who were being poisoned by what they'd read in the press concerning the trusteeship agreement and the apparent inability of the companies to refinance themselves.

Stanley M. Lazarus, attorney, on behalf of Ira M. Gast, charging "mismanagement and maladministration resulting in serious and threatening financial difficulties," filed application for an equity receivership for Fox Film on January 18. The papers filed requested that the "Fox Securities Corporation," W.F.'s brainchild, be restrained from selling, pledging or encumbering any of the properties transferred to it.

Matter-of-factly, Untermyer responded to the press from his hotel in Atlantic City, "The application for receivership will be vigorously opposed. The corporation is overwhelmingly solvent with a surplus." Untermyer had his assistant, Abe Shamos, draw up affidavits and answers for the receivership suits pending in several courts. Shamos used the standard legal argument that creditors were to be treated *pari passu* (literally, at an equal pace, or side by side)—no creditor could collect individually and take advantage over other creditors.

W.F. often said, if there were an Olympic medal for the number of times a businessman were sued frivolously, he'd hold the gold many times over. Throughout the course of his ordeal, there were some 25 legal actions brought against the companies. The court's dockets were clogged with Fox litigation.

A lawyer named Arthur Berenson brought a receivership action against the companies, claiming he represented 620 shares of stock whose value was less than $12,000 at that time. Berenson had a reputation as a frequent representative of minority stockholders in many corporate struggles, and in a suit against the New Haven Railroad was said to have earned $800,000. Berenson was the type of predatory lawyer who'd come to annoy W.F. even more than the dark-suited Wall Street types.

There was something else about Berenson's action that made the whole suit smell a little fishy. Wasn't this the same Arthur Berenson who Louis B. Mayer had used to litigate against Vitagraph when he'd pilfered Anita Stewart?

There followed a suit by Mrs. Susan Dryden Kuser, widow of W.F.'s Newark friend who had invested in Fox Film in 1915, and who in the course of 14 years had received dividends amounting to $10 million. For 15 years Anthony Kuser had been a close friend to W.F., a great believer in William Fox and in the Fox enterprises. Any time he had wanted some money, he'd sold a few shares. There were at least 15 Kusers who were stockholders and they stood behind W.F.

It became apparent that General Heppenheimer, president of the Trust Company of New Jersey, one of the 13 banks from which W.F. had borrowed money, was a confidential adviser to Mrs. Kuser. W.F. presumed that either the Telephone Company or the Chase Bank at one of the bank meetings asked Heppenheimer if he knew a substantial holder of Fox Film stock who would start an action.

The lawyer who brought this suit was Isador Jacob Kresel, general counsel for the Bank of United States, the Marcus bank. Sad-faced Kresel, 52, had ample experience in dealing with demanding situations. A product of the Columbia Law School, he had been Assistant District

Attorney for New York County and had helped impeach Governor William Sulzer in 1913. As a prosecutor, he had probed insurance irregularities, meat packers and ambulance chasers.

Throughout this difficult period of time, banker friends told W.F. privately they wanted to help him but dared not as it would bring upon them the enmity and resentment of the most powerful Wall Street forces. "The gods of Wall Street had practically ordained my doom and nothing on earth could prevent this great money machine from mowing me down," W.F. said.

W.F. sat across a dinner table from dark-haired, heavily built Bernie Marcus and his brother-in-law, Mr. Singer. "Now, Bernie, I don't believe you think you are fooling me. I know definitely you are now in the employ of the Chase Bank and the Telephone Company. You are acting under orders. They are telling you what to do. I would like to make you this little prediction. Some day the Chase Bank won't like what you do. Some day the Telephone Company won't like how you did this job. Whenever they reach that conclusion, two things will happen to you. Only one thing is happening to me—my business is being taken away. But two things will happen to you: One, they will take your bank away and shut its doors and two, they will indict you and send you to jail as sure as your name is Bernie Marcus."

Bernie smiled and said, "You're being a little melodramatic, aren't you, Bill?"

"Just wait and see."

To pursue a restructuring of the companies, W.F. met again with Bancamerica-Blair, Lehman, and Dillon, Read to formulate a financing plan. These three houses ranked with the most powerful on Wall Street. As lead negotiator, Bancamerica-Blair nominated Elisha Walker, supported by the resources of the Blair and Giannini organizations. Philip Lehman represented Lehman Brothers; his house the prior year had floated a $100 million investment trust.

In a relatively short period of time, Bancamerica-Blair produced a plan whereby, through the issuance of debentures and stock, Fox could raise $65 million and pay its debts. It was now a matter of appearing before the Honorable Judge Frank Coleman, who was hearing the receivership suits, to explain that W.F. was in a position to meet the companies' obligations, and secure the dismissal of the suits. The elements of the Blair plan, wrangled over for several days, contemplated an issue of $40 million of 10-year, 7-percent debentures and $25 million of 7-percent cumulative preferred stock, which was convertible at its par value at the option of the holders at any time into class A common stock.

The Blair plan stipulated the disposition of the proceeds: $18 million was for the payment of Fox Theaters' existing debt; $15 million was going directly to the Telephone Company; $3.4 million was for miscellaneous Fox Theaters' corporate expenses; $18 million for the payment of Fox Film's underwriting obligations to Fox Theaters; $12 million for the payment of the $12 million Halsey, Stuart loans of 6 percent Gold Notes of Film dated April 1, 1929, due April 1, 1930; $14.3 million for the payment of obligations incurred in connection with the acquisition of an interest in Gaumont-British Picture Corporation Limited; $5.8 million for the payment of unsecured bank loans; and $9.05 million and any part of the aforementioned $18 million not required to meet said underwriting obligations, for payment of indebtedness, construction requirements and miscellaneous corporate purposes.

Obviously, W.F. would have to offer something from his personal hide, which he gladly would do. He would assign all of his interest in Fox-Hearst to Fox Film; enter into a royalty-free, nonexclusive license to use the "worthless" Tri-Ergon patents; assign his Grandeur shares to a new company; create a new voting trust arrangement with class A stockholders; and it went on and on, no panacea for William Fox, he assured everyone, but a lot better than the alternative.

A process server advised W.F. that a judgment of default for $342,158 in favor of the Public National Bank and Trust Company, 76 Wall Street, had been awarded against Fox Film. In response, Samuel Untermyer advised the court that it was Fox's intention to pay and take over the judgment and eliminate interference with the Blair plan to refinance the company. Untermyer told W.F. that all judgments would be held in abeyance until the receivership litigation was settled.

The 13 creditor banks were becoming a sore spot, and W.F. instructed Untermyer to fight their actions with everything he had to gain time for presenting the Blair plan to stockholders.

Fox Gets Two Days to Avoid Receivership

65 Million Reorganization Plan Meets Objection of Stockholders

Exclusive-Dispatch to The Herald

New York, Feb. 12.—The tangled finances of the William Fox amusement enterprises, after being aired again in court yesterday before Federal Judge Coleman, were left in a state of suspension for another 48 hours pending a final decision tomorrow on acceptance of a $65,000,-000 reorganization plan.

This plan, publicly announced yesterday, is the result of the joint efforts of Lehman Brothers, the Bancamerica-Blair Corporation, and Dillon, Read & Company, the three banking houses Mr. Fox recently called to his aid. Failing acceptance of this plan, Judge Coleman indicated, the two entities which comprise the amusement enterprise, Fox Film Corporation and Fox Theaters Corporation, must go into receivership, a contingency which all parties involved in the present difficulty have expressed themselves anxious to avoid. The plan, with possible minor alterations, is therefore considered practically certain of adoption.

Judge Coleman's pointed remarks to this effect were made when, directly on announcement of the plan, criticism was expressed from two sources. Lawrence Berenson, counsel for petitioning stockholders, maintained the proposed refinancing will cost the Fox companies $20,000,000, and is too expensive. He advocated sale of the Fox Pacific Coast Theaters to Loew's, Inc., for $23,000,000 and the raising of an additional $50,000,-000 through sale of the Fox group's Loew stock.

Judge Coleman called for a private conference with all the parties and their counsel. W.F. was there with Untermyer as well as his enemies, Gast and Susan Kuser. Seated in the hearing room were more lawyers than could actually fit around the table. Some were assigned to a row of chairs along the wall.

Gast had filed the first petition for an equity receiver. The second petition, which contended mismanagement on W.F.'s part, was filed on behalf of Susan Kuser. As Judge Coleman spoke, W.F. looked Susan Kuser in the eye, but she lowered her head, afraid to let him confirm she was being used as a pawn. How long was W.F. expected to control himself?

Among the most painful charges was that Eve Fox had participated in graft; that she had performed work in designing and decorating the theaters of the Fox Theaters Corporation and had received profit from this. The truth was this: Eve Fox had spent from 1915 until 1930, 15 years of solid labor, day and night, sometimes until the small hours of the morning, giving the best that her brain had, for which she never received a penny of compensation.

Untermyer wanted to establish that there was a plot afoot to bankrupt companies that were financially sound. "It is most peculiar that a party who is a trustee for a business under an agreement—and an agreement which he maintains is still in effect—should try to throw that business into receivership with the consequent disruption of management, loss of employee morale, failure of confidence by the business community, drop in the price of the stock—ruination, indeed, of a thriving business that is temporarily embarrassed."

At adjournment, W.F. was advised by a clerk to meet with Judge Coleman at 1:00 in his chambers. He had a prior commitment with someone important, so he arrived at 1:45 p.m. Judge Coleman's court was scheduled to convene at 2:00.

The courtroom was not located in a building where justice was supposed to be dealt out, but rather in an ordinary loft space. Because of a case overload, Judge Coleman was holding court in the Woolworth Building, a graceful Gothic-style office building on Broadway and Park Place.

Lawyers, curiosity seekers and newspapermen packed the terra cotta-colored room to suffocation. The corridors leading to this room were lined with men mumbling and talking. Everyone seemed to know that William Fox had been sent for, and that

Judge Coleman was waiting for him, that he was supposed to appear at 1:00, and here it was 1:45 p.m. and still no William Fox.

On the ride downtown, Harry Sundheim, one of his battery of lawyers, accompanied W.F. and Sundheim rehearsed him on what to say to the judge.

"I know, W.F., your inclination is to become loud, and you may irritate the judge. Be sure you don't do that. If his judgment sounds wise, follow it."

Outside the tallest building in Manhattan, W.F. met Untermyer, who looked a bit agitated. He told W.F. the judge was upset because W.F. was late. W.F. was ushered into a room that he guessed was about 10 by 5 feet. This was the room where the judge and he were to have this confidential talk.

Judge Coleman said, "How dare you disobey my instructions!"

The magistrate was about six feet tall, wore glasses and had a head of gray hair, a very dignified-looking jurist. Making a limp excuse, W.F. indicated he was late because he had several important matters to resolve.

"I need you to comply with the trusteeship agreement, Mr. Fox. Give me the resignations of your board."

"I am not going to give you any resignation papers, Judge Coleman."

"I warn you that I will appoint a receiver when I walk out of here."

"You must hear my side first."

"Mr. Fox, will you go through with this trusteeship in modified form?"

"No. No, I won't, Judge Coleman."

"I will sign this application for receivership."

"No, you won't."

"Yes, I will!"

Judge Coleman scurried out in a huff, but the curious, inexplicable thing was that he had not signed the application for a receiver. If it were true, as Untermyer had said, that Judge Coleman was one in a thousand, which W.F. didn't believe for a minute, the tide might be changing.

As W.F. left the ad hoc courtroom, news reporters hurled questions at him. "Are the Fox companies bankrupt, Mr. Fox?"

"Let me answer that," Untermyer said. "How can a company whose assets exceed its liabilities by many millions of dollars be bankrupt?"

The other objection was voiced by Morton G. Bogue, counsel for Harry L. Stuart of Halsey. Stuart & Company, one of the present Fox trustees, who would be supplanted by the trusteeship proposed before Judge Coleman by Mr. Fox two weeks ago. Mr. Bogue requested his client be allowed 48 hours to study the plan, and said Halsey. Stuart & Company. is willing to float a stock issue similar to that proposed in the plan offered by the other bankers at a cost to the corporation of only 9 per cent of the aggregate sum received and without a stock bonus. At this point Judge Coleman interrupted to say "Mr. Fox has assured me he never would agree to anything with you."

The reorganization plan which has the approval of Mr. Fox. as outlined by Samuel Untermyer, his attorney. provides for an issue by Fox Film Corporation of $40,000,000 worth of 7 per cent debentures, carring warrants which entitle the holders to buy within 10 years 25 shares of Class A common stock at not less than $20 a share during the next three years and $30 a share during the last four years. Twenty per cent of the corporation's net earnings are to be set aside for redemption of the debentures at a p̲r̲e̲m̲i̲u̲m̲ o̲f̲ 1̲0̲ p̲e̲r̲ c̲e̲n̲t̲ f̲o̲r̲ t̲h̲e̲ f̲i̲r̲s̲t̲ three years, 7½ per cent for the next three years and thereafter 5 per cent. The other $25,000,000 would be raised by the issuance of 7 per cent cumulative preferred stock, convertible into Class A common stock at not less than $25 a share during the first five years and thereafter at $30 a share. The new banking group pointed out through counsel, Robert T. Swaine, that its offer will not be available after tomorrow. Directors of the two Fox corporations will vote on the plan tomorrow prior to the adjourned hearing at 3:15 P.M.

When W.F. got downstairs, he met Harry Sundheim. The aftermath of W.F.'s encounter with the judge was of vital concern to him. "I was standing right outside that door, and while I could not hear what you were saying, I knew that you were talking too loud. You must have disobeyed my instructions." In no uncertain terms, W.F. told him what he had said to Judge Coleman.

Shaking his head in disbelief, Sundheim said, "Long before we get back to your headquarters, you will read in the papers that a receiver has been appointed for your companies."

"Don't be so pessimistic, Harry."

To outward appearances, W.F. acted as if he had triumphed over his enemies in the court-room. Certainly, things could have gone worse, and maybe they did, but W.F. had spoken his mind and all he could pray was that the learned judge had understood that he was not about to give up his companies because of some sinister plot led by Chase Bank and its friends. Even if the opposition stuck to its demand for receivership, W.F. was going to fight until he had no more fight in him.

This he made clear to Samuel Untermyer and the other lawyers who surrounded him.

When W.F. got back to his suite he took a long hot bath. Lately, he was bathing more than usual because his body got itchy and someone with experience told him it was because he was spending so much time around lawyers. W.F. hadn't seen a director, producer, actor, actress, stuntman, grip, cameraman or anyone else faintly connected to the motion picture business in ages. Creditors, lawyers and auditors were to become a staple for some time to come.

A fatigued Samuel Untermyer retreated to his estate at Greystone in Yonkers, New York, well aware of the fact that the biggest battles still were in front of him. It was his habit, before entering

the litigious phase of a lawsuit, to sleep extra hours and play a set or two of tennis, so that when he appeared in the courtroom he would be steady and prepared to go the distance if need be.

His son Alvin joined him. The younger Untermyer kept his jumping horse, Cinelli, boarded on the estate. On top of a hill were many greenhouses growing melons, grapes, hot-house flowers and orchids, many of which Samuel Untermyer used in his lapel.

Samuel Untermyer's estate, Greystone

CHAPTER 30

.   It was important not to confuse lawyers with one another because, although they sprouted from a common genealogical tree, each one claimed a unique pedigree when it came to the practice of law. Hence, there were those who were constant winners and others who were perennial losers. In the case of the Fox litigation, with but a few easily identifiable exceptions, what was on display in the courtroom were Wall Street's most celebrated jurists.

The big-name law firms, with an average of 13 to 20 partners and a regiment of underpaid law clerks, inhabited the buildings of 15 Broad Street or 63 Wall Street. These illustrious barristers served as directors on the boards of Dow 30 companies, and knew by first name any banker who was worth his salt. Their cases were not cases at all, but industrial and financial problems of legendary complexity and importance. Their fees would, in a lengthy and complicated corporate reorganization like that of the Fox companies, exceed a quarter or a half million dollars.

Of course, the epicenter of big-time corporate litigation was Manhattan, an island studded with rare and unusual legal heads. For example, Sherman & Sterling were counsel for the National City group; Sullivan & Cromwell for Harris Forbes and Goldman Sachs; White & Case for Bankers Trust and New York Trust; Rushmore, Bisbee & Stern for the Chase group and Stone & Webster; Carter, Ledyard & Milburn for the Stock Exchange and Lee, Higginson; Davis, Polk, Wardwell, Gardiner & Reed for J.P. Morgan and the Guaranty Trust; Winthrop, Stimson, Putnam & Roberts for Bonright & Company, and Commonwealth & Southern; Cravath, de Gersdorff, Swaine & Wood for Kuhn, Loeb and Bethlehem Steel.

Even though Jewish law firms represented 50 percent of the lawyer population, this did not readily translate into 50 percent of New York's lawyer power. The most important law firms were those that counseled banking, insurance, trust companies, investment bankers, railroads and manufacturing on important corporate matters. These firms had no Jewish partners. Instead, the Jewish lawyers labored in the bankruptcy courts, real estate, tort, divorce, collections and litigation.

In W.F.'s corner stood Samuel Untermyer, one of the most respected litigators of his time, and W.F.'s personal attorney, Benjamin Reass, who had settled Mona's nasty divorce from Taussig.

Attorney for Fox Film was a tall, thin, white-haired Republican, a former political leader named Robert O. Levy, who had been counsel for Mrs. Florence Knapp, New York State census-taker convicted of misappropriating public funds.

Cravath, de Gersdorff, Swaine & Wood were counsel for the Blair syndicate. The partner in the Fox matter was the Harvard-educated Robert T. Swaine, a man in his early 40s, who was considered to be one of Manhattan's most brilliant legal minds. A prize scholar, Swaine graduated at the head of his law school class. He was said to detest litigation and thought it wasteful and uneconomic.

Advocating for Harry Stuart and John Otterson—in their capacity as trustees—was Hughes, Schurman and Dwight. Richard E. Dwight, a bulky, good-looking Princetonian, was lead counsel. Halsey, Stuart had their own legal representation provided by Morton C. Bogue of Beekman, Bogue and Clark. Otterson's employer, Electrical Research Products, the Telephone Company subsidiary most directly involved with the Fox companies, had George C. Pratt as their general counsel, supported by the firm of Green and Hurd.

Winfield Sheehan's attorney, Nathan Burkan, was more noted for his theatrical practice than commercial litigation. While Burkan guided Sheehan through the Fox legal maze, he was also counsel for Mae West in the *Pleasure Man* case.

There were lesser-known types like Martin Conboy and Arthur Berenson—who might have been fronting for Louis B. Mayer.

With so many lawyers feeding from the same trough—the coffers of Fox Film and Fox Theaters—one could see why no one was in any particular rush to negotiate a settlement and jeopardize a stream of constantly increasing fees. W.F.'s only concern was, would there be anything left once the mess was settled?

W.F. entered Judge Coleman's court on January 27 for a hearing on the motions for equity receivership. A bailiff lifted his arm, shouting, "Please rise for the Honorable Judge Coleman." Everyone rose and then sat down again.

W.F. rotated a fresh cigar to light it, settling in for what promised to be a long and arduous hearing. Behind and to one side of him were three rows of dark suits, their faces glowering. The rest of the room was packed with courthouse regulars who were there for the drama.

"We're here to discuss the issues in the applications for equity receivership made by Susan Dryden Kuser, executor of her husband Anthony Kuser's estate, Henry Gast and Benjamin Rudnick and Abraham Snyder."

The makeshift courtroom in the Woolworth Building was bursting at the seams and Judge Coleman decided to clear it, requesting that those only having an academic interest to leave. There was a lot of groaning as he insisted a second time.

"I do it with regret and with my apology." The grumbling gathered momentum and then abruptly subsided as the guards cleared the room.

Untermyer sat at a table with his older son Alvin and his assistant, Shamos. On the other side were seated those who were prepared to litigate for receivership.

"Mr. Untermyer, you may make an opening statement."

"Thank you, Your Honor."

Untermyer stood up and faced the judge.

"My understanding, Your Honor, as a result of the conference in your office today, is that I am to procure for you the resignations of at least a majority of the directors of the Fox Film Corporation and the Fox Theaters Corporation—"

"Do you have a majority?"

"Yes, Your Honor, we do."

"Please continue, Mr. Untermyer."

Untermyer fingered his thick, gray mustache. "Yes, Your Honor. In addition to this, you want the resignations of all the officers of both corporations. It is your purpose to deposit these resignations with the court, with the stipulation that they are to be held by the court until such time as the court receives from John E. Otterson and Harold L. Stuart their resignations under the trusteeship agreement entered into between William Fox, John Otterson and Harold Stuart on December 3, 1929."

Untermyer explained that W.F. would deposit his shares with a new board of trustees of seven to consist of William Fox, Jack Leo, Winfield Sheehan, Bernard Baruch, Jr., E.R. Tinker, Louis Abrons and a seventh board member to be named by the trustees. Clearing his throat, Untermyer looked at opposing counsel to see if his posturing had provoked any kind of reaction. It hadn't. They merely shrugged. They would have their turn to respond to what they considered to be a preposterous stance on the part of William Fox.

In spite of regular interruptions, Untermyer was eloquent in his delivery. His words flowed in studied deliberation.

Judge Coleman was forced to caution several members of opposing counsel to be quiet. "You'll have your turn in a few minutes, counsel!"

"Thank you, Your Honor. All we ask is that our bankers be given sufficient time to work out the details of refinancing two very solvent companies."

"Do you find this financing plan satisfactory, Mr. Kresel?"

"Your Honor, we were never notified and know nothing about this proposal."

"Mr. Untermyer?"

"Your Honor, we could not notify them. We just completed it 10 minutes before we came here."

"May we have a copy of the plan?" Kresel asked.

Swain stepped in and clarified the matter for the court. "There is no plan as yet."

"Your Honor, if it please the court?"

"Yes, Mr. Bogue."

"Your Honor, we categorically object to the stipulation that our clients, who represent $27 million of unsecured debt, resign from the board of trustees."

Realizing the litigants had reached a standoff, Judge Coleman called for a conference at 3:15 p.m. that same afternoon. "This hearing is adjourned!"

A light lunch was followed by a quick trip to the W.C. W.F. witnessed the longest row of New York's most expensive lawyers lined up at the urinals. Then it was back to the courtroom.

By this time W.F. was beginning to feel a certain degree of respect for the judge. He was not overly impressed by the pedigree of the lawyers involved in the litigation. It seemed that Judge Coleman was a practical and honest man; W.F. hoped that common sense would somehow prevail in his courtroom.

Dropping into his chair, Judge Coleman leaned forward on his elbows. "Before I render a decision on your motions, I would ask the counsel for the plaintiffs to state why this court should not stay these motions for equity receivership to give the bankers sufficient time to complete their refinancing plan?"

Bogue jumped to his feet and said, "It is not our financing program, Your Honor, and although we are here trying to protect our clients, and we want to protect all creditors, we would rather have the receivership immediately, and if this plan could be worked out, the receivership could be terminated quickly."

Judge Coleman looked at Untermyer. "Counsel?"

"Your Honor, the refinancing plan is the result of a week of constant effort by day and night. Halsey, Stuart is pressing for payment, although by their terms, the notes are not due until April 1. They claim that the giving of obligations by the Film Company, having more than 120 days to run, on the purchase of the English chain of theaters, constituted a default that matured the notes before their due dates, although I understand, and the papers submitted to you show that Halsey was not only familiar with but assented to the deal to consummate the English purchase, and in a sense, participated in the negotiations."

"Halsey was not a party to the Gaumont purchase, Your Honor." Bogue interjected.

"If it please the court, I want to enter into the record an affidavit signed by William Fox addressing the issue of the Gaumont purchase."

"Are there any objections?"

"None, Your Honor," Bogue replied.

"The affidavit is made part of the record."

Untermyer fumbled in a pocket for his reading glasses and put them on. "I'll read a small portion of Mr. Fox's affidavit, if it please the court."

"Please proceed, Mr. Untermyer."

"'This matter was discussed at great length with Mr. Ernest Niver, manager of the New York branch of Halsey, Stuart, with whom I had almost daily contact, not only in this matter, but in other matters, and he was the authorized agent at all times for Halsey, Stuart and Company. It was he who sent cables about this matter to Harold Stuart while Stuart was in London, and received replies and informed me of them. It was he for the firm of Halsey, Stuart who urged as hard as he knew how that the acquisition of the Gaumont Company be made. When Stuart returned from abroad and called on me again in August, as he says he did, the matter of the Gaumont acquisition was fully and completely discussed. He commented on the cables he received and sent, and inquired whether the information he had transmitted through his office was of any assistance to me."

Bogue was desperately trying to get Judge Coleman's attention. He wanted him to focus on the matter being litigated, Fox's insolvency.

"Mr. Bogue?"

"There is no money in sight, and I don't see why we should be asked to forgo our interests or to desert the other creditors and consent to a new management where there is no promise before the court that our debt will be paid, or that anybody else will be paid."

Untermyer responded: "Mr. Bogue, did not Mr. Swaine invite you to a conference..."

Bogue got red-faced. "This is a preposterous suggestion. I saw no point in getting into a discussion representing bankers and those supposed to have an interest in the new financing, and being there in a position to help Mr. Fox break his agreement with my clients."

Raising his head and squaring his shoulders, Judge Coleman spoke forcefully. "Gentlemen, I've heard enough and will render my decision tomorrow at 9 a.m. This conference is adjourned."

Early next morning, W.F. met Untermyer and Reass outside of the Woolworth building. Untermyer said he wanted to have a few words with W.F. before going into the courtroom. They all stood in a semi-circle and kept their voices low since opposing counsel was arriving in dribs and drabs. Maybe because of their shared experience, Untermyer and Fox were getting to know and respect each other.

Untermyer said, "We've got a 50-50 chance Judge Coleman will rule in our favor, Bill. I think he'll grant us a stay."

"What does that mean, Samuel?"

"Just enough time to draw up that financing plan with Blair. The question now becomes, how much time do you really need?"

"At least 30 days."

Untermyer thought for a moment and said, "We'll be lucky to get a couple of weeks."

Untermyer read to the court a revised voting trust agreement that immediately provoked a strong objection from Bogue.

"So far as my clients are concerned, they feel that they should not withdraw from the position they took yesterday in requesting a receivership, because they feel that there is a possibility that no plan will be presented, and we will be that much further behind; and they feel also that there may be a plan that will not be agreeable to Mr. Fox, and we will be that much further behind, and we may come to a point where we will have to have a receivership at a very unseasonable time of the year in the film business."

Untermyer pressed: "Are you saying that Mr. Harold Stuart is not interested in fulfilling his duty as a trustee and refinancing the companies?"

"Mr. Stuart's first duty is to his firm and to the investors to whom he sold Fox Corporation notes for $12 million. And his duty as a trustee is to the whole corporation and all its stockholders. They own the corporation—Mr. Fox's stock has control but it is only 20 percent of that total stock."

"Is Mr. Stuart's counsel saying that his only interest here is to get the notes paid?" Untermyer asked.

"Yes, in effect, I am. With Mr. Fox fighting us, we cannot launch a successful refinancing. But at least we aim to protect the note holders." That was the admission Untermyer was hoping for. Now he could inform other bankers that they could finance Fox—without cutting in on Halsey, Stuart's turf.

Untermyer directed his comments to the bench. "If Your Honor grants the petition for receivership now, overnight the 20,000 employees of the Fox companies will face unemployment and despair as this worldwide enterprise crumbles. Will Your Honor add another business collapse to these distressing times? I ask for two weeks adjournment in which time there is no doubt whatsoever that a refinancing plan will be developed to preserve this thriving business under Mr. Fox's imaginative leadership."

Instantly five lawyers sprung to their feet to lodge a protest before Untermyer's logic could take hold of Judge Coleman's very open mind. But Judge Coleman would have nothing of it.

"Gentlemen, I will not hear you further at this time. All applications for an equity receivership are stayed as I'm granting a two-week adjournment in the matter of the voting trust agreement."

Judge Coleman added, "While the voting trust agreement is thus held in abeyance, the banks involved should not execute any judgment against Mr. Fox or his interests; no properties should be alienated and no consent judgments be obtained against the corporation or Mr. Fox. The case is set down for Tuesday next at 9:30 a.m."

Reporters gathered around Untermyer—who was very adept at using the press to gain the favor of public opinion—as he assembled his papers from the counsel table. No, he couldn't divulge who the other bankers were, but he'd have an announcement shortly. Yes, it was true that Fox Film's earnings had never been so good and patrons were filling the theaters in spite of the state of the economy.

Half an hour later, Untermyer and his squad of lawyers were in his suite at the Ambassador. A teakettle was whistling and Untermyer was outlining the next steps in the litigation.

"First, we address the public. We'll need their sympathy if we are to prevail."

The next morning, Untermyer released a statement to the press:

> In response to inquiries from stockholders concerning the meaning of large judgments entered against the Fox Film Corporation by banking interests, Samuel Untermyer reiterated today that these entries were measures of overabundant caution in case their financing plan now in progress should unexpectedly fail.

"What can we expect from them now, Samuel?"

"Bill, I'm hoping we can convince Judge Coleman that our financial plan addresses every outstanding obligation and that, therefore, the equity receivership doesn't have any legs to stand on."

Creditors of Fox Film filed two judgments in the Supreme Court because of the company's failure to answer the suits. One was for $392,898 due on a note for $450,000, made by the Corn Exchange Bank Trust Company. Bankers Trust Company filed the second judgment for $298,248 due on a note for $400,000.

Just as Untermyer had predicted, they had bought themselves a little breathing room until February 11 at 3 p.m., when the two competing camps would present their refinancing plans. Although it was a shallow victory for W.F.'s side, it gave him the strength to continue the fight against Otterson, Stuart, Wiggin, Gifford and Sheehan.

On another front, Rothapfel began fomenting discord among the shareholders in the Roxy Theater Corporation, the voting control of which was held by Fox Theaters. W.F.'s only consolation was that Rothapfel was a very small stockholder and carried little weight before those who had a bigger stake in the theater.

On January 29, Samuel Untermyer submitted an affidavit to Judge Coleman in which W.F. denied allegations made against him in the suits for equity receivership. This was one of those formalities with which he had to comply.

At a spontaneous luncheon W.F. was told by John Otterson and Harry Stuart "to leave the country for six months as the co-trustees intended to do many drastic things during that time and it would be impossible for him to suffer the humiliation that would be heaped upon him."

"I'm not about to abandon the presidency of the Fox companies, gentlemen."

A waiter brought them coffee and a piece of layer cake. Otterson toyed with his serving while Harry Stuart ate heartily.

Otterson said, "I'm sorry you can't see it our way, Bill."

"That's the way it is, John."

They went out of the restaurant into the cold air and shook hands. There was a tight, glazed look around Stuart's tired eyes. "Bill, I'm sorry we can't come to an understanding."

"No more sorry than I am, Harry."

W.F. watched Otterson and Stuart walk off side by side, and after another quick glance backward they were gone. W.F. knew things were about to get progressively worse.

To counter the arguments offered by Susan Kuser, W.F. presented an affidavit where he indicated that Mrs. Kuser was not representing the Kuser interests because other members of the family who were stockholders of record were against receivership. These individuals were John L. Kuser; the estate of Mary D. Kuser, J. L. and D.M. Kuser, trustees; John L. Kuser, Jr.; Walter G. Kuser; R. Victor Kuser, Jr.; R. E. Kuser; Frederick Kuser; and Frederick A. Kuser, Jr.

Summarizing his arguments, W.F. stated the three main reasons for the failure to carry out the refinancing plan: his inability to complete the proposed consolidation of Fox with Loew's, the motorcar accident, and the stock market crash.

Chase National Bank kept up the pressure. On January 30 they entered a default judgment against Fox Film for $353,740. Payment was demanded on December 28; Fox paid $48,233 on December 30.

The holders of the $12 million, 6 percent Gold Notes formed a protective committee that included George W. Davison, president of the Central Hanover Bank and Trust Company; Andrew J. Miller of Halligarten and Company; Frederick T. Moses, president of the Fireman's Mutual Insurance Company of Providence, R.I.; and William Buchsbaum, vice president of Barstow, Tyng and Company.

On February 2, Bankers Trust Company entered a judgment for $501,939 against Fox Film. The bank's attorneys, Davis, Polk, Wardwell, Gardiner and Reed, served the papers on C.B. Levin, the secretary of Fox Film. On February 4, Fidelity Trust Company filed a default judgment for $53,833 against the Fox Film Corporation based on a note for $125,000 made on October 10, 1929 and payable on January 10.

Fortunately, Judge Coleman had ruled that no judgments could be enforced during the stay. However, this did not preclude the filing of such actions.

On February 11, the litigants all gathered again in the same foul-smelling room, as directed by Judge Coleman. The courtroom and corridor were packed with all sorts of onlookers.

Surrounded by his retinue, Untermyer proceeded to the Fox side of the hearing room and remained standing. Responding to the bailiff's charge, Judge Coleman entered and greeted them with a warm smile as a still larger group of suits assembled on the other side of the room. Everyone sat down. Swaine advised the bench that the Fox side was ready to present the Blair plan.

Untermyer requested permission to address the court. A deep resonance in his voice, he said, "If it please the court, Your Honor, I would like to submit a statement here showing that the Fox Film Corporation earned over $2 million the last four weeks, and that its business is greatly on the increase, notwithstanding the troubles that it is having now in the way of financing."

Staring directly at Bogue, Judge Coleman asked, "Any objections, counsel?"

"None, Your Honor."

"There being no objection, the statement is made part of the record. Is your side ready to present its financing plan, Mr. Untermyer?"

"Yes, we are, Your Honor."

"Then, please do commence, Mr. Untermyer."

"Before I do, Your Honor, I request that letters signed by Bernard Baruch and two equally reputable figures in the financial community be made part of the record. For the public good and to preserve this worldwide business, they hereby agree to serve as trustees of Mr. Fox's voting shares under a new refinancing plan. I also have a signed letter from Mr. Fox agreeing to deposit his shares with the new trustees."

"Any objections, counsel?" "None, Your Honor." "There being no objection, the letters are made part of the record. Please continue, Mr. Untermyer."

"Thank you, Your Honor. Mr. Fox hereby deposits with this court the resignations he has procured from his entire board of directors, conditional on the acceptance of the new voting trustees by this court."

Facing opposing counsel, Untermyer waved several documents in the air. "These charges of mismanagement and speculation against Mr. Fox are entirely false and malicious, but in any event no further heed need be given them, for these eminent trustees will be complete assurance against any possibility of mismanagement."

Raising one eyebrow, Untermyer looked at the judge again. "Now I would like to read to the court a proposed financing plan—it is full of mistakes—we have only completed it in the last 10 minutes." Momentarily, there was a buzz of activity in the courtroom, causing a temporary disturbance.

Judge Coleman banged his gavel. "Quiet in the court! You may proceed, Mr. Untermyer."

Kresel was on his feet, vigorously waving his hand. "If it please the court, may I be heard on the matter of the trustees?" "Yes, Mr. Kresel."

"This offer of the director's resignations and turnover of Fox's stock to trustees is nothing but an elaborate gesture. Mr. Fox doesn't even have his shares, they're at Bankers Trust Company, and the courts may hold that they will stay right there."

"May I address the court, Your Honor?" "Yes, you may, Mr. Bogue."

"Hundreds of note holders are looking to this court to see that Fox Film pays back the money they lent it. As in all insolvencies, we hear about new financing, but no money is forthcoming. The receiver must be appointed now. He will not necessarily break up and sell the business. If refinancing becomes available, it can be undertaken in an orderly manner under the court's aegis."

"Your Honor must bear this in mind," Untermyer said in a tragic tone, "that once the court takes the fatal step of appointing a receiver and brands these companies with that badge of failure, the wheels of this thriving business will halt. Stockholders will suffer tremendous losses and thousands of employees will walk the streets."

"Mr. Berenson?"

"Your Honor, this plan is going to cost the stockholders too much money."

"How so, Mr. Berenson?"

On one computation it was $20 million, and on another computation it would run up to as much as $35 million. He was figuring in the 10 percent redemption fee of the bonds.

"Mr. Untermyer?"

"Your Honor, do not the stockholders get a premium if they take the bonds?"

Well beyond his understanding of finance, Berenson dropped the argument and sat down looking like a fish out of water.

Judge Coleman glared at opposing counsel's table. "Who else has a plan? Mr. Bogue, does your client have an alternative plan?"

"Your Honor, the Blair plan is taking the only free asset that Fox Theaters has, the Loew's stock, and is proposing to pledge this equity."

Samuel Untermyer reminded the court, "It is pledged now, Mr. Bogue!"

It was fairly obvious that Judge Coleman was irritated that Halsey, Stuart didn't have a plan. Directing his piercing eyes at Bogue, Judge Coleman said, "Will you consent that your arrangement for future financing be withdrawn? Will you consent to that if the present bankers go ahead with the plan?"

"I am not prepared to say that, Your Honor."

Untermyer said, "But, Your Honor, this plan proposes to pay these gentlemen every dollar of their debts. What are they doing there? What is it they want? They do not want their money. Evidently they want something else."

Bogue tried to say something, but Untermyer wouldn't let him interfere. "This is a matter of some importance, Your Honor, and I think we should be heard upon it."

"Yes, I agree. Go ahead, Mr. Untermyer."

"Your Honor realizes, of course, that as far as these gentlemen are concerned as creditors of these corporations, this plan proposes to pay them principal and interest."

"Yes, that is apparent."

"Your Honor realizes that the securities that they may have issued on various theaters in the past are very much increased in safety by the furnishing of this additional money to the Fox Theaters Company."

"I understand that, Mr. Untermyer."

"They are not jeopardized. They are helped and materially helped by that fact, so that there must be something else behind it. Let us see what there is behind it."

In a grand pose befitting a veteran stage player, Untermyer faced his adversaries' table as he spoke. "These gentlemen have a bankers' agreement for a 15-year preferential contract. It is a most unusual thing. In other words, Fox Films and Fox Theaters could not do any financing without first giving these gentlemen the opportunity to do it."

Red in the face, Judge Coleman interjected, "Mr. Untermyer!"

"I'm not going to go into that."

"It is my judgment that we ought not to."

"I do not understand Mr. Bogue's attitude, Your Honor, and I would like to be heard on it. I understand Mr. Bogue is representing Halsey, Stuart. This plan proposes to pay them cash for notes that have been selling at 50 cents on the dollar, for which their clients are to get 100 cents on the dollar. What is this policy of theirs? It looks a good deal like a dog in the manger policy, and that is all there is to it, I think."

"I do not think you ought to characterize it, Mr. Untermyer."

It was getting late in the day; Judge Coleman glanced up at a wall clock and said, "Will counsel please approach the bench."

In an off-the-record conference, Judge Coleman sought a compromise. After 15 minutes of a soft-toned, back-and-forth conversation, Judge Coleman said he'd give Untermyer one more week to settle the last few details of his financing. Speechless, Bogue shook his head, now thoroughly frustrated with the outcome of the hearing. Kresel put on a long face.

The lawyers resumed their places at their assigned tables and Untermyer requested on the record an additional week's adjournment. "There being no objection, the motion is approved."

The press reported: "William Fox yesterday made the most spectacular gesture in his whole spectacular career. In open court, he handed over his own resignation and the resignations of his boards of directors."

While all of this was taking place, Walter Gifford was giving testimony to a Senate Committee on Interstate Commerce in Washington, D.C.

One of the Senators asked him, "What about the loan you've made to the Fox companies?"

"I'm not worried. The companies are perfectly sound."

"That'll be all, Mr. Gifford."

There was an urgent call from Sol Wurtzel advising W.F. of the death of director Kenneth Hawks and nine other men in an airplane accident during the filming of a Fox picture. The tragedy took place when two big Stimson-Detroiters, carrying Hawks and cameramen and assistants, went up to film a parachute jump. A small Lockheed, carrying stunt men, was to come between them and the jump was to be made and photographed from both big planes. One of the Stimsons came up under the other and they locked, exploded and burst into flames.

Kenneth Hawks was the brother of Fox director Howard Hawks, and was married to Fox actress, Mary Astor.

On the fourth adjournment of the receivership hearings, Blair finally let Untermyer announce that they were proposing a plan for refinancing the companies. The syndicate would include Dillon, Read and Lehman Brothers. Halsey, Stuart immediately said they would compete with Blair for the underwriting business on the new Fox stock.

On February 13, the parties to the proposed receivership were back in court again and the imperturbable Bogue was doing his best to dissuade Judge Coleman from accepting the Blair plan as a realistic alternative.

"They said this—"

Unable to stomach Untermyer's portrayal of what was going on, Bogue leaped out of his chair, interrupting Untermyer. "Just one second, please!"

"May I finish?"

"Yes, you may, Mr. Untermyer." Judge Coleman said, leaning back in his chair. "You'll have your turn, Mr. Bogue."

Upset, Bogue returned to his chair rather than risk the wrath of a presiding judge. Slowly but surely he began to see a pattern in Untermyer's statements. The old man was out to establish the credibility of William Fox and the financial worthiness of the Blair syndicate.

"Please continue, Mr. Untermyer."

"Thank you, Your Honor. The position taken by Mr. Bogue is an extraordinary one. He said that in years past, Halsey, Stuart has made loans on various pieces of real estate, has issued bonds that have gone to the public of Fox Theaters—by the way, it is not here—the Fox Film Corporation is here, but the company has made a loan. Now they seem to think that a receivership will be better security for those underlying loans than would the putting of $35 million behind them."

Bogue rose and returned to his principal argument, namely, that W.F. had signed the trusteeship agreement and had given his client certain preferential treatment in refinancing and that was that.

Pratt followed and presented an argument that challenged common sense. "In spite of the fact that this plan provides for our amount in full, we object to the plan for this reason: We have a 15-year contract with the Fox Company covering talking motion pictures, and we do not feel that this plan provides sufficient latitude for future financing for them to properly carry on the business that is contemplated by the contract. It it is necessary to work out a plan that is comprehensive for the future, as well as taking care of present needs."

In a convoluted sort of way, Pratt was alleging that letting the Fox companies become solvent through an alternate plan of financing was jeopardizing the Telephone Company's future earnings. A noticeably frustrated Judge Coleman said, "We seem to be at a deadlock here." Looking daggers at Untermyer and then at Pratt, Judge Coleman asked, "Can you point out any way in which I can prevent Mr. Fox from blocking the trust agreement except by receivership?"

Pratt said, "I cannot, sir."

"There is no way, is there?"

"There is no other way, Your Honor."

"Mr. Pratt, I am absolutely convinced from my talks with Mr. Fox and my observation of his conduct in this case that he will never consent to entering an agreement with Halsey, Stuart and with the Electric Research Laboratories. The plan that you suggest as possible can only be worked out by means of a receivership. I am convinced of that."

Untermyer wasn't going to go down without a fight. He masterfully laid out the heart of the matter. "I object to the responsibility for this situation being placed to any extent on Mr. Fox or his unwillingness to go on with Halsey, Stuart or anybody else. The responsibility for this situation rests right at the door of Halsey, Stuart and of the Electric Research Laboratories."

"Mr. Untermyer, I cannot permit you—"

By this time Untermyer was getting a little hot under the collar, too. "Your Honor does not seem to want me to be heard!"

In a quieter voice, Judge Coleman said, "I want you to be heard on matters that are up for discussion. On those matters, I am glad to hear you. But on matters that we cannot do anything about, I think it would be a mistake to attempt to deal with them."

Untermyer said, "But Your Honor, you started by saying that Mr. Fox would not do this and Mr. Fox would not do that, and these gentlemen have made certain objections and I am answering them. A week ago or two weeks ago, Mr. Bogue stood up here and said he wanted a receivership for Halsey, Stuart and Company. This is about as extraordinary a situation, I think, as has ever been presented in a large transaction. Here are two creditors, one for $12 million and the other for $15 million, who are confronted by a plan of three of the most reputable banking houses in the country to pay their principal and interest in full, and they are objecting to that plan."

Martin Conboy stuck his two cents in. "That might be an alternative that would be the lesser of two evils, because if Your Honor appointed a receiver for this corporation, then there would be somebody who would have in mind not merely Mr. Fox's individual and personal and selfish interests, but the interests of all the parties concerned."

W.F. fumed and Untermyer tapped his hand, as if to say, bear with me, Bill, in a court of law you can say almost anything.

Judge Coleman was ready to rule on the matter before his court. "Gentlemen, it is the decision of this court not to appoint a receiver since we have on the table a refinancing plan developed by reputable bankers that should be submitted to the stockholders for their approval. I would also suggest that Halsey, Stuart submit their proposal in the same fashion. This court will recommend neither plan nor any other plan. Court adjourned!"

W.F. wanted very badly to believe that Judge Coleman could push the litigation to a reasonable conclusion. He wanted him to declare null and void that confounded trusteeship agreement. He wanted Judge Coleman to force Otterson and Stuart to sign off on the Blair plan, so that he could refinance his companies. He wanted Judge Coleman to tell everyone that Mr. William Fox could go back to running his businesses.

He wanted Judge Coleman to rule that there was a semblance of sanity left in the world.

For all of five minutes, Samuel Untermyer, Jack Leo and William Fox rejoiced in their narrow victory over Halsey, Stuart and the Telephone Company, and then immediately went to work on the next two important steps: board approval of the Blair plan and a stockholders' meeting where they'd strive to win approval for refinancing the companies.

One of the obstacles to refinancing was the government's reluctance to authorize the Fox-Loew's merger. On the morning W.F. and Reass were leaving for Washington, W.F. received a letter from Senator Thomas Walsh of Montana, whom he had known, expressing his regrets for the difficulties that W.F. found himself in, and so when he arrived in Washington, D.C. he met with Colonel Huston, who read the letter. Huston asked to keep the letter and encouraged W.F. and Reass to wait in their hotel for his call in the evening.

Later that evening, Huston, elated, brought W.F. a letter signed by William Mitchell in which the Attorney General outlined the plan of the method that could be employed to consolidate the Loew and Fox companies.

Because W.F. still controlled the board, a majority of the directors adopted the refinancing plan offered by Bancamerica-Blair Corporation, Lehman Brothers and Dillon, Read and Company. They also addressed letters to the stockholders requesting their proxies for votes favorable to the plan at a special stockholders' meeting scheduled for March 5.

Working diligently at the Fox headquarters, Alvin Untermyer said, "There's no use sending this final telegram to any stockholders west of the Mississippi. They couldn't get their proxies here in time anyway."

A class A stockholders' committee, headed by Morton F. Stern of J.S. Bache, issued a statement on behalf of the Blair plan. "Proxies will be sought broad enough to permit the committee to vote for this plan and any other plan submitted to the stockholders."

Next morning, W.F. awoke as a breakfast tray was placed across his middle. He immediately went to the newspaper, searching for anything to do with the litigation. An article on page three caught his eye. "Listen to this, Eve."

"What is it?"

"Sheehan and Rogers object to the Blair plan."

"Don't let it bother you, Bill. The stockholders will have the final say, won't they?"

"Remember, my voting shares are in that damnable trust."

Ten minutes later, an annoyed W.F. was on the phone with Untermyer. "Do you know, Samuel, this Sheehan is the man I brought into the business in 1915 after he'd been thrown out of a newspaper job? He was nothing when I gave him a job and made him millions—now he's gone over to Stuart."

The question surrounding W.F.'s voting stock, which had been deposited in the trusteeship, began to haunt him. W.F. met with Samuel Untermyer and Benjamin Reass to discuss what they should do to prevent John Otterson and Harry Stuart from voting the stock against the Blair plan. Everywhere he turned, he was reminded of the mindless act he'd committed by signing that infernal trusteeship document.

Exchanging ideas, Untermyer, Reass and W.F. sat around the stained-glass office, smoking. This went on for over an hour; around noon, W.F. saw a harried-looking Jack Leo poke his nose in just as Untermyer finished loading his pipe. "Mr. Leo, so good to see you."

"Mr. Untermyer, I'm happy to see you again."

W.F. motioned for Jack Leo to sit in the chair next to him.

"Let's get down to the issues that face us, gentlemen," Untermyer said. "What do you think, Bill?"

"I don't want to see Otterson and Stuart voting my shares at the stockholders' meeting."

Untermyer came out firmly against complicating the litigation any more than it was. "I've filed an injunction with Supreme Court Justice Nathan Bijur and he has issued a temporary stay preventing the stock from being used until certain issues are decided."

"Is that good enough to permit me to vote my shares for the Blair plan?"

The Waldorf-Astoria in 1915, when William Fox's filmmaking dream was just beginning.

"You're still the holder of record, W.F.," Leo noted.

"Which helps us a little, Bill," Untermyer said.

Having suffered together through the first round of a contentious legal battle, they were now becoming as friendly as one might dare with a lawyer. W.F. reminded himself he was still Untermyer's client, and the old warhorse owed him the best advice money could buy.

Untermyer took his pipe out of his mouth and said, "That trusteeship agreement is still the fly in the ointment, Bill. If the court rules in favor of the trusteeship voting those shares, well, we'll be looking in from the outside."

"I should have never listened to Hughes!"

Leo said, "Default judgments continue to plague the company, W.F. Manufacturers Trust Company filed for $250,941."

"Bastards!"

Untermyer said, "The stay order issued by Judge Coleman is the only thing standing between the stockholders' vote on the Blair plan and receivership."

That afternoon, after eating lunch alone at his desk, W.F. had his chauffeur drive him to see the old Waldorf-Astoria where he could reminisce about that day, February 15, 1915, when he'd formed Fox Film. Since a builders' syndicate had announced the demolition of the hotel, he hadn't been near the area. It was a terrible disappointment for W.F. to drive around the block on Fifth Avenue between 33rd and 34th streets.

To make way for what the press was calling the tallest building in the world, the once haughty edifice had been completely cut down by an iron ball. There were a few chunks of mortar and some fragments of the walls of the old hotel along the north side of the block. In the center of what was once an elegant ballroom, W.F. saw a series of gaping excavations. There was a long, curving wooden ramp for the trucks and not much more.

Fifteen years later, the Waldorf-Astoria is just a hole in the ground.

"George, pull over for a minute."

"Yes, Mr. Fox."

Stepping out of the motorcar, W.F. studied what was now a busy construction site. Looking around with his red-rimmed eyes, he whispered, "It's only been 15 years."

Strange, wasn't it? Just 15 years and how things had changed.

CHAPTER 31

As in all good pictures, the villains—Halsey, Stuart and the Telephone Company—weren't about to give up without a struggle. Their next move was to circulate a letter to the stockholders of the Fox companies charging W.F. with the sole responsibility for the "financial embarrassment of both concerns."

"Do not be frightened by talk of receivership," read the first paragraph of the letter. "There will be no receivership if Mr. Fox and the board of directors, which he dominates, work in the interests of all the stockholders instead of looking to Mr. Fox's own selfish desires. We believe further that, regardless of who sponsors the same, a more advantageous plan of financing will be submitted to the stockholders' meeting and that the stockholders should judge for themselves as to the plan they wish to support."

In reply to their accusatory letter, W.F. fired off an immediate response and invited the *Times* to his office on 10th Avenue. He specifically requested that Emory R. Buckner, counsel for the independent Fox Film stockholders' committee headed by Morton F. Stern of J.B. Bache, be there.

Buckner was a member of the potent Manhattan law firm of Root, Clark, Buckner & Ballantine, and was one of the city's great trial lawyers. In a calculated show of solidarity, Untermyer and Buckner stood by W.F.'s side. W.F. studied intently the faces of the reporters who had gathered for the press briefing. They were expectant, and anxious to report any semblance of a breakthrough in the Fox mess.

The first question was directed to Mr. Buckner. "Sir, what plan does your client support?"

"We fully support the Blair plan as the only practicable plan thus far suggested."

"Mr. Fox, how do you respond to the charge that you are attempting to manipulate the refinancing plan for your own personal gain?"

"Halsey, Stuart and the American Telephone and Telegraph Company have been trying to buy my voting stock in the Fox companies ever since the Bancamerica-Blair group submitted their plan. At the same time that they were trying to buy my majority stock of 50,100 shares for $10 million or $200 a share for my film shares, their plan offered other stockholders the equivalent of $50 a share for the remaining 49 percent of B stock. I told the stockholders in my previous circular that I would not sell my stock, but I intend to stand by the stockholders to the end, and that is what I am doing at great personal sacrifice. I am entitled to have them stand by me and by themselves."

Once the briefing adjourned, Buckner approached W.F. and shook his hand. "Once you have stockholders' approval, we should be able to move quickly with financing."

"I hope so, Mr. Buckner."

The moment of truth was quickly approaching. There'd been 14 annual meetings of the Fox Film Corporation, and there was present at each of these meetings, other than officials of the company, one lone stockholder, a doctor who lived in Newark, New Jersey. W.F. considered him the mascot of Fox Film.

But this was 1930 and things had changed. A great struggle pitted William Fox against Halsey, Stuart, the Telephone Company and the Chase Bank.

On the top floor of Fox Film's headquarters on 10th Avenue were two spacious rooms, recently whitewashed, where the studio had made many a silent picture. These rooms began to fill at 10:00 on the morning of March 5, 1930, the date set for the special Fox Film stockholders' meeting.

The agenda announced in the proxy statement listed four points:

To consider and take action upon the plan of financing of the corporation set forth in a proposal submitted to the corporation by Bancamerica-Blair, Lehman Brothers and Dillon, Read and Company; to consider and take action upon the proposal to authorize and consent to the creation and issue by the corporation of additional equity and debt; to authorize the directors, officers and agents of the corporation to make, execute and deliver such agreements, consents and other documents, and do such acts and things as may be necessary, convenient or desirable to carry into effect the plan; and to transact such other business as may properly come before the meeting or any adjournment thereof.

Among those who attended the meeting were Winfield Sheehan, James Grainger, Clayton Sheehan and Courtland Smith, part the gang of six, all busily trying to drum up proxies for W.F.'s enemies. They were a pathetic sight to behold, these traitors dressed in their pinstriped suits who owed W.F. so much for the years he'd invested in their careers.

The shares necessary to ensure a positive outcome lay in the 50,100 shares of stock W.F. had deposited with the trustees at the Bankers Trust Company. As the holder of record, W.F. theoretically had the undisputed right to vote these shares unless somehow his enemies managed to find a court where a judge would determine whether William Fox could vote his block of B shares or whether it would be voted by John Otterson and Harry Stuart.

Unfortunately, they found that judge, Aaron Levy.

On Tuesday, March 4, a day before the meetings, briefs were filed; Judge Levy heard arguments on an injunction suit and announced that the question was much more complicated than he had anticipated. He would spend the night studying the documents and hand down his decision the first thing in the morning, March 5.

The morning of March 5, Judge Levy refused to enjoin John Otterson and Harry Stuart from voting W.F.'s shares because of the trusteeship agreement. "This court is not at all impressed by Mr. Fox's disingenuous charges that the agreement was induced by fraud and that it was violated by the other two trustees."

Who was this Judge Levy? It turned out that Judge Levy was an intimate friend of Sheehan and an active Tammany politician. W.F. also discovered that Sheehan had given an important position at a high salary to a friend of Judge Levy.

Standing resolutely before a gathering crowd of stockholders, W.F. thought of what he was going to say.

About 15 minutes before the Fox Film meeting was scheduled to begin, Richard Dwight approached the dais and announced to W.F. that he had just been informed of Judge Levy's decision and that Halsey, Stuart and the Telephone Company intended to vote his shares.

With his knees a little wobbly and his heartbeat a bit accelerated, W.F. felt as if he had come to his own execution and there was nothing more he could do. He breathed out, then slowly in again, and mustered up the courage and fortitude to confront whatever faced him. He decided he had to go on. He would fight for the Blair plan and pray that the stockholders would see the wisdom of refinancing the companies with William Fox still at the helm.

It was in that frame of mind that he sat down to open the meeting. This was a man who on October 28, 1929 weighed 182 pounds, and on March 5, 1930 weighed less than 150. He had had no new clothes made between the time he weighed 182 and the present. At 182 pounds, he was a man robust and healthy; now he looked haggard, tired and worn, with not enough vitality left to assert himself and his rights, but rather happy and glad that he was still alive and wondering whether he would be able to finish it out, whether he would be able to complete the job before his widow and daughters would hear a Rabbi say: "And here lies William Fox. He wasn't a bad man. He lived a good life."

From across the room came Untermyer, approaching W.F. He advised him that the directors would have to meet before commencing the stockholders' meeting.

"Let's follow protocol and get the full board or a majority to approve the latest version of the Blair plan before putting it to a stockholders' vote, Bill."

In agreement, W.F. had Jack Leo rustle up the directors and escort them into the boardroom. It was unsettling to see Winfield Sheehan sitting across the table, but under the circumstances, W.F. comported himself as a gentleman. In stark contrast to W.F.'s gaunt look, Sheehan appeared to be sitting on top of the world.

Several material modifications to the Blair plan were made by W.F.'s side, anticipating objections by the stockholders, such as abandoning the preferred issue of $25 million and replacing it with 1,250,000 shares of common stock. The Fox Theaters issue of convertible debentures was changed to provide $40 million of 7-percent debentures bearing stock warrants.

W.F. also reasserted his unwavering stand against the Halsey, Stuart plan. "Gentlemen, there is no plan." Outnumbered on the board, there wasn't much Sheehan could do except cast his vote against any recommendation W.F. made.

Nobody said anything in protest and W.F. surmised that Sheehan had been instructed not to wage war at the board meeting, a board that both Otterson and Stuart held in contempt.

Since the Fox forces outnumbered the opposing element, the board approved the modified Blair plan by a vote of four to three, with affirmative votes coming from Jack Leo, Aaron Fox, Charles S. Levin and Jacob W. Loeb. Voting against the plan were the Halsey and Telephone Company stooges, Winfield Sheehan, Saul Rogers and Nathaniel King.

It all came down to this: Since the Blair plan involved the issuance of stock, a two-thirds vote was required by law. W.F. came to the meeting with 62 percent of the proxies. Halsey, Stuart had about 7 percent, and 26 percent was in the hands of the stockholders' committee that had been organized by Morton F. Stern of Bache. The remaining 5 percent of the stock was W.F.'s voting shares, which were sitting in escrow at Bankers' Trust. If W.F. could vote these shares, he would have 67 percent and be over the two-thirds requirement.

W.F. called the stockholders' assembly to order at 11:32 a.m. Twenty policemen were scattered about the building in case of demonstrations. Charles Hall and Henry Mendes were named inspectors and 10 tellers were appointed. The 1,500 folding chairs that had been set up were full. News reporters assembled along the walls. The Fox stockholders' meetings were to become front-page news.

More prevalent than stockholders were the number of agitators representing the Telephone Company, whose job it was to hooray everything the Telephone Company wanted and shout down everything that W.F. wanted. Gifford's "Information Department" had orchestrated a well-set plan to sway investor opinion to his side.

A Mayer surrogate, Lawrence Berenson, got up and addressed the meeting.

W.F. introduced him. "This is the man who has filed a receivership petition, although he only represents 440 shares."

"I object!"

"Sit down, you bum."

Ignoring the epithets, Berenson made a bitter speech, full of attacks on the Blair plan. He concluded, "It is better for every stockholder in the corporation to stand behind the petition for the appointment of a receiver under the guidance of the United States Court."

There were hisses and cries of, "No, no."

W.F. said to Berenson, "Now will you please sit down, Mr. Berenson. You are out of order!"

"I am not out of order. I decline to sit down. I am going to be heard. There are stockholders here that want to hear me."

"No, there are not," Untermyer said.

There were several cries of "sit down!"

"Mr. Berenson, just a moment. Is there anybody in the room who wants to hear Mr. Berenson any further?" W.F. asked.

"No! Put him out!"

From the back of the room someone shouted, "Whoever heard of him before this?"

Berenson played his voice like a shrill musical instrument; every word he said was irritating. "I want to be heard."

"The man has a legal right. Let him say it!" someone shouted from the back of the room.

"Mr. Berenson is your man, gentlemen," W.F. responded.

Incensed, W.F. gave Berenson seven minutes more to complete his tirade. Finally, he quit.

Martin Conboy, representing another small group of dissident shareholders, got up to attack the Blair plan and blamed the situation on W.F.

"You seem to like Berenson."

"Well, I am not an enemy of his. I like you, too, Mr. Untermyer," Conboy stated.

"But Mr. Conboy, you ought to have a great deal of sympathy for Mr. Berenson, because you too ask for a receivership."

"There is not any question of sympathy. I did not ask for a receiver."

"You did."

"I told the court there were worse things than a receiver. Don't interrupt me with statements of that kind. You know that is not quite an answer to what I am saying. We are talking about receivers for a moment."

"He wants to razz you, too," Berenson said.

The patrician-looking Emory Buckner got up and spoke. "There may be those who have Mr. Berenson's fancy for a receivership, but I think the stockholders are ill-advised if anything they can do to prevent a receivership is left undone. We lawyers know, even if you have not had experience, that in a receivership it is mostly the lawyers and the trustees and the new bankers or new organizing gentlemen who come around who do nearly all the receiving, and the common stock is generally wiped out to make a reorganization more practicable."

Buckner concluded and emphatically stated that the Stern Committee would cast its 26 percent for the Blair plan. As if scripted, Martin Conboy quickly challenged the vote of the Stern committee, cast by Bruckner, demanding that Bruckner be sworn, according to section 20 of the General Corporation Laws.

A bit flustered at Conboy's insistence, Bruckner rose and repeated the oath: "I do solemnly swear that in voting at this election I have not, either directly, indirectly or impliedly, received any promise or any sum of money or anything of value to influence the giving of my vote or votes at this meeting or as consideration therefor."

Not satisfied with Bruckner giving the oath, Conboy demanded it from Swaine.

Untermyer suggested they ought to have the same oath from Stuart and Otterson. "Are you voting, too, Mr. Conboy?"

"Yes."

"We might have one from you, too."

"I move the swearing be closed."

Now all W.F. needed was the right to vote his B shares.

Next up was Richard Dwight, representing Otterson and Harry Stuart as trustees. "I am acting for all the trustees, including Mr. Fox."

There was a dramatic lull in the conversation, or at least a pause aimed at letting the audience digest what was going on. This was a dangerous moment in the proceedings when it became apparent to the stockholders that there were two different camps in support of two unique solutions to Fox Film's financial problems. Throughout the meeting there were rumors regarding the dilution of stockholders' ownership as a result of the Blair plan.

Rising, Untermyer reacted to Dwight's preposterous assertion and politely said, "I am afraid Mr. Dwight is just a trifle disingenuous. He says Mr. Fox is one of the trustees, but the trustee agreement says that the two other trustees can vote without him, so that he is in a peculiar position."

"It says nothing about that in the voting trust agreement."

With a due show of professionalism, Untermyer said, "It does say that any two or a majority can act."

"Not the voting trust agreement."

Determined to deny Dwight the litigator's rhythm, he replied, "Yes, and so much so that this Halsey, Stuart plan, which has the approval of the trustees and is really made by the trustees, was considered and put out in your office."

"That is correct," Dwight had to agree.

Lunchtime came and went. During a brief pause there was no stopping the extraneous talk. At 3:00, the proposed time for the Fox Theaters meeting had passed. Finally, Fox Film recessed until evening to begin the Fox Theaters meeting.

In the evening session, voting was put off until morning. In the Fox Film meeting, unofficial tallies gave the William Fox side 573,000 out of 602,000 proxies of A stock. Both sides voted W.F.'s B shares, so it was impossible to determine how everyone stood.

At the behest of several long-time stockholders, W.F. was invited to speak. He rose slowly and peered over a pair of smudged glasses. "I cannot promise you that I am going to work any harder from now on than I have in the past, because I don't believe that I have the same vitality left. After all, I gave this company my best years, from 21 to 51, and I do not believe that I have got 30 years more left. I am sure that if I had, they won't be years with as much energy as I was able to expend in the last 30. But all that I have belongs to these companies, I pledge you that."

Following the stockholders meetings' adjournment, Untermyer told the press, "The result of the stockholders' meeting is an overwhelming victory for Mr. Fox and is a complete refutation of the false and reckless charges made in heated controversy." In declaring victory Untermyer was following the golden rule. Never admit to anything when the votes are on your side.

When the votes were counted the following morning, the tellers reported the official results in favor of the Blair plan carried by a vote of 914,405 against 33,085.

Before leaving for the night, Untermyer approached W.F. "This is only the beginning of the fight. Stay by the telephone—I'll have some points to check with you this evening."

On the way back to the Ambassador, Untermyer worked through his options. They were lost unless they could get a favorable decision on the voting trust agreement. There was a regular stockholders' meeting in the offing, scheduled for April 15, where Stuart and Otterson would surely vote W.F.'s shares. Since Judge Levy's decision rested on findings of fact, Untermyer couldn't win in a state court. The only possibility was to move the litigation to a federal court. And, for that, he needed to raise a separate issue to avoid a *res judicata* ruling—an affirmative defense barring the same parties from litigating a second lawsuit on the same claim.

A meeting was called in Judge Coleman's chambers; he had invited Otto Kahn, Harry Stuart, John Otterson, Clarence Dillon, George Kindsay of Bancamerica-Blair and Philip Lehman. Before anything new was added to the agenda, the lawyers for each side presented their own particular version of what had transpired at the stockholders' meeting.

Untermyer handed the judge the official vote tally and he jotted it down in a notebook he was using to record the highlights of the hearing.

Kindsay told Judge Coleman that Bancamerica-Blair was ready to put the finishing touches on their financial plan and requested that the court make some kind of ruling in their favor.

Otterson got red-faced and said the Telephone Company and Halsey, Stuart were of a mind to offer an alternative plan, and since the trusteeship controlled the voting stock of the company, it would probably be necessary to hold an extraordinary stockholders' meeting to consider their plan where all of the voting stock would be taken into consideration.

Never a phrasemaker, Otto Kahn spoke in simple terms and said, "The Blair plan represents a realistic refinancing for the Fox companies." Harry Stuart replied, "The Halsey alternative will not dilute the stockholders as much as the Blair plan. They ought to have a choice."

By this time, Judge Coleman's expression was troubled; he seemed anxious to close the hearing and said he'd take everything he had heard under advisement and call for another hearing. The *Times* reported the "banker's presence was viewed as a sign of probable mediation in the fight."

As a practical matter, the companies still didn't have the money in the bank, and the implementation of the refinancing plan would take some time.

The Atlantic National Bank of Boston filed a judgment for $390,119 in the Supreme Court against Fox Theaters.

Negotiations for a merger of the Equitable Trust Company and the Chase National Bank reached a more active stage. A meeting was held between Winthrop W. Aldrich of Equitable and Albert H. Wiggin, chairman of Chase. Experts placed the probable terms of the merger at four shares of Chase for five of Equitable. Control of Equitable was largely in the hands of the Rockefeller interests.

Appropriately, Untermyer proceeded on the basis that he had won a battle but not the war. He filed suit in W.F.'s name in federal court to restrain Harry Stuart and John Otterson from voting the stock of the companies, and requested that W.F. be declared sole owner of that stock on the ground that Stuart and Otterson had breached the trusteeship agreement.

Since W.F. hadn't received any satisfaction in Levy's state court, Untermyer decided a change of venue was in order.

In response to Untermyer's motion, Otterson's and Stuart's lawyers brought another suit in the State Supreme Court to halt by injunction Untermyer's action in the federal court. There was no way they would let W.F. and his legal counsel remove the Honorable Aaron Levy from the scene. Their man was in place and it was now important to litigate everything in front of him.

By this time, there were so many lawsuits filed that even the lawyers were confused as to who was suing whom, so everyone decided on a truce. The attorneys agreed that the federal court hearing be put off for a few days until the state court could sort things out.

The three receivership actions, the hearing for which had been scheduled for March 17, were postponed until March 20. In the meantime, trading in rights to subscribe to additional class A shares and debentures of Fox Film started on the Exchange.

On March 18, in the Supreme Court of New York County, Sheehan was deposed and began his incredible story of how he, and he alone, was responsible for any of the success enjoyed by the Fox Companies.

> I have a more intimate knowledge of the general business details, production
> details, distribution details and all other fields that are under my supervision
> than any other official, executive or employee of the company.

Sheehan and his mentors, Otterson and Stuart, hatched this affidavit. It was not only filed in court but also was printed and distributed by Halsey, Stuart to the companies' stockholders, undoubtedly at company expense.

Two days later, while the Untermyer lawyers worked until the early hours of the morning in preparation for the federal court, Abe Shamos appeared at the Ambassador suite. It was past midnight.

"What's wrong, Abe," Alvin asked.

"They got a temporary stay from Judge Manton until April 7 of any hearing in the federal court on the voting trust agreement."

"Damn!"

"And they smacked us with an order to show cause on April 7 in the Circuit Court of Appeals why a writ of prohibition should not issue."

In effect, Dwight was petitioning the higher federal court to forbid the lower federal court from hearing Untermyer's new case on the voting trust.

All Alvin Untermyer could say was, "Very clever."

As in any title fight where in the late rounds the challenger seems to be ahead on a couple of points, there comes the time to put in the "fix," time to remove an honest referee from the ring because he has shown rectitude in ensuring the combatants of a fair outcome.

A man not easily persuaded by wealth and power, this Judge Coleman. Incorruptible. Fair-minded. Diligent. Reasonable. Every positive adjective in the book fit Judge Coleman.

Lawyers employed by Otterson and Stuart submitted to Judge Martin T. Manton, Senior Judge of the United States Circuit Court of Appeals, the affidavit of Harold L. Stuart alleging prejudice on the part of Judge Coleman, asking why he should not be restrained from "taking any steps whatsoever" in the actions brought by William Fox against the trustees.

The affidavit cited a long laundry list of the things that Coleman had done to favor Fox and to deny Stuart. The document requested that Judge Coleman "enter upon the records of this Court the certificate of disqualification." Now hamstrung, Judge Coleman could no longer decide on any of the Fox issues before the court.

It was time for Sheehan to earn more of those gold coins. The bag was not yet full. His allegations were the standard arguments developed by his new employer, the Telephone Company. Sheehan was treating W.F. like an incompetent, using phrases like "the attitude of Mr. Fox has been harmful to the best interests of the companies and to his own interests as well," which made W.F. want to vomit. He'd had a belly full of this perfidious ingrate and was finding it very difficult to be around him.

In one of the worst moments of his life, W.F. was forced to respond to Sheehan's duplicitous accusations and issue a long statement refuting point by point every allegation, stating in no uncertain terms, "Sheehan wants to wreck this great enterprise by forcing it into receivership. Sheehan has entered into a bargain by which he is to replace me."

On March 19, a production supervisor on the Fox lot, William Goetz, married Edith Mayer, Louis B.'s daughter. The event was said to have cost $25,000, Hollywood's biggest wedding to date. W.F. now had a Mayer "plant" in his organization. He'd always felt the meddling hand of Louis B. Mayer behind the scene, somehow beholden to Albert Wiggin.

Judge Coleman once again opened proceedings in a crowded courtroom in which he had just finished charging a jury in a criminal case. The idea was to comply with Judge Manton's order removing him from the Fox case for "prejudice."

For all that, he gave the impression of being unaffected and would conduct his court in the usual expedient manner, much as he customarily did every day of the week. His tone perfectly conveyed how he viewed his position in the most practical of terms. "Recently, there has been filed with me an affidavit of prejudice; my impression of the law is that the mere filing of this affidavit divests me of discretion in the matter."

Muttering a profanity, Untermyer pleaded, "If Your Honor pleases, we believe that we can convince you that you can act."

"Gentlemen, I am willing to turn this entire matter to another judge, if you so desire. I will not consider it a personal reflection if you will express yourselves freely. I believe that this is a legal and not a personal matter."

"We do not want this to go to another judge," Untermyer said. "No other judge will do so much as Judge Coleman has done to avoid the disaster of receivership."

"Perhaps that is the trouble," Judge Coleman said cynically.

"Can't the court, Your Honor, let us provide for refinancing of the Fox companies without receivership but under the mandate of the court?" Untermyer queried.

"How can I do that without a receivership?" Judge Coleman asked.

A radiant Bogue rose in support of his allegation of bias and said, "The court has accepted Mr. Fox's statement that he would not do business with Halsey, Stuart at face value."

"It's over, Bill." That was what Untermyer whispered to W.F. Judge Coleman would have to step down and could no longer hear the case.

A hundred questions raced through W.F.'s mind, but he knew they would remain unanswered. The first and most important question was why he had signed the trusteeship.

Almost nothing in W.F.'s life seemed to be going well. Even his wife, dear Eve, was losing her strength to continue the battle with these corporate giants. And now Samuel Untermyer was conceding defeat.

"We go on, Samuel!"

On the ride back to the Ambassador Hotel, a more subdued Samuel Untermyer asked W.F., "What in the hell do they really want, Bill?"

"The Tri-Ergon patents."

"What in God's name are they?"

"Part of the technology the Telephone Company will need to run its sound projectors. Without them, they'll never be able to run sound-on-film."

"Let me use them to negotiate a settlement, Bill."

"I can't."

"Why?"

"If I lose control of the company, Samuel, I'll make them pay through the nose for these patents."

"Once they've got your shares, Bill, they'll go after those patents with a hundred lawyers. You won't have enough money to defend them."

"We'll see."

While the legal struggle proceeded unabated, the companies were anxiously trying to fill their treasury with real money. Jack Leo notified the New York Stock Exchange that the companies wanted to extend the rights to subscribe to the new common stock and debentures from March 31 to April 10. Under the agreement with the Blair group, Fox Film and Fox Theaters had to do their financing no later than April 15.

Federal Judge Frank J. Coleman disqualified himself on March 27 "from further judicial participation" in the legal maze surrounding William Fox and his companies. William Fox and his enemies were all there for this momentous decision, both sides with their respective legal counsel.

For the last time, Judge Coleman spoke of the William Fox matter. "This action is essential under the law and I have no discretion in the matter. I was to rule on whether the affidavit filed stated facts that in themselves or by reasonable inference did or might show my bias or prejudice in this case. The law did not permit me to ask whether the statements or inferences were true. I was to accept them as sufficient and rule that they were.

"If the inferences were true, I am not only disqualified in this case but I am unfit to be a judge in any case. I took the matter up with my associates, and they have assigned Federal Judge John C. Knox to the case."

"These statements are false, Your Honor. Mr. Bogue, counsel for Halsey, Stuart has assured me that his only interest lay solely in the payment to his clients of $27 million."

Nodding, as if to accept what Swaine was saying, Judge Coleman said, "It's useless to go any further into this matter as I am bound by the affidavit of prejudice."

"My only purpose, Your Honor, is to defend this court. My clients do not need a defense," Swaine said.

"The implication being," asked Judge Coleman with a smile, "that this court does?"

Bogue got in the last word. "My clients are trying to form a refinancing plan. There has been no attempt to impugn this court's integrity and I resent the implication that my own veracity has come into question."

"Your conduct throughout," said Judge Coleman, "has contained nothing pusillanimous. It has been free from anything one could criticize."

Untermyer told W.F. to go back to his office and said he would attend to the next steps in the process. W.F. left with Jack Leo.

Arrangements were made for the lawyers to appear before Judge Knox in another courtroom in the federal building. When Knox took the bench, he told the lawyers the case was new and they would have to start all over again. After clarifying several points of order, Samuel Untermyer was granted the opportunity to review the case and summarize the legal procedures to date. Ralph Harris, one of the lawyers representing Stuart and Otterson, accused Untermyer of presenting a biased statement of the case. He then read a long statement of the case from his point of view.

Judge Knox announced that he would hear the case again at 4:30 p.m., Monday, March 31, and he would be prepared to hold an all-night session.

At this point in the legal struggle, Harry Stuart, John Otterson and Albert Wiggin were back on track. Win or lose, time was on their side and their idea was to delay, delay, delay, knowing well the Blair syndicate would eventually fall apart, afraid of getting mired in the spider's web W.F.'s enemies were spinning.

For the first time W.F. began to have serious thoughts of quitting, selling his shares while they still had some value, halting the time-consuming, money-draining litigation that was taxing not only the Fox companies but his personal wealth as well. He told Samuel Untermyer to drop a comment here and there with his adversaries that he might be open to a reasonable offer.

The Public National Bank and Trust Company entered a default judgment for $553,874 against Fox Film. Three Fox suits were put off until April 2 in accordance with stipulations presented by the lawyers. First was Sheehan's motion to "have William Fox and the film and theaters corporations restrained from financing under the Bancamerica-Blair plan."

Sheehan alleged that W.F. "railroaded" his proposal through at the board meetings, declaring that the four directors who voted with W.F. were relatives and one was a life-long friend.

Another was a similar motion by E. Clay Krebs and other minority stockholders. The third action referred to Untermyer's request for an injunction action against the co-trustees, Otterson and Stuart, on the grounds that W.F. had brought a more comprehensive suit in the federal court.

The Fox litigation wound its weary way through three courts with no definite resolution. Justice John Ford in the Supreme Court heard arguments on the motion of William Fox to discontinue his action against Otterson and Stuart, co-trustees, and on the motion of the co-trustees to restrain W.F. from prosecuting his federal court suit. Decision was reserved on both motions.

Newly appointed Judge Knox expressed his displeasure at the delaying tactics of opposing counsel. He said, "Will you gentlemen be prepared to argue then? I cannot waste my time coming in here just to hear a request for adjournment."

During the first meeting in Judge Knox's courtroom, W.F. tried to remember how long it had been that he'd thought about making pictures. That, after all, was his business. He'd encouraged Sol Wurtzel to conduct business as usual with California production, and Jack Leo was keeping his finger in Fox's East Coast operations. Surprisingly, thanks to W.F.'s excellent organization, they were meeting production schedules and making good pictures. Sound engineering was progressing satisfactorily and whenever he could, W.F. called someone in the company and discussed what he'd always discussed, producing good pictures. He hated every minute of this constant contact with judges, lawyers, process servers and all the other parasites who lived off the difficulties of others.

A bailiff announced the arrival of Judge Knox.

After discussing various legal motions, Judge Knox invited the parties to conference in his office. "I shall not be a negotiator, gentlemen. My position might as well be understood first as last; it will be strictly judicial. I am willing to do anything I can to help settle this case, but it will be as a judge, not a negotiator."

For the better part of an hour, Judge Knox walked both sides through the legal issues as he saw them and said, "The potency of this trust agreement must be determined before either of these plans can be put into effect. It doesn't seem to me that any plan can go through until we get some of this litigation out of the way."

Bogue got up on his high horse and bitterly defended a strict interpretation of the trusteeship agreement.

Judge Knox quickly silenced him. "The court will decide this matter, Mr. Bogue."

One thing was fairly obvious. The judge was in no mood for any more discussion. "I'll decide this case tonight. It seems to me to be an impossible situation. With all these legal actions, it is a treadmill."

Untermyer added, "It is a disgrace."

"Hearing adjourned."

While the antics of the courtroom were entertaining one group of lawyers, another equally forceful group was actively trying to dissuade the Blair syndicate from proceeding with their refinancing plan. Their ace in the hole was the threat of a legal quagmire. It was important to recall that the Blair group was committed up to the 15th of April. After that, they could drop Fox and his companies without incurring a penalty.

In the midst of all this, W.F. received a hand-delivered letter from the Blair group, informing him that they no longer held him bound by his promise not to sell his voting shares.

W.F. thought that strange. What were they telling him?

Meanwhile, W.F. wanted to get a decision on the trust as soon as possible. He told Untermyer, "It seems to me as if this law business with Judge Knox is going to take a long time. You ought to give me some idea how long you will take in court, and then we should meet these bankers and get an extension of time."

"This will take us into June, Bill."

"Let's request an extension to June 15."

"I'll ask for a meeting."

It was Monday, March 31. The following day was Belle's birthday. W.F. sat slumped in his darkened office, trying to catch up with business matters. He was interrupted by a messenger boy, who brought him a hand-written note from Jack Leo. W.F.'s presence was urgently needed at Bancamerica-Blair.

Something was wrong? He buried his face in his hands. In the dark of an overcast day he read the letter once more. It read "urgent."

Samuel Untermyer and his son, Alvin, were chauffeured to the meeting place. They met W.F. in an anteroom. For over an hour, they were kept waiting in the outer office.

W.F. said, "I think we ought to plan out our program when we go in there, and I wish it would be followed as I suggest—that neither Alvin nor myself open our mouths, but that you, Samuel, do all the talking, and we be allowed to observe the banking group and their lawyers."

"That's fine by me, Bill."

In a little more than an hour they were ushered in. There sat a group of 15 men. As W.F. came into the room, they appeared to him as though they were all Japanese. Every man in that room knew that Judge Coleman was no longer on the case, that Halsey, Stuart had filed the affidavit of prejudice, that the court that had held this thing together was no longer there to do it. He felt that every man there knew that Halsey, Stuart had played their final trump card and won the game.

As W.F. observed each of man's face, he was receiving mental communications that something had gone terribly wrong. He was not in the presence of the tremendously friendly group who had been arguing in court that their plan should be the only one submitted to the stockholders. At the stockholders' meeting these men had been like schoolboys in a contest.

What in God's world could they be thinking about now?

Untermyer said, "Gentlemen, because of this great amount of litigation, and because of the removal of Judge Coleman, Mr. Fox has requested that we have this meeting to inquire from you whether you would be willing to renew your contract to supply this financing for 60 days longer."

There was dead silence. Robert Taylor Swaine, of the prestigious law firm of Cravath, de Gersdorff, Swaine & Wood, asked several legal questions and Untermyer took 15 minutes to answer them. It was the same Robert Taylor Swaine who had acted as counsel for the Bancamerica-Blair group, who had considered litigation wasteful and uneconomic, who had assured William Fox that his client would finance his companies. Robert Taylor Swaine was now giving him the runaround.

Untermyer queried again, "Gentlemen, we are asking whether you will extend the contracts to June 15?" Again, silence.

A lawyer for the Lehman group, Mr. Royce, then asked Untermyer a question, again a carefully prepared one. Again it took Untermyer 15 minutes of explanation before he could conclude the answer. There was not a sound out of all these bankers, not a word, not an eyelash movement—they were just Japanese diplomats.

And then Untermyer for the third time asked whether they could extend the contract, and this time Robert Taylor Swaine, who had asked the first question, asked a second question.

W.F. went over to Alvin and said, "Go and tell your father not to ask our question again, but to leave with our question unanswered."

And so they left. The question was never replied to.

William Fox in his garden at Woodmere

CHAPTER 32

Shortly after the banker's meeting, W.F. left for Woodmere and called Albert Greenfield, telling him he'd be willing to sell his voting shares.

Greenfield said Harley L. Clarke wanted to buy them and he would get W.F. a letter from Clarke, which constituted an offer. As part of the purchase, Clarke wanted W.F. to surrender his Fox Movietone stock, his Grandeur patents and the Tri-Ergon patents, all of which were W.F.'s personal property.

In his negotiations for the sale of W.F.'s voting shares, Greenfield had included the rights to the Tri-Ergon patents. He took the position that he had been informed repeatedly that these patents were valueless, so W.F. might as well throw them into the deal. Suffering from an acute case of fatigue, W.F. was ready to surrender the patents.

Eve Fox was in the doorway, with only a curtain between them, listening to Greenfield's conversation. She came into the room, and went into a rage of a kind W.F. would never like to see her or anyone in again; it resulted in a terrific expression of frenzy, and she finally dropped to the floor and passed out. For a while W.F. thought she was dead; it took them half an hour to bring her to again. It was then that Greenfield realized he must never mention the Tri-Ergon patents, and if there were ever to be a sale, it would have to be done without those patents.

There came a time when W.F. had to break the news about selling his stock to his family. They all met in the spacious living room at Woodmere. Eve and the girls were there as well as Jack Leo, Benjamin Reass and Samuel Untermyer.

Outside the sky was a cloudless blue and the gulls were singing because decent weather had finally arrived. One could not imagine a more fitting backdrop for the final scene of a great melodrama. It was picture perfect. John Ford could not have come up with a more appropriate set.

Emotionally and physically spent, W.F. was not looking forward to facing the inevitable. After fumbling for a few moments, W.F. lit a cigar. He took a long drag and blew out a stream of smoke. "What are my chances, Samuel?"

Before responding, Untermyer tapped his pipe into an ashtray. "Not good. At the annual stockholders' meeting they'll vote your stock and elect new directors. You'll be forced out, Bill."

"Is there anything we can do?" Eve pleaded.

There really wasn't much Untermyer could do, except for litigating ad nauseam. "We can continue to litigate the validity of the trusteeship agreement, Eve, but frankly speaking, Bill will be looking from the outside in."

W.F. had reflected on the significance of his decision to sell for a long time. Cut your losses short, he had always cautioned his staff. Besides, the sale wouldn't be the end of it. There remained several thorny financial issues, like the matter of personal guarantees.

"I'm giving up the fight. I cannot risk deliberately wasting our remaining fortune on lawsuits. It wouldn't be fair to any of you—Eve, Mona or Belle. Nor to your children. There will be problems ahead because I've personally guaranteed many things. William Fox is tired. Samuel, I'm prepared to sell my shares to Mr. Clarke."

"I'll talk to him in the morning."

"No, have Greenfield set up the meeting."

Exchanging warm glances with Eve, W.F. smiled for the first time in a long time. "Help me up, Eve. I want to go to sleep."

W.F.'s meeting with Harley Clarke and his band of lawyers included Alvin Untermyer and Albert Greenfield. The site was W.F.'s Ambassador suite, the one he had been using as his battle headquarters.

With bowed head, Blumy showed up several minutes later and sat with the Clarke entourage.

W.F. wanted Blumenthal out of the room. "Get that little son-of-a-bitch out of here!"

Mad as a wet hen, Blumy looked to Clarke for instructions.

"If you don't mind, Mr. Blumenthal."

William Fox glared at Blumenthal. "God will strike you dead for what you did to me!"

His tail caught between his legs, Blumy left the room.

"After we finish our business, Harley, permit me to tell you the true story of Alfred C. Blumenthal. Before he gets in your good graces, you had better hear from my lips just what he is."

"I appreciate that, Bill."

To kick off things, Clarke put his wish list on the table. Surrender the Fox-Movietone stock. Surrender the Tri-Ergon patents. Surrender the Grandeur patents, which were all W.F.'s personal property.

Not so surprisingly, Greenfield was taking the position that W.F. accede to Clarke's demands because Fox Film owed him $10 million, which was almost half the capital of his company. He had a lot at stake and wanted a good outcome.

As part of the deal, W.F. was to receive a certified check for $15 million, $3 million in a note and 20 percent of the fees in any new financing because W.F. wanted to stay involved until the companies could be put on sound footing again. W.F. wanted to be a director for five years; he wanted Clarke to establish an advisory board and make W.F. chairman; and he wanted a salary of $500,000 for five years. In return, W.F. would agree to give Fox Film a royalty-free license for the use of the Tri-Ergon and Grandeur patents.

Then W.F. hit Clarke with a peculiar condition: "When the bankers sent me a letter stating they no longer objected to my selling my voting shares, they extracted from me a promise that the purchaser of my shares, if he did any financing, would have to do it through them; they would have to be in the syndicate, and at least three-fourths of the financing would be handled by them."

"Bill, Chase and Halsey, Stuart will handle things."

"I gave my word, Harley."

"Would you like me to prove you have no bankers?"

"Yes, I would like to have proof of that."

"All right. Do you know Tinker?" "No."

Tinker was president of Chase Securities Corporation. To assuage W.F., Clarke got him on the phone. When Tinker answered, Clarke explained who W.F. was and then passed the phone to him.

THE REFINANCING

NEW YORK, April 7.—INS—The gigantic financial battle for control of the Fox Theater and Motion Picture enterprises ended today when William Fox announced a final peace move. The magnate relinquished control of his $300,000,000 movie business in the sale of his 151,000 shares of "B" stock to a syndicate headed by Harley L. Clarke, president of General Theaters Equipment, Inc., Clarke is a Chicago Public Utilities Company head.

In a formal statement, Samuel Untermeyer, Attorney for Fox, said the conflicting banking interests, involved in refinancing the Fox Companies, will participate jointly in a new refinancing plan that will feature a $60,000,000 issue of six and one-half debentures.

The price received by the magnate from the Chicago syndicate was not revealed.

Fox, although selling control, will continue as chairman of an advisory board of the company for five years. Both Halsey, Stuart and Co., and the Bancamerica-Blair-Lehman-Dillon-Read banking groups will aid the refinancing, it was announced, and both have approved the new organization plan.

W. R. Sheehan, vice president of the Fox companies, who backed the Halsey-Stuart re-financing plan, said Clarke has provided ample finances to cover an expansion program.

Untermeyer said that all the debts of the Fox companies would be paid at once with interest. He said all pending litigation "will doubtless" be dismissed.

Fox's financial and legal troubles were revealed last October, shortly after he recovered from injuries sustained in an automobile accident. Two stockholders' suits, demanding an equity receivership were filed, and these started an amazing succession of legal actions, climaxed in recent weeks by several injunctions.

"Mr. Tinker, Harley Clarke tells me that last Monday you met my banking group and that you reached an agreement with them that they would be willing to take 50 percent of the financing. With whom did you have that understanding?"

"I have had that understanding with your group, and particularly with Elisha Walker."

W.F. thanked him and called Elisha Walker at his home. W.F. told him he was selling out. Walker confirmed what Tinker had said. W.F. insisted on 20 percent of bankers' fees.

"Here, your bankers have 50 percent and our bankers have 50 percent, and where are you going to get 20 percent?"

In a fit of temper, Clarke said the deal was off and he was taking the train back to Chicago. He was not above attempting to frighten W.F. into thinking he was prepared to walk away from the negotiation.

Suffering from an acute case of fatigue, W.F. headed to his apartment at the Marguery for momentary solace. Greenfield decided to stay overnight at the Ambassador with Alvin Untermyer. They weren't about to abandon the city until an agreement was signed.

Before departing, W.F. told Greenfield that if he were awake, he would be glad to see him at his home at 3 p.m.

A timetable said the Twentieth Century train left New York at 2:45 p.m. W.F. posted a man at the Grand Central Station to see if Clarke would go back to Chicago on that train. The hour came, and W.F.'s man phoned and said Clarke had not taken the train.

While waiting, Greenfield had some tea. The phone rang. It was W.F. "That fellow Clarke didn't go back to Chicago. He didn't call the deal off. He is right across the street. He's got an apartment at 277 Park Avenue," W.F. said.

"I will go right across the street and see him," Greenfield said.

It wasn't too difficult to find Clarke at home. Within an hour Greenfield returned and said Clarke had agreed to the 20 percent participation. Now it was a question of waiting for Samuel Untermyer to arrive and read the contract. There was a slew of paperwork to deal with before the closing.

When he got there, W.F. said to Untermyer, "Before we sign the contract, be sure you have a perfect arrangement whereby these companies are going to pay you the million dollars that I had arranged with you."

There was this one last item to negotiate. Greenfield escorted Untermyer across Park Avenue to Clarke's apartment and they discussed Untermyer's fee. With little debate, Clarke agreed to pay it.

There were no remaining obstacles to the sale of W.F.'s shares. He had a deal. Ten lawyers were working around a massive mahogany table in Untermyer's office, writing, crossing out, handing clean sheets back and forth for typing. On only one other floor of the Equitable Building were typewriters clicking that Saturday afternoon.

For some reason not fully understood by W.F., Untermyer insisted that the contract could not be signed until after the stroke of midnight. This was Sunday, April 6. W.F. suggested that in view of the importance of the deal they wait until 10 or 15 minutes past 12—perhaps the watch they were going by did not keep accurate time. So sometime between 5 and 10 minutes past 12, William Fox signed an agreement ending his long career at Fox Film and Fox Theaters.

As consideration there was a certified check for $15 million, a note for $3 million and a five-year advisory contract worth $500,000 annually. It was curious that the check was drawn on the Chase Bank.

Clarke and W.F. sat at opposite ends of a table, facing each other. There was a pause before W.F. spoke. "I just thought of something funny, Harley. I just sold you my voting shares, and I can't deliver them. They're in that damn trust."

Clarke smiled. "Oh, don't worry about that little matter, Bill. They're on their way to my office in Chicago."

It was less than a 10-minute walk to the Marguery. Tonight, W.F. would sleep in his own bed.

It was by no means easy for W.F. to accept the offer. There was his own reluctance to quit the battle, and the inevitable questions as to whether the offer constituted a fair deal. When he did accept it, he had at least the conviction that he had done very best he could and had not totally destroyed his family's nest egg.

A week later, Winfield Sheehan hosted 50 or 60 representatives of newspapers, trade periodicals and fan magazines in his suite at the Savoy-Plaza. He told the reporters: "The new controlling ownership and the banking association of Halsey, Stuart and Company and others are welcome. I have the highest admiration for Harley L. Clarke."

Untermyer responded: "Mr. Fox sold his shares under conditions that Mr. Fox is satisfied will safeguard the future prosperity and expansion of the companies. He has consistently refused to sell his controlling shares until it could be accomplished so as to fully protect the rights of every stockholder and the future of the companies."

"The new plan is exactly that proposed some time ago by Halsey, Stuart," Sheehan told reporters. One of Sheehan's assistants remarked: "Fox will be chairman of the advisory board, but by the time that board meets, all of you will have gray beards."

There came that last day W.F. would spend alone in his office, picking up personal things and saying fond goodbyes to the many people who'd toiled with him day and night, loyally helping him turn a small studio into a magnificent enterprise that had gained a worldwide reputation for making and exhibiting quality pictures.

The shimmering lights and the shifting imagery of the sun's rays piercing through the stained glass created a funereal effect in the office. While examining personal correspondence, W.F. noticed, out of the corner of his eye, the snub-nosed profile of that treacherous Brutus. Sheehan was halfway through the door.

Cautiously, the round-faced Sheehan approached W.F.'s desk.

"What are you doing here, Winnie?"

"I just wanted you to know that what I did, I did for the sake of the company."

W.F. could have reacted in many ways, some of them violent, but he chose not to reward this Brutus by getting out of character, even though he was seething deep inside.

Slowly, W.F. got up and came around his desk to look deeply into those ice-cold blue eyes Sheehan possessed.

"The company, you say? The company? You've destroyed everything I've worked for! Thirty years of my life! Get out, you treacherous bastard! Get out!" Recognizing he'd ignited something in W.F. whose outcome was no longer predictable, Sheehan shrank, and walked out the door.

W.F. stood there for a good while, his hands balled into fists. He was trembling, acutely aware of the fact that he had lost the most important battle of his life. He was no longer in control of his companies.

W.F.'s eyes swung around in time to catch Eve looking at him. "Eve?"

She was quiet for a moment. Then she said, "Bill, let's go home."

"Yes, Eve. Let's go home."

EPILOGUE

By 1930, the population of the United States was 122 million, with New York, Chicago and Philadelphia the three largest urban areas.

The 12 leading film producers in 1930, Paramount, Warner Bros., Fox, MGM, R.K.O., United Artists, First National, Pathé, Universal, Columbia, Tiffany and Educational, made 400 feature pictures and more than 1,000 shorts.

The motion picture industry was enjoying healthy theater receipts and film production revenues of $1,200,000,000.

In spite of the technical revolution in sound, Hollywood still used nitro-cellulose film because it was cheaper by a half cent per foot, and it lasted longer.

Led by Harley Lyman Clarke and his new ally, Winfield Sheehan, Fox produced 48 pictures at a cost of $25 million.

The Fox Film board included Harley Clarke; Matthew Brush—president of the American International Corporation; Charles Higley—president of the Hanover Fire Insurance Company; Oscar Qurelman; and Charles Stuart.

The Fox Theaters board consisted of Harley Clarke; Arthur LaFrente—president of the American Surety Company; Samuel Fordyce—attorney; Robert Winmill—member of Gude, Winmill and Company; Charles Stuart; and Walter Herrick—member of Herrick, Berg and Company.

Since the government never approved the acquisition of the Loew's interest, the shares were turned over to a separate company called Film Securities Corporation, controlled by three trustees appointed by a federal court.

Putting things in perspective, the 660,900 Loew's shares that W.F. purchased for $74 million were sold to Film Securities for $29 million, at a loss of $45 million.

The Chase National Bank got Fox's voting trust certificates with Harley Clarke, W.F. Ingold (Pynchon & Company) and W.S. Hammons (Hammons & Company) becoming voting trustees and the Corporation Trust Company of Chicago acting as the depository for the 50,101 shares of Class B common stock of Fox Film Corporation. The chairman of the Corporation Trust Company was none other than Samuel Insull.

In connection with General Theaters Equipment Incorporated's acquisition of the controlling interest in the Fox companies, Pynchon and Company, West and Company and W.S. Hammons underwrote the issuance of 433,000 of GTE's shares at $48.50 a share.

Isador Ostrer, the seller of the British Gaumont chain, received $14 million in cash, and $6 million was still due.

The number of affiliated chain theaters in 1931 was:

Paramount-Publix Corporation	971
Warner Bros. Pictures	529
Fox Film Corporation	521
Loew's Incorporated	189
R.K.O. Corporation	161
Universal Theaters Corporation	66
Total	2,437

Fox Metropolitan Playhouses, which operated 175 theaters in the greater New York area, was placed in receivership. The same bad fortune befell Fox Brooklyn, Fox Detroit and Fox St. Louis.

Greek-born Spyros P. Skouras—who had sold most of his theaters to Warner Bros. in 1928—took over the Fox Metropolitan group and rescued it from bankruptcy.

On June 22, 1932, Fox Theaters wound up in receivership, upon a petition filed by the Chicago Title & Trust Company, a creditor claiming $410,190.

The Roxy Theatre filed for bankruptcy, and with a single stroke of a pen, 13,000 small investors were wiped out. Howard Stix Cullman, whose business was tobacco and whose passion was theater, was appointed by the receivers to run it. Within the first year, he turned a weekly loss of $4,000 to a profit of $6,500. Five years later the Roxy was sold to Twentieth Century-Fox.

The stock market's volatility didn't spare Fox Film's stock price. Right before the crash, Fox Film stood at $101 a share. By July 1932, the price plummeted to $1.

Sometime in April 1930, when he arrived at Fox headquarters on 10th Avenue, Saul Rogers found his corner office heavily padlocked, his career at Fox now history. Not long thereafter, moon-faced James R. Grainger was escorted to the door by Clarke's successor, Sidney Kent.

Two Philadelphia building and loan associations, which won judgments totaling $115,637.50, sued round-robin conspirator John Zanft, once a vice president of the Fox Theaters Corporation.

Per his consultancy agreement with Clarke, William Fox attended a director's meeting, and never got word when another was to be held. The message was clear. His services were no longer required by the Clarke regime. In substitution for W.F.'s participation in Fox Film's financing, Clarke agreed to pay him $3 million in the form of 10 one-year notes for $300,000 each.

In July 1931, "William Fox Presents" was quietly removed from picture titles and film posters and Glendon Allvine, Fox's PR man, got word to eliminate "William Fox" in all copy.

The two Leos, Jack and Joe, were given their walking papers and told to stay home and wait for a call. The call never came. Since severance was due under their respective employment contracts, Clarke paid them for a year without giving them anything to do, and finally settled in cash for the remainder of their contracts.

Maurice and Aaron Fox were summarily dumped from the Fox payroll.

Still towering over Clarke and his minions was the $55 million of short-term notes that had to be refinanced by April 1931. Fox's old bankers, Halsey, Stuart and Company announced they were retiring from the whole Fox affair. Rumored as the principal reason for their decision was the intimate relationship between Fox Film and General Theaters Equipment, which sold a lot of equipment to Fox-controlled theaters.

When Halsey withdrew from the creditor syndicate, Clarke called upon Fox's shareholders to elect six new directors. At the head of the list was Albert Wiggin with Cornelius Vanderbilt, Phillip Reame Clarke, Frank Overton Watts and George Monroe Moffett standing beside him.

The following article appeared in the June 1931 issue of *Fortune:*

> The troubled waters surrounding Fox Films were not calmed by President Harley L. Clarke's rejection of the audit of Fox books prepared by Price, Waterhouse & Company. Claiming amortization charges on films were excessive in the new audit, President Clarke declared that the company would continue its old (and much criticized) system of bookkeeping. But Chase National, banker for Fox, has used the new audit in its recent offering of $30 million Fox debentures. All of which worries Robert L. Clarkson, youthful Chase executive, in his new job: chairman of the executive committee of Chase Securities Corporation. As such, he shares with President Clarke the task of solving Fox's financial problems. The apathetic reception of the Fox debentures recently offered by Chase is not encouraging.

A total of $75 million was raised, $30 million of it other people's money, obtained by selling new bonds to the general public. The bankers invested $45 million in the Fox businesses and were expected to sell these holdings to the public later. Wall Street shuddered to think of what might have transpired with the markets had Fox defaulted on a $55 million issue.

Lacking the creativity required to manage a factory of dreams and illusions, the Harley Clarke regime lasted for a relatively short 19 months.

A Chase-dominated board—Matthew C. Brush, Samuel W. Fordyce, David K.E. Bruce and Cornelius Vanderbilt—elevated Clarke to the inconsequential position of chairman, inserting Edward Tinker, a former chairman of Chase Bank and Chase Securities, to run the business. A man indebted to Albert H. Wiggin, much like Harley Clarke before him, Tinker knew absolutely nothing about making motion pictures. Under Harley Clarke, Tinker discovered that Fox Film had a net loss of $4 million.

Tinker, 53, Yankee born and bred, was a close confidant of Albert Wiggin.

Broadway and Hollywood were asking: "How long will he be there? What will he do?"

Much as William Fox had predicted, Sheehan fed his weakness for the old-fashioned epic—the big, expensive picture that had to gross millions to return a decent profit. Sheehan spent a tidy sum—$2 million—on a saga of the West, *The Big Trail,* which brought in only $1.5 million.

He continued to produce big-budget films like *Liliom,* which were out-and-out failures. An occasional big success kept the studio afloat. *Calvacade,* which cost the studio $1,115,000, brought in nearly $3 million.

Shirley Temple and Will Rogers took over where Buck Jones and Tom Mix had left off, starring in cheap pictures that earned tremendous profits. Neither the curly-topped child nor the cowboy jester ever grossed much less than $1 million on a picture, making up deficits from Sheehan's bad films.

Tinker authorized a distressed Sheehan to take a three-month leave of absence. Once again, Sol Wurtzel was called on to deliver the film product the studio so desperately required for its survival.

Fed up with the Fox's lackluster box office, the board chose another president to run the studio, Sidney R. Kent, replacing Edward R. Tinker, who had replaced Harley Clarke, who had replaced William Fox.

Changes in personnel were commonplace. Those that Kent dropped from the payroll included Maitland Rice, formerly in charge of the music department; Archie Buchanan, assistant director and unit manager; Orville Dull, unit producer manager; and Sid Bowen, former head of the personnel department, which was also discontinued.

When Kent joined Fox Film in January 1932, he inherited an operating loss of nearly $3 million for the prior year.

In the basement of the Chemical Bank and Trust Company, W.C. Michel, vice president, Sydney Towell, treasurer, and Felix Jenkins, general attorney, put the finishing touches to the reorganization of Fox Film by throwing into a furnace $29,600,000 worth of canceled Fox bonds.

The following article appeared in the April 24, 1933 issue of *Time* magazine:

> Darryl Zanuck, for five years general production manager of Warner Bros.' First National Studios, resigned "due to a disagreement of policy in company management." The emergency board of the Academy of Motion Picture Arts & Sciences had ruled the bank holiday cut of 50 percent in studio salaries should be ended by Warner Bros. and full pay be restored April 10. When Warner Bros. refused to restore full pay until April 17, Mr. Zanuck, who had given his word to employees, resigned.

For guidance on his next move, Zanuck called on Joe Schenck, the boss of United Artists. Before the meeting was over, Zanuck and Schenck had drawn up a contract and formed Twentieth Century pictures.

What Sidney Kent needed most was another Irving Thalberg, a young, hard-working producer to supplement the work of Sheehan and Wurtzel; a producer, for instance, like Darryl Zanuck—who was at that moment making a series of hits for United Artists.

Sidney Kent met with Joseph Schenck, the biggest stockholder in Twentieth Century. "If you still want that merger between Fox and Twentieth Century, I'm willing. I'll take over your production in Hollywood and keep Sheehan on with Zanuck."

Twentieth Century-Fox was born on May 28, 1935, 20 years after the formation of Fox Film. All William Fox could do was quietly observe from the sidelines. He could only imagine what might have been.

The merger was complicated by the asymmetry of the two enterprises, particularly the valuations placed on each company, the smaller—Twentieth Century—a prolific generator of profits and cash with no fixed asset base to speak of, and the larger—Fox Film and Fox Theaters—asset-rich, with mediocre performance and a poor return on investment.

Based on its most recent financial results, Twentieth Century had a theoretical earning power of $1,700,000 a year. Against that, Fox had generated a surplus of $3 million built up under Kent in one year, nine months, and Fox's earnings for the first quarter of 1935 were $600,000. Based on that performance, Fox Film's average annual profit at the time of the merger was $1,800,000.

Given Fox's $36 million in net worth as compared to Twentieth Century's $4 million, Fox insisted on 1,200,000 preferred shares in exchange for 2,400,000 common shares, with a fixed dividend of $1.50 a share. This guaranteed Fox shareholders a payout of $1,800,000 before any additional distribution of earnings.

Twentieth Century shareholders would receive 130,000 preferred shares, guaranteeing them an automatic payout of $195,000 a year.

The profit of the two companies was approximately equal, $1,700,000 against $1,800,000. So, the common stock was split equally, 613,264 shares to Fox stockholders, 613,264 to Twentieth Century's—214,642 shares each to Schenck and Goetz, and 183,979 shares to Darryl Zanuck. As a final protection to Fox, it was agreed that the preferred stock could be converted at any time into common, one and one-quarter shares for one.

Thus, if the new company should turn in stellar profits so that Twentieth Century threatened to collect a disproportionate share of the earnings through big dividends on the common, Fox could convert to common. Ultimately, if the preferred stock were all converted, Fox stockholders would get 2,100,000 shares and Twentieth Century stockholders 780,000.

When Sheehan heard that he was going to have to report to Zanuck, he bolted. He adamantly refused to share responsibilities with Zanuck, so Kent agreed to pay him $360,000 to tear up his contract, which had 14 months to run. Sheehan also kept a healthy block of stock.

Upon announcing the departure of Sheehan, Kent said: "It was accepted with regret. The corporation and I extend our best wishes to Mr. Sheehan. This matter has been settled amicably."

As a result of Sheehan's unscheduled departure, Darryl Zanuck, who had expected to make just 12 pictures a year, found himself in sole charge of the Fox lots, with the unenviable task of giving personal supervision to 29 productions before him. Thus Sidney Kent, instead of adding a producer to his staff, merely exchanged one for another.

Zanuck was pleasantly surprised by Fox Hill's size and sophistication. There were over five miles of streets, 12 sound stages, and a complex of administrative buildings.

In the process of taking over Fox, Albert H. Wiggin angered the Rockefellers with his stock market manipulations, driving into bankruptcy the Philadelphia banking house of West & Company. In 1931, Harris, Forbes merged with Chase Securities forming Chase Harris Forbes. The era of Albert Wiggin was over.

Wiggin's successor at the helm of Chase was Winthrop W. Aldrich. Aldrich was Rockefeller's brother-in-law—John D. Rockefeller, Jr. married Winthrop Aldrich's sister, Abby—and he produced a series of records for a Senate hearing indicating that his bank had a total investment of $89,330,047 in Fox Film and General Theaters Equipment. Aldrich further stated that the investment had been written down to $19,757,866 for a loss of $69,572,180.

Harley Lyman Clarke's financially troubled Utilities Power & Light Company rested on two main assets: (1) all the common stock of the then $80 million Indianapolis Power & Light

Company, and (2) control of a group of British properties worth about $25 million. There was $50 million in debentures outstanding against these assets.

Early in 1935, the government took control of the $400 million public utility holding company serving 570 communities in the United States and no less than 503 cities in England. Clarke controlled the holding company through a small issue of voting stock held by a super-super holding company called Public Utilities Securities Corporation.

In early 1936, Clarke was sued for alleged misappropriation of $3 million by Utilities Power & Light Corporation, whose presidency he resigned October 29 of the same year under pressure from Odlum's Atlas Corporation, which had bought control. Clarke charged that Odlum and the Chase National Bank, among others, had conspired to bring about the financial ruin of Utilities Power & Light.

The fate of Harley Clarke was sealed. By 1938 his own lawyer admitted that Clarke was too broke to be sued. His personal fortune was once estimated at $60 million. Clarke died in his home in suburban Mount Prospect, Illinois, at age 73.

After leaving Fox, Winfield Sheehan joined the ranks of unsuccessful independent producers, giving the world such unmemorable works as *Florian* (1940) and *Captain Eddie* (1945).

During the shooting of *Captain Eddie,* Winfield Sheehan died from a relapse following an abdominal operation. He was 61.

Fox's long-time director, Raoul Walsh, made his last film for Fox in 1932, *Me and My Gal,* with Spencer Tracy and Joan Bennett. After nearly two decades with Fox Film, Walsh moved on to the Warner Bros. lot, where he directed several great pictures including *High Sierra* and *They Died With Their Boots On.* Following a long and productive career in Hollywood, Walsh retired from film in 1964 and died in 1980 at age 93.

Fox's Pantheon director, John Ford, shot his first talking picture, *The Black Watch,* in 1929. Although Ford suffered losses during the crash and the Depression that followed, mostly in Fox companies' stocks, his earnings materially increased during 1933-41. Pictures like *The Grapes of Wrath, The Long Voyage Home* and *How Green Was My Valley* firmly established Ford as an outstanding director. John Ford died in 1973 after some 50 years of quality filmmaking.

Frank Borzage, winner of Hollywood's first Academy Award for *Seventh Heaven,* died from cancer at age 67 in 1962.

Sol Wurtzel was the only Fox executive whose contract was gladly renewed by Zanuck. By then Wurtzel owned an Italian marble palace on Stone Canyon Road in Bel-Air and was being chauffeured to the lot in a Rolls Royce. Recognizing that he was in dire need of assistance, Zanuck made him executive director of all "B" pictures that were being filmed on the Sunset lot. Wurtzel spent the rest of his career with the company that had taken him from stenographer to motion picture producer. Sol Wurtzel died in 1958.

While at the helm of Twentieth Century-Fox, Russian-born Joseph Schenck acted as go-between and problem-solver for Zanuck and his roster of temperamental stars. The man who had sparked the merger between Fox and Twentieth Century resigned his position in 1941 after being sentenced to a year in jail on charges involving income tax violations and union bribes. Schenck became a victim of the infamous "Willie Bioff scandal," for which many said Schenck accepted the role of fall guy. After serving four months in prison, Schenck returned to film as an executive producer with Fox. In 1949 he resigned from Fox and decided to spend all of his time managing Fox's 364 theaters in preparation for a government antitrust order, which was expected to force Fox to separate its production and distribution activities from its theater operations. Joseph Schenck died in 1961.

In early 1921, Theda Bara and Charles Brabin married and returned to California, where he continued to direct films while she entertained offers from small producers. Theda Bara appeared onscreen in *The Unchastened Woman,* which Chadwick Pictures released. Her last film role was in *Madame Mystery,* a satire of the screen vamp produced by Hal Roach. On February 13, 1955, Bara entered the California Lutheran Hospital and underwent four operations for abdominal cancer. Lapsing into a coma, she died on April 7, 1955 at age 65. Charles Brabin died in a hospital in Santa Monica in November 1957. Of her 39 Fox Films, she would always be remembered for *A Fool There Was.*

After a three-year tour with Ringling Brothers Circus, Tom Mix returned to the silver screen and made sound Westerns at Universal. The Western genre was in sharp decline, so Mix retired from films in 1932. His congenial persona lived on through a popular radio series (1933-50). In 1932, Mix, 52, married Mabel Hubble Ward, 28, circus aerialist. On October 12, 1940, Tom Mix roared down Route 89 in his beloved Cord, somewhere between Florence and Tucson, Arizona. When Mix approached a detour that required a zigzag maneuver at slow speed, he couldn't quite adjust and veered down into a gulch and tipped over. One of the big metal trunks that carried his precious "gear" shot forward and struck him in the head. Western legend Tom Mix was dead at age 60.

Two years after Tom Mix's death, Tony, 39, the famed Wonder Horse, was euthanized in San Fernando, California. Never considered a trick horse, Tony was intelligent, fully understood Mix and had what Mix called "a genius for acting." Together, they'd earned over $4 million during the length of their association.

Fox's other cowboy, Buck Jones, also went on to make more films but by 1941—when he signed with Monogram to co-star in the *Rough Rider* series—his popularity had diminished at the box office. In December 1942, while on a tour to sell war bonds, he perished in a Boston nightclub fire. It was reported that Buck Jones lost his life while trying to save others.

Truman Hughes Talley, 50, died in 1942. Talley was executive vice president of Movietone News.

Sidney R. Kent, 56, the super-salesman who was president of Fox Film, died of a heart attack in Manhattan in 1942.

Frank Ellis Campbell, 61, famed Manhattan undertaker—Valentino, Hammerstein, Woolworth—died of heart disease in 1934.

Pearl White, 41, died in 1938 in Paris of a liver ailment. She was past her prime when she joined Fox, and her pictures floundered at the box office. She had retired to Paris with a considerable fortune.

Warner Baxter, 58, Hollywood's second actor's Oscar winner, died in 1951 after a long illness. He played the Cisco Kid in the industry's first outdoor, all-talking Western, *In Old Arizona.*

Al Jolson, 64, died in 1950 of a coronary occlusion. The musical/comedy star would always be remembered for his role in *The Jazz Singer.*

Showman Sid Grauman, 70, died in 1950. His theaters—Million Dollar, Egyptian and Chinese—are lasting tributes to Hollywood's Golden Age.

Muscular star George O'Brien died in 1985 at age 85.

First best-actress Oscar-winner, Janet Gaynor, died in 1984 at age 78. Teamed with Charles Farrell in the early 30s, they became "America's favorite lovebirds."

Studio workhorse Shirley Mason died in 1979 at age 78.

John Otterson had a short, uninspired stint as head of Paramount and was soon ousted. In 1942, he headed the New Jersey Shipbuilding Corporation and East Coast Shipyards, concerns that built landing craft and tankers. He made his home in Ridgefield, Connecticut. He died at age 83 in 1964.

The sound-on-film system was constantly improved over time and became the standard bearer of talking pictures. Vitaphone was obsolete by 1932.

Ted Case, the dynamic inventor, who had first opened William Fox's eyes to the limitless possibilities of sound, lived off his money in Auburn, New York, the site of his laboratory. Ted Case died in 1944.

For whatever reason, things went bad for Alfred Blumenthal, who lost his wealth doing deals in Mexico. When he died there wasn't enough money to pay the hospital bills and bury him. Harry Warner got wind of Blumy's unfortunate death and anonymously donated enough to settle the account. Harry Warner had never forgotten the little man who had helped him gain control of William Fox's First National shares.

Albert Greenfield collected the $10 million he'd lent to the Fox companies and went on to face the vagaries of the Great Depression. He died on January 5, 1967.

Before a Senate committee, William Fox was able to tell his side of the story of how he had lost control of the companies that bore his name. "I was forced to enter into that under duress; I had not any choice except to sell out."

"Who forced you?"

"Halsey, Stuart and Company; Mr. Albert H. Wiggin of the Chase Bank; Mr. John Otterson of the American Telephone and Telegraph Company; Mr. Harley Clarke and 12 or 13 bankers in New York to whom Fox Film was indebted."

There remained that one face card, the Tri-Ergon patents.

The whole struggle had been about substantiating their validity and enforcing them against the infringing motion picture industry. Millions of dollars were at stake. More money than W.F. could possibly count.

The fact was that the fly-wheel patent and the double print patent were being used in thousands of theaters equipped by both Western Electric and RCA, and according to William Fox's counsel, Ward, Crosby and Neal, "Every sound picture produced in the United States had violated these patents."

In holding the patents valid, the lower courts made it seem as if Walter S. Gifford's nightmare had finally come true. AT&T would have to pay W.F. a fortune to license those patents. To further complicate things, the U.S. Supreme Court refused to hear an appeal filed by Paramount. The issue was no longer one of patent validity, but one of patent infringement. Or was it?

In its response, the Supreme Court had not actually awarded W.F. any damages, or said that his patents were infringed on, or ruled that he owned the patents. In fact, Fox Film was alleging that W.F. had improperly obtained control of Tri-Ergon and that he had no right to the patents.

On the evening of his victory, William Fox purportedly said: "Now I've got the sonsabitches by the balls, and don't think I won't twist them."

In a foolish move that was to cost him public support, William Fox issued 14,000 warning letters to exhibitors and published ads in trade journals reminding theater owners that every projection of any sound picture was a patent violation. He was causing more furor in the motion picture industry than it had experienced in many a year.

The telephones of important Manhattan law firms were all buzzing. It was time, once again, to mount a major offensive against William Fox. Time to teach the old man a lesson, remove him from the industry once and for all.

W.F. sought an injunction against all Paramount-Publix theaters showing motion pictures that used the patented technology. Estimates of the amount due Fox through his control of these processes ranged as high as $100 million.

Otterson reacted: "We don't know yet how far the court's decision goes. The legal departments of several large companies interested must first make a study of the whole matter. It certainly is not a desirable situation for any one man to be placed in the position of being able to control the whole industry."

The caustic manner in which William Fox attempted to enforce his victory produced an unexpected result: He antagonized public opinion. Rumors abounded that W.F. had been offered millions to sell out. His answer was the same: He sued virtually the whole industry, 11 companies in all. By this time the defendant's army of counsel included onetime Attorney General, William D. Mitchell.

Just 22 weeks after the Justices of the Supreme Court had refused to entertain an appeal on a case holding the Tri-Ergon patents valid, these same dark-robed men changed their minds, ruling that in the public interest, these same patents were not valid. They declared the sound patents were based on ancient mechanical devices and lacked invention. The Tri-Ergon patents that William Fox had acquired for $60,000, and could have sold for $10 million or more, were

William Fox in the 1940s

now utterly worthless. In the process of defending the Tri-Ergon patents, William Fox had spent over a million dollars in legal fees.

Vindicated, John Otterson informed the press, "The so-called Tri-Ergon patents in question, originally taken out by German inventors, have been used as the basis for numerous infringement suits brought against American manufacturers, motion picture producers and exhibitors, in connection with which extravagant claims for damages were made. The decision of the Supreme Court declaring these patents to be invalid finally and effectively dispose of all of these suits and claims incident thereto."

Contrary to sporadic press reports, William Fox made no further attempts to return to the industry.

Belle Fox with son William Fox, Jr. and family dining at the Laurent in New York in 1985. Seated left to right: Barbara Weil Fox, William Fox, Jr., Belle Fox; standing left to right: Lucille Weil, Alan Weingarten, Jo-Ann Fox-Weingarten, Susan Fox Rosellini and Donald Rosellini.

After a long struggle with his health, William Fox died on May 8, 1952, at age 73. Death came in Doctor's Hospital, New York, where he had been under treatment for nearly a year. In recent years he had lived quietly at his home, Fox Hall, Woodmere, Long Island.

No one from Hollywood's power circle took note of the passing of William Fox, except for Sol Wurtzel. He told the press, "William Fox was a great man and a wonderful pioneer in the industry. I started with Fox as his secretary in 1914. He sent me out here to take charge of Fox Studio in 1917 and I was with him until he sold out. It was a blow to the industry when he discontinued."

W.F.'s father, Michael Fox, died in 1936 at age 80. His mother, Anna, died in 1925 at age 44. Sister Tina Fried died on June 24, 1957 at age 72. The youngest of the family, Malvina, died on July 26, 1952 at age 47. She was a dramatic coach and talent scout at Twentieth Century-Fox. Aaron Fox died in 1962 at age 67. Outliving all of the Fox siblings, Maurice died in 1987 at age 91.

Max Leo, Eve Fox's father, a retired clothing manufacturer, died at his home in Lakewood, New Jersey in 1933. Surviving him were his wife, the former Sophie Rosenblatt; three daughters, Eve Fox, Bess Rosenbluh and Sadie Sareky and three sons, Benjamin Leo, Joseph Leo and Jack G. Leo, all of New York.

After Eve Fox died on December 29, 1961, the family disposed of the nine-acre Woodmere estate, which was purchased by Woodbay Estates, Inc., builders of custom homes. The new owners built 19 houses, which sold at $55,000 and up.

The Marguery on Park Avenue was demolished and replaced with an office building.

William Fox, Jr. poses with his daughters Susan and Jo-Ann.

Mona's son, William T., spent most of his life doing things unrelated to the motion picture industry. He died in 1998, leaving a daughter, Mona.

Douglas Taussig worked in the film industry doing publicity and public relations for United Artists. He died on Long Island on August 5, 1962. He was 69 years old.

Belle, the youngest of the Fox girls, divorced Milton Schwartz and never married again. She died in 1989.

Belle's only son, William Fox Junior, lived in New York. There are two great-granddaughters, Susan and Jo-Ann, both of whom have two children of their own.

William Fox Junior died in 1987, two years before the death of his mother, Belle.

Eve, Belle and Mona in happier times

A SPECIAL TRIBUTE TO THE FOX FILM/THEATERS TEAM, CALIFORNIA, JULY 1, 1929.

I want to recognize and thank those who contributed so much to the success of Fox Film. Most of their work was done behind the scenes. They were the unheralded warriors who kept the studio going through good and bad times. I'm happy to say that Sol Wurtzel and his team survived all of the turmoil described in this book. I know my great-grandfather was eternally grateful to him.

The names were taken from a partial directory I came across in Twentieth Century-Fox's research library. I want to apologize to the many Fox associates whose names do not appear in this book for lack of a complete directory. However, I will mention their departments and hope that someone out there has a copy of the directory, which I will gladly publish in later editions of this book.

Just e-mail me at sfoxrosellini@aol.com. Also let me know if you knew any of these individuals or are somehow related to them. Tell us their story.

Departments for which I found no 1929 directory:

Acoustical Research Laboratory
Camera Research
Casting
Contract Players
Directors
Director of Safety
Dialogue and Scenario Writers
Drapery
Drafting and Technical
Electrical
Film Editing and Cutting
Fox Film Corporation Exchange
Fox Hills Studio
General Manager's Office
General Superintendent's Office
Grandeur Film
Laboratory
Legal
Music
Movietone News
Movietone Studio Executives
New York Offices of Fox Studio
Paint
Production Cabinet
Projection
Publicity
Purchasing
Photographic
Property Rental
Reading
Scenic
Script
Special Effects
Sound
Sound Effects
Stage Directors
Studio Manager's Office
Technical Advisors
Unit Managers
Still Cameramen
Studio Fire Chief
Studio Hospital
Supervisors
Telephone and Telegraph
Test

Title Camera
Transportation
Wardrobe Rental
William Fox Studio
William Fox West Coast Theaters

OFFICIAL DIRECTORY

EXECUTIVE OFFICES
Sol M. Wurtzel, 828 S. Longwood Ave., Hollywood   WH-3137
Al Lewis, 723 N. Roxbury Dr., Beverly Hills   OX-3928
Edward W. Butcher, 8356 Fountain Ave., Hollywood   CR-9230

ACCOUNTING AND FINANCIAL DEPARTMENT
George L. Bagnali, 1336 N. Harper Ave., Hollywood   CR-9545
H.A. King, 343 Riverside Drive, Glendale, Calif.   DOUGLAS 1581
Carl Brady, 2551 Silver Lake Court, Los Angeles
Lloyd Nobles, Box 248, N. Hollywood   N. HO-533W
Margaret Millen, 1055 N. Wilton Pl., Hollywood   HE-9620
Earl Rettig, 525 S. Kenmore Ave., Los Angeles   EX-6739
Katherine McCarthy, 4539 Ambrose Ave., Hollywood   MO-16271
Allen Maynard, 1632 N. Normandie Ave., Los Angeles   MO-14237
R.C. Barrows, 669 S. Westlake Ave., Los Angeles   WA-2611
George Hellgren, 6064 1/2 Selma Ave., Hollywood   GR-6930
James Engle, 10552 1/2 Easthorn Ave., Westwood
Dwight B. Culver, 1412 Poinsettia Pl., Hollywood   GR-5418
Lillian L. Phillips, 5146 1/4 Sunset Blvd., Hollywood   HO-4514
Henrietta Ginsberg, 1510 N. Kingsley Dr., Hollywood   HO-4721
George C. Roberts, 5616 Lexington Ave., Hollywood   H0-8010
James Weisser, 1954 Canyon Dr., Hollywood   H0-3847
H.F. Connolly, 1831 W. 24th St., Los Angeles   EM-9017
G.J. Fischer, 6035 Madden Ave., Los Angeles
A.E. Gibson, Fox Hills Studio, Westwood   GR-3151
Dan Pinck, 414 S. Chevy Chase, Glendale   DOUGLAS 7704J
Wm. Crawford, Asst. Counsel, 4957 Melrose Hill   GR-2879
Christina Shultz, 177 N. Reno St., Los Angeles   DU-8261
Mary Yost, 1437 N. Las Palmas Ave.   HE-9205

LIBRARY AND RESEARCH DEPARTMENT
Frances C. Richardson, 1562 N. Serrano, Hollywood   HO-4482
Kathrine Webb, 5615 Fernwood, Hollywood   HO-4072
Gertrude Kingston, 1309 3/4, North Hobart, Hollywood   HE-3516
Estelle Beshon, 6337 Fountain Ave., Hollywood   GL-7312
Jack Wiggins, 117-A E. Fairview Ave., Glendale
Edwin K. O'Brien, 1627 1/4 N. Hudson, Hollywood   R-6731

LOCATION DEPARTMENT
R.E. Goux, 6059 Carlton Way, Hollywood   HO-8307
Clay E. Crapnell, 1927 Hyperion Ave., Los Angeles   MO-14438
Lee Gerstenfield, 5602 Fernwood Ave., Los Angeles   HE-8372
George P. Busch, 228 Doheney Ave., Los Angeles   CR-7136

MAINTENANCE DEPARTMENT
Ben Wurtzel, 1025 N. La Jolla Ave.   CR-7269
M.M. Miggins, 1000 N. La Jolla Ave.   CR-6763
John Hilliard, 7970 1/4 Sunset Blvd.   GR-2230
Mabel Beshon, 6337 Fountain Ave.   GL-7312
G.H. Muldorfer, 536 N. Oxford   HO-2651

William Werner, 1859 West 25th St.   EM-2874
R.L. Smith, 5345 Sunset Blvd.   HE-8505

MAKEUP DEPARTMENT
Charles Dudley, 1210 N. Wilton Pl., Hollywood   HE-9256
Jack Dawn, 4555 William St., Los Angeles   OX-7357
Paula Sielaff, 1519 S. Manhattan Pl., Los Angeles   EM-4689
William Huntington, 4353 Kingswell Ave., Los Angeles   OL-1261

MECHANICAL AND PLUMBING DEPARTMENT
Robert Falconer, 712 N. Hobart, Los Angeles   HO-7430
Don Summers, 373 W. 108th St.   TH-1933-R-I

MILL AND CARPENTER SHOP
A. R. Field, General Construction Superintendent, 33454 Casitas, Ave., Los Angeles
                                                                               OL-3454
Gus Lehman, 1242 S. Sierra Bonita, Los Angeles   WH-4398
Phil Adams, 5523 Bayer St., Hollywood   GR-0267
R.P. Knoche, 428 S. Lincoln St., Glendale   DOUGLAS 8069W
Charles Rabold, 5131 5th Ave., Los Angeles   UN-4065
A.P. Case, 1748 Woodland Ave., Glendale   DOUGLAS 9502W
J. Girton, 6640 Colgate Ave., Los Angeles   CR-7882
Ike Rosen, 642 N. Grand Ave., Los Angeles   MU-2673
W.L. Jones, 4507 Ambrose Ave., Los Angeles   MU-19083
E.D. Johnson, 131 S. Louise St., Glendale   DOUGLAS 1159W
W.E. Ritchey, 1412 1/2 Courtland Ave., Los Angeles   BE-2061
A. Bell, 2743 Glen Eden St., Los Angeles   OLY-5635
C.M. McCormick, 5353 Fountain Ave.   HO-7578
A. Jett, 1245 Vine St., Los Angeles   GR-1005
C.R. Wanamaker, 825 N. Wilcox St., Los Angeles   HE-6847
T.C. Cloud, 1153 N. Western Ave., Los Angeles   GL-6592
A. Piellusch, 5624 Santa Monica Blvd., Los Angeles   GL-6608

MINIATURE DEPARTMENT
Ralph Hammeras, 1562 W. Avenue 46, Los Angeles   AL-2005
W.L. Vogel, 6212 Leland Ave., Los Angeles   ————
E.M. Hammeras, 1568 W. Avenue 46, Los Angeles   AL-2251

MODERN WARDROBE DEPARTMENT
Sophie Wachner, 456 S. Occidental Blvd.   WA-8464
Helen O'Brien, 442 Wittmer St.   TU-3413
Birdie Chambers, Hotel Rector   HO-0713

ART DIRECTORS
William Darling, 216 W. Maple Dr., Beverly Hills   OX-6322
Ben Carre, 2754 Woodshire Dr., Los Angeles   HO-6563
Harry Oliver, 1849 Kenneth Ave., Glendale   DOUGLAS 6495
Jack Schulze, 5272 Hollywood Blvd., Hollywood   GR-7258
William Moll, 506 Croft Ave.   OX-4684
Joe Wright, 10524 Whipple St., N. Hollywood   N. HO-175W
Duncan Cramer, 8016 W. 4th St.   WH-4879
Lance Baxter, 9038 Rosewood Ave., Los Angeles   OX-5952
Lionel Margolies, 514 N. Beverly Dr.   OX-5419
David S. Hall, 636 S. Plymouth St.   WH-5442
Rudolph Bylack, 2445 N. Gower St.   HE-4423
Fred Stoos, 4517 Melbourne Ave.   OL-8972
Harry Johnson, 5510 Lexington Ave.   ————
Nick Timchenckoe, 8571 3/4 Rugby Dr., W. Hollywood   OX-0835

ASSISTANT DIRECTORS

D.M. Abrahams, 7944 Blackburn St., Los Angeles	OR-0327
C.J. Baker, 1320 Lake Shore Ave., Los Angeles	DR-3689
Jasper Blystone, 141 S. Serrano Ave., Los Angeles	WA-8466
Lew Borzage, 3944 Wilshire Blvd., Los Angeles	WA-9285
Sidney Bowen, 2254 Manning Ave., Los Angeles	S.M. 33236
Lou Breslow, 435 N. Alta Vista, Los Angeles	OR-1083
Archie Buchanan, 6613 Whitley Terrace, Hollywood	GR-9754
Frank Dettman, 1928 Franklin Circle, Hollywood	HO-4592
Eli Dunn, 1382 Ridgewood Place, Hollywood	HO-6474
R.A. Flynn, 802 N. Gardner St., Hollywood	GR-1429
Max Gold, 350 N. Orange Dr., Hollywood	WH-3781
J. Edmund Grainger, 815 S. Genesee St., Hollywood	OR-5346
L. Virgil Hart, 529 N. Huntley Dr., West Hollywood	OX-3846
Leo Houck, 2175 Fairfield Ave., Los Angeles	GR-4827
R.L. Hough, 534 Sierra Bonita St., Hollywood	OR-7472
Horace Hough, 1204 W. 74th St., Los Angeles	TH-3201
Ralph Kaufman, 2117 Rockledge Road, Los Angeles	HE-7209
George McNulty, 2176 N. Argyle Ave., Hollywood	HO-8944
Clark Murray, 3079 Belden Drive, Hollywood	HO-8970

Phone numbers were illegible for the following individuals.

Wm. A. O'Connor, 2500 N. Highland Ave., Hollywood   ———
Edward O'Fearna, 9019 Vista Grande, West Hollywood   ———
Marty Santell, 5680 Reseda Blvd., Reseda   ———
Ad Schaumer, 1152 N. Poinsetta Drive, Hollywood   ———
Sam Schneider, 5921 Barton Ave., Hollywood   ———
Ewing Scott, 3073 Girard St., Los Angeles   ———
Willis Tinling, 8731 Bonner Drive   ———
William Tummel, 362 N. Sierra Bonita Ave., Hollywood   ———
Sam Wurtzel, 1015 N. Orlando Ave., Hollywood   ———

CAMERAMEN

Lucien Andriot, 8506 Holloway Dr., Los Angeles   ———
Alfred Brick, 741 N. Croft Ave., Los Angeles   ———
Daniel Clark, 4601 Sunset Blvd., Los Angeles   ———
Charles Clarke, 6275 Selina, Los Angeles   ———
George Eastman, 2022 Fairburn, Santa Monica   ———
Sol Halprin, 1194 S. Bronson Ave., Los Angeles   ———
Joe Kealey, 4608 Kingswell, Los Angeles   ———
Glen MacWilliams, 11972 Dorothy St., Santa Monica   ———
Ernest Palmer, 8604 W. Knoll Dr., W. Hollywood   ———
Hal Rosson, 105 N. Rexford, Beverly Hills   ———
John Schmitz, 914 N. Ridgewood, Los Angeles   ———
Walter Scott, 1516 N. Hobart Blvd., Los Angeles   ———
J.O. Taylor, 3535 Clarington Ave, Palms   ———
Joseph Valentine, 410 N. Genessee St., Los Angeles   ———
Sidney Wagner, 6416 Drexel Ave., Los Angeles   ———
Conrad Wells, 6626 Franklin Ave., Los Angeles   ———
George Schneiderman, 1324 Fuller St., Hollywood   ———
L.W. O'Connell, 427 Camden Drive, Beverly Hills   ———
Arthur Edeson, 2050 Laurel Lane, Laurel Canyon   ———
Curtis Fetters, 1417 N. Bronson Ave., Hollywood   ———
Hatto Tappenbeck, 7168 Lexington Avenue, Los Angeles   ———
Vincent Farrar, 502 1/2 N. Gennessee, Hollywood   ———
Don Anderson, 6275 Selma Ave., Hollywood   ———
J. Ross Fischer, 615 N. Gramercy, Los Angeles   ———

A SELECTED BIBLIOGRAPHY

Aitken, Roy E. *The Birth of A Nation Story.* Middleburg, Virginia: William W. Denlinger, 1965.

Alleman, Richard. *The Movie Lover's Guide to New York.* New York: Harper & Row, 1988.

Allvine, Glendon. *The Greatest Fox of Them All.* New York: Lyle Stuart, Inc., 1969.

Altman, Diana. *Hollywood East.* New York: Carol Publishing Group, 1992.

Behlmer, Rudy. *Inside Warner Bros.* New York: Simon & Schuster, Inc., 1985.

Berg, A. Scott. *Goldwyn.* New York: Alfred A. Knopf, 1989.

Berger, Miles L. *They Built Chicago.* Chicago: Bonus Books, Inc., 1992.

Birchard, Robert S. *King Cowboy: Tom Mix and the Movies.* Burbank, Calif. Riverwood Press, 1993.

Bowser, Eileen. *The Transformation of Cinema. 1907-1915.* New York: Charles Scribner's Sons, 1990.

Brouwer, Alexandra and Wright, Thomas Lee. *Working in Hollywood.* New York: Crown Publishers, 1990.

Brown, Gene. *Movie Time.* New York: Macmillan, 1995.

Brownstone, David and Franck, Irene. *Timelines of the Twentieth Century.* Boston: Little, Brown and Company, 1996.

Brownlow, Kevin. *The Parade's Gone By.* Berkeley: University of California Press, 1968.

Bryson, A.E. *Halsey, Stuart & Co., Inc.* Chicago: Halsey, Stuart & Company, 1945.

Calistro, Paddy and Basten, Frank E. *The Hollywood Archive.* New York: Universe Publishing, 2000.

Carr, William H.A. *From Three Cents a Week.* Englewood Cliffs, N.J.: Prentice-Hall, Incorporated, 1975.

Carter, Joseph H. *Never Met a Man I Didn't Like.* New York: Avon Books, 1991.

Collins, Theresa M. *Otto Kahn.* Chapel Hill, NC: The University of North Carolina Press, 2002.

Crowther, Bosley. *Hollywood Rajah: The Life and Times of Louis B. Mayer.* New York: Holt, Rinehart & Winston, 1960.

Day, George S., and Schoemaker, Paul J.H. *Wharton on Managing Emerging Technologies.* New York: John Wiley & Sons, Inc., 2000.

Dearing, Albin Pasteur. *The Elegant Inn.* Secaucus, N.J.: Lyle Stuart Inc., 1986.

DeMarco, Mario. *Tom Mix.* Published by author.

De Mille, Cecil B. *Autobiography.* Edited by Donald Hayne. Englewood Cliffs, NJ: Prentice-Hall, 1959.

Donbitz, Nanette. *The Fox and the Reptile.* Unpublished manuscript.

Dreher, Carl. *Sarnoff.* New York: Quadrangle/New York Times Book Company, 1977.

Drinkwater, John. *The Life and Adventures of Carl Laemmle.* New York: G.P. Putnam's Sons, 1931.

Dunlap, David W. *On Broadway.* New York: Rizzoli, 1990.

Erdlich, Lisa. *Goldman Sachs.* New York: Alfred A. Knopf, Inc., 1999.

Everson, William K. *The Hollywood Western.* New York: Citadel Press, 1992.

Eyman, Scott. *The Speed of Sound. Hollywood and the Talkie Revolution 1926-1930.* New York: Simon and Schuster, 1997.

—*Print the Legend.* New York: Simon and Schuster, 1999.

Fell, John L. *Film Before Griffith.* Berkeley: University of California Press, 1983.

Flamini, Roland. *Thalberg.* New York: Crown Publishers Inc., 1994.

Fox-Bordega, Barbara. *An Oral History.* New York: Unpublished manuscript, 2001.

Franklin, Joe. *Classics of the Silent Screen.* New York: Citadel Press, 1959.

Freedland, Michael. *The Warner Brothers.* New York: St. Martin's Press, 1983.

—*Jolson.* New York: Stein and Day, 1972.

Gabler, Neal. *An Empire of their Own.* New York: Crown Publishers Inc., 1988.

Gallagher, Tag. *John Ford. The Man and His Films.* Berkeley: University of California Press, 1986.

Geisst, Charles R. *Wall Street: A History.* New York: Oxford University Press, 1997.

Genini, Ronald. *Theda Bara.* North Carolina: McFarland Press, 1996.

Golden, Eve. *Platinum Girl. The Life and Legends of Jean Harlow.* New York: Abbeville Press, 1991.

Graham, Sheilah. *The Garden of Allah.* New York: Crown Publishers, Inc., 1970.

Grun, Bernard. *The Timetables of History.* New York: Simon and Schuster, 1982.

Gussow, Mel. *Darryl F. Zanuck.* New York: Da Capo Press, Inc., 1971.

Hamilton, Ian. *Writer in Hollywood 1915-1951.* New York: Harper & Row, 1990.

Hampton, Benjamin B. *History of the American Film Industry.* New York: Dover Publications, Inc., 1970.

Hawes, Elizabeth. *New York, New York.* New York: Alfred A. Knopf, 1993.

Hays, Will H. *The Memoirs of Will H. Hays.* New York: Doubleday, 1955.

Heide, Robert & Gilman, John. *Box-Office Buckaroos.* New York: Abbeville Press, 1989.

Higham, Charles. *Cecil B. De Mille.* New York: Charles Scribner's Sons, 1973.

—*Merchant of Dreams. Louis B. Mayer, M.G.M. and the Secret Hollywood.* New York: Donald I. Fine, Inc., 1993.

Hirschhorn, Clive. *The Universal Story.* New York: Crown, 1983.

Jackson, Kenneth T. *The Encyclopedia of New York.* New Haven, Conn., Yale University Press, 1995.

Jasen, David A. *Tin Pan Alley.* New York: Donald I. Fine, Inc., 1988.

Katz, Ephraim. *The Film Encyclopedia.* New York: Harper Perennial, 1994.

Kerr, Walter. *The Silent Clowns.* New York: Alfred A. Knopf, 1979.

Kobal, John. *Hollywood. The Years of Innocence.* New York: Abbeville Press, 1985.

Koszarski, Richard. *The Astoria Studio and Its Fabulous Films.* New York: Dover Publications, 1983.

—*History of the American Cinema. An Evening's Entertainment: The Age of the Silent Feature Picture 1915-1928.* New York: Charles Scribner's Sons, 1990.

Lasky, Jesse L. *I Blow My Own Horn.* New York: Doubleday & Company Inc., 1957.

Lasky Jr., Jesse L. *Whatever Happened to Hollywood?* New York: Funk & Wagnalls, 1975.

Levin, Martin. *Hollywood and the Great Fan Magazines.* New York: Arbor House Publishing Company, Inc., 1977.

MacCann, Richard Dyer. *The First Tycoons.* Metuchen, N.J.: The Scarecrow Press, Inc., 1987.

Margolies, John & Gwathmey, Emily. *Ticket to Paradise.* Boston: Little, Brown and Company, 1991.

Martin, Albro. *Railroads Triumphant.* New York: Oxford University Press, 1992.

Marx, Samuel. *Mayer and Thalberg.* New York: Random House, 1975.

Mast, Gerald. *A Short History of the Movies.* New York: Macmillan Publishing Company, 1986.

McBride, Joseph. *Frank Capra.* New York: Simon & Schuster, 1992.

—*Searching for John Ford.* New York: St. Martin's Press, 1999.

Mix, Paul. *Tom Mix.* Jefferson, North Carolina: McFarland & Company, 1995.

Morehouse, Ward. *George M. Cohan.* New York: J.B. Lippincott, 1943.

Morden, Ethan. *The Hollywood Studios.* New York: Simon and Schuster, 1988.

Mosley, Leonard. *Zanuck. The Rise and Fall of Hollywood's Last Tycoon.* Boston: Little, Brown and Company, 1984.

Musser, Charles. *Edison Motion Pictures, 1890-1900.* Italy: Smithsonian Institution Press, 1997.

Naylor, David. *Great American Movie Theaters.* Washington, D.C.: The Preservation Press, 1987.

—*American Picture Palaces.* New York: Prentice Hall Press, 1981.

Norris, M.G. "Bud." *The Tom Mix Book.* Waynesville, North Carolina: The World of Yesterday, 1989.

Okrent, Daniel. *Great Fortune. The Epic of Rockefeller Center.* New York: Viking, 2003.

Oppel, Frank. *Tales of Gaslight New York.* Secaucus, N.J.: Castle, 1985.

Parish, James Robert. *The Fox Girls.* New York: Castle Books, Inc., 1972.

—*Growing Up in Hollywood.* Boston: Little, Brown and Company, 1976.

Pfeiffer, Lee. *The John Wayne Scrapbook.* New York: Citadel Press, 1993.

Place, J.A. *The Western Films of John Ford.* Secaucus, N.J.: Citadel Press, 1974.

Purdy, Ken W. *Motorcars of the Golden Past.* Boston: Little, Brown and Company, 1966.

Rainey, Buck. *The Life and Films of Buck Jones.* Waynesville, North Carolina: The World of Yesterday, 1988.

Robinson, David. *Chaplin. His Life and Art.* New York: Da Capo Press, 1994.

Saint-Etienne, Christian. *The Great Depression 1929-1938.* Stanford, Calif.: Hoover Institution Press, 1984.

Sarris, Andrew. *The American Cinema. Directors and Directions 1929-1968.* Chicago: The University of Chicago Press, 1968.

Schickel, Richard. *D.W. Griffith.* New York: Simon and Schuster, 1984.

—*The Men Who Made the Movies.* New York: Atheneum, 1975.

Schulberg, Budd. *Moving Pictures.* New York: Stein and Day, 1981.

Sennett, Mack. *King of Comedy.* San Francisco: Mercury House, 1954.

Sennett, Ted. *Warner Bros. Presents.* New York: Castle Books, Inc., 1971.

Shipman, David. *The Story of Cinema.* New York: St. Martin's Press, 1982.

Shulman, Irving. *Valentino.* New York: Simon & Schuster, Inc., 1967.

Silver, Charles. *The Western Film.* New York: Pyramid, 1976.

Silverman, Stephen M. *The Fox That Got Away.* Secaucus, N.J.: Lyle Stuart, Inc., 1988.

Sinclair, Upton. *Upton Sinclair Presents William Fox.* Los Angeles: by the author, 1933.

Smith, Sally Bedell. *In All His Glory.* New York: Simon & Schuster, 1990.

Sobel, Robert. *Coolidge. An American Enigma.* Washington D.C.: Regnery Publishing, Inc., 1998.

Solomon, Aubrey. *Twentieth Century-Fox: A Corporate and Financial History.* Metuchen, N.J.: The Scarecrow Press, 1988.

Sperling, Cass Warner, and Millner, Cork with Warner Jr., Jack. *The Warner Brothers Story.* Rocklin, Calif.: Prima Publishing, 1994.

Swanberg, W.A. *Citizen Hearst.* New York: Galahad Books, 1961.

Thomas, Bob. *Crown Prince of Hollywood.* New York: McGraw-Hill Publishing Company, 1990.

—*Thalberg.* Garden City, New York: Doubleday & Company, Inc., 1969.

Torrence, Bruce. *Hollywood. The First Hundred Years.* Hollywood, Calif.: Hollywood Chamber of Commerce, 1979.

Trager, James. *Park Avenue.* New York: Atheneum, 1990.

Tye, Larry. *Rising from the Rails.* New York: Henry Holt and Company, 2004.

Vermilye, Jerry. *The Films of the Twenties.* Secaucus, N.J.: The Citadel Press, 1985.

Walker, John. *Halliwell's Film Guide.* New York: Harper Perennial, 1996.

Walsh, George. *Gentleman Jimmy Walker.* New York: Praeger Publishers, 1974.

Warner, Jack. *My First Hundred Years in Hollywood.* New York: Random House, 1965.

Weidman, Bette S. and Martin, Linda B. *Nassau County Long Island in Early Photographs 1869-1940.* New York: Dover Publications, Inc., 1981.

Weis, Elisabeth and Belton, John. *Film Sound.* New York: Columbia University Press, 1985.

Wheeler, George. *Pierpont Morgan & Friends.* Englewood Cliffs, New Jersey: Prentice-Hall, Inc., 1973.

Wiley, Mason & Bona, Damien. *Inside Oscar.* New York: Ballantine Books, 1987.

Willensky, Elliot. *When Brooklyn Was the World. 1920-1957.* New York: Harmony Books, 1986.

Wurtzel-Semenov, Lillian. *William Fox, Sol M. Wurtzel and the Early Fox Film Corporation.* North Carolina: McFarland & Company, Inc., 2001.

Yagoda, Ben. *Will Rogers.* New York: Alfred A. Knopf, 1993.

Yenne, Bill. *All Aboard!* Greenwich, Conn.: Barnes & Noble, 1989.

Zierold, Norman. *The Moguls.* Los Angeles: Silman-James Press, 1969.

Zukor, Adolph. *The Public Is Never Wrong.* New York: G. P. Putnam's Sons, 1953.

Also consulted were the following articles from *Fortune* magazine:

"Kuhn, Loeb." *Fortune* (March 1930): 89

"The Times and the Times and Their Times." *Fortune* (April 1930): 57

"The Case of William Fox." *Fortune* (May 1930): 48

"Cloak and Suit." *Fortune* (June 1930): 92

"Wiggin." *Fortune* (June 1930): 90

"Pullman." *Fortune* (July 1930): 64

"Trends & Men." *Fortune* (July 1930): 107

"Faces of the Month." *Fortune* (July 1930): 111

"Career Milestones." *Fortune* (July 1930): 112

"A.T.&T." *Fortune* (September 1930): 37

"Newspictures." *Fortune* (September 1930): 60

"Skyscrapers." *Fortune* (September 1930): 54

"Swimming Pools." *Fortune* (September 1930): 74

"The Forty Ranking Cities." *Fortune* (September 1930): 136

"Movies." *Fortune* (October 1930): 33

"Radio Advertising." *Fortune* (December 1930): 64

"Stained Glass." *Fortune* (December 1930): 74

"The $3,000,000 Machine." *Fortune* (December 1930): 98

"Uniforms of the U.S." *Fortune* (January 1931): 74

"Life of Owen D. Young." *Fortune* (January 1931): 30

"Transamerica Corp." *Fortune* (January 1931): 68

"Faces of the Month." *Fortune* (January 1931): 137

"N.Y. Corporation Lawyers." *Fortune* (January 1931): 61

"The Grand Central Terminal." *Fortune* (February 1931): 97

"Faces of the Month." *Fortune* (February 1931): 137

"Gallery of Calamity." *Fortune* (April 1931): 89

"Faces of the Month." *Fortune* (June 1931): 152

"Body and Soul Budget." *Fortune* (August 1931): 26

"Girls Schools." *Fortune* (August 1931): 26

"Chicago Banks." *Fortune* (September 1931): 60

"Insull Heir." *Fortune* (September 1931): 74

"A Hotel is Built." *Fortune* (October 1931): 57

"The White House Goes to Work." *Fortune* (October 1931): 94

"American Board Rooms: Directors and Decorations." *Fortune* (October 1931): 96

"Career Milestones." *Fortune* (October 1931): 150

"Rockefellers in Finance." *Fortune* (December 1931): 50

"Servants." *Fortune* (December 1931): 44

"Eastman Kodak Co." *Fortune* (May 1932): 50

"Citadel of Conservatism." *Fortune* (September 1932): 33

"An Appraisal." *Fortune* (September 1932): 37

"Blue Chip." *Fortune* (September 1932): 45

"Fifth Avenue Tailors." *Fortune* (November 1932): 66

"Fifteen U.S. Corporations." *Fortune* (November 1932): 18

"National Horse Show." *Fortune* (November 1932): 26

"Metro-Goldwyn-Mayer." *Fortune* (December 1932): 50

"Rockefeller Center." *Fortune* (January 1933): 62

"$100,000 Worth." *Fortune* (May 1933): 58

"Budget for a Bride." *Fortune* (June 1933): 38

"Gardens." *Fortune* (August 1933): 67

"Bernard Mannes Baruch." *Fortune* (October 1933): 30

"The Astors." *Fortune* (October 1933): 71

"Faces of the Month." *Fortune* (October 1933): 135

"Armour." *Fortune* (June 1934): 58

"The Ritz." *Fortune* (June 1934): 69

"Faces of the Month." *Fortune* (June 1934): 178

"U.S. Hairdressing." *Fortune* (September 1934): 83

"Color in the Movies." *Fortune* (October 1934): 92

"Public Service of New Jersey." *Fortune* (November 1934): 96

"Diamonds." *Fortune* (May 1935): 66

"New York Pushcarts." *Fortune* (May 1935): 100

"Columbia Broadcasting." *Fortune* (June 1935): 80

"Faces of the Month." *Fortune* (June 1935): 166

"Faces of the Month." *Fortune* (August 1935): 118

"Odlum of Atlas." *Fortune* (September 1935): 50

"In the New Wall Street." *Fortune* (October 1935): 78

"Madison Square Garden." *Fortune* (October 1935): 84

"Twentieth Century-Fox." *Fortune* (December 1935): 85

"Faces of the Month." *Fortune* (December 1935): 202

"Chase National Bank." *Fortune* (January 1936): 55

"Faces of the Month." *Fortune* (January 1936): 154

"Palm Beach." *Fortune* (February 1936): 55

"Jews in America." *Fortune* (February 1936): 79

"Faces of the Month." *Fortune* (October 1936): 200

"Massachusetts Tech." *Fortune* (November 1936): 107

"Richest Women." *Fortune* (November 1936): 115

"Faces of the Month." *Fortune* (February 1937): 180

"Paramount." *Fortune* (April 1937): 87

"Wall Street." *Fortune* (June 1937): 69

"Faces of the Month." *Fortune* (June 1937): 192

"Cafe Society." *Fortune* (December 1937): 123

"Warner Bros." *Fortune* (December 1937): 110

"Will Hays." *Fortune* (December 1938): 69

"Fire!" *Fortune* (March 1939): 61

"The Public Is Not Damned." *Fortune* (March 1939): 83

"Loew's Inc." *Fortune* (August 1939); 25

"United Artists." *Fortune* (December 1940): 95

"Hollywood's Magic Mountain." *Fortune* (February 1945): 153

"More Trouble in Paradise." *Fortune* (November 1946): 154

"Paramount: Oscar for Profits." *Fortune* (June 1947): 89
"Movies: End of an Era?" *Fortune* (April 1949): 99
"Mr. Odlum Gets the Business." *Fortune* (September 1949): 90
"Let's Ask Sidney." *Fortune* (October 1953): 172
"What Caused the Great Depression?" *Fortune* (February 1955): 94
"MGM: War Among the Lion Tamers." *Fortune* (August 1957): 98
"The Cliff-Hanger at MGM." *Fortune* (October 1957): 134
"The Bustling House of Lehman." *Fortune* (December 1957): 157
"It's Hertz Itself in the Driver's Seat." *Fortune* (October 1963): 119
"The Dream Factories Reborn." *Fortune* (February 1998): 107

Archives consulted:

Case Research Lab Museum, Auburn, New York
Twentieth Century-Fox Studios, California
Museum of Modern Art, New York
Sinclair Manuscripts, Manuscript Department, Lilly Library, Indiana University, Bloomington, Indiana
New York Times Archives, New York Public Library, New York
William Fox File in the New York Public Library of the Performing Arts at Lincoln Center
William Fox File in the Motion Picture Academy in Hollywood, California

Other materials consulted:

Daily Variety
Exhibitors Herald
Photoplay Magazine
Motion Picture Classic
Motion Picture Magazine
Motion Picture Story Magazine
New Movie Magazine
Talking Screen
New York Clipper
New York Herald Tribune
New York Review
Time Magazine 1923-30
Time Capsule 1923-29
Variety

Catalogue of the Stories and Plays Owned by Fox Film Corporation,
    Twentieth Century-Fox Library, July 1, 1935